Prisoners of the Good Fight

Prisoners of the Good Fight

The Spanish Civil War, 1936–1939

by CARL GEISER
with a Preface by ROBERT G. COLODNY

Lawrence Hill & Company
WESTPORT, CONNECTICUT

Published in the United States by Lawrence Hill & Company,
520 Riverside Avenue
Westport, Connecticut 06880

Library of Congress Cataloging-in-Publication Data

Geiser, Carl.
  Prisoners of the good fight.

  Bibliography: p.
  Includes index.
  1. Spain—History—Civil War, 1936–1939—
Participation, American. 2. Spain—History—Civil
War, 1936–1939—Prisoners and prisons. 3. Spain—
History—Civil War, 1936–1939—Campaigns. 4. Spain.
Ejército Popular de la República. Brigada Internacional.
XV—Biography. 5. Prisoners of war—Spain—Biography.
6. Prisoners of war—United States—Biography.
7. Soldiers—Spain—Biography. 8. Soldiers—United
States—Biography. I. Title.
DP269.47.U6 1986   946.081   86-18431

Contents

Preface

▬▬▬▬▬▬▬▬▬▬▬▬▬▬▬▬

. . . Spain tore the earth with her nails
When Paris was most beautiful.
Spain poured out her enormous tree of blood
When London tended it's gardens and its lake of swans . . .
    —Pablo Neruda

The International Brigades have fought for an ideal, even though the
ideal is a heresy. They have proven that they know how to die: they
remain disposed to die, just as though they were all Spaniards.
    —General Francisco Franco to the
    Italian Ambassador, March 1937.

Comrades of the International Brigades: Political reasons of State, the
welfare of the same cause for which you offered your blood and bound-
less generosity, are sending you back, some of you to your own countries
and others to forced exile. You can go proudly. You are history. You are
legend. You are the example of democracy's solidarity and universality,
in face of the shameful, "accommodating" spirit of those who interpret
democratic principles with their eyes on the hoards of wealth and
industrial shares which they want to preserve from any risk . . .
    When the olive tree of peace puts forth its leaves again, entwined
with the laurels of the Spanish Republic's victory—come back!
    —From La Pasionaria's Farewell Address
    to the International Brigades, 1938.

WHEN Carl Geiser's history of the travail of the American prisoners of war in Franco's prisons is published, the world will pause in the midst of its current calamities to observe the fiftieth anniversary of the conflict in Spain (1936–39). This means that for the young of this generation, and perhaps even for their fathers, the war in Spain, with its million casualties, is as remote as the Napoleonic wars or the struggles between the Romans and Carthaginians.

This historical myopia is both tragic and unnecessary, because few wars have been so thoroughly chronicled as the Spanish—with its bibliography totaling some 25,000 volumes. It is tragic because, at the time, the flames devouring Spain lit up the entire global, moral, and political landscape—indicating for all but the self-blinded the apocalypse to come and gave fair warning that a second world war, instigated by the Rome-Berlin-Tokyo axis, would see the civilized world pounded to the edge of oblivion. Furthermore the motives and commitment of the defenders of the Republic should mean something to the young of this generation, who confront the prospects of United States sponsored counterinsurgencies in Central America, Africa and Southeast Asia. When the generals of the Spanish army rose in re bellion against the duly elected Republican government, with the open support of Church and aristocracy and with the promise of necessary support from Rome, Berlin, and Lisbon, the continent of Europe was al ready harvesting the dragons' teeth sown by World War I. Wilson's war to end war and to make the world safe for democracy had produced the Russian Revolution of 1917 and the emergence of fascism in Italy in the 1920s.

Mussolini's example and the Western gleeful response to his "curbing of the Red menace" was soon to find imitators in the rest of Europe, and the Italian blackshirted thugs who murdered unionist and socialist leaders would soon be copied in their lethal campaigns by other mercenaries in the service of the conservative continent-wide counterrevolutions. The term "death squads" had not yet been invented, but the reality of the mode of counterrevolution had been established. The melancholy calendar appended to the end of these notes makes this clear.

What should be noted is that after the Great Crash of 1929, the temp of counterrevolution accelerated, and after 1934 the drift toward World War II became irreversible. It should never be forgotten that while the Spanish Republican soldiers fought on against ever-increasing odds, German seized Austria and Czechoslovakia and Japan pursued its imperial adven tures in Asia. Thus, when the first American volunteers died in Spain, it was only three years until Dunkirk and four until Pearl Harbor.

This chronicle of disasters is the context of the Spanish conflict. What remains to be explained is the reaction of the peoples of the world and the radically different response of the ruling groups in London, Paris, Wash ington, and Moscow. I will give a brief account of this by referring to earlier works of mine that were published a generation ago, but have stood up a more of the secret archives of the Western powers have been opened to scholars.

"The resistance of the Spanish Republicans to the rebellion of the Generals had set off a political chain reaction in Europe whose ultimate result was the appearance of the International Brigades at the gates of Madrid. The first centuria were spontaneously formed by the men on the spot and these were continuously reinforced from France. The news that foreigners were fighting with the militia, that Germany and Italy were supporting the rebels, was spread across the continent by the socialist, communist and anarchist press, and served to stimulate the flow of volunteers. That this took place before the Soviet government denounced the Non-Intervention Agreement and openly championed the cause of the Spanish Republic is an indication of the wide response the first armed resistance to fascism evoked in the European working class in general and among the German, Italian, Austrian and Polish emigres in particular.

"The concept of the war in Spain as a crusade against fascism was born in the West, not in Moscow, and was concomitant with the proclamation of the crusade against Bolshevism in Iberia proclaimed in Berlin, Rome, Burgos, Lisbon and Vatican City. The political season was propitious for forming a legion to fight for the Republic (and another to fight for the rebels). The left had gone down to ignominious defeat in Germany in 1933: the Vienna workers had gone down fighting, but fighting alone in 1934, as had the miners of Asturias. The Popular Front policy proclaimed by the Third International at the VIIth World Congress in 1935 had led to electoral victories in France and Spain in 1936. That the Popular Front on an European or on a world scale should defend a Popular Front Government under armed attack in Spain was simple political logic, and the implementation of this logic was first seen in the Aragón in the summer of 1936. It was also not surprising that the German and Italian volunteers formed the hard core of the International columns and gave them the character that made them militarily potent."*

In 1965, one of my graduate students, Margaret George, published a beautiful book entitled *The Warped Vision, British Foreign Policy, 1933–1939*. She asked me to write a foreword, and because what I wrote then sheds some light on Carl Geiser's history, I quote a few passages from that foreword:

"That the errors and crimes of the Munichmen were redeemed by Churchill, his colleagues, and allies, suggests that there were alternatives to conservative policies as these evolved in the interwar yars. Only a believer in malignant goddess of fate would assert the contrary.

"But it is equally the case that in the practice of global politics, actions and their consequences tend to restrict the range of future alternatives. Appeasement practiced without immediate calamity in Asia does not predispose a British cabinet to resist naked Italian agression in Africa. Furthermore, the act gives rise to a rationalization which in turn produced a tenuous theory about the world in which further appeasement is implicit. Thus the cycle of action and justification began in Manchuria and culminated ten years later in the awful ruin on the beaches of Dunkirk.

"It is the merit of Margaret George's study that it centers attention on

---

The Struggle for Madrid, written in 1950, published by Paine-Whitman, New York, 1959.

the inner political grouping of the Tories, the tight circle of political activist
who throughout this period possessed both legal authority and real power in
the community. It is not the intra-party maneuvering, nor the sharp rivalrie
of shifting cliques that concerns her, but rather the *world view* of those wh
from positions of impregnable authority and unassailable power dictated th
diplomatic decision so pregnant with disaster. It is this vision of the extern
world nurtured by narrow caste interests and constantly reinforced by clas
prejudices that engendered a morbid and unreasonable fear of social revolu
tion from the Left and predisposed the Tories to view the German Naz
thugs as counterweight to the Soviet Union on the international scene, an
fascists in general as guardians of the established order in all those parts
the world where there existed a real or imagined manace of socialism. Th
irony of this, of course is that the paragon of aristocratic and imperi
traditions, Winston Spencer Churchill, in virtue of his intellectual powe
and political sagacity, understood both the threat of German imperialis
and the necessity of the Soviet alliance; whereas the amateur Machiavell
around Baldwin and Chamberlain, prisoners of a Uriah Heep mentalit
understood neither and bartered away with peevish stubbornness the ba
tions of national and imperial security.

"However plausible the reasons were which Tory officialdom advance
to mask retreat in Manchuria, Ethiopia, or the Rhineland, these attitud
and calculations proved inadequate to explain the Establishment's respon
to the conflict in Spain. For here for the first time since Allied intervention
the Russian civil war, ideological issues were sufficiently clear for th
politically dormant public to stir from its slumbers and question the wisdo
of Establishment decisions. The Spanish struggle evoked passionate pa
tisanship amongst large segments of the European world, forcing gover
ments, parties, and peoples to reveal their hidden hopes and fea
concerning the human condition in the twentieth century and the way th
world was heading.

"Ducal Britain heard in the anguished echoes from Spain the sound
tumbrels rumbling through revolutionary streets and opted openly f
Franco, his Moors, and fascist legionnaires. A few thousand Britishers we
off to die at Madrid, but the Tory elite's prize contribution to the decad
melancholy history was the invention of the London Non-Interventi
Committee, whose supreme achievement was to make a political hypocri
a fine art and to doom the Spanish Republic to thirty months of valia
dying.

"In this episode, those with prophetic instinct foresaw London put
the torch by the Luftwaffe arsonists, and perceived in the ruins of Mad
the fate of Europe's cities of the 'peaceful tomorrows' purchased by Cha
berlain at Munich."

               *   *   *   *   *

On every battlefield, there is a four-part litany of sorrows: killed in action, wounded in action, captured in action, and, ambiguously, missing in action. For Generalissimo Franco's Christian crusade, one will want to add the category "butchered in cold blood after surrender." Those Americans and other International Brigaders who survived the other battlefield calamities and ended in Franco's jails are the subject of Carl Geiser's history. He has searched the archives in a half dozen countries to tell this all-but-forgotten epic of American fortitude in the presence of appalling privation and humiliation. This alone would justify the publication of this study. It is true that anonymous millions suffered in the prisoner-of-war camps of World War II—and in the Asian conflicts that followed. In the Stalags of World War II, the American prisoners knew that a grateful government would use its immense power to try to guarantee the enforcement of the provisions of the Geneva Convention. And by 1943 they could hear the roar of Allied armadas bringing retribution to Hitler's Third Reich, and they knew that, month by month, powerful armies were advancing from the East and the West. Victory and liberation were but questions of when. For the prisoners in Franco's hellholes, there were no such certainties. Their government was at best indifferent to their cause, and at times openly hostile.

For a time, Republican successes, as at Teruel and in the crossing of the Ebro river, kept their spirits high and their morale undamaged. And when the tide turned, as it inevitably had to, and the Republic lay shattered, they, behind prison walls, retained a faith, not in their government, but in their people, in the wisdom and insight of that common folk from whom they had sprung. In this they were not mistaken. Carl, who shared in full measure all their suffering, has, in writing this book, restored a page torn out of American history. For this his countrymen will thank him.

ROBERT G. COLODNY
Professor Emeritus, History
University of Pittsburgh

Dedicated to the memory of the International Brigaders who were captured, both the killed and the survivors. May the courage they displayed and the suffering they endured serve to inform and strengthen all who are striving for a peaceful and a more just world.

Acknowledgments

BOB STECK, a fellow prisoner, contributed mightily to this history by his research in the newspapers of 1937 to 1940; by preparing biographies of 120 captured Americans; and by his fund-raising activities. Without Bob's help, this history would not have been written.

Nor would it have been written without the financial support of Ring Lardner, Jr., his friends, and supporters of the Lincoln Brigade, some seven hundred in all. Special thanks go to William McCarthy, a Lincoln volunteer, for a very large contribution.

I am also indebted to Victor A. Berch, the Special Collections Librarian at Brandeis University, and Richard T. Gould at the National Archives in Washington, DC, who have been very helpful, and to Linn Shapiro for her valuable research in the National Archives.

In Madrid, I owe a large debt of gratitude to Don José Manuel Mata Castillón, subdirector general of Spain's archives, and to Don Javier Rubio, director general of Foreign Affairs; General Don Carlos Alvarado at the Servicio Histórico Militar; Don Miguel Molina Campuzano, director of the Hemoreteca Municipal de Madrid; and to Don Pedro Ruiz de Ulibarri, secretary general of the Archivo Histórico Nacional in Salamanca. I want to thank them for their cordial reception and the aid given by their able assistants, especially Dona Luisa María Diez de los Rios at Salamanca and Director Maria José Lozano Rincón at the Consular Affairs archives.

I owe special thanks to Mr. Tom Entwistle, who opened many doors for me, and also drove Bill Rubens, a photographer, and me to Burgos, Zaragoza, Alcaniz, Belchite, Quinto, Gandesa, and Barcelona, introducing us to Spaniards who had fought with us, or recalled the fighting, or had been prisoners or guards at San Pedro de Cardena, greatly enriching this history. Particularly valuable was the introduction to Prior Garcos García, head of the Cistercian Order now occupying San Pedro de Cardeña, who showed me a lovely monastery we did not see as prisoners, and provided me with information about its history as a concentration camp. An emotional part of the trip was seeing again the wall where sixteen of us had faced a firing squad.

At the International Committee of the International Red Cross in Geneva, Madame C. Rey-Schyrr, Director of the Archives, and Herr Boleman, head of the Tracing Agency with 55 million names of prisoners and ref-

gees, did all that their regulations would permit in order to provide me with
nformation. Ernst Linggi in Zurich, head of the Swiss Spanish veterans
rganization, and Otto Hafner in Basel, a former prisoner at San Pedro,
riefed me on what had happened to the Swiss veterans and prisoners.

In the Federal Republic of Germany, Dr. Klaus A. Maier, a military
istorian at the Militargeschichtliches Forschungsamt in Freiberg im
Breisgau, and Dr. Maria Keipert at the Auswartiges Amt in Bonn directed
ne to the pertinent material in their archives. I am particularly grateful to
Robert Weinand in Essen for a manuscript copy of his *Nie Vergessen*, which
escribes his experiences at San Pedro de Cardeña and subsequent Franco
oncentration camps, and his three years at Dachau concentration camp,
ntil freed by the US Army on April 29, 1945.

In the German Democratic Republic, I had the great pleasure of inter-
iewing four Germans I had known at San Pedro: Georg Heinzmann in
rfurt: Karl Loesch in Dresden: and Herman Streit and Alfred Zarth in
erlin. I want to thank the Spanish veterans Kurt Hofer, Heinz Priess,
George Henke, and Kurt Goldstein of the Komitee der Antifaschistischen
Widerstandskampfer der DDR; they not only very efficiently organized my
tay but also paid my expenses while in the GDR. And not least, I must
hank Willi Schutt for his generosity and Karl Kormes for information about
hose I was unable to meet.

In Warsaw, Eugeniusz Szyr, a minister in the government, Dr. Zygfryd
eer, and military historian Michal Bron—all had served the Spanish Re-
ublic—took time to provide me with information about Polish prisoners.

In Moscow, the Spanish Section of the Soviet War Veterans Committee
indly arranged an interview with Aviation Colonel Alexander Stchukaev,
ne of the first Soviet pilots to go to Spain in October 1936. Shot down in
ecember, he underwent two mock executions before he was exchanged in
une 1937 for a pilot from the German Condor Legion.

In Britain, James Cameron, a former prisoner, provided rent-free quar-
rs and pleasant company for five weeks. Through Bill Alexander I was able
reach seven more prisoners: James Moon, whose father kept a diary in
hich he copied all of Jim's letters, which provided precise dates for many
ents in San Pedro; Dougal Eggar, Tony Gilbert, and Maurice Levitas, who
ere with the British Battalion when it unexpectedly ran into Italian tanks;
eon Tenor, now a sculptor in Leeds; Tom Jones in Hawarden, Wales, who
as imprisoned with Frank Ryan; and Frank West, who was captured just
fore the British left the front for the last time.

Dr. Humberto Sinobas del Olmo, Evelio Aneiros Subirats, and Eladio
ula Bolanos in Cuba—all former San Pedroites—told me how the thirty-
ght Cubans sent back to San Pedro were finally freed. Former Canadian
isoners Frank Blackman, Jules Paivio, and Reverend Jack Firmin were
ry helpful, as were veterans Lee Burke and Wally Dent. Luigi Totis and
varo Lopez in Italy forwarded to me valuable documents describing the

Republic's treatment of its Italian prisoners. Dr. Gabriel Ersler and Janin Ersler sent me important information from the Archivo Histórico Naciona in Salamanca.

Among those who have read the manuscript and made valuable sugges tions are Ted Cogswell, Robert G. Colodny, Leonard Levenson, Albert Prag Bill and Irene Rubens, Max Shufer, Randall B. Smith, Bob Steck, and H Wallach. Ann Warren and Donald Davidson have my deepest appreciatio for their skillful and understanding editing.

To Doris, my wife, and to Frances Goldin, my persistent literary agen who have encouraged and assisted me during five years of research an writing, I owe my heartfelt thanks.

Events on the Road to Fascism and World War II

1921	German democrat, Mathias Erzberger, assassinated.
1922	German democrat and foreign minister, Walter Rathenau, assassinated.
1923	Bulgarian agrarian leader, Alexander Stambolinsky, assassinated. Coup d'états staged by Primo de Riviera in Spain and Smetona in Lithuania.
1926	Military dictatorship set up in Greece by General Panaglos; coup d'état in Poland by Marshal Pilsudski.
1928	Military dictatorship set up by Salazar in Portugal.
1929	Royal dictatorship set up in Yugoslavia. Stock market crashes on Wall Street.
1931	King leaves, and Spain becomes a Republic. Japan invades Manchuria.
1933	Nazis burn Reichstag on February 27 and blame Communists, winning 43.9 percent of the vote two weeks later. Seventeen days later Hitler becomes dictator. In Spanish elections, Anarchists refuse to vote, and the Right wins.
1934	Dollfuss crushes socialists in bloody battles in Vienna. Dictatorship set up in Estonia by Patz. Hitler assassinates rivals during Night of the Long Knives. German Nazis assassinate Dollfuss. Revolt of Asturian miners against entry of fascists into Spanish cabinet brutally suppressed. First clash between Italian and Abyssinian (Ethiopian) troops.
1935	French Minister Laval proposes free hand for Italy in Abyssinia. Baldwin government in Britain signs Anglo-German Naval Pact, legitimizing expansion of German Navy. Seventh Congress of Communist International in Moscow urges a worldwide popular front against war and fascism. Italy invades Abyssinia.
1936	Popular Front wins majority in Spanish parliament; generals, monarchists, and large landowners prepare to gain by force what they cannot win by elections. Hitler occupies Rhineland, weakening France's security and voiding the Locarno Pact.

July 17. Fascist revolt begins in Spanish Morocco.

July 25. German ambassador cables Hitler revolt is lost without help

July 29. German and Italian planes ferry Franco's troops in Morocco to mainland.

August 8. France closes Spanish border.

August 14. Franco's troops (supported by foreign planes and artil lery) capture Badajoz and murder about four thousand in the bull ring.

September 9. British sponsored Non-Intervention Committee, in cluding Germany, Italy, and the USSR, forbids sending arms to either side.

October 7. The USSR announces it will feel free to help the Republi if Germany and Italy continue to send arms and men to Franco.

November 8. Franco's troops stopped at gates of Madrid by Re publican militia, people of Madrid, 11th International Brigade, and Soviet planes and tanks.

November 18. Germany and Italy recognize rebel junta.

December 26. Ninety-six Americans sail from New York to fight fo the Republic.

1937   January 28. US Neutrality Act bars shipment of war supplies t either side, but Secretary of State Hull secretly allows shipment o gasoline and military trucks to Franco.

February 13. British Battalion suffers heavy losses, with 30 captured

February 16. Lincoln Battalion loses 17 Americans and Canadian when two trucks mistakenly drive into the fascist lines.

March 8–15. Italian plans to take Madrid via Guadalajara are fiasco, with 496 captured.

March 9. Franco announces all foreigners caught with arms will b shot.

April 11. Republic decrees lives of all captured must be respected.

May 3–5. POUM and some anarchists revolt in Barcelona.

May 14. Juan Negrín replaces Francisco Caballero as prime minis ter.

May 28. Neville Chamberlain becomes prime minister of Britain.

May 30. Franco frees 23 of the British captured on February 13.

July 6–20. International Brigades take part in Brunete offensive.

August 24–September 5. 15th Brigade takes hundreds of prisone while helping to capture Quinto and Belchite during Republic offensive toward Zaragoza. Negrín moves government from Valenc to Barcelona.

December 14. Republican forces surround Teruel in one day.

1938   January 1. 15th Brigade joins defenders of Teruel.

February 20. Franco recaptures Teruel.

March 9–16. 15th Brigade, hit by overwhelming fascist forces, su fers heavy casualties, is rebuilt by March 29.

March 30–April 3. Outnumbered thirty to one, 15th Brigade is crushed by fascist forces, which reach the Mediterranean on April 15.

March 10–April 15. Fascists capture 230 Americans, of 144 are killed. Most of those taken alive end up in the San Pedro de Cardeña Concentration Camp with several hundred other Internationals.

June 11. Colonel E. C. Martin visits the British prisoners at San Pedro.

June 24. US Consul Bay visits San Pedro.

July 9. *New York Times* correspondent William Carney visits San Pedro.

July 25. Rebuilt 15th Brigade takes part in recrossing of Ebro River.

September 7. Twenty captured Americans are machine-gunned to death.

September 25. International Volunteers withdrawn for repatriation.

September 29. Chamberlain signs Munich Agreement, dooming Czechoslovakia.

October 8. Fourteen Americans are exchanged for fourteen Italians held by Republic.

October 18. Republic releases 97 Italian prisoners.

October 25. One hundred exchanged British prisoners begin to arrive in London.

November 15. Barcelona bids emotional farewell to Internationals.

December 23. Franco begins offensive against Catalonia.

1939   January. Republican military leaders Casado and Mattalana, anarchist leader Cipriano Mera, and socialist Julian Besteiro plot to surrender remaining 500,000 soldiers in Central Zone to Franco.

January 26. Barcelona falls.

January 29. Republic releases 70 Italians to be exchanged for British.

February 6. Franco releases 67 British prisoners.

February 27. Britain and France recognize Franco.

March 2. Casado leads successful revolt against Negrín, sets up "National Defense Council" to arrange surrender.

March 16. Hitler completes occupation of Czechoslovakia.

March 28. British Consul Gooden evacuates 167 Italian prisoners held by the Republic. Franco's army occupies Madrid.

April 1. Franco announces the war is won. US recognizes Franco regime.

April 5. 31 Canadians and 11 Swiss are exchanged.

April 22. 71 Americans plus 34 Internationals are exchanged.

April 26. 2 Canadians and 8 British are freed.

August 25. 11 Americans are freed.

September 1. Germany invades Poland.

September 3. England and France declare war on Germany.

1941   June 22. Germany, having conquered western Europe, attacks Soviet Union.

December 7. Japan attacks Pearl Harbor. US at war against Fascist Axis.

Prisoners of the Good Fight

1 Why Did We Go to Spain?

WHY DID 2700 young American volunteers, of whom about 800 would give up their lives, go to Spain to fight in the Abraham Lincoln Battalion between December 1936 and July 1938?

We went because we were alarmed about what was happening both in our country and in Europe as well as in Spain. The Great Depression, which had begun in 1929, had brought widespread unemployment and hunger worldwide, except in the Soviet Union. By 1932 25 million were unemployed in the United States of America—there was no unemployment insurance then—and farmers were plowing under their crops and slaughtering new-born pigs while millions went to bed hungry. That November, Franklin D. Roosevelt, promising a New Deal, was elected president. Although by 1935 the New Deal had put many millions back to work, millions were still unemployed and hungry. Attacking the New Deal for this, Father Coughlin, a Catholic priest, preached that we needed a strong man (read dictator) in the White House to set things right. He had a weekly radio audience of between thirty and forty million. His National Union for Social Justice had organized chapters in every large town. Also openly promoting a dictatorship were such organizations as the Nazi Bund, Christian Front, Ku Klux Klan, and Black Legion.

Millions of Americans were trying to solve the problems of unemployment, hunger, and low wages democratically, through many organizations. The Unemployed Councils, the budding Congress of Industrial Organizations, the ethnic fraternal organizations, farmers' unions, the Bonus March to Washington by war veterans, the hunger marches, the campaign for social security—all stood for broadening our democracy, not curtailing it.

Through the National Student Union, students, too, were fighting for academic freedom, civil and economic rights, and peace. Then a student, I helped arrange an Ohio Student Congress against War and Fascism in Cleveland over Thanksgiving weekend in 1932. Several weeks later, seeking funds to rent a bus to take students to Chicago for the National Student Congress against War and Fascism over the Christmas holiday, I approached Newton D. Baker, Hoover's secretary of war. He said, "Maybe we need a little war to get rid of some of the unemployed," then slammed the door in my face. President Green of the Ohio Bell Telephone Company received me cordially and made a $10 donation, equivalent to about $100 today. We obtained enough money to hire the bus.

The congress of a thousand students surprised me when they chose me to represent them at the Latin American Congress against War and Fascism to be held in Montevideo, Uruguay, in February 1933. In the fall of 1934, an American delegation attended the World Congress against War and Fascism in Amsterdam, Holland.

The people of Europe had suffered from unemployment and hunger since World War I. Labor unions and unemployed factory and farm workers tried to organize to improve their living conditions. The large landowners, the industrialists, and the aristocracy were afraid their wealth and privileges would be endangered if they permitted the people to organize and run their own candidates in elections. They sponsored and financed organizations that deceitfully claimed to be defending religion, the flag, social justice, and freedom, while in practice they promoted nationalist feelings and racial hatreds, blaming all evils on the socialists and communists. Democratic institutions and practices were illegalized. Dictatorships were set up, in emulation of Mussolini's Italian fascism, to "set things right," but in practice to look after the interests of the wealthy. Unions, farmer organizations, and left political parties were outlawed and their leaders imprisoned and frequently tortured. The establishment of fascist dictatorships in country after country was becoming worrisome to Americans who believed in democracy (see "Events on the Road to Fascism and World War II").

To our surprise and joy, a move toward a democratic society took place in 1931 in an impoverished and illiterate but proud corner of Europe: Spain. On April 14 King Alfonso XIII decided he would be safer outside his country, and amid wild rejoicing the people of Spain set up a republic. A national election on June 28 gave the Republican and Socialist parties a large majority, but the old bureaucracy was able to hold back making needed reforms in education, land ownership, and labor laws.

In 1933 the anarchists refused to participate in elections, and the reactionary forces won a majority. When the government brought pro-fascists[1] into the cabinet, a general strike was called for October 5, 1934. It was effective only in Asturias, where the miners seized power. At the suggestion of a cruel disciplinarian, General Francisco Franco, Moroccan and Foreign Legion troops were used to restore "law and order." The brutal treatment of the miners and the jailing of some 35,000 Spaniards led to a strong campaign for amnesty and the release of the political prisoners.

Out of this campaign came a People's Front embracing all organizations that supported a democratic Republic, and in the February 1936 elections the People's Front won a substantial majority in the parliament. Generals, large landowners, and the wealthy businessmen, supported by the hierarchy of the Catholic Church realizing it would be difficult to obtain power through elections, started a revolt against the Republic on July 17, 1936. They miscalculated: at the end of a week they held only a small part of Spain. On July 25 the German ambassador in Madrid cabled Hitler: "Unless there occurs something out of the ordinary, it is now difficult to understand how the military rebellion can succeed."[2]

"Something out of the ordinary" did occur. Two fascist governments, Italian and German, intervened militarily to overthrow the democratically elected government of Spain. The untrained and poorly armed people were no match for the well-trained and well-armed Moroccan troops backed up by German and Italian planes, tanks, and artillery. By the first of November, Madrid, Spain's capital, was being bombed and shelled, and a fascist army was at its gates.

What did the democratic countries do about this? Great Britain, acting through France, set up a Non-Intervention Committee (NIC) on September 9, 1936. All European countries except Switzerland agreed not to supply war material or manpower to either side, and all kept their word—except Germany, Italy, and Portugal. The result was that the Republic was unable to purchase arms, while Germany and Italy poured arms into the fascist side.

Enrique Líster, in my opinion the Republic's greatest military leader, told me in 1982 that we would have had no business coming to Spain in 1937 if it had been only a civil war there between classes or regions; but the invasion of Spain by the armed forces of Germany and Italy had transformed the conflict into an international war against fascism on Spanish soil, and therefore the Republic had welcomed us. I shall not use the term "civil war" to describe the war after the intervention began.

On October 7, 1936, the Soviet representative announced at a meeting of the NIC that if Germany and Italy did not stop sending in arms and men, the Soviet Union would consider itself free of its non-intervention obligations. Hitler and Mussolini did not stop. Soviet planes and pilots and tanks arrived in Spain at the end of October, barely in time to help keep the fascists from capturing Madrid.

Before the first American volunteers left for Spain, there were anti-fascist Germans, Italians and Poles who, having fled to France from their fascist governments, had gone to fight with the Republican forces. Hundreds joined anarchist military units in Barcelona. The first volunteers to reach Madrid as an organized unit formed the 11th International Brigade, composed of 1900 Germans, French, Belgians, and Poles, with a British machine-gun section. They arrived in Madrid on November 8, 1936, at a critical moment and contributed far more than their fighting ability, which was considerable. They served as a model of organization and discipline for the newly forming Republican Army. Above all, they told the people of Madrid that they had friends abroad who cared enough to offer their lives for the Republic. Despite daily shelling and bombing, the Republican Army, supported by the people of Madrid, held off the fascists until betrayed by several treacherous colonels and generals in March 1939.

When we learned that Germany and Italy were sending men and arms to help the fascists, and that the Republic was fighting for its life, many of us wanted to go to fight for the Republic. But how could we go to Spain without money? By December 1936, a way had been arranged. We went for interviews, and then for physicals. All antifascists who passed the physical exam and were free of family responsibilities were accepted, regardless of party affiliation, told to get a passport, and given third-class tickets to France. We didn't ask who had made the arrangements (a group set up by the Communist Party) nor did we ask who was paying our fare, for we were glad just to go. The first ninety-six left New York on December 26, 1936, on the SS *Normandie*.[3] They were followed by about 2600 more in 1937 and 1938.

The antifascists who could not go collected funds for medical aid to the Republic. Over a hundred ambulances with supplies plus doctors and nurses were sent from major cities and medical institutions, joining medical personnel from many countries to save the lives not only of International Brigaders but also of many Spaniards, both military and civilian.

Profascist groups, the Catholic hierarchy· and Father Coughlin proclaimed that Franco was fighting communism. On January 8, 1937, the US Congress enacted into law a ban on shipment of war materiel to Spain, making no distinction between the elected Republic and those trying to overthrow it. Congressman John T. Bernard, Farmer-Laborite from Minnesota, cast the single dissenting vote.

Some American businessmen deliberately helped the fascists. When the rebellion occurred, Texaco had five oil tankers at sea fulfilling a contractual agreement with the Republic's oil company, CAMPSA. Captain Thorkild Rieber, Texaco's director, ordered all tankers to go to ports controlled by the fascists. Texaco, helped by Standard Oil, supplied three and one half million tons of aviation and truck gasoline to the fascists that Germany and Italy could not supply, much of it on credit. While Hitler and Mussolini were able to supply 3,00 military trucks, General Motors, Ford, and Studebaker provided 12,000. These transactions were violations of the Neutrality Act and though known to Secretary of State Cordell Hull were kept secret.[4] Without the gasoline and trucks, the fascists would have lost.

Volunteers came to Spain from fifty-three countries to join the International Brigades. The first went to Spain by train, but France closed its borders early in 1937, forcing all later volunteers except medical personnel to follow Spanish guides over the Pyrenees. The Soviet Union sent planes and tanks, and pilots and tank drivers until Spanish pilots and tankists could be trained. It also provided trained military advisers at division and army corps levels and occasionally at brigade.[5] Without Soviet aid, the fascist forces would have quickly overthrown the democratic Republic.

2 A Short History of the First War Against Fascism

BRIEFLY, THE REPUBLIC built an army and set up a war industry, and was able to hold its own and even make advances through most of 1937 with the aid of arms bought from the Soviet Union and Mexico. By May 4, 1937, Italian submarines and aircraft had made 86 attacks on Soviet freighters. Three were sunk, and four had been captured. According to the Italian Stefani press agency, Italian military aircraft hit 224 ships of various nations between 1936 and 1938.[1] Soviet efforts to ship war materiel through the Baltic and overland through France were stymied by the closing of the French border with Spain except for short periods when it looked as if the Republic might fall. Soviet war materiel was still on French soil when the Republic fell, and those items ended up in Nazi hands. The NIC served throughout the war to prevent the Republic from purchasing arms to defend itself, but did nothing to prevent the fascists from getting everything Hitler and Mussolini were willing to supply.

About 45,000 volunteers came to defend the Republic, of whom fewer than 15,000 were in the front lines at one time. They formed five brigades. The 11th took in those who spoke German. The 12th was the Italian Brigade, known as the Garibaldis. The 13th was made up of Slavs and Poles, the 14th was French, and the 15th took in the English-speaking volunteers. The 129th and the 150th Mixed Brigade had some Balkan volunteers. The 14th and 15th Brigades included a battalion of Spaniards with a sprinkling of Internationals. By July 1938, the Brigades had as many Spaniards as Internationals.

The International Brigades formed part of a strike force which included the Spanish soldiers commanded by Líster, El Campesino, and Juan Modesto, considered the Republic's best troops. An International Brigade remained in action until it had about 500 killed and 1500 wounded, which could occur in one to eight weeks of fighting. Then the brigade would be given two to ten weeks to rebuild its strength. This cycle was repeated five times after July 6, 1937. For example, on November 27, 1937, after the 15th Brigade had been out of the lines for five weeks for rebuilding, it had 79 commissioned officers on duty and 39 in hospitals, and 2388 soldiers and noncommissioned officers on duty and 725 hospitalized.[2]

Mussolini sent Franco about 100,000 men, mostly infantry. Hitler supplied about 50,000, of whom not more than 15,000 were in Spain at any one time, staying three to six months to obtain battle experience. They manned the German antiaircraft guns, much of the artillery, tanks, planes, and many auxiliary services, such as radio, telegraph, aerial photography, and military

training schools for officers and specialists.[3] In addition, the fascists ha
about 75,000 Moroccan and several thousand Portuguese troops.[4] Thu
Spain was invaded by about 230,000 trained and armed troops during th
war.

Franco first tried to take Madrid, but was unable to do so. The Italia
command tried to take it, and suffered a fiasco in March 1937 with 49
Italians taken prisoner. On March 31, Franco began an attack on norther
Spain, which was isolated from the rest of the Republic.

Help for the North required the launching of a republican offensiv
from Catalonia. However, no significant offensive was possible as long a
Catalonia remained under the control of leaders who insisted a worker
revolution must have priority over the war against fascism. These leade
were Anarchists and members of the ultra-left POUM (Partido Obrero c
Unificación Marxista), some under the influence of Leon Trotsky. Th
Republican government held that all must unite to defeat the fascist forc
before any radical social changes should be considered, a position supporte
by the Republican, Socialist, and Communist parties. Under the rule of th
Anarchists and the POUM in Catalonia, the farmers and middle cla
became dissatisfied; industrial production fell by a third, and there we
long queues to buy bread.[5] Military units in Catalonia, under Anarchist ar
POUM control, paid little heed to the Republic's army command and we
incapable of mounting an offensive.

The problem was not solved until after Dr. Juan Negrín, a Socialis
became premier on May 17, 1937. The POUM was dissolved on June 1
and its leaders were arrested. The Council of Aragon, through which th
Anarchists and the POUM had exercised their power, outraging both th
Catalan and the Republican governments, was dissolved on August 10.

Two weeks later, the Republic began an offensive to try to relieve th
pressure on the North by directing an attack from Catalonia towar
Zaragoza. Although the offensive captured several towns, including Quin
and Belchite, it was too late and too weak. Gijón, the last major city in th
North fell on October 19, 1937.

Before Franco could get his forces in position for another assault o
Madrid, a Republican army surrounded a provincial capital, Teruel, in o
day, December 14, 1937. It would take Franco seventy days to retake th
city.

Since Franco had large offensive units, including the Italian and M
roccan divisions and artillery and planes, conveniently located, he decid
to cut the Republic in two by driving to the Mediterranean Sea along th
south side of the Ebro River. Starting March 9, 1938, he was at th
Mediterranean in 37 days. The Republic was now divided into two unequ
parts—a small Catalonia with a third of the army and a much larger Centr
South zone area with two thirds of the armed forces. Alarmed, the Fren
government opened the borders for three months, and with the new Sov

arms thus made available, the Republic launched a surprise attack from Catalonia across the Ebro on July 25, 1938. It would take Franco almost four months and over 100,000 casualties to drive the Republican army back across the river. Republican casualties were about 50,000.[6] However, the Republican forces in Catalonia had used up most of their planes, tanks, and artillery, and they could not be replaced because of the coastal blockade and the closed French border.

All Internationals were withdrawn from the front on September 27, 1938, for repatriation in the hope that the League of Nations and the democratic countries would then force Hitler and Mussolini to withdraw their armed forces. The League of Nations sent a commission to count the foreign volunteers in Republican Spain and found there were 12,673.[7] Mussolini then withdrew 10,000 wounded and exhausted Italians, but sent in more officers. The French, British, American, and Scandinavian volunteers were repatriated in December; but those who had fled from fascist countries could not return to them.

Franco began his attack on Catalonia on December 23. The poorly armed Republican forces were unable to hold back his Italian and Moroccan troops and his air force. By February 10, 1939, fascist troops had occupied all of Catalonia. Some 300,000 civilians fled, mostly on foot, into France, along with some 100,000 soldiers, including the remaining Internationals.

When it was too late, the French reopened the border to allow passage of Soviet war materiel. The Republic returned the equipment so it wouldn't fall into Franco's hands. Republican soldiers who wanted to return from France to the Central region of Spain were held instead in concentration camps enclosed with barbed wire, without shelter or medical care, and with very little food and water. The only way out of the camps was to return to Franco Spain.

Negrín returned from France to the Central zone where a half million men were under arms to continue the war, only to face a revolt organized by treacherous army officers and political leaders who had been negotiating a surrender to Franco. On April 1, 1939, Franco was able to announce the war was over.

The Republic Was Not Defeated! It Was Betrayed!

A British intelligence officer who had just spent four months with Franco reported on December 14, 1938, that the Republic had

. . . the better fighting troops from the point of view of organization, morale, their belief in themselves, and their production of war materiel and the Government's new Commissariat is considerably superior to Franco's . . . and the higher command and staff are decidedly superior. . . .

If we on the other hand look at Franco's troops—there has been too much cocksureness and the many foreigners, Italians, Germans and Portuguese, have ha◆ their demoralizing influence. Instead of being taught to rely on themselves, Franco' soldiers have to rely on the foreigners . . . there are as many generals in the Italia◆ Division and the Italian-Spanish one as there are colonels in those opposing them

Franco has used up most of his ammunition and a portion of his guns on th◆ Ebro, so that he is now frantically calling for further amounts from Germany an◆ Italy, the latter being more and more reluctant to send them. . . .

Concluding, the intelligence officer said that if the government were t◆ have a moderate military success, Franco would be in serious trouble with war-weary population, unhappy foreign allies, and division among his sup porters.[8]

What made it possible for Franco's forces to occupy all Republica◆ territory within the next three and one-half months?

When Franco's forces had cut the Republic in two in April 1938, Negrí◆ and his cabinet were in the Catalonian half. The major part of the Army, half million strong, was in the Central-Southern zone under the comman◆ of the Central General Staff. The offensive mounted from Catalonia acros◆ the Ebro River on July 25 not only halted Franco's drive against the Centr◆ zone but also forced him to use his best units and aviation and artillery fc the next three and a half months to drive the Republican troops across th◆ Ebro.

That the Central Staff did not mount a significant attack again◆ Franco's weakened lines around the Central zone during this time is su◆ picious. But even more suspect are the Central Staff's operations in D◆ cember and January. Under pressure from the government and the peop◆ in the Central zone to relieve the pressure on Catalonia, the Central Sta◆ prepared a large offensive on the southern front, starting with a naval attac◆ near Motril between December 8 and 11. After the navy was at sea, th◆ attack was called off. However, the army had orders to start an offensiv◆ between Seville and Badajoz on December 18. If successful, it would hav◆ cut Franco's territory in two.

When the army was in place, it received orders to attack toward Gr◆ nada instead; that meant moving the army rapidly some two hundred mil◆ east over impassable roads. When it was ready, orders came to make th◆ attack wherever the army commanders thought it would be most effectiv◆ Since they preferred the first plan, they moved the army back to its origin◆ positions, now quite exhausted and in considerable disorder. Neverthele◆ when it struck on January 5, it broke through the fascist lines. But th◆ General Staff had made no plans for advancing into the unfortified areas and the offensive, which would have been a disaster for Franco, was halt◆ just as Franco was threatening Barcelona.

The Republican army in Catalonia, unable to replenish its armamen◆ (although Soviet arms were on the other side of the closed French borde◆ was pushed across the French border by February 10. Líster's 5th Arm◆

Corps, which began with 22,000 soldiers, many of them new recruits, had offered the main resistance; it was reduced to 8,000 when it crossed the border. Lister describes the disarming of his men and their imprisonment as "the most bitter moment of my life."[10]

Negrín and J. Alvarez del Vayo returned to the Central area on February 10. Colonel Segismundo Casado, commander of the Center Army defending Madrid, informed Negrín that continued resistance was impossible due to lack of food, aircraft and artillery. Negrín told him that negotiations for an honorable peace had failed, that food was on its way, that 600 Soviet aircraft, 500 pieces of artillery, and 10,000 machine guns were in Marseilles and would soon reach Spain, and that surrender would lead to more deaths than continued resistance.[11]

When Líster returned to Spain on February 15, Negrín asked him to visit the armies holding the front to find out whether they were willing and able to continue to fight. Líster reported all were able and wanted to do so, but that the morale was bad at the top of the Army of the Center, headed by Casado. Líster intimated he could make the most important contribution as head of the Center Army. But Negrín did not act to remove Casado.[12]

In *Los Cien Ultimos Dias de la República* José Manuel Martínez Bande, a pro-Franco historian, reveals some details of the activities of the treacherous officers' group headed by Casado. Martínez Bande had access to Franco military intelligence files on the negotiations with Republican officers for the surrender of the Republican Army, dating back to early February 1939. He hints that negotiations may have occurred earlier.

Franco's espionage network, the Information Service and Military Police headed by Colonel José Ungría Jiménez from Franco's General Staff, used the underground fascist Falange organization for its espionage. Casado's intermediaries contacted the Falangist organization in January, and on February 11 Ungría received a telegram: ". . . Casado in agreement with Besteiro asks that the life of decent military leaders be respected."

On February 15, Casado received a letter from Franco's General Fernando Barrón y Ortiz saying Casado "should have blind faith in the treatment which would cure him of his illness." Casado, greatly moved by Barrón's words, stated that "all is prepared for the assault on the Communist strongholds, with the cry of 'Long live Spain and death to Russia!'" Franco now pushed Casado to depose Negrín and get rid of the Communists before they got rid of him.[13]

Casado, aware of the strong sentiment for continuing the war, delayed his coup until March 5. Even then a counterrevolt almost overthrew him. Casado was saved by timely attacks by Franco's forces and the help of Anarchist units under General Cipriano Mera.[14]

On March 11, Casado came to an agreement with those who wanted to continue the war. He would free all "noncriminal" Communist prisoners and listen to the views of the Communist leaders. All anti-Casado military units returned to their former positions on the twelfth. On the thirteenth Casado had Colonel Luis Barceló, the popular commander of the 1st Army Corps, and José Conesa, its commissar, who strongly opposed surrender court-martialed and shot.[15]

Casado was not the only traitor. On March 5, Franco had received from General Matallana Gómez, the chief of the General Staff, a map showing where the Republican lines were weakest. Franco already had the information from General Enrique Jurado Barrio.[16]

Casado took no chances on Franco's "justice." Fearful of attacks by betrayed Republicans, he was given a secluded hideout in England. Matallan Gómez, who handed over the Armies of the Center to the fascists, was tried, and died in prison in 1952.[17]

The number of Spaniards killed after the war, by death squads or after court-martial, is not known. The killing on the fascist side is described by Ramón Serrano Súñer, Franco's brother-in-law, who, though minister of the interior, was not in charge of the "political cleansing":

It is shameful to say it, but it must be said because it is the truth, that the brutal cruelty in the rear caused more deaths than the open fighting at the fronts. . . . The military legal adviser of the General Staff, Martínez Fusset, daily during coffee time after lunch received the sinister report of the punishments by death for The Chief of State's information.[18]

Serrano Súñer did not exaggerate. The total battlefield deaths were about 100,000. The number killed and executed behind Franco's lines during the war was about 200,000. The number executed after the war was about 200,000.[19] The ratio of deaths caused by "the brutal cruelty in the rear" to those on the battlefield was about four to one.

Additional hundreds of thousands were held in concentration camps, prisons, and labor battalions. The people of Spain paid a heavy penalty in lives and suffering because of betrayal by military leaders, and by democratic countries that refused to help the Republic stop the advance of international fascism. And the people of the world would pay for this with fifty million lives in the second war against fascism—World War II—which began exactly five months after the Republic fell.[20]

3 The First to be Captured

THE FASCIST OFFICER approached the young soldier standing quietly before the firing squad to offer him a blindfold. The soldier refused it.

The officer asked, "Is there anything you would like to say?"

"Yes, I would like command of the firing squad."

Surprised, the officer looked into the fearless eyes in the long angular face with a large forehead, hesitated a moment, then replied: "Sir, the firing squad is at your command."

In a firm voice, the young soldier ordered, "Get ready! . . . Aim! . . . Fire!"

So died the first of 176 American nationals who were killed after capture by fascist troops. He was Carmelo Delgado Delgado, one of nine children of a poor Puerto Rican family. Born in Guayama on April 20, 1913, Carmelo completed elementary school in six years and high school in three, always at the head of his class.

Carmelo took a very active part in the fight for Puerto Rican independence led by Columbia Law School graduate Pedro Albizu Campos. After a brief period at the University of Puerto Rico, Carmelo used a small inheritance to go to Madrid to study law. To his dismay, Spanish laws did not allow him to work. He shared a small room without heat with two students. His roommates, greatly impressed by the fervent Puerto Rican nationalist, shared their meager stipends with him.

When the fascist uprising began, Carmelo helped form a student column to stop the fascist advance in University City on the outskirts of Madrid. In December 1936, Carmelo joined a Colombian and a Venezuelan student on a scouting patrol. They didn't hear the signal to withdraw and were captured. After interrogating them, the fascists asked them to choose between having their embassies arrange their return home, or execution. The Venezuelan and Colombian chose to return home.

Carmelo answered that he preferred to die rather than beg for his life from a representative of the Yankee invader of his country. On April 29, 1937, in Valladolid, the brilliant and brave young Puerto Rican was executed.[1]

In 1964 Carmelo's parents went to Spain to find Carmelo's grave. They learned there were no graves for the executed, but they did find a Spaniard who had been in prison in Valladolid with Carmelo. He told them how their son died.

* * * * *

Sixteen Americans and one Canadian of the Lincoln Battalion head quarters staff felt their hearts beat faster late in the afternoon of Februar 16, 1937. They were on their way to their first battle against the fascists. Th Spanish drivers of their two small trucks had difficulty maneuvering aroun the shell and bomb holes in the road. All eyes were scanning the road ahead searching for the Republican troops holding the front.

At 5:15 P.M. they saw soldiers standing along the road waving to them to come on. As the trucks slowly drew up abreast of the soldiers, the Spanis drivers swore, "Fascists!" Since there was neither time nor space to tur around, they floored their accelerators. The soldiers who had waved at them now fired at the trucks. Bullets were also coming from the nearby hills c both sides.

One shot damaged the steering mechanism on the first truck and th driver was barely able to keep it on the road. At the first bend, it rolled ove on its side, and the second truck ran into it. Those who were not wounded injured and who had rifles took up positions alongside the trucks or in th ditch along the road to fire at the large number of fascist soldiers runnir down the hills toward them from both sides.

Five Americans, who had only a pistol among them, made a run for bent over, along the road in the direction the trucks had been going. Seeir soldiers coming off the hill on their left, they took refuge in a culvert, whi one tried to hold the soldiers off with the pistol. According to a fasci sergeant, Santos Clemente García, interviewed in 1982, one of his men wa able to roll a grenade into the culvert, killing all five.

Of the fourteen who remained with the trucks, thirteen were killed an one was taken prisoner. The fascist soldiers, members of the 1st Company the 7th Ceuta Light Infantry Battalion, were ordered to return items take from the trucks. The battalion commander, Don Luis Riera Guerra, made detailed inventory of the captured materiel. It began with two light truck 13 rifles, and included among its 26 items 185 blankets, 96 khaki berets, spoons, and one butcher knife. The last item, "various documents," i cluded the American passports. The pistol did not appear in the invento

One fascist soldier had been wounded, though not seriously. R publican troops held both ends of the road, making it impossible to bring an ambulance. The sun had set. The officers decided it would be better wait until daylight before carrying the wounded soldier over the hills. Th made him as comfortable as they could near the trucks. That night Moro can troops from an adjoining unit came down to loot the bodies. Finding th wounded soldier and believing him to be a Republican, they killed him The name of the American prisoner and what happened to him are n known. The names of fifteen, the first to die, are known:[3]

1. Hans Adolphi, young German-born electrician from New York.
2. Thomas Beckett, Canadian. (Not to be confused with Thoma Beckett from Kansas City, Mo.)

3. Thomas Cox, Jr., 45, Douglas, Alaska. Chauffeur.
4. Steve Dabelko, 28, New York, NY. Evening student at City College of NY.
5. Russel Dempsey, 23, New York, NY.
6. Edward Freed, 29, New York, NY. Artist.
7. Walter Fairbanks Grant, 28, Marion, Ohio. Writer and organizer.
8. Everett Hobbs, 25, Inglewood, Calif.
9. George Webster Leap, 24, Winnetka, Ill. Musician and painter.
10. John William Parks, 25, Pittsburgh, Pa. American Indian and organizer.
11. Michael Ransel.
12. Dominick Represas.
13. George Werner Stark.
14. Leon Sloan Torgoff, 21, New York, NY. Student.
15. Leo Turner, San Francisco, Calif.

Two lucky volunteers became separated from the ill-fated trucks. They had been in them the day before, when a convoy picked up the Lincoln Battalion at its training base at Villanueva de la Jara to take it to the front for the first time. Two trucks had been assigned to carry the battalion headquarters staff and its records and supplies. One also carried several volunteers who had slight illnesses.

Assigned to that "hospital" truck was Irving William Rappaport, better known as "Rappy," who had the grippe and a sore throat but insisted he had to go along. Rappy, twenty-seven, was a bare five feet six and weighed only 120 pounds. Among the first Americans to volunteer to fight for the Spanish Republic, he had left a job with a grocery chain in New York, where he had helped organize the union.

The convoy carried the Americans to the bullring in Albacete, the base of the International Brigades. Here Rappy received a scarf from Milton Rappaport—no relation—to protect his throat. Then he listened to the send-off speeches. The fascists were trying to cut the main highway between Madrid and Valencia on the Jarama front, endangering Madrid. It would be the Lincoln Battalion's job to help stop the fascist drive. Each man received a new rifle (covered with Cosmoline), 150 bullets, a bandolier, and a steel helmet. Rappy, determined to help save Madrid, left the hospital truck and climbed into one assigned to his company.[4]

Norberto Borges Aldama, also one of the first to volunteer, was a thirty-year-old Cuban who had spent the previous eight years working in New York. Now he was on the headquarters staff and therefore on one of the two trucks. The convoy stopped at dawn, between Chinchón and Morata de Tajuña, not far from the front. The volunteers dismounted, cleaned the protective Cosmoline off their rifles, and were shown how to fire them. They were each permitted five test shots into an adjoining hillside to prepare them to meet the enemy. Norberto, after his fifth shot, found his truck had left without him, taking his knapsack and blanket roll. He hitched a ride on another truck.[5]

Late that afternoon the two headquarters trucks went on ahead. A short distance past Morata de Tajuña on the road to San Martín de la Vega the drivers turned right on the first road going north, unaware that the fascists had seized part of it and that no Republican troops were in front of them.

The Lincoln Battalion took up positions along the north side of the road, knowing only that two trucks were missing. Word of what must have happened to them and the possibility that some men might have been taken alive did not reach the United States until seven months later. Letters to the State Department asking it to intervene for the safety of the men who were on the trucks brought replies that the Department was unable to obtain information about them.

Among those on the trucks was twenty-eight-year-old Walter Fairbank Grant, born in Marion, Ohio. He was the son of a Congregational minister and his ancestors were rebel Scots who came to America on the *Mayflower's* second trip. Seeing two black youths lynched by the Ku Klux Klan in spite of his desperate efforts to save them led Walter eventually to "indict the whole of society of which I and my church were part." He earned an MA in English at Indiana University, and that got him a job with the WPA Writers Project at $23.86 a week. Another was creative twenty-one-year-old Leon Torgoff, born in New York. He had left his studies and newspaper column, "Moods and Muses," at Denver University to go to Spain.

*   *   *   *   *

Before the Lincoln Battalion arrived, the British Battalion had prevented a fascist breakthrough on the same front. In four days of very bitter fighting, British casualties were close to 75 percent.[6] On the second day, February 13, 30 members of the Machine Gun Company were captured. In 1981, Bill Alexander, a former commander of the British Battalion who had interviewed survivors and studied the terrain, told me about it.

The Machine Gun Company had placed their guns in a forward position with a good field of fire except on their left. That flank was defended by a rifle company on a hill a hundred yards away. On the first day, they had held off a strong fascist attack. On the second day, a group of soldiers suddenly appeared from the left. A member of the Machine Gun Company yelled "Don't shoot! They are ours!" But even though the uniforms of the newcomers looked similar to their own, several men reached for their rifles. The newcomers shot them.

The rest, realizing that these were fascist troops who would shoot them, raised their fists in the antifascist salute and sang "The International." To their surprise, an officer ordered them taken alive. The thirty, holding their hands over their heads, were marched back over the route the fascists had taken. Among the captured were Harold Fry, the company commander, and Ted Dickinson, the second in command.

A British rifle company began firing, at the column, but stopped when the escorts placed the prisoners between themselves and the British. When they were out of rifle range, Phillip Elias used the little Spanish he knew to ask permission to smoke a cigarette. Permission given, he dropped his hands to get a cigarette and lighter out of his pockets. Immediately, a burst of gunfire killed Phillip and John Stevens the man, behind him.

The British were enraged. Even though others sought to restrain Dickinson, his contempt for his captors caused them to halt the column. Stood against a tree, Dickinson realized he was to be executed. He smiled, raised his clenched fist, and called out *"Salud"* as they fired.

A little later the others were lined up before a firing squad. They were saved by the arrival of an officer who called off the execution. Instead, their hands were tied tightly behind their backs with telephone wire. Moors on horseback, using their whips freely, marched them to San Martín de la Vega. The prisoners were depressed by the large numbers of fascist tanks, artillery and men they saw along the road.

Two days later, Civil Guards loaded the British on a truck and took them farther back to Navalcarnero. Here a London *Daily Mail* photographer took a picture of them on the truck. The publication of this photo not only informed relatives and friends that they were prisoners, but also meant that the fascists could not longer deny that they had captured them.[7] (A United Press dispatch on February 18 saying that thirty Americans were being held at Navalcarnero was an erroneous reference to the 27 British prisoners.)

The British were held at Navalcarnero for eight days. Their heads were shaved and they were fingerprinted. Alfonso Merry del Val, son of a former Spanish ambassador to England, interrogated them. Their next move was ninety kilometers farther west to Talavera de la Reina. There the main prison was too crowded to hold them, and so they were placed in an old factory. It, too, was overcrowded with local residents. A covered van, the "Agony Van," called every evening and took away a group of handcuffed Spaniards. They were executed on unconsecrated ground, and their bodies were buried in large pits in the cemetery.

Bill Alexander describes life at Talavera de la Reina:

Groups of British prisoners were taken out every day to work, some on the roads, some to cover the bodies in the cemetery pits. One sergeant in charge of the armed escort, however, would take them back to prison through the working-class streets. Women from the houses would give them small gifts—bread, cigarettes, fruit.[8]

One of the prisoners, twenty-two-year-old James E. Rutherford, described their plight in more detail:

. . we were put to work chiefly on roads. Our conditions were almost unendurable. We were starved. Our only food was two helpings of beans per day, served in the crudest fashion possible. In our cells we slept on the ground without straw or covering. Some of us who had overcoats when we were captured had been relieved of them by the Moors, and our suffering during the cold nights was almost unendurable. We huddled together for warmth. The sanitary arrangements were primitive and during the whole term of our imprisonment we had no facilities for a decent wash. In addition, some of us had been wounded in the battle in the trench, and our wounds were left unattended. Our Commander, Harold Fry, had been wounded in the arm and had to attend to it himself under these conditions. Most of us fell ill; one contracted lung disease.[9]

*   *   *   *   *

On March 9, 1937, General Francisco Franco issued a proclamation that all foreigners captured with arms would be shot. This led the British Foreign Office to send a stiff note to Franco, threatening "the strongest possible reaction on the part of H.M. Government"[10] if the 1929 Geneva Convention[11] was not observed in their treatment of British prisoners of war.

The Republic published very different guidelines for the treatment of prisoners. On April 11, 1937, President Manuel Azaña·and Premier Francisco Largo Caballero signed the following decree:

Article 1. That the lives of the insurgent combatants, whether Spaniards or foreigners, shall be respected and they will be delivered without loss of time to the competent authorities, it being forbidden to bring them to trial without previous decision of the Council of Ministers.

Article 2. With regard to the combatants of the rebel camp who voluntarily present themselves to our ranks not only will their lives be respected but an inquiry will be instituted and, if their adherence to the Republic is proved as a result thereof, the Government will recognize their positions, situations and ranks which they may prove that they enjoy or have enjoyed, whether in civil or military life.[12]

On May 18, after three months at Talavera de la Reina, all the British prisoners except Charles Martinson and Robert Silcock were transferred to Salamanca to be court-martialed. No interpreter was provided, and they were tried as a group. The prisoners agreed no one would speak in court. Having come to Spain to defend its legally elected government, they were astonished to be charged with "aiding a military rebellion." The defending officer, whom they had not seen before, pleaded for mercy on the ground that they had been misled.

Five were sentenced to death: Harold Fry, Morry Goldberg, George Leeson, James Rutherford, and Charles West. James Pugh and G. Watters were condemned to twenty years in solitary confinement. The rest were sentenced to twenty years' imprisonment.

All were returned to the Model Prison at Salamanca. Every evening the guards would unlock all cell doors and call out the names of Spaniards to be executed that night. A few days later, the British were called out one forenoon and taken before a board of Italians, seven men and one woman who informed them that Franco had decided to pardon them and send them home. They would be given new clothes and money, and then be allowed to cross the border into France. They were taken to a hotel, where they enjoyed their first baths since capture and were given clean, lice-free clothes.

Five days later, all but two were taken to Fuenterrabia. Morry Goldberg and George Leeson were held back as hostages so that the others would not say anything unfavorable about the Franco regime when they returned to England. At Fuenterrabia, the twenty-three were paraded before a Movietone Newsreel camera as proof of "Franco's great generosity." A fascist sergeant was photographed with them, holding in his arms packets of cigarettes to issue to them. The pictures were taken—and the sergeant walked off, with the cigarettes.

The prisoners were then taken to the French border. Less than two weeks before, they had received death and twenty-year sentences. Now they were joyous, about to be free men again. Then a hitch arose. They would have to give the Franco salute for the benefit of photographers before they could cross the border. When they refused, they were informed they would be returned to prison.

Given a short time to think it over, the prisoners proposed: One would give the salute for all. The fascist authorities accepted the compromise; a prisoner stepped out, raised his arm, and gave a feeble "Viva Franco" and the twenty-three happy men crossed over to France. They reached Britain on May 31, 1937.[13,14]

*   *   *   *   *

The fascist leaders were certain they would take Madrid. On February 26, General Gonzalo Quiepo de Llano, Franco's most comical radio broadcaster (he had a large audience on both sides of the front), announced that Madrid would fall between March 12 and 14. The Falangist Party's press and propaganda sections had met in Salamanca to discuss who was going to get what building in Madrid. Mussolini, certain that Franco would need no more arms or men, instructed Count Dino Grandi, his representative at the Non-Intervention Committee, to vote in favor of the proposed withdrawal of all foreign troops from both sides.

For the first three days, the Italian offensive to take Madrid, begun on March 8, 1937, went better than planned. The Italians suffered only five hundred casualties while routing ten thousand poorly organized and poorly led Republican troops. They appeared to have no Republican troops left in front of them.

On the eleventh, an Italian reconnaisance patrol met another Italian speaking patrol and asked how to get to their next objective, Torija. "We know the way, just come with us," was the reply. A little farther on they met more Italians, and by the time the patrol realized these were the Garibaldi of the 12th International Brigade,[15] it was too late: they were prisoners.

The Garibaldis were fascinated by a picturesque and talkative prisoner who wore an astrakhan cap, a shiny brown jacket, and black riding pants and carried a map case. They were more than fascinated when they found the case held not only a map but also Italian General Mario Roatta's plans for the capture of Madrid, including the manpower and armament at his disposal. The prisoner was Major Antonio Luciano, commander of a machine gun battalion attached to the Black Arrow Division. He was carrying documents he should not have had. As a result, the Republican units moving up to stop the Italians received extensive information about the Italian divisions and their weapons and their plans to capture Madrid.[16]

How a rout of Republican forces was turned into a rout of a much larger number of Italian troops cannot be told here, except to pay tribute to the foot soldiers who under the leadership of men like Enrique Líster, commander of the 11th Division, fought grimly, without rest or food, in sleet and snow, to halt and then pursue the Italian invaders.[17] They saved Madrid and the Republic, and by capturing 496 Italian soldiers and officers, they also saved the lives of some 500 Internationals who were captured a year later, for whom the Italians would be exchanged.[18] Among the 500 were 98 American volunteers, including myself.

The first large group of Italians was taken to Madrid. On March 16 they were visited by leading Republican Army officers, Minister of Education Jesús Hernández, and press correspondents from all over the world. Speeches made during the visit were broadcast. After the reading of the prisoners' names, Hernández spoke to them.

We fight so that the tragic problem of hunger may vanish from every home. We fight so that unemployment may be ended. And we fight above all, soldiers of Italy, to prevent the forces of fascism, which are preparing a world war, from causing your wives, your children and your parents to weep tears of blood, for you are one of the peoples who must be hurled into the war which is being prepared, and you will suffer only to benefit the imperialists whom fascism represents.

General José Miaja, president of the Defense Council of Madrid, said

They told you that we, the so-called reds, the defenders of the Republic, murder for the pleasure of killing. You see now this is a lie, yet all their propaganda is based on it. Think for a moment what would have happened to our brothers if they had been taken prisoner by the enemy; they certainly would have been shot. Have no fear; we are defending the Republic, and therefore freedom and justice, and we shall do nothing which is not in accordance with these.

The prisoners applauded and many were in tears. They were invited to speak freely. Three spoke of their poor life under fascism and in the Italian Army. One concluded, "I am ready to join you in the cause you are defending."

As General Miaja and the others left, the prisoners shouted "Viva" for him and the Republic. Foreign journalists were greatly impressed,[19] but the New York Times did not find the Republic's treatment of its prisoners news fit to print. The fascists did monitor Republican broadcasts, and it is probable that it was the Republic's treatment of the Italian prisoners that made Franco decide to free twenty-three British prisoners.

The Italian prisoners were taken to the San Miguel de los Reyes Castle to be housed with thousands of Spanish prisoners. There they were fed well, had comfortable sleeping quarters, and received a generous ration of tobacco. There were no beatings or trials, and they were encouraged to correspond with their relatives. Many wrote: "They treat us as brothers." In the first four months, some thirty asked for permission to join the Garibaldis.[20]

On March 17, General Roatta informed all under his command that captured International Brigaders should be held as prisoners.[21] He may have suspected that the Republic would want live International Brigaders in exchange for Italian prisoners.

Seven members of the International Brigades who were captured in the fighting at Guadalajara survived. All were from the 11th Brigade. They were taken to Gumora prison and then to a concentration camp at Soria.[22]

On March 29, the Republic delivered to the League of Nations, and to the British, French, and Soviet governments, a 320-page volume that contained irrefutable proof of a massive invasion by the Italian Army to overthrow the legally constituted government of Spain. Included were copies of 101 documents seized from the Italian Army in Spain and the statements of many soldiers and officers. When the leaders of England and France still insisted that their non-intervention policy was working, they were lying.[23]

Major General Sir Maxwell Walter Scott, after a ten-day visit in Franco's territory, wrote the Foreign Office that he had visited the British prisoners. He falsely reported the prisoners had no fault to find with the food or general treatment and that many had enlisted for the pay offered by the Republic, and that only one or two had joined because of their convictions. Major General Scott also revealed what had happened to the SS Mar Cantábrico, which had left New York with munitions and food a few hours before the US Neutrality Act took effect, and was reported sunk.

. . I had been told this amusing incident about the so-called British ship, Adda, really the Mar Cantábrico. When the Nationalist cruiser Canaris saw four British destroyers coming up to help the supposed British vessel which had wirelessed for help to the English Navy instead of the British Navy, she signalled our destroyers to stand off as this was not a British ship but a Spanish one. The destroyers turned around and went off signalling "Good luck." The Mar Cantabrico is now safe in the Ferrol Harbor [in Franco Spain] and was not sunk. She contained 48 airplanes about 150 crew, 7 passengers including 5 Italian and 2 French, 1050 machine guns 30 lorries, 14 million rounds of ammunition.[24]

But Scott did not mention that the Spaniards in the crew had been executed.[25]

*   *   *   *   *

In the United States, a nationwide one-day student Strike Against War on Thursday, April 22, 1937, was sponsored by the United Student Peace Committee. The committee consisted of representatives from all national student organizations, from the American Student Union on the left to the National Student Federation on the right. The strike was supported also by the National Council of Methodist Youth and the National Councils of the Student YMCA and YWCA.

James A. Wechsler and Joseph P. Lash, editor and associate editor of The Student Advocate, published by the American Student Union, in an editorial supporting the strike wrote:

If, while fascism throws all its resources into Spain, the allies of the Spanish Government remain inert, the simple and inevitable consequence will be World War in which the chances of American involvement are vast.[26]

This student analysis proved to be much more accurate than those made by Congress, the State Department, and the hierarchy of the Catholic Church.

*   *   *   *   *

Dr. Marcel Junod, representing the International Red Cross (IRC) suggested an exchange of prisoners to a Franco general, Emilio Mola. Mola exclaimed: "How can you expect us to exchange a red dog for a Spanish gentleman?"[27] Evidently, "red dogs" were worth more than Spanish gentlemen, because Mola refused to make an exchange.

General Mola was in charge of a fascist offensive begun on March 31 1937, to take the northern provinces of Vizcaya, Asturias, and Santander which had remained loyal to the Republic. On June 3, the fascists reported that Mola had died when his plane hit a mountain. British Ambassador Sir Henry Chilton on June 12 informed the Foreign Office:

I learned . . . that General Mola's death was caused by a bomb placed under his seat in the airplane, possibly by some mechanic whom the Nationalists had been obliged to employ because they are short of labor. Mola's body was apparently pretty well blown to bits. . . .[28]

The logical way for the Republic to come to the aid of the North was by launching an offensive from Catalonia. Because of the Anarchist and POUM policy of first making a workers' revolution, no offensive had been launched against Franco from Catalonia since the early days of the revolt. Franco also boasted to the German ambassador that he had thirteen agents in Barcelona who could cause fighting to break out whenever he wished.[29]

After the Republic took steps in April to mobilize the people and industry of Catalonia in order to defeat fascism first, a battle broke out inside Barcelona on May 3 between the POUM, supported by some anarchists, and those forces supporting the Republic. The arrival of government forces on May 6 ended the revolt. This was my introduction to Spanish politics when I crossed the Pyrenees on May 1. Along with several hundred volunteers, I was held back at Figueras until May 7, when we were taken in covered trucks to the train station in Barcelona. These events made us question the antifascist credentials of the leaders of the POUM and the anarchists.[30]

*   *   *   *   *

Franco, too, had problems with conflicts between the two main organizations supporting him. He solved them by announcing on April 19 that he had merged the two organizations into one, with himself at the head of it. His brother-in-law, Ramón Serrano Súñer, would be the organization's secretary-general.[31]

In the Republic, widespread dissatisfaction with Premier Largo Caballero, led to his resignation.[32] President Azaña on May 18 named Juan Negrín, formerly minister of finance and a Socialist, to take his place. Negrín proved to be an excellent choice. He quickly prepared and launched an offensive from Catalonia, but it was not powerful enough to save the Basques. Bilbao fell on June 19.

Franco had other, more serious problems. One was the scarcity of labor; large numbers of workers had been executed or were in jails and concentration camps. And what should be done with several hundred thousand imprisoned Republican supporters? Civilians who had supported the Republic before or after the revolt, and who had not supported Franco's seizure of power, were held under the "special offenses" charge. He solved both problems with Decree No. 231 on May 28, 1937: "Article I: The right to work is conceded to prisoners of war, and to those imprisoned for special offenses, under the circumstance and conditions established below."[33]

The decree set up a central office to prepare and organize the prisoners for employment and to receive requests from those wishing to employ them.

Working prisoners were to be paid the equivalent of thirty cents a day, but they would actually get only seven and a half cents a day, paid weekly, the remainder being deducted for maintenance. Wives of working prisoners on the fascist side without property or support would get another thirty cents plus fifteen cents for each child, provided that the total did not exceed the average wage for a laborer in the district.

The inspector general of prisons and the commanding general of each military district were responsible for listing the prisoners in their areas. A judge would decide which prisoners would receive a work permit. Prisoners would be under military command and subject to the army's Military Code of Justice and to the Geneva Convention of June 27, 1929.

It would be safe and profitable to employ the prisoners in labor battalions under military control, providing the judges had eliminated those most likely to cause "trouble." The decree did not mention foreigners, nor did it specify that lives of POWS must be respected at the point of capture. The reference to the Geneva Convention was window dressing.

*   *   *   *   *

Four members of the 11th International Brigade were taken alive on June 10, 1937, on a reconnaisance mission on Mount Picarón in the Utande sector of the Guadalajara front. They were Randulf Dalland, a Norwegian Communist leader; Karl Kormes, twenty-two, from Berlin; and Max Allenspach, twenty-six, and Ulrich Lörrach, twenty, Swiss citizens. Karl and Ulrich, wounded, were hospitalized and treated well by the staff. Cured, they were imprisoned with Max and Randulf for several weeks before being transferred to the concentration camp at Soria, where they met the seven who had been captured in March. They would remain there for eight months.[34]

*   *   *   *   *

On May 18, the US ambassador to Spain, Claude Bowers, sent a confidential message to Secretary of State Cordell Hull:

This station [the Italian radio station in Salamanca] solicits war correspondents to make propaganda speeches for them for from one to ten thousand lire. . . . One American, Mr. Carney of the New York Times responded. I am informed . . . that one of the conditions . . . is that they shall close their talks with the fascist cry "Arriba España!" That may account for Mr. Carney's use of the phrase.[35]

4 Captured at Brunete

My INITIATION into battle, in which two large organized groups of men try desperately to kill one another (and do so), came in the Republic's first big offensive at Brunete. It began at 5:30 A.M on July 6, 1937. I was the third ammunition carrier for a machine gun, at the bottom of the military totem pole. My task was to lug two heavy cases of ammunition for the gun, plus my rifle and knapsack, and then defend the gun from a nearby foxhole.

Our objectives were to relieve the pressure on Madrid and to slow the fascist drive on the North, where the provinces of Santander and Asturias were still holding out.[1] Within the first two days we had helped capture over two hundred prisoners, all of whom were sent behind the lines to prisoner camps.[2]

On our third morning we received orders to follow several tanks that would pass over our trenches. The tanks flushed out a line of enemy troops. They retreated rapidly, and we hurried after them, down a long grassy slope, across a dry riverbed, and up a gulley toward Mosquito Ridge. A quarter of the way up, I saw a very dear friend who had been a frequent guest in my home, Paul Anderson. He was dead, a bullet hole squarely in the center of his forehead. A battalion scout came down the gully urging us to hurry because the fascists had evacuated the ridge. We scrambled up as rapidly as we could, carrying our heavy Maxim machine gun, ammunition, and rifles. When we were within three hundred yards of the top, we came under rifle and machine-gun fire. We pushed on a short distance farther until our company commander, Walter Garland, was wounded. Garland, a black, was beloved for his splendid amalgam of discipline, fairness, and concern for us and for his courage and military competence. We then dug gun pits and foxholes for the night. Subsequent attempts to take the ridge were unsuccessful.

Later I learned this ridge had been one of the major objectives of the offensive, for from it we could have shelled the fascist positions attacking Madrid. On May 18, 1981, I visited Albares, a small village fifty kilometers southeast of Madrid, where we had rested between major campaigns. There I met Ricardo Sánchez, a short round-faced Spaniard about my age who had fought in Franco's army. I invited him to lunch and then learned he had been among those we had chased up Mosquito Ridge.

I asked him, "Did you leave the top of the ridge?"

"Yes. We went right over it and down into a woods on the other side."

"Why did you come back up on top?"

"Our commander ordered us to go back, and so we did, just in time to

stop you," Ricardo said it with a smile. If only we had been briefed ade
quately beforehand about the strategic importance of Mosquito Ridge,
thought, we might well have summoned up the energy and determination 1
capture it, and so relieved Madrid of shelling by artillery.

Eight Americans were captured in this offensive.[3] One of them was Le
Grachow. Abe Sasson, a fellow soldier, later wrote about the twenty-three
year-old Grachow, who did not survive capture. Abe had known Leo at th
Hebrew Orphan Asylum as a promising poet and journalist: "Leo had to h
in the most furious fighting for humanity and progress. Into this flame h
great brain and heart forever plunged him: he would burn or put it out. Ar
burn he must for his poetic genius flung him to the forefront. . . ."

Lou Ornitz was the only survivor of the eight. "*Ruso! Ruso!*" the Moo
shouted as they pointed their rifles at him.

"*No, no, americano!*" Lou insisted. One of the Moors forced Lou's jav
apart; he looked in, and seemed disappointed. Fortunately, an officer ran t
and ordered Lou and five Spaniards taken back to headquarters.

Brooklyn-born, and just twenty-five, Lou was muscular, nearly six fe
tall, with a broad, open face. He had organized textile workers in New Yo:
and Massachusetts and coal and steel workers for John L. Lewis and th
United Mine Workers in Pennsylvania. In February 1937 he had come
Spain, and had been assigned to the 5th Transport Regiment.

On July 26 Lou had driven a truck with a crew of four up to the Brune
front to retrieve empty artillery casings. A roadside guard informed him th
he should pick up two pieces of artillery in danger of capture, and a memb
of the artillery crew was put on the truck as a guide. They loaded one pie
and were chaining the second so they could tow it when they found ther
selves surrounded by Moroccan troops.[4]

Captured, and marching back as ordered, Lou noticed some Moc
pecking away at the teeth on dead bodies, collecting gold caps and filling
He was thankful he did not have any. The sergeant in charge of the prison
detail pointed to the star and Republican emblem on the ring on Lou's le
hand. He said Lou would be safer without the ring, and reluctantly Lou ga
it to him. The sergeant pointed to a hole with partly buried bodies and sa
they had been shot recently. But before he turned the prisoners over
headquarters, he slipped Lou some fascist pesetas and two cigarette pacl
with a low "*Viva la República!*"

Lou was put in a cellar. Soon the five Spaniards who had been on h
truck joined him. Lou shared his tobacco with them, but they had bare
finished their cigarettes when guards entered and took the Spaniards awa
Soon he heard shouts of "*Viva la República!*" followed by a volley of rifle fi

After a restless night preparing himself for execution, Lou was rea
when the guards came the next morning, only to find himself handed a c
of coffee and some bread. All day he waited. At dusk two guards came t
tied Lou's hands behind his back, and then ordered him to march. They to

him to a church crowded with prisoners. The officer in charge insisted Lou was a Russian and put him into a room with other foreigners.

Before Lou could become acquainted with the others, two Moors came in and took out an International Brigader. Screams followed. Soon the bruised and bloody body was dragged in. Another International and a third received the same treatment. Then it was Lou's turn.

Two Moors grabbed me by the arms and dragged me into the next room. I . . . can remember nothing more than the sight of huge Moors armed with clubs, and a little Spanish captain who spoke in broken English. He said something about showing the American what Franco thinks of those who believe in democracy. . . . Then I was beaten and kicked. Those kicks and blows seemed to come from all directions. They poured against me without a stop until I lost consciousness.[5]

Some did not recover, but Lou survived, thanks to his strong physique and the care he received from two other survivors; Albert, a young German; and Fritz, a nineteen-year-old Austrian. They were trucked about eighty kilometers west to a concentration camp near Talavera de la Reina. It was a walled compound that appeared to have been a warehouse or factory. It had one entrance, a runway through the center, with two forty-foot-square rooms on each side, and a yard open to the sky in the rear. Against the back wall a trench had been dug and a big plank laid over it to serve as a latrine.

Here Lou found guards were still free to use their clubs as they saw fit. The loss of a relative at the front was sufficient excuse for whacking an international. Fortunately, one of the younger Civil Guards stationed there had a brother in Chicago. After he found out Lou was an American, he would call him over to his post to talk about the United States. He even gave Lou some tobacco and grapes. But his friendship didn't go so far as to protect Lou from occasional beatings. Prisoners were constantly coming and going, and groups were being called out daily for execution.

In the second half of September, Lou, Fritz, and Albert were moved a hundred kilometers farther behind the lines to a dungeon in the bullring in Trujillo, then a concentration camp for several thousand prisoners. Lou is uncertain how long he was held in the completely dark dungeon, but he does recall vividly the pain in his eyes when he was brought out and the whacking he got because he couldn't see to follow the guard's orders.

Lou and his comrades were assigned to one of the stables under the stands, where Spanish prisoners made room for them. Allowed to walk around in the bullring, Lou found more Internationals, among them Robert, a tall, thin Frenchman from whom he learned there was a prisoner organization. Through it, Lou sent letters to his family to inform them where he was held.

During their first two months at Trujillo, Lou's closest friend, Albert, the young German anti-Nazi, developed severe headaches and began to have fevers and chills; his eyes began to bulge. As there were no beds—

everyone slept on the stone floors—Lou or a friend would lie beside Albert trying to warm him, but his condition grew steadily worse. When they finally got a doctor to look at him, he merely nudged Albert with his foot. Lou protested that Albert would die without treatment, and the doctor responded he would be better off dead. Soon the guards had him carried away.

A Basque priest refused to conduct religious services praising the Franco regime and protested the brutal treatment of the prisoners. When he died of a beating, several other Basque priests, also prisoners, arranged a secret 4 A.M. mass for him. Lou and Robert attended, representing the International Brigades, and in his halting Spanish, Lou paid tribute to the brave Basque priest.

Three months later, a representative of the International Red Cross asked to see Lou and gave him an IRC form to fill out for delivery to his family, asking for eyeglasses and some money.

The next day Lou was called before the prison commander to explain he had come in without glasses, why did he now ask for a new pair? Lou informed him that an officer had taken the glasses when he was captured, perhaps for the gold-plated rims. To Lou's astonishment, the commander in a very civil manner said he would have given him a pair of glasses if he had asked him for them. The commander ordered the beating of International stopped. Then, were it not for the continued calling out of prisoners for execution, the lack of medical care, the elementary toilet facilities, and the hunger, the lice, and the fleas, life might have been bearable.[6]

Lou became acquainted with some twenty Internationals at Trujillo including two Germans and one Italian, two Poles, two Yugoslavs, an Austrian, half a dozen Frenchmen, Bobbie Beggs from Dundee, Scotland, and Julian Ben Raadi from Morocco. Julian was only seventeen and had been captured on the Madrid front. Usually, a Moor who fought on the Republican side would be beaten to death by Moors on Franco's side. But Julian had been brought gifts of food by the Moors because his father had been an important leader in the Rif wars in North Africa against France and Spain during and after World War I. Julian and Lou became very close friends.

Called again into the commander's office, Lou saw sitting beside him the IRC representative. Lou was told to open a small package. It contained eyeglasses, socks, and some hard candy from his family. Lou was overjoyed especially when he also received five dollars in pesetas, and he hurried back to share his good fortune with his comrades.[7]

Lou was joined by another American early in January 1938—Jesús de la Casa Barro, twenty, born in Philadelphia. His family had been visiting northern Spain when the uprising began. He and his brother, Joseph, had stayed to fight for the Republic. Jesús, better known as Andy, had been captured when the North fell, and had been assigned to a labor battalion repairing docks and railroads. When he said he was an American, he was sent to the Trujillo bullring. Andy, a sturdy five foot four, wrote letters in Spanish for those who didn't know how to write and served as a Spanish-English interpreter.

The fascists had not established a policy on what to do with International Brigaders who were not killed immediately upon capture. Lou heard from Spanish prisoners about Internationals they had met in other prisons who were believed killed. He reports a few Internationals were called out at Trujillo; according to the grapevine, they were killed.

Late in January, Lou, Andy, Fritz Riegler, Bobbie Beggs, and several other Internationals were moved to Santander, into a large stone building filled with Spanish prisoners. A high fence on each side ran down to a small beach. They were pleased when they were able to wash themselves for the first time since their capture, even though the water and air were cold.[8]

A week after his arrival at Santander, Lou was delighted when Ben Raadi joined him. Then an unusual prisoner came in, a Chinese, twenty-four years old, powerfully built. The three soon became fast friends. Chang Aking had been born in Shanghai. When life became dangerous for him under Chiang Kai-shek because he had helped some Communists form a union, he shipped out on a French freighter as a cook's helper. The cook came from French Indo-China, now Vietnam, and turned out to be the most brilliant and wisest man Chang had ever met or heard. From him Chang learned not only about politics and the struggles of the Indo-Chinese to free themselves, but also how to speak French. The cook persuaded Chang to leave the ship to join the Loyalist forces in northern Spain. But when Chang asked the cook to come with him, he explained that he was already in an army and had been ordered to go to a school in Moscow. Lou later suspected that the cook had been Ho Chi Minh, who later would lead the struggles to drive the French and the United States out of Vietnam. Chang had joined an Asturian miner's battalion, and when the North fell, he was captured near Mieres.

Lou and the rest of the Internationals were transferred to the San Pedro de Cardeña Concentration Camp on April 5, 1938.

*   *   *   *   *

Harold ("Whitey") Dahl was the first American to be reported captured by the press, the first to be court-martialed and sentenced to death, and then the first to be court-martialed and sentenced to death a second time.

Dahl, who graduated from the US Army Air Corps flying school at Kelly Field in 1933, was discharged from the Air Corps on February 10, 1936. In need of funds—he had paid some bills in California with checks that bounced—Dahl went to the Spanish embassy in Mexico City and signed a contract to fly for the Republic for $1,500 a month.

In February 1937 he started flying fighter planes. On the eighteenth he was shot down over Republican territory, bailed out, and returned to his base to resume flying. On April 12, Dahl went to France for an appendectomy and was joined there by his wife, Edith Rogers, a nightclub singer and entertainer. He returned to Spain on June 24 to collect back pay and to fly another month, but before he left Paris he gave the US military attaché full details, with photographs, of the Soviet pursuit plane I-5.[9]

On July 12, at Brunete, Dahl tried to escape from a fascist attacker by a power dive; he lost a wing. Barely managing to bail out, he landed in fascist territory. Moroccan troops caught him and began clubbing him, but he was saved by the timely appearance of an officer. In a filthy guardhouse, various officers tried to get him to talk by jabbing their pistols into his ribs. He was transferred to Salamanca by three Civil Guards, who also pressed their pistols hard into his ribs trying to get him to talk, warning him that if he didn't they would execute him as an example so other American pilots would think twice before aiding the Republic.

William Carney, the *New York Times* correspondent on Franco territory, interviewed Dahl at Salamanca on July 21, and then reported that Dahl had been treated with "exquisite courtesy" by officers after his capture.[10] Secretary of State Cordell Hull ordered US Consul George M. Graves at Vigo to visit Dahl to find out whether he had been recruited illegally in the United States; Graves reported on July 28 that Dahl had signed his contract in Mexico City, and that the judge who would try Dahl said the court-martial would unquestionably sentence him to death.[11]

On August 23, US Consul Charles Beylard at Nice, France, asked the State Department for instructions on what to do with $100 given him for Dahl by his wife. He was told to return the money to her and the same instructions went to Consul Graves. But Beylard, at the insistence of Mrs. Dahl, had already forwarded it to Graves under the assumption there would be no objection to sending funds to an American citizen in danger of losing his life. Graves returned the money.[12]

Ambassador Bowers, after talking with Flight Lieutenant Juan Castillo, who had sat on Dahl's court-martial, telegraphed Hull on September 1 that Dahl had been condemned to death. He asked for instructions. The *New York Times* reported the next day that Dahl had been court-martialed. In the next two days telegrams came to the State Department from Dahl's mother and from the mayor, city council members, and Chamber of Commerce of Champaign, Illinois, urging the Department to intervene to save Dahl's life.[13]

On September 14 Bay reported that General Queipo de Llano had informed him that Franco said Dahl had not been condemned to death and was on a list of prisoners to be exchanged. Then, on the twenty-seventh, Bay reported that Dahl would be tried at 11 A.M. on October 5.[14] Dahl described the trial preparations graphically:

. . . military court. . . . Tried and *convicted*, I was assured by my cheery guards! And the charges? Here's where you get a laugh! We were charged with "taking up arms against the Spanish Government." Can you match that for sheer ironical effrontery? A charge like that brought by a bunch of revolutionists who were engaged themselves in an attempt to overthrow that same government![15]

This time it was a public trial, the courtroom packed with reporters. Dahl was tried with three Soviet and three Spanish fliers. He had been given a court-appointed counsel, the Marqués del Merito, who began his defense by making a trip to Burgos to confer with Franco.[16]

The court, consisting of nine officers resplendent in military regalia, adjourned after a four-hour trial. When they reconvened several hours later:

At a word from their ranking officer, they drew their swords and laid them on a small table in front of them. One glance was all that was needed, the point of every sword was directed towards us. . . . The points spelled death.

Dahl's execution was set for 6 A.M. on October 8. While he waited, he saw one of his Spanish co-defendants, David Gómez Varela, taken to be shot. On the seventh Dahl heard a crowd coming down the prison corridor. Then he heard almost hysterical voices: "Whitey! Old boy, you've been pardoned! There'll be no execution!" A crowd of newspaper men had come up to congratulate him.[17]

The three Soviet aviators had their sentence reduced to life imprisonment, and were exchanged not long afterward. While the Republic exchanged a number of German and Italian pilots for Soviet pilots, Dahl was never included, possibly because of Carney's reports that he was willing to fly for Franco, which Dahl has denied. He was paroled on October 10, 1937, and assigned a private room in the officer's wing of the military hospital at Salamanca after taking an oath he would not try to escape.[18] He enjoyed considerable freedom and was able to receive funds from abroad. Dahl was freed on February 22, 1940, and returned to the United States on the SS *Ixiria* on March 17 with the next-to-last group of American prisoners.[19]

5 Quinto, Belchite and Teruel

ON AUGUST 14, 1937, Franco began an offensive against Santander in northern Spain, using several Italian divisions. The Republic, wanting to relieve the pressure on the North, strengthened Catalonia for an offensive toward Zaragoza. But it was August 24 before the Republic was able to get troops and materiel in place to launch the offensive—too late to help Santander, for it fell the next day.

Although the Lincoln Battalion was part of the strike force, no Americans were captured in this offensive. We took hundreds of prisoners, and am ashamed to report that a few officers and three fascist officials were killed without trial.

In this offensive I was the observer for the Lincoln Machine Gun Company. After passing the silent Anarchist troops holding the front line we advanced over their soccer field (where they had played with the fascists) to attack Quinto. We drove the fascists out of their fortifications in a well-coordinated fifteen-minute attack that included concentrated artillery fire, aerial bombing and strafing, tanks smashing barbed wire defenses, and an infantry charge under cover of our machine-gun fire.

Some of the retreating troops had taken refuge in the church, always built on high ground. Taking the church proved to be difficult. I wrote to my wife:

Finally some 57 prisoners crawled out a window, most of them kids 18 and 19 years old. They told how the officers tried to keep them from surrendering, and how the officers killed a number who tried to surrender.[1]

I have learned since that among the fifty-seven were two civilians identified as hated fascist officials by the young soldiers. At their request the two were executed by two Americans.[2] A more serious blot on the reputation of the 15th International Brigade was the execution of some officers and noncommissioned officers later that day. I have received varying accounts of how it happened, but there is no doubt that it did happen.

We were commanded by General Walter (Karol Swierczewski), head of the 35th Division. He and his staff were always close at hand when we were in action. While he demanded excellence in performance from his staff, he was very loyal to them. His friendship with and esteem for the chief of the Division Medical Services, Dr. Domanski Dubois, were especially great. Dr. Dubois was killed by a sniper in the church steeple. The next day we took Quinto and captured some two hundred men, including several commis-

30

sioned officers. The officers were brought before General Walter. After questioning them, he held his pistol against each officer's head, and saying *"Za Dubois"* (For Dubois), he shot every one, except a doctor.[3]

Walter then ordered the killing of a small group of noncommissioned officers who were standing to one side. American and Spanish troops opened fire on them. An American who was in the Machine Gun Company and who took part in the shooting informed me in 1981 that he recalled some were still living after they had fallen. The coup de grace was given to all except one—a particularly good-looking young Spaniard who had only a very bad leg wound. Some Americans, revolted, wanted to call the political commissar to decide whether the young Spaniard should be hospitalized or shot when someone known as "Crazy O'Leary" put a bullet into his head. My informant has had many nightmares about this. An indication of the shame Americans felt over this event is that they kept quiet about it. I did not hear about it until forty-five years later.

The next morning the Machine Gun Company received orders to help take Purburell Hill, a well-fortified ridge some eight hundred feet high, with steep and bare sides. That evening I wrote my wife:

About one kilometer from the town on a very high bluff, the fascists had built a beautiful system of trench-works and block houses, and a number of them were in these. This morning we prepared to attack. . . . But a few minutes before we were ready to storm it, they waved a white flag and some 600 surrendered. . . . these troops looked more like candidates for a Boy Scout camp than real soldiers, and they were extremely happy when they were safely in our hands, safe from their officers and our attacks.[4]

We learned that here again some who had wanted to surrender were shot by their own officers. All officers and soldiers were taken to POW camps.

Our next assignment was to help take Belchite. We arrived there on the afternoon of the second day, after the town had been surrounded. The fascist military command in Zaragoza was encouraging the military and civilian authorities inside Belchite to resist by radioing them that a relief column was on the way. Supplies were dropped from planes to them at night. They held on for six more days and inflicted heavy casualties on us from the two church towers jutting above the town.

In 1981, in the archives of the Servicio Histórico Militar in Madrid, I saw aerial photographs made by German reconnaissances planes showing the location of our machine guns, artillery, and trucks. Throughout the siege, Franco's 5th Army Corps Command in Zaragoza had known the strength and the disposition of our forces. The Republic had had neither radio communication nor aerial photography at its disposal.

For example, Belchite Comandante Santa Pau radioed at 5 P.M. on September 3, 1937, about sixty hours before Belchite fell:

The enemy attack continues with extraordinary intensity situation most difficul [due to] infiltrations. Most urgent send medical supplies and sand bags. Number o casualties extraordinary nevertheless the defense will be continued with unlimitec enthusiasm. Viva España!

And at 12:15 P.M. two days later, Santa Pau radioed, without a *Viva España,* "Tell me situation [of relief] column." He then received an order foi thirty top officers to break out that night. A bonfire would be built on Sillerc peak to serve as a beacon to guide them through the night.[5]

In 1981, when I mentioned Belchite to Ricardo Sañchez, my luncheor guest at Albares, he remarked: "I was there, too."

"You were! How did you get out?"

"At night we tried to break out through you, and we didn't make it, so w tried to go east and got stopped, and then we went south and broke througl and got back to our lines."

Ricardo did not tell me the whole story. According to a secret report tc the General Staff by Franco's 5th Army Corps, based on interviews witl those who had escaped on the evening of September 5, some five hundrec soldiers tried to break out along Main Street (held by the Lincolns) at 8:15 but they had to withdraw because of the intense enemy fire. At 9:30 the' failed to break out at another point, and at 10 they failed again at a thirc point. At 11:10, now desperate, they gathered a group of some three hun dred, soldiers, *women, and children,* and decided to break out on the soutl side. "The reds, disconcerted by the violence of the attack and the boldnes of our troops, hesitated for some seconds, long enough for the heroi survivors to get away into the fields. . . ."[6]

The report omits an event that explains the decrease from five hundre soldiers to three hundred, including women and children. Dave Doran, thei brigade commissar, commandeered a passing sound truck, from which Spaniard that evening told soldiers and civilians that no relief column wai coming, that they would die if they fought on: "But we don't want to die. . . Come over to the people's side, where you will have freedom, where a ne\ life awaits you. . . . Drop your arms and come over the barricades one b one. All who come over to us will live." Some soldiers came over th barricades; others decided to wait until the officers had left and thei surrender to us.

Lieutenant Hernández y Alcana, a Republican staff officer who was a the breakout point, described the approach of a group of civilians, includin women, who yelled "Comrades!" Believing they were more of the civiliar who had managed to get away, the Republican troops asked them to halt t be identified, and were greeted with a shower of grenades. The lieutenar reported: "The whole affair had taken us by surprise. Then, we had hes tated too long for fear of killing the civilians. So the fascists were able t attack us first."[7]

I described what I saw the next morning standing on the bank of a sunken roadway looking down on the last to surrender: "Just at dawn, the last garrison surrendered, and some 160 soldiers and over a hundred old men, women and children marched out. Every third soldier had a bandage around his head from a head wound. Many were trying to sing the Internationale and the majority greeted us with raised fists."

From civilians we learned how "morale" had been maintained: the fascists killed some three hundred soldiers and civilians during the eight days the town was besieged in order to maintain law and order.[8]

After dawn we searched the houses for hidden officers. Ralph Thornton, a black from Pittsburgh, Ben Findley from Turtle Creek, Pennsylvania, and I entered a house on Main Street where we found a very old couple lying on blankets on the basement floor. At the end of a passageway we found a small opening into an adjoining room. My flashlight revealed a pile of hay against a wall. I entered the room, kicked the pile, and brought out a frightened young soldier. While one of us took him to the collection point for prisoners, the other two continued the search. Upstairs, in the attic, its sloping roof blown away,

I saw a sniper in civilian clothes sitting on a box with a rifle across his knee. The moment he saw me, he stood up, raised his left hand, shouting "Viva la República!" but keeping the rifle in his right hand. Then he began to beg me not to shoot him, that he had been fighting for the Republic for 40 years and could prove it, etc. By that time the others came up. But when we felt the barrel of his rifle, it was warm, there were empty cartridges lying about, and his rifle was loaded.[9]

We delivered him to the prisoner collection point. That night I met a fellow soldier who had to get something off his chest. The civilians from Belchite had insisted that one of the prisoners be executed. They said he was the vice-president of the Falange of Zaragoza and had killed many people who had not shown the proper zeal for the "Nationalist" cause. My friend was finally told to take him out and shoot him. It had been an unnerving experience, the prisoner clinging to his knees and begging incessantly for his life. But my fellow soldier, aware of the man's brutality, carried out the order. When he described the man, I recognized our sniper prisoner. We agreed he had earned his fate, but we would have preferred to have had him brought before a court.

When I was in Belchite in June 1981, I asked a shopkeeper who was in his fifties whether he remembered the siege.

"I shall never forget it. My father was killed in it."

"Who killed him?"

"The fascists. They thought he had Republican ideas."

Another man (Mariano, then a boy of thirteen) remembered the siege and said the soldiers and civilians had decided to surrender to the Lincolns because they believed we would spare their lives. I have found no evidence

that we shot any captured soldiers or officers; all were turned over to
Spanish authorities.

According to Hugh Thomas,

. . . Belchite and the other little towns had been defended by their Carlist or falangist
defenders most courageously and republican morale on this front had been severely
damaged by the political upheavals which had preceded the battle.[10]

I strongly disagree. What stubborn resistance there was had been
gained by the use of deceit, violence, and terror by the fascist officials at a
horrible cost to civilians and soldiers. Our offensive only became possible
after what Thomas chose to label "political upheavals."

*   *   *   *   *   *

Visitors and news from overseas cheered us. In August 1937, Louis de
Brouckére, the venerable president of the Second Socialist International
visited the Internationals. He spoke about the need for a world-wide front
against fascism to aid Republican Spain. (He was removed from office for
having said this.) President Roosevelt in his "Quarantine the Aggressor"
speech on October 5 in Chicago condemned the invasion of other countries
by certain powers. We hoped it would lead to the lifting of the embargo. Two
Congressmen—Jerry O'Connell, a Montana Democrat, and John T. Bernard, a Minnesota Farmer-Laborite—expressed their views over radio station EAR in Madrid on October 22. O'Connell stated:

After seeing the situation at first hand, I, for one, do not believe that this kind of one
sided non-intervention can be permitted to continue. It is an open invitation to the
Fascist aggressors to provoke so-called civil wars and then move in with their armed
battalions to carry Fascism throughout the world.

John T. Bernard proved himself prophetic when he added:

Continued failure to grant the Spanish Republic its proper rights will, we fear
hasten the coming of a new world war with all its consequent dangers to liberty and
democracy, as President Roosevelt so well pointed out in his Chicago speech.[11]

*   *   *   *   *

On October 21, Gijón, the last important Republican town in the North
was captured by Franco's armies. The fascists jailed and began to execute
large number of people. Appalled, the Republic offered to allow some 7,000
fascist civilians and military personnel who had taken refuge in foreign
embassies and legations in Madrid, plus all German, Italian, and Spanish
POWS, to leave the Republic if Franco would allow all civilians and soldiers
in Asturias, Santander, and Vizcaya who wanted to leave to do so. Franco

made a counterproposal, and negotiations were placed in the hands of British Field Marshal Sir Philip Chetwode. Additional thousands were executed in the North before an agreement for a large exchange was reached on March 23, 1938.[12] Even that was called off by the fascists when they decided the Republic would collapse within a month.

*   *   *   *   *

On November 6, Hitler signed an Anti-Comintern Pact with Italy and Japan, making it appear that their alliance was directed solely against the Soviet Union. Many important political and religious leaders believed this. But as revealed at the Nuremberg trials, Hitler had called together his top military commanders only the day before to announce to them his plans for a war of extermination against Britain and France and to declare that the war in Spain had to be supported to maintain Italian control of Spain's Balearic Islands.[13]

Fighting at Spain's Coldest City: Teruel

I visited the Lincoln and MacPap (Canadian Mackenzie-Papineau) battalions in their front-line trenches at Teruel at the end of January 1938. I was to direct a school for political commissars, and I went there to recruit students. I found the battalions fighting in temperatures as low as eighteen degrees below zero Fahrenheit and snow three feet deep. Food froze before it reached the trenches, and anyone who received a very bad wound froze to death before he could be taken to a first-aid station.

Both battalions were helping to hold off Franco's frantic efforts to retake the provincial capital, Teruel. No Internationals had helped take the city. Yet on January 7, a front-page article in Franco's *El Diario Vasco* claimed that, of the troops who had captured Teruel, "40 percent . . . are . . . Jews, North American Negroes and Czechs. . . ."

In that bitter weather, patrols were going out into no-man's-land at night to check on the enemy's activities. One night three men did not come back: Clyde Taylor from Louisville, Kentucky, a twenty-one-year-old Antioch College graduate who was the MacPap mapmaker; Yorki Burton from Vancouver; and another Canadian. Fascist prisoners taken the next night hinted that the three had been caught, questioned, and shot. Two Americans from Boston were captured at Teruel; Henry Shapiro, born in 1910, was reported captured and killed on January 1; the date of capture of Antonio Flores González, twenty-four, is not known.

The 15th Brigade was relieved on February 3, and the exhausted survivors caught a train to Tarazona to rest and refill their ranks. However, before they reached their base, they were ordered to return to the Terue front. On February 16, they made a night attack near Segura de los Baños i snow and icy winds. In a very successful action, the MacPaps and Lincoln captured about five hundred enemy troops. All were taken alive and treate well, except a very arrogant commander who demanded special treatmen Milton Wolff, the Lincoln Battalion commander, reported: "I gave it to him. booted his ass down the side of the hill in full view of his troops—and I' sure they appreciated it."[14]

*   *   *   *   *

Premier Negrín had moved the Republican government to Barcelon during the fall of 1937. Public trust had been badly damaged by the sun mary justice meted out by Anarchist groups and the "uncontrollables." government decree ordering a mandatory review of all death sentence helped restore public confidence. Other decrees reorganized Catalonia industrial production to meet the vital needs of the people and the militar Negrín was handicapped by a minister of defense, Indalecio Prieto, who wa convinced the war could not be won, and by a president, Manuel Azaña, foreign minister, José Giral, and several other Cabinet members who we very pessimistic about the war's outcome. However, strong public suppo for Negrín's measures, sparked by the PSUC, the Unified Socialist Party Catalonia, had greatly increased Catalonia's contribution in war materi and manpower.

*   *   *   *   *

Franco also reorganized his government. On February 1, 1938, he s up a conventional cabinet, with himself as president and General Francisc Gómez Jordana y Souza as vice-president and foreign minister. The mo powerful man in the cabinet was Franco's brother-in-law, Serrano Súñe the minister of interior. Súñer did not have responsibility for public orde military courts-martial and fascist death squads took care of that.

In brief, a totalitarian state was set up: The right to strike and to barga collectively was banned. Industry was placed under the direction of th state. Public companies and banks no longer had to hold shareholde meetings or provide a public audit of their books. Farmers had to sell the wheat and other produce at fixed prices to state organizations. All educati was placed firmly under the control of the Catholic Church.[15]

Under Franco, the state intervened in all phases of economic and soci life, supposedly for the benefit of all, but in practice for the benefit of th wealthy, the military leaders, and the church. Anyone who expressed a opinion that this was not the ideal form of society could expect a brief tr before execution or years of service in a labor battalion—if the death squads didn't get him, or her, first.

*   *   *   *   *

On January 21, the *New York Times* reported that a tanker flying an American flag and operating with an American crew had been captured by two Franco warships and taken to Franco's naval base at Palma on the island of Majorca. The ship was the Gulf Oil Company tanker *Nantucket Chief,* which had sailed into the Mediterranean bound for a Republican port.

On February 10, the State Department announced that the ship's captain, J. E. Lewis, had been released and had been treated well in prison. On the twelfth the *Times* carried an interview with Lewis in Gibraltar. He stated he had been beaten with a rubber hose every day of the sixteen days he and his crew were imprisoned: "My body was a mass of bruises." In an emaciated condition after the ordeal, the skipper said: "I am the happiest person in the world. I am lucky to have escaped a firing squad."

Lewis had been told that he had been sentenced to seventeen years imprisonment for trading with the Spanish Reds. Meals in prison consisted of a plate of soup, a few beans, a jar of water, and a bit of bread daily.

Alf Andreasen and Reuben Barr

Alf Andreasen's experience after capture was unique. Alf, born in Bergen, Norway, in 1901, became a naturalized citizen in Brooklyn, served two years in the US Coast Guard, then worked as a seaman and carpenter before sailing for Spain on June 5, 1937, to fight with the Lincolns. Wounded twice, he could have returned home, but decided to fight on.

On January 17, 1938, at Teruel, Alf volunteered to retrieve an ambulance abandoned in no-man's-land. The fascists were lying in ambush and captured him. He was sent to Zaragoza to be court-martialed, but his pretrial interrogation file was mislaid. Consequently, no judge was named to hear his case, and he remained lost among the thousands of Spanish prisoners for eighteen months.

On March 14, 1939, two weeks before the end of the war, the State Department received a report that two Americans, Alf Andreasen and Conrad Stojewa (Reuben Barr), were in the provincial prison at Zaragoza. Four and a half months passed before the State Department authorized Vice Consul John D. Jernegan at Barcelona, to visit them. In his memorandum on his August 3, 1939 visit to Zaragoza, Jernegan reported:

Andreasen says that he is treated as well as the other prisoners but that conditions in general in the prison are very bad. He says that for breakfast they receive only a cup of imitation coffee without sugar or milk, and for lunch and dinner one or two potatoes and a piece of bread. He also says that the prison is intended to hold only 400 and that actually there are about 4000 being held there, with the result that the men are obliged to sleep so packed together that they cannot even change position during the night. They have only one blanket for every two men. Andreasen says that as a result of these conditions virtually all of the men suffer from sores, and that many have died of illness. He himself, he says, was for a time in very bad physical condition but was able to obtain special food from the hospital and is now somewhat better. However he does not look very strong and is still suffering from sores.

Alf had gained the right to send and receive mail in June 1939, but having no money for postage, he had only managed to send a letter to the US embassy in San Sebastian. He had received a reply saying that food, medicine, and clothing would be sent him on request. Alf requested these items and a salve to treat his sores, since the prison authorities no longer provided either bandages or medicines. Jernegan gave Alf money for stamps.

Jernegan was told by the prison authorities that Alf's records had been lost but that a search would be made. If found, the records and Alf would be sent to Burgos, since all foreigners were to be placed under the jurisdiction of the Sixth Military Region.

Alf expressed concern for Francisco Robles, who he heard had received a death sentence. Francisco's father, José Robles, a professor at Johns Hopkins University, had met his death in Spain under suspicious circumstances. Although Francisco was a Spaniard, Alf thought an expression of concern by a US official could save his life.[16]

Jernegan also spoke with Reuben Barr, a slender, fine-featured thirty-six-year-old who was fighting and imprisoned under the name Conrad Stojewa. Reuben, born on New York's East Side, was selling newspapers and candy at age eight, and at fifteen rode the freight trains west. He worked the wheat fields of Kansas and the Dakotas and fought forest fires in Idaho. When he became secretary of an IWW (Industrial Workers of the World) hall in Kansas and was indicted for criminal syndicalism, he defended himself and won an acquittal that set a valuable precedent. He returned to New York and joined some ten thousand applicants for a few post office jobs. Scoring among the top five, he worked until they found out he had been in the IWW and fired him.

In Spain, Reuben rose to the rank of company political commissar in the Lincoln Battalion. At Teruel, on January 4, 1938, he walked up to a group of soldiers he thought were from his company during a lull in the fighting. By the time he realized they were Moors, it was too late to withdraw. Reuben believes that what saved him from being killed was the fact that he was unarmed and wearing glasses. Poor people didn't wear glasses, so the Moors believed Reuben when he told them he was a reporter. They sent him behind the lines for questioning; there he said only that he was an American.

On January 22, Reuben was charged by the military prosecutor of the 5th Region with being a foreign volunteer in the service of the enemy aiding the "rebellion," and on February 3 he was sent to the Provincial Prison at Zaragoza to be court-martialed.

The Provincial Prison consisted of four new buildings set at right angles to each other. Each opened up on its own pie-shaped exercise yard between adjacent buildings. The center was occupied by a building where guards monitored the traffic between exercise yards and buildings. Reuben and Alf were in different buildings and heard of each other through the grapevine.

Reuben smuggled a letter out to his family to let them know where he was and of his need for funds. On September 2, 1938, eight months after his capture, Reuben was tried by a military judge, a military prosecutor, and a translator who spoke excellent, even if sneering, English. The trial was brief. He was asked whether he was a volunteer and whether he had seen action at the front. He stuck to his original story that he was an American reporter.

Pending the court's decision, Reuben was returned to his quarters. When he received some funds from his family, he tried to arrange a Thanksgiving Day party. A young Norwegian who had become expert at passing from one exercise yard to another, carried an invitation for all Internationals to come to Reuben's yard on Thanksgiving Day. But on his way back the Norwegian was searched and a reply note was found.

Reuben was accused of organizing a conspiracy and placed in solitary confinement in a small room with no furnishings except a bucket and a blanket, with no light except that coming through a small corridor window near the ceiling. There was a continuous stench from a sewer. The servings of lentils and beans in the two meals a day were so small that Reuben lost weight steadily. To pass the time he paced back and forth in his cell, telling himself stories or playing mental games. Unable to communicate with anyone, he could tell the passage of days only by assuming he was being served meals twice a day. Louse-ridden, filthy, hungry, losing his teeth, living in the stinking darkness, Reuben was glad to be transferred to the death cell early in March 1939.

The death cell, a room about twenty feet square, held thirty to forty Spaniards awaiting execution. Every morning ten to fifteen would be called out for execution, and during the day another ten to fifteen would replace them. Reuben recalls:

A finer, more courageous body of men I never met. Mornings when names were called, kisses and embraces were exchanged, final heart-breaking farewells by heroes. They left all their belongings, pictures, money, clothes, and blankets to those left behind, who would be executed on following days.

Reuben admits he was quite depressed when he entered the death cell, having resigned himself to execution. When the Spaniards learned he was an American and had fought with the Lincolns, they tried to cheer him up. "We can't let the fascists kill you. We will do something to save your life."

"But how can you do anything when you are in here?"

"The first thing to do is to send a letter to your family so they can help you."

"But I'll be dead long before they get the letter."

"Send it anyway. At least they will know what happened to you."

When the Spaniards gave him several sheets of paper and envelopes, Reuben had an inspiration. He would write not only to his family but also to President Roosevelt and his two senators. Suspecting that censors might open the letters, Reuben wrote, "I am suffering from the same disease Nathan Hale succumbed to."

When his cellmates saw the address, President Franklin D. Roosevelt, the White House, Washington, DC, they asked in awe; "You know President Roosevelt?"

"He's my president, and if anyone can help me, he can."

"Why, of course, of course. Now we'll take the letters and arrange to get them mailed."

When Reuben was introduced to new men put into the cell, they would express surprise and their gratitude to him for having come so far to help them, and their deep regret that they had to meet under such circumstances. Each morning that passed without Reuben's name being called, the others would congratulate him and try to convince him that their efforts to save him had succeeded. When a week had gone by and all those who had been in the cell when Reuben first entered it had gone to their deaths, Reuben was torn between the thought that surely tomorrow he would be on the list and the hope that help might reach him in time.

Reuben's emotions ranged from the deepest anger at the death of these fine brave Spaniards to a great love for his cellmates of only a few days as he saw the heights of their courage and generosity.

The condemned men were supplied little food, but they were allowed to receive food baskets from their families. Generously, they shared their food and tobacco with Reuben. It hurt deeply to see such fine men go to their deaths at the hands of the barbarous fascists, who were maintaining their grip on the people through brutal terror while they claimed to be building a new nationalist and Christian Spain. Reuben understood why these men reviled and even spat upon the priests who came into the cell to extract confessions of penitence for their opposition to the Franco regime. Many of the guards had obtained their positions to avoid service at the front, and some tried to help the condemned men.[17]

The letters that President Roosevelt and all Congressmen received about prisoners and from them were passed to the State Department, which eventually sent them to the National Archives. But Reuben's letters are not here; they were either intercepted at the prison or caught by the censor. It is possible that his "high connections" may have led the prison officials to decide to let Burgos handle Reuben's fate.

When Reuben's name finally was called out, he was transferred to a cell for prisoners considered dangerous. He quickly became friendly with the seven Spaniards in that cell. They could send letters and receive mail, money, food, and clothing, but Reuben was not allowed to do so. Called out to see Jernegan on August 3, Reuben wore all his clothes. Jernegan noted that he was

badly in need of all sorts of clothing, especially underwear, shirts, socks, shoes (size 9), trousers and handkerchiefs. His present wardrobe consists of a very ragged shirt, wornout trousers and a pair of old sandals. He also needs food to supplement the prison diet of potatoes and cereal, and would like to have some cod liver oil. Any money that may be obtained from his family or other sources would also be of great assistance to him, as the prisoners are ordinarily permitted to make small purchases with their own money.

Jernegan was informed that Reuben had been punished the previous November not for passing the note, but for "spreading anti-Franco propaganda among the prisoners, which is a very serious offense." He was also told that Reuben would be returned to the normal life of the prison and permitted to receive and send letters and to receive money. But a special watch would still be kept on him.[18]

Reuben now met Alf for the first time. They became very close friends. VALB began forwarding funds to Reuben, sending $10 on September 5 and $15 on October 4, 1939. Gladys Barr, Reuben's sister-in-law, sent $25 on December 14.[19]

Reuben's next visitor was Earl T. Crain, the third secretary at the embassy in Madrid, who had come to Zaragoza by plane on December 11, 1939. He presented Reuben and Francisco Robles with a package prepared by Mrs. Weddell, the ambassador's wife. Each package contained a blanket, two pairs of socks, two undershirts, two handkerchiefs, one knitted shirt, two towels, a pair of gloves, fifteen tins of condensed milk, two pounds of lump sugar, canned sardines, one carton of cigarettes, magazines, and soap. Reuben and Francisco were overcome with gratitude for such riches. Though Crain was told by the prison authorities that Alf had been sent to San Pedro de Cardeña, he was still at Zaragoza. Crain had also brought a package, money, and a questionnaire for a Swedish prisoner.[20]

Alf and Reuben remained separated from the other Internationals. They would be the last two Americans to be freed.

6 The Retreat from Belchite

MARCH 1938 was a rough month. Seventy-one Americans were captured in one week of fighting, and forty-three of them were killed.

During the bitter fighting at Teruel, Franco had received additional manpower and armaments from Italy and Germany, but the Republic was unable to replace the planes and arms it had lost there. Its best units had been withdrawn for rest and rebuilding after the loss of Teruel on February 22

At 6:30 A.M. on March 9, a massed artillery barrage along a one hundred-kilometer front east and south of Zaragoza announced that Franco had decided to cut the Republic in two along the south side of the Ebro River to the Mediterranean. Hundreds of planes bombed and strafed the front lines. Some 150,000 fascist troops, many motorized, then attacked the 35,000 poorly fortified and badly armed Republican troops, breaking through their lines within a few hours. Those Republicans who stood and fought were killed or captured.

The only units in immediate reserve were the 11th and 15th International Brigades. They, with the remnants of the front-line units, would have to hold until the 35,000 troops, regrouping in the rear, could be brought up to the front.

The 15th Brigade was integrating into its ranks 800 replacements, and had about 1400 American, Canadian, and British volunteers and 1000 Spaniards. Orders to defend Belchite reached the 15th Brigade Staff at Hijar on the afternoon of the ninth. The Mac-Paps were immediately ordered to make a night march to Azuara, fifteen kilometers southwest of Belchite. The British and the 59th Spanish Battalion were to be at Belchite by dawn. The Lincolns were there already, and the brigade staff moved there that evening.

*   *   *   *   *

Let's follow a Lincoln Battalion soldier—we'll call him Lucky Lou—as the battalion does its best to delay the fascist advance.

On March 10 Lou is awakened at 2:30 A.M. and told the Lincolns are to set up a secondary line of defense along the road to Fuendetodos, without delay. By three he is marching along the road in the dark, where he meets troops moving toward him. Lou assumes they have been relieved by other troops at the front.

Shortly after dawn his company climbs a hill and is told to dig trenches. Soon bullets begin to whistle menacingly. As he digs more energetically, he thinks, "What the hell's wrong with the Brigade? Don't they know the difference between a front line and a secondary line?"

At eight sharp the artillery opens up on him with shrapnel. Then come the planes, bombing and strafing him. A movement in the distance catches his eye. "Hey, Sarge, get a load of those tanks, will ya? Got any antitank ammo?" and then he mutters to himself: "What a day this is going to be!" Had he known the tanks were running on gasoline supplied by Texas Oil Company, much of it on credit, his language would have been more foul.

What our soldier doesn't know is that two hours later a bomb will land on the battalion staff, mortally wounding Dave Reiss, his battalion commander, and killing Eric Parker, the battalion commissar, and several staff members. Sidney Rosenblatt, a twenty-three-year-old volunteer from the Lower East Side of Manhattan, will try to keep Reiss's intestines from popping out of his ripped abdominal wall, and will be captured when he delays leaving in spite of Reiss's entreaties for him to do so.

Fortunately for Lucky Lou, his squad received an order to retreat in time to avoid capture.

*   *   *   *   *

Franco's staff was jubilant. On March 10 *Diario de Burgos* had already reported the destruction of two International Brigades. The Republic was in serious straits. It lacked both arms and equipment to stop the fascist blitzkrieg. Minister of Defense Indalecio Prieto was telling everyone who would listen that the war was lost. The Cabinet sent Negrín to France to insist that Soviet arms piled up on the other side of the closed border be allowed to cross. Emissaries were sent to all training bases, hospitals, and convalescent homes to call for volunteers to return to their units. As early as the eleventh, the lightly wounded and the convalescent were mounting trucks to stop the fascist drive.[1]

*   *   *   *   *

The 15th Brigade was fighting desperately. The brigade staff remained in Belchite, in spite of the shelling and bombing, to indicate to its battalions its determination to hold there. When enemy troops attacked the staff, in the late afternoon of the tenth, Robert Merriman, brigade chief of operations, escaped by driving a car over open fields, as did others in a second car. Among the staff members captured were Lieutenant Peter Hampkins, the brigade paymaster, forty-three years old, from Kenosha, Wisconsin, and

Marshall Garcia, forty years old, a U.S. citizen (though born in northern Spain) and the brigade interpreter.

Carl Herman Riffe, a strong, six-foot, blond nineteen-year-old from Portsmouth, Ohio, was in a squad that had been posted early that morning on the south side of the road running west from Belchite. They had wondered why troops were coming back along the road during the early morning hours, past the heavy machine gun they had positioned to cover the road. The squad survived the shelling and bombing that forenoon. By noon they saw enemy troops advancing far to their right and also on their left along a ridge overlooking their position. No order to retreat had reached them, and Carl and his comrades waited too long before deciding to withdraw. When they reached Belchite, the enemy was already there, and several, including Carl, were captured.

The sun was about to set when an order was given for all Internationals to step forward. Carl stepped forward, but Marshall Garcia made a split second decision to remain with the Spaniards. Then Marshall saw those who had stepped forward lined up against a wall, facing a firing squad.

Lieutenant Peter Hampkins was the first to be shot. After several others, it was the turn of a short stocky man who cried, "No! No!" as he ran along the waist-high wall. Carl took advantage of this to vault the wall and run as fast as he could. The soldiers fired at him repeatedly, and one bullet went through his arm just above his wrist. Another bullet entered one side passed under the navel and exited on the other side. Another passed through his shoulder and a fourth struck him in the hip.

He could hardly run, but he reached an irrigation ditch and flopped into its black, muddy bottom. He felt faint and splashed water on his face. Afraid they would look for him, he crawled a short distance. Then, ignoring the pain, Carl stood up and walked bent over, even though his right leg didn't want to function. It was growing dark, so he rested behind a small hill, glad he had hung on to his army overcoat.

Carl checked his wounds. Fortunately, the soldiers had used steel bullets, so the holes were small. His ribs had not been hit. He couldn't tell how much damage had been done by the bullet that went through his belly. And while the shoulder wound was painful, it did not handicap him as much as the right hip wound.

A small group of soldiers came by, whispering in English. Carl wanted to go with them, but found he was no longer able to walk, even with help. They gave him a blanket, and he gave them directions on the best way to retreat.

During the night enemy artillery set up on top of the hill and began firing over Carl's head. The next morning he lay low until noon, when deciding his situation was hopeless, he called up to the artillerymen. A half dozen came down. An old leathery-looking Spaniard wanted to cut Carl throat, but several soldiers held him off. A sergeant who spoke English tol

Carl he liked Americans. Several helped him onto his feet and wanted to take him up to the battery, but it was more than Carl could stand. They placed him on the blanket, but he was too heavy to carry that way, and at that point Carl thought they would shoot him. But they left him lying there. A half hour later they returned with a stretcher and carried him to an ambulance in Belchite. The sergeant accompanied them and advised Carl not to say anything until he was in a hospital, so no one would try to kill him. After a brief stay in a hospital in Zaragoza, Carl was transferred to a ward for prisoners in a Bilbao hospital.[2]

* * * * *

Max Shufer not only was a champion gymnast at City College of New York, but also had earned a BS in physics and a Phi Beta Kappa key. Enrolled at MIT for graduate studies, he left to join the Lincoln Battalion. Before dawn on March 10, dark-haired, twenty-three-year-old Max was leading his squad, which was pulling a heavy Maxim machine gun out along the Belchite-Fuendetodos road. They were puzzled by the hundreds of straggling soldiers going the other way, some without arms or equipment. Not long after the sun rose, they passed the formidable stone fortress of the Sanctuary of Pueyo on a high ridge on the left. A little farther on, they came under small-arms fire. Taking shelter on the left side of the road, they set up their Maxim to cover the road. The battalion staff, located in a tunnel on the east face of the ridge just behind the sanctuary, instructed them to hold there.

All morning and into the afternoon they were shelled and bombed. One shell fell within fifteen feet of them and ricocheted away; if it had exploded, there would have been no survivors. That afternoon several enemy tanks approached along the ridge. Since they had no antitank ammunition or grenades, they had to choose between retreating without orders or staying to be run over.

Max decided it was time to retreat. Strong and tall twenty-one-year-old Henry Giler, from Brooklyn, carried the heavy machine-gun carriage on his back. They found only dead bodies at the battalion headquarters. No one was in sight. They hurried down toward the road and came under tank fire. Hiding the machine gun's breechblock, they abandoned the carriage and started running back with their rifles. The squad members became separated. Max Shufer, Henry Giler, Charles Hall (a twenty-three-year-old volunteer born in Canning, South Dakota) and a Kentuckian dropped into a deep gulley. They found the gulley led only toward fascist territory. Any more to leave the gulley brought a hail of bullets, but they decided to make a run for it anyway. The Kentuckian went first. He came right back with a bullet wound in the buttock. They decided to hide in the gulley until dark

and then sneak away. Soon they heard *"Manos arriba!"* and looked up into
the barrels of rifles held by two Spanish soldiers. Charles Hall describes
what happened next:

We put up our hands, were searched, and had to surrender most of our valuables.
One of the fascist soldiers explained that if he didn't take our watches and money, his
sergeant would. Somehow I got away without having to surrender my Stateside
leather boots which I had dragged over the Pyrenees. We were marched back to the
fascist outfit's headquarters, past the 75mm guns which were still firing away at the
Republican lines, if I may use that term for our then shattered front. There was some
interrogation, not much, and no brutality.

As the Americans were marched back, they were astounded at the
number of troops and the amount of equipment the fascists had already
brought forward. Entire hillsides were covered with men, mules, and artillery. Later that evening they were taken to a stable with a straw-covered
floor, where they received some food. The next day the nonwounded were
loaded into boxcars. Hall describes the trip:

Our car was pretty crowded, and there were no sanitary facilities. The train made a
lot of stops but nobody ever came to open the door. We were able to urinate through
the cracks where the doors didn't close tightly, but those with more challenging
problems had to improvise. The most enterprising got two buddies to hoist him up to
the little two foot square opening near the ceiling of the box car, where steadied by
the friendly hands holding his feet, he bared his ass to the evening breeze, stuck it
through the opening and defecated on the right of way.

Morale was good in the box car, with little apprehension. I do recall though that
two of our comrades, names now unknown, started rehearsing the fascist anthem
"Cara al Sol," thinking it might be some form of insurance for them. They were
rather rudely told to knock it off, and did. Thinking back over the whole experience
from capture to our release, that is the only incident I remember of anything close to
collaboration or cowardice.[3]

Charles A. Barr, from Steubenville, Ohio, was possibly the youngest
American volunteer. He had managed to sail for Europe on the SS *Laconia*
on September 25, 1937, just eleven days after his eighteenth birthday. Here
Charles tells how he lost his eye:

My best buddy was Charles Youngblood, a young Negro soldier who was an expert
marksman. He was the salt of the earth. When this Belchite retreat began we were
cut off and were crawling along a wall. We saw we weren't getting any place and
Youngblood whispered to me, "Charlie, it looks bad." I said it sure does and he said
"If anything happens to either one of us the other one'll look up his family when he
gets back.

Barr said "OK" just as a bullet passed through Youngblood's chest, and
while Barr was trying to stop the bleeding in his comrade's chest, a bullet
entered his own left eye, passed under the bridge of his nose and came out
through his right cheek. Barr reported later it didn't hurt much at first, but

he was hazy about what happened next.[4] He was taken to Zaragoza and then to a Bilbao hospital. Luckily, the bullet had caused no other serious damage.

Fred Stix, a twenty-three-year-old volunteer from Suring, Wisconsin, lay outside Belchite with two bullet wounds. When fascist stretcher-bearers came along, they helped him onto his feet and told him to walk to their first-aid station a few hundred yards away since they had too many of their own to carry in.

I stumbled on to the first aid station—all by myself. There they were busy bandaging their own men. I felt like a damn fool coming up to them and saying "Here, I'm a Loyalist. Fix my wounds." But I had to do it and did it. There happened to be no officers around so it worked like a charm. The Franco troops crowded around me, wide-eyed when they heard I was an International Brigader. They searched me and found the circus union card on me. "Artista!" one of them exclaimed.

That got them more excited than before. They were wonderful to me, these ordinary peasant lads who had a Franco uniform on but were no more fascists than I am. They were just kids. I told them about Carl [Belau] laying out there in no man's land and asked them to go bring him in. But they wanted to talk more with the "artista." . . . This went on until the officer came around to question me. He asked me a few questions I refused to answer. That burned him up.

He whipped out a command: "Shoot the bastard." They lined me up against a wall ready to do their stuff. Just then a car came up with some German officers in it. They asked what was going on here . . . I answered them, telling them that I came from America, was an International Brigader. I told them I was going to be shot. That seemed to surprise the Germans. They called the Spanish fascist officer down. "You got orders now to keep International Brigaders prisoners, see." That saved me. When they left, the Falangista kicked me a couple of times, sent me on to the rear guard. I would have been done for if it wasn't for those two Nazi officers. They were looking to exchange prisoners, I figured.

Stix, too, was sent to the hospital in Bilbao.

Carl Belau, for whom Stix tried to get help, was a thirty-year-old railroader from St. Paul, Minnesota. He had nine wounds, including one in his jaw. He called to fascist stretcher-bearers for help. They looked at their officer, who ordered Carl to stand up. When he was unable to do so, the officer threatened to shoot him. Only when he saw Carl was really too weak to stand did the officer order the first-aid men to carry him in.

Once the officer was out of sight, the stretcher-bearers searched Carl. They found a membership card in Socorro Rojo—the Republican version of the Red Cross—and tore it up. They also threw away a sergeant's stripe they found in Carl's pocket. Then, giving him the Republican closed-fist salute, they carried him to a first-aid station.[5] Carl also was taken to the military hospital in Bilbao for prisoners.

Growing up in Brooklyn hadn't let Leopold Berman become very bi
but it had made him tough. With no prospects for a job in 1930, he wangle
his way into the US Navy at seventeen. Without work in 1933, he rode th
freights for a year before he signed on to a banana boat. He graduated to th
transatlantic run. In Hamburg an English-speaking Jewish girl, who wore
yellow armband with the Star of David, taught Leo the meaning of fascisn
he had already seem the broken Jewish shop windows and the *"Jude"* sign:

Spain was a short jump for Leo. His naval gunnery experience lande
him in the John Brown Artillery Battery. Dissatisfied with the antiquate
guns and the lack of action, Leo and several buddies deserted to the Lincol
Battalion. Leo fought in its ranks from Fuentes del Ebro through the cru
winter campaigns until March 10 at Belchite. That day a strafing plane pu
two bullets through his left leg. Unable to walk, and with a bootful of bloo
he hid under an olive tree. Two fascists in an armored car spotted him. On
cursed him and struck him on the head with his rifle butt. Just then a
officer ran up shouting, *"No! No! Prisonero!"* Leo was loaded onto a mu
and taken to a first-aid station and then to a hospital train. Three Moo
came into the car; one spat in his face and then pulled out a stiletto.
Spanish guard came into the car just in time to explain that Leo was neede
for interrogation. Leo was relieved when he arrived· safely at a Zaragoz
hospital.[6]

Many were not so lucky; they were killed. One was Paul MacEachro
whose father, Malcom MacEachron, was Nevada state secretary. Paul ha
been a sophomore at Oberlin College in Ohio and a member of the Nation
Executive Committee of the American Student Union. His machine-gu
squad, without orders to retreat, held their position. None survived.[7]

Lucky Lou is having a very rough time. He hears panicky rumors th
the brigade and battalion leadership have been wiped out and that tl
fascists are already ahead of him. He has had no food or sleep since l
awakened at 2:30 A.M. on March 10. He doesn't know where he is going. H
only possessions are his rifle, ammunition, entrenching tool, and tl
clothes he is wearing. When he is told to dig in and fortify, he does so, for tl
shelling, bombing and strafing are the worst he has seen.

Under these conditions the Lincoln Battalion in five days, bombed ai
shelled while fighting off enemy attacks during the day and retreating
night, travels on foot from Belchite twelve kilometers south to Lécer
sixteen kilometers southeast to Albalate, five kilometers northeast towai
Hijar, twenty-five kilometers southeast toward Alcañiz, and anoth
twenty-five kilometers across country north to Caspe. Lucky Lou is woi
out.

Dr. Edward Barsky had brought his mobile operating unit to Munies
thirty kilometers south of Belchite. A bombing raid killed Robert Webste

the driver, and wounded nurse Helen Freeman and Gabriel Quinones, all Americans. Dr. Barsky, though covered with earth by the blast, was unhurt, but the mobile unit left Muniesa. The next day a new ambulance donated by members of the staff of New York's Bellevue Hospital was driven past waving roadside guards by Merriman's chauffeur. He was hurrying to get wounded Americans to Dr. Barsky at Muniesa, unaware the fascists had already taken the town.[8] The chauffeur and the wounded men in the ambulance were killed.

At 4:30 A.M. on the fourth day of the retreat, a group of Americans was told to withdraw by any means possible. Three stuck together; blond and slender nineteen-year-old Richard Browne, a graduate of Manual Training High School in Kansas City; tall, Lincolnesque, twenty-one-year-old Homer Chase, a graduate of Hillsboro High School in New Hampshire; and David Kachadorian, from Boston. They and four German volunteers mounted a kitchen truck of the 11th Brigade, which tore down the road toward Alcañiz. The driver turned off the road to pick up some kitchen utensils, and all seven jumped off hurriedly to load them. Then the driver, deciding there wasn't time to pick up anything, shot out of the driveway, unaware that they were not on the truck.

One of the Germans had a map, so the seven set out cross-country toward Alcañiz. As they approached the town, they could hear rifle fire. Afraid that the fascists had taken it, the three Americans turned back, but the Germans continued on. When the Americans came to the road again, they saw a truck and a man lying about 150 away from it. Richard ran over to him. He was dead. Richard looked up and saw a tank trying to aim its gun at him.

Richard scrambled to one side and managed to get behind the tank, and then on top of its rear. To hang on, Richard grabbed the only thing that stuck out, the exhaust pipe. It was very hot and burned his hand. While the tank driver kept searching for him, Richard was hanging on for dear life. An International Brigade ambulance stopped alongside the tank. Richard and one of his comrades jumped on the ambulance and screamed at the driver to get out of there. He floored the accelerator to reach a dip in the road before the tank got their range. They reached it, only to run into a motorized Italian unit. This time there was no escape.

Taken by truck to a church in Alcañiz, the men were lined up inside with about four hundred other prisoners. The fascists took the officers away. Next the Internationals were separated from the Spanish prisoners and herded down to one end of the church. All expected to be shot. But that evening they and the Spaniards were marched outside to attend a fascist rally where the Italians sang songs and listened to speeches. Richard later wrote:

I wish to say here that all the time we were in the hands of the Italians, the common soldiers treated us well, even going so far as giving us cigarettes. Some of them asked us questions as to conditions on the other side. On the whole they seemed to be indifferent to the war.

They spent the night in an open field; it was cold and few had blankets. The next morning the Spanish prisoners were taken away, leading to rumors that the Internationals were to be shot. An officer interrogated the prisoners about the morale and supplies behind the Republican lines. Trucks then took them to a railroad terminal, where they were directed into boxcars, their home for the next four days. People from the town brought them water and tobacco and greeted them surreptitiously with the Popular Front salute. On the fifth day the boxcars were taken to Bilbao. There the prisoners were put in with hundreds of Basque and Asturian prisoners, who, in spite of their defeat in the North, still believed that the Spanish government would eventually drive the fascist invaders out of Spain.[9]

Three days before his fortieth birthday, John Clarence Blair, company commissar in the 1st Company of the Mac Paps, was sideswiped by a truck on a narrow street in Hijar. John sat down on some debris from a bombed-out building and soon had stiffened so much from his injuries that he could not move. He sat there until late at night. Villagers brought him food, including a raw egg. Some Internationals came along, picked him up and tried to carry him out. John could see they were very tired. Finally they gave up, placed him in a bed in an empty house, and left.

John spent the day there. An elderly Spaniard noticed him and that evening civilians came with a mule and took him to a fascist field hospital or the road to Albalate. John lay there a day, and then was moved to a hospital in Zaragoza and later by train to Deusto hospital in Bilbao.[10] Thus began a journey that was to take John to more Franco prisons than any other American.

*   *   *   *   *

Dave Doran, commissar of the 15th Brigade, and Milton Wolff, the twenty-two-year-old commander of the Lincoln Battalion, cut short their leaves and rejoined the 15th Brigade in the fighting around Hijar and Alcañiz. Doran received orders to hold Caspe until a new defensive line could be set up. He rounded up seven hundred exhausted, hungry, battered International and Spanish troops, and they held off twenty thousand fascist attackers from March 15 to 17.[11]

On the sixteenth, bombs, shells, and machine-gun fire poured down on the weary defenders holding Caspe. They did not know that a new French government had been formed under Léon Blum and that, the border having been opened that day, much-needed arms were flowing into Spain. Nor did they know that a quarter million people were demonstrating in Barcelona under the leadership of the trade unions and the Socialist, Communist, and Anarchist parties demanding that resistance be continued and the cabinet ministers who had lost faith be replaced. Nor did they know that evening that Italian planes (from an air base on the island of Majorca, only fifteen minutes away) had begun three nights' bombing of Barcelona, in which they would kill over two thousand people and wound between three and four thousand, angering the Republican population and horrifying the rest of the world.[12] The men fighting at Caspe knew only the roar of exploding bombs and artillery shells and the continual whistle of bullets. They knew only that in spite of incredible weariness and frightful scenes of destruction and death, they were being called upon for the last ounce of their strength and the last bit of their willpower to hold back the fascist advance.

Miraculously, Lucky Lou has escaped being killed, wounded, or captured. Hungry, dirty, ragged, lousy, and fleabitten, he is the only one left of his squad of six. He is still shaking from the last bombardment, which ruined his rifle. Now, on the evening of the sixteenth, he is listening to a lieutenant.

"Comrades, we can only hold Caspe if we retake those heights on the north side we lost today. Tonight we've got some moonlight. We're going to bring up all the tanks we have left to fire on the heights to make the fascists keep their heads down, while we climb up as close as we can. When the tanks stop firing, we charge, yelling like hell, firing our rifles and throwing our grenades, and scare the hell out of them."

Lucky Lou explains to the lieutenant that there is no point to his going along since he doesn't have a usable rifle.

"You can yell, can't ya? And get yourself a couple of good rocks to throw at them."

And the wonder is that Lucky Lou does just that, muttering, "Damn, what'll they think of next in this war?"

In the final charge, his yelling of obscenities undoubtedly helps more than his rocks, for the fascists flee in panic.

But next morning Lucky Lou finds he and his comrades are surrounded, the only way out over a narrow railway trestle under enemy fire. He reaches the other side safely and learns the 12th and 14th International Brigades have arrived to relieve them. Along with less than a hundred surviving Americans, Lucky Lou reaches Corbera, finally out of the hell of the last ten days and scarcely able to believe himself still alive.

"Regroup, reorganize, and rearm!" they are told. But Lou says, "You got it all wrong, buddy. Eat, drink, and sleep!"

But twelve days later they would be marching back to the front again in a regrouped, reorganized, and rearmed 15th Brigade. I still recall coming up with eight hundred from Albacete and the training base at Tarazona (the commissar school was suspended) and having to spend the first night out in a field in the melting snow and mud. Merriman, 15th Brigade chief of staff, had told me very firmly that the survivors of the brigade had first priority for shelter.

*   *   *   *   *

Franco's newspaper, *Diario de Burgos,* on March 12 announced that over two hundred Yankees had been captured near Belchite. *Diario de Vasco* reported on the eighteenth that the 11th, 12th, 14th, 15th, and 16th International Brigades had been destroyed. But in another article the same day, it also reported that only the International Brigades were keeping the war going.

There was no 16th International Brigade, and the 12th and 14th Brigades had just arrived at the front on March 18 and had few casualties. Only the 11th and 15th were hurt, though not as badly as it seemed at first. As those who got lost during the night marches returned, their battalions were approaching half their original strength. The "destroyed" 15th Brigade was restored to a battle-ready unit in less than two weeks.

On March 22 the New York Times printed William Carney's dispatch from Burgos that three thousand foreigners had been killed and nearly two thousand captured. He had interviewed prisoners of many nationalities. They were to be sent to a camp near Burgos.

The seventy Americans who were captured had failed to get orders to retreat and stayed at their posts until it was too late to escape, gotten lost during the night marches, or become so fatigued they were unable to fight any longer.

An unknown number of Internationals were caught asleep at Hijar, unaware that there were no troops in front of them. The Italians entered Hijar that night and took the Internationals alive. They turned them over to Spanish troops, whose officers had them killed. It is not known whether any were Americans.

It wasn't only Franco's generals who were predicting the war would soon be over. On March 20, Ambassador Bowers informed Secretary of State Hull:

One fact is beyond question, that at this hour Germany and Italy are acting openly and on a very large scale in Spain, and that the Government deprived of the artillery and planes for which she has always been prepared to pay in gold, cannot compete. Man to man, the loyalist army can hold its own: but when the rebels are backed with the latest mechanical instruments of destruction on a great scale no army can stand against such odds.

This is all due absolutely to the non-Intervention scheme of the British which has tied the hands of France and the other Democracies while making no pretense to enforcing the agreement upon the Fascist Powers.

Negrín's minister of the interior, Julian Zugazagoitia, told a US consular member that without outside aid the end was merely a matter of weeks away.[13] Ernest Hemingway was making arrangements to evacuate the American nurses and doctors along with the 537 wounded Americans in hospitals. Hull stated US naval vessles would evacuate all Americans when the Republic collapsed.[14]

Our thoughts were not on defeat as we joined Internationals and Spaniards rushing to the Aragon front from training bases, convalescent homes, and hospitals in order to stop the fascist advance. We went, feeling both the heavy responsibility and our pride in the task of fighting fascism where it mattered most at that critical moment. The call to resist in Negrín's radio speech on March 28 expressed not only our desire and determination but also that of the people of Republican Spain. Defeatism existed in the group around Prieto and some Anarchist leaders.[15] For us, turning Spain over to the fascists was unthinkable.

7 Captured! Survivors and Killed

"IT'S THE BULLRING!" Memories of what they had read and heard about the murder of thousands with machine guns in the bullring at Badajoz quickened the pulse of the surviving captured Internationals brought to Logroño by boxcar. Here Max Shufer and his comrades found hundreds of Spanish prisoners. They learned prisoners weren't shot inside the bullring, but every day names were called of those to be taken out for execution.

The next day they listened intently whenever names were called out and marveled at the composure of the Spaniards being escorted to their death.

"What do we do? Wait until they call our names?"

"The most important thing is to let our relatives and friends know we are here, then the fascists can't execute us without expecting some kind of an uproar."

"But how can we get our names out of here?"

"You saw the Spanish women outside the gates who bring baskets of food to their men who are in here. Maybe we can get one of the Spaniards to have his wife smuggle out our letters."

"How about just making a list of our names and the name and address of a person to be notified, and maybe we can find someone who will write letters to them?"

A list was prepared and a Spaniard chosen who assured them he could get it out. Now they could only wait, fearful the list would be intercepted or would be too late. A very brave Spanish woman, Felipa Soto, wrote to two individuals named by the prisoners, asking them to contact the others. To Vera Rifkin on Townsend Avenue in the Bronx, Señora Soto wrote in Spanish:

Milady:

During a visit to a relative of mine who is a prisoner in Depósito de Evadidos y Prisoneros, Plaza de Toros, Logroño, he told me that in this prison is a person by the name of Irving Rabinowitz [Max Shufer] who asked him to get in touch with you and to tell you that he is well, but that he needs a little money to buy supplements.

With him are the following countrymen of his who need money for the same purpose and who also wish you would write to their relatives.

Señora Soto then listed the relatives of Joseph Radacoi, (Radacoy), a twenty-one-year-old born in Hutchinson, West Virginia, who became a coal miner while a teenager; Charles Hall; Walter Hannigan, forty-two, born in Altoona, Pennsylvania, who had worked as a machinist in Des Moines

54

Iowa; Sam Koneski, a twenty-eight-year-old chauffeur from New Ken-sington, Pennsylvania; Howard Earl, a thirty-year old aircraft worker from Santa Monica, California, and one of the sit-down strikers at Douglas Aircraft Company; Sidney Rosenblatt; Joe Karinsky and Oscar Pikalchuk, of Ottawa, Canada; George Severdia, twenty-two, a clerk from Clifton, New Jersey; and Louis Kocelic, from Woodside, New York.

She sent a similar letter to Irene Soames in New York, for Leon Tenor, twenty-six, born in Beaver Falls, Pennsylvania, and jailed several times for his leadership in the Ohrbach Department Store strike in New York City; John Higgins, a twenty-seven-year-old chauffeur from New York; Frank Grodski, a twenty-seven-year-old Brooklynite who had led delegations of unemployed for food and clothing, and who had been wounded in Spain; twenty-one-year-old Mike Goodwin (Henry Giler), expelled from City Col-lege for political reasons, who had spent six months in the Civilian Con-servation Corps; and John Pierkarski (Piekarski), born in Poland forty years earlier, a cook and a naturalized US citizen. Felipa Soto daringly included her address, but did take the precaution of adding *"Arriba España, viva Franco."*

The letters arrived at their destinations on April 20, 1938, and were taken to FALB.[1] Phone calls and letters then went to the relatives. But it was too late to reach the prisoners at Logroño; they had already been moved to the concentration camp at San Pedro de Cardeña.

*   *   *   *   *

Leo Berman made a deal in the hospital at Zaragoza. He would give the priest who came to the ward every day lessons in conversational English in return for a daily package of cigarettes. Leo remained there until he was able to walk again, and then was transferred to San Pedro de Cardeña.[2]

The wounded who were taken to the Deusto hosptial in Bilbao experi-enced both brutality and kindness. Carl Riffe had a bad scare one day when an elderly Spaniard threatened to shoot him. A Spanish lieutenant came along just in time to stop him.[3] John Blair describes his first hours in the same hospital:

I had just been in bed for an hour or so on the day 4 or 5 of us arrived on a train from Zaragoza. There were about 15 Internationals in this room, probably a class-room in normal times.

A man in a bed to the right of me and somewhat in the rear was screaming in pain. He appeared to have an injured leg. Shortly, a large husky man came in and sat next to the bed. I thought he might be a doctor as he was well dressed in civilian clothes. But suddenly I saw him bring his arm way back and then strike the patient with all his might in the face with a large beefy hand. The patient stopped screaming and I heard the big bully speaking in a threatening tone to him.

The fascist bully left, but the patient continued to groan. Shortly they moved

him to another part of the building where he died within a couple of days. I was told
that he was a Brazilian who had part of the calf of his leg shot away and gangrene
had developed because of lack of care.

There was a large Englishman in a bed next to me whose only injury was a
broken arm caused by being struck with a guard's gun-butt after he was captured.
The broken arm was never set and caused a series of problems with the result that a
fascist bully appeared one day, stuck a 45 caliber pistol muzzle against the head of
the Englishman and told him any further problems would get him shot. [Blair heard
later that he either died or was killed.]

Most of the common labor was done by Basques whom we could trust in most
matters. They told us that a sister of Pasionaria was working in the place and made
arrangements for her to appear one day. They got her to come into the room when
the coast was clear. She stood in the middle of the room for about a half minute so we
could all get a good look at her and then left. She certainly had a strong resemblance
to her famous sister and appeared to be as old or older.[4]

John Blair, Carl Riffe, an Irishman, and several others were transferred
to San Pedro de Cardeña in the middle of April. Carl was still unable to walk.
The Spanish lieutenant who had saved his life earlier carried him from the
ambulance into a third-class compartment on the train and tried to make
him comfortable on a wooden bench.

It Helps to Have a Friend

Guy Castle's mother, fearful that her son had joined the Lincoln Battalion, asked her family friend, Secretary of State Cordell Hull, to find out
where he had gone. Within two days, helped by three US consuls, Hull
informed her that Guy had enlisted in Franco's Foreign Legion on July 9,
1937. She was much relieved.

Guy's unit of the Foreign Legion was sent to Brunete to help stop our
July offensive, and Guy was wounded. His mother went to Spain to see that
he was properly cared for. Seven months later, when Guy had recovered, he
obtained permission from the Foreign Legion to accompany his mother to
La Linea at the Gibraltar border. His mother went on to Gibraltar, and that
night Guy tried to swim there from La Linea. He was a good swimmer, but
came ashore a little too soon, and was caught by sentries alerted by guard
dogs on the Franco side of the border.

Hull learned on February 16 from a brief press dispatch that a Guy
Castle had tried unsuccessfully to escape from the Foreign Legion and faced
a court-martial for desertion. Immediately, Hull telegraphed Consul Charles
S. Bay for the facts. Within an hour after a confirming cable the next day
Hull instructed Bay to arrange with Franco authorities for Guy's release in
the custody of his mother.

Three weeks later, Bay cabled Hull that Guy was leaving with his mother for Gibraltar. On March 25, the consul at Gibraltar supplied the happy ending when he cabled that Guy and his mother were sailing that night on the SS *Conte de Savoia*.[5]

Hull's prompt and vigorous intervention with the Franco authorities had accomplished a small miracle. To obtain an exception to the Foreign Legion's standard death penalty for desertion was most unusual. Of course, Hull had some powerful, even if unmentioned, bargaining chips—the oil and trucks Franco had to have to win the war.

Nine days before Guy sailed for home, Hull's attention was drawn to a dispatch in the morning's *New York Times*. William Carney was reporting that he had talked with four Americans captured by Franco's troops, Sidney Babsky, Michael (Morris) Ecker, Ralph Neafus, and Leon Ticer. That afternoon Hull received eighteen telegrams on their behalf. FALB asked him to check immediately on their safety. Another, including a copy of a cable to Franco that thirty professors at Columbia University had sent asking for assurance of the four men's safety, urged Hull to "render every possible aid in securing safety American prisoners." Another telegram came from Charles J. Hendley, president of Local 5 of the American Federation of Teachers.[6] Hull did nothing.

Babsky's parents had contacted former Congressman Vito Marcantonio. He phoned Adolph A. Berle, assistant secretary of state, and he, in turn, sent a note to Eric C. Wendelin in the Division of European Affairs, asking him "to take whatever measures are possible through our officers in Spain." In a note, Wendelin asked the Passport Division to check on the citizenship records of the four.[7]

On the second day, many more telegrams and letters arrived. One was from Dean Morton Gotschall of City College of New York, signed by seventeen faculty members. Another came from the noted composser Wallingford Riegger.[8]

On the third day, the Passport Division informed Wendelin that Babsky and Ecker had been born in New York in 1906 and 1912 respectively, Neafus in Tucumcari, New Mexico, in 1910, and Ticer in Alfalfa, Oklahoma, in 1915.[9]

On the fourth day, Raymond Edward Murphy, an assistant in the Division of European Affairs (not to be confused with Robert Daniel Murphy in the Paris embassy), sent Wendelin a note having an anti-Semitic and antilabor tone:

The mass of night letters in the Babsky case is the greatest example I have seen of the use of pressure by a minority group in a specific case. The letters appear to emanate from union locals of the Teachers Union of New York. That union has long been regarded, even though a member of the A.F. of L., as a radical organization in its sympathies at least. Isidor Begun, at present a suspect in Spanish recruiting, had a close tie-up with it.[10]

A snide remark came from another State Department official who noted that no word had arrived from Babsky's parents. Within two hours Mr. and Mrs. Max Babsky's telegram was received from the president's office, with a note from his aide. Marvin McIntyre.[11]

Within a few days Hull had received some six hundred telegrams and nearly one hundred letters and postal cards from individuals and organizations urging him to intervene to assure the safety of the captured Americans.[12] After the second day, an unusual decision was made not to include the telegrams and letters on the "List of Papers" for the National Archives, except those forwarded by the president and congressmen and the parents. The total number of telegrams and letters the Department received is unknown.

A news item had mobilized the full power of the State Department on behalf of Castle, but the pleas of leaders in education, science, religion, and law, plus hundreds of friends and relatives of these four Americans, were ignored.

Sidney Babsky had graduated from Morris High School with awards for scholarship and mathematics and obtained his MA in Education from the City College of New York in 1931. Appointed as an elementary teacher at P.S. 5, he later transferred to P.S. 188 in Harlem, where good teachers were needed. Sidney was also studying law at New York University.

Sidney was not only active in his union, American Federation of Teachers Local No. 5, but also in the committee for Better Schools in Harlem and in the Harlem Housing Development. Sidney had left for Spain early in March 1937 and served with the Mackenzie-Papineau Battalion. A fellow soldier remembered him as a "gentle, strikingly handsome and very nice, thoughtful, decent guy."[13]

Sidney's wife and mother saw Wendelin at the State Department on March 23 or 24.[14] Normal procedure was to write a short memo for each visitor, to be placed in the subject file. None appears in the Babsky file.

It was ten days before the State Department made its first reply to the thousand-odd telegrams and letters it had received. On March 26 it sent a letter to Mr. and Mrs. Babsky responding to the letter FDR had forwarded saying that the American consul was trying to effect the release of their son.[15] On the same day the State Department sent its first instructions, in code, to Consul Bay in Seville.

In view of statement made by General Quiepo de Llano that a considerable number of Amricans were captured recently by forces of General Franco, you are requested to make inquiry through him regarding whereabouts and welfare of following American citizens reported captured by Franco forces while serving with the armed forces of Spanish Government: Ezak Babsky, Morris Ecker, Ralph Lawrence Neafus, Leon Norvell Ticer and Paul McEachron, Jr. [Inquiry should also be made regarding Americans mentioned in previous telegrams from the Department.]

Department's position regarding protection of American citizens serving with the armed forces in Spain was set forth in its telegram of November 6, noon. [It would, however be helpful if assurances could be given by General.] However, in view of reports circulated in this country that Americans captured in Spain are in danger of execution it would be helpful [to us] if Franco authorities would confirm our assumption that rules of war respecting treatment of prisoners are being respected.[16]

Sections enclosed in brackets were struck out of the original draft of the cable. Contrary to the letter to the Babskys, the cable did not call for obtaining the release of those captured. The Department's telegram of November 6, 1937, had stated that American volunteers could not expect the protection ordinarily accorded American citizens, and that consular action was to be limited to requesting information through unofficial sources as to their welfare and whereabouts.[17] Paul McEachron's name was included because Hull, two days before, had received a letter reporting his capture from Joseph P. Lash, the executive secretary of the American Student Union.[18]

Parents and friends of Morris Ecker, Ralph Neafus, and Leon Norvell Ticer were also unable to obtain any information about their sons from the State Department.[19] If Hull had acted on March 16, he might have saved the lives of the four interviewed by Carney. But the fascist authorities received no indication of concern from the State Department, and Sidney Babsky, Morris Ecker, Ralph Neafus, and Leon Norvel Ticer paid with their lives.

That they were killed was confirmed indirectly by Carney's dispatch in the *New York Times* on May 30. He had learned from unofficial but well-informed sources that some Americans he had talked with had been shot without trial.

Two days before Hull sent his instructions to Bay, he had received from his legal adviser, Ralph Hill, an analysis of a twenty-page legal brief prepared by Herman E. Cooper, "The Right of American Citizens Imprisoned by the Spanish Insurgent Military Forces to Diplomatic Interposition on their Behalf" (summarized in Appendix I). It had been formally submitted to Hill on February 14 by a distinguished group of veterans of the Abraham Lincoln Battalion led by David McKelvy White, who had served as the clerk for the Lincolns and the MacPaps, and who was a son of a former governor of Ohio. With White were Hans Amlie, former commander of the Washington and Lincoln battalions and brother of Wisconsin Congressman Thomas Amlie; Paul Burns, Lincoln captain wounded at Jarama and Brunete; and twice-wounded Walter Garland, the first black to command a white machine gun company.

Hill informed the State Department that diplomatic protection, while a moral right, was not enforceable by legal methods. But past US custom had

seen to it that Americans who became prisoners of war were treated hu
manely according to the usual rules of warfare. Additional protection coul
be given if the State Department wished.[20] The State Department's replie
to relatives that it could not go beyond seeking information about a pris
oner's whereabouts and welfare were not true; that position did not eve
follow past precedents, let alone do what it had done for Castle.

Hull ignored White's requests for comments on the brief until FDR o
March 16 forwarded a telegram White had sent him. Hull's reply to Whit
on March 28 disposed of the brief in thirty-one words:

> The Department has given careful consideration to the statements contained i
> the brief, and its position remains the same as set forth in previous communicatior
> to your organization on this subject.[21]

Spain, March 30–31, 1938

The 15th Brigade was rearmed shortly after dawn on March 30, an
that afternoon the Lincoln and British battalions received orders to move u
during the night to take up secondary positions. At dawn the Britisl
marching in single file on both sides of the road, moved up through Ca
aceite. Captain Frank Ryan, from brigade staff, a well-known leader of th
Irish Republican Army, was up front with an Irish light machine gun cre
that included Bob Doyle, Peter Brady, and John Lemmon.

Tony Gilbert, barely five feet tall, an amateur boxer and very fit, was
battalion runner. He was out front with Taffy Adams, commander of the 1
Company, which was leading the battalion. All were puzzled by the ap
pearance of a single horseman, who, after waving and shouting, rode bac.
Ordering Tony to stay with Ryan, Taffy went back to see George Fletche
the battalion commander, about the horseman.

Having heard the noise of engines, Ryan instructed Bob to set up th
light machine gun to cover the bend in the road they were approachin.
After part of the battalion had passed by, Bob and his crew fell back in lin

Some minutes later, tanks came out of an olive grove on the left. Wal
Tapsell, the battalion commissar, was right behind Frank and Tony, ar
since he believed Líster's men were in front of them, he cried out, "Dor
shoot! They're the Lísters." He went up to the first tank to convince th
driver that they were both on the same side, but the driver settled the matt
by shooting him down. At that point the First Company scrambled for cov
and started firing at the tanks.

Tony and Frank jumped into the nearest ditch. Tony began to fire at th
tanks and at motorcycles which had appeared with swivel-mounted m
chine guns. Suddenly they heard a command behind them: *"Manos a
riba."* When Frank and Tony looked around they found themselves starii

into a rifle barrel whose owner was pleading with them: *"Abajo fusil! Abajo fusil!"* Tony reports: "I put my rifle down, and that was it."[22]

Before the firing started, Bob put down his gun and went over to look at a tank that had stopped near him. By the time he saw the Italian colors on the tank, he could no longer reach Ryan. Infantry appeared and marched Bob and additional British prisoners off with their hands over their heads.[23]

Farther back, Dougal Eggar, a runner for 1st Company and not much taller than Tony, had just carried a message to Fletcher, and was hurrying back. Shots caused him to look up. He saw tanks coming down the road and heard someone yell, "They're fascists!" He jumped into an adjoining field and fired at the tanks, but he too was rounded up by the infantry.[24]

Maurice Levitas was with a light machine gun grouped a little behind the center of the column. When the group heard the firing, they dashed off the road behind some cover in the adjacent field and began to fire at the tanks. Some tanks appeared to be disabled. Low on ammunition, the men decided to try to work their way back. Heavy fire forced them to hide in a gulley.

An Italian patrol found them late in the afternoon. They were taken before an officer for questioning, but refused to give more than their names and nationality. Later that evening they were set to work digging a pit. They assumed it was to be their grave, but before it was finished, they were marched to a barbed-wire compound. There they met Ryan, Gilbert, Eggar, and scores of other British prisoners, and an American, Max Parker.[25]

Garry McCartney, from Glasgow, Scotland, was in the machine-gun company bringing up the rear of the battalion. Much of the company had passed around the bend when Garry heard gunfire up ahead. His crew set up their gun on high ground with trees. When a Fiat tank nosed around the bend, their bullets set it afire. One of its inmates was hit when trying to escape and slumped over the side of the turret. Another tank came around the bend but scuttled back when it saw the first one burning.

When nothing happened during the next half hour, Garry's crew dismantled the heavy machine gun so they could carry it up higher and see farther. After they had climbed about thirty yards, Italian soldiers from the Black Arrow Division suddenly appeared from behind the trees and bushes, yelling *"Manos arriba!"* Caught completely by surprise, Garry's crew had their valuables taken from them, and they were marched down to the road. Along with another dozen captured British, they were ordered to stand against a wall. The soldiers said they would be shot.

An Italian officer then ordered them marched up the road with their hands behind their heads. The tank was still burning, but the body had been removed. The bodies of the dead British—Garry recalls the bloody red entrails of some—were still on the road. Rifles and equipment were scattered around.

Morgan Harvard, a Welsh coal miner, could put only one hand behind

his head; the other, bleeding profusely, hung limp at his side. Garry told one
of the guards that Morgan needed immediate attention. To his surprise,
Morgan was taken aside. An Italian officer later informed Garry that Morgan
was being taken to a hospital. There his arm was amputated without
anesthetic after he was given a shot of cognac.[26]

Garry was impressed by the large number of soldiers, trucks, and guns
filling the road as they marched toward Alcañiz. After crossing the Matar-
raña River, they were shunted into a clearing where Frank Ryan and about
a hundred British prisoners were being held.[27]

*   *   *   *   *

Max Parker, twenty-five, came from the Lower East Side of New York
and had had to leave school after the tenth grade to support his family. He
had been driving a truck on the hectic Aragon front for six days and nights,
only occasionally catching a nap. On the seventh day he arrived at his base
to sleep. A few hours later, he was awakened and told that another driver
had gone to pieces. He would have to drive some thirty telephone linemen
under the command of a Spanish lieutenant to repair communication lines
to the front. As Max dropped and picked up linemen, he wondered where
the front was. He saw one bridge blown up after he had crossed it. Around
midnight he was halfway across another bridge before he found out the far
end was missing.

A little later he was stopped at a roadblock and ordered out of the cab by
a tall lieutenant and a short soldier. Since the lieutenant identified himself
as an Italian and asked Max if he was one, Max's first impression was that
he had run into the Garibaldis. But when he heard the short soldier say
"Shoot him!" repeatedly in Spanish, Max knew he was in fascist hands.
When he identified himself as an American from New York, the lieutenant
who had lived in New York, talked with him about the city and paid no
attention to the short soldier. But Max's heart almost stopped when he saw
them line up the Spanish linemen and shoot every tenth man, killing three.

Max was taken to a hut where some happy Italian officers were eating
and drinking. When Max said he was hungry, they gave him bread and
wine.

Soon after I was led from there to what appeared to be a small stable. My hands were
tied behind my back and I was shoved to the floor. I remember the guard urinating
against the wall and splashing me. By this time it was almost light and I was taken
outside where an officer, Italian I think, pushed me to the ground, cursed me, spat
on me, called me a red bastard, etc. and kept threatening me with his gun. The
Spanish comrades who had been on my truck were watching nearby and I was
convinced the fascists wanted them to see me beg for my life, which I was determined not to do. I knew that I had to keep my wits about me and I kept repeating
that I knew nothing about the disposition of troops or anything else of importance.

invented the name of a Spanish officer who was supposed to be my commanding officer.

At that point an Italian soldier approached the officer who was questioning me and spoke to him. The officer left. The soldier lifted me up from my kneeling position and said in Spanish: "You're a lucky man!" He untied my hands and told me to follow him. He went to the side of the road where I found a group of English prisoners seated on the ground. I sat down near them. In a little while, someone, I don't who, asked: "Who is the officer here?" A man stood up despite the protests of the men. It was well known that the fascists shot captured officers. The man gave his name, Frank Ryan. The interrogator asked if anyone in the group could talk Spanish. There was no reply, and after some hesitation, I spoke up and interpreted for him. I don't recall what questions were asked other than his rank. He replied: "Captain."

Across the road was a farmhouse with a fenced-in yard. We were taken to this yard where we waited apprehensively for perhaps two hours. I had the feeling they didn't quite know what to do with us. We were on a country road but there was a constant stream of traffic, military vehicles, all going in one direction.

As I recall, there were close to a hundred English prisoners. . . . A remarkable aspect of their story was that they had been surrounded by Italian troops who appeared to be trying to keep them alive, telling them to stay down. . . .

When we were moved out of the yard, we were marched against the oncoming traffic—vehicles and foot soldiers. Since I was the only person there who admitted knowing Spanish, I became the official interpreter and was at the head of the procession with Frank Ryan. He kept shouting words of encouragement to us; to remember who we were; why we were in Spain, to maintain discipline. Large convoys of Italian fascist troops rolled slowly past us, spitting at us and yelling obscenities. They shouted that they wanted to get La Pasionaria and mutilate her.

It was late in the morning and we had marched a long way. We had had no food or water. We were taken off to the side of the road and . . . they strung up barbed wire around us. Frank insisted that I . . . talk to the commanding officer and demand food and water. I did so and we were given water. A Gestapo man came to talk to Frank. They had a conversation in English. Among other things, he wanted to know why Frank was fighting in Spain instead of in Ireland. Frank told him it was the same fight in both places. After several minutes the Gestapo man told Frank that he was a brave man, wished him luck and left.

Covered trucks took them to Alcañiz that afternoon. Parker recalls a huddled conference in the dark over what to say when questioned. These principles were agreed upon: give no information that could harm the Republic; say "I came to Spain to help the Republic."[28]

*　　*　　*　　*　　*

The Lincoln Battalion also met the enemy on March 31, but in a less disastrous fashion. While marching toward the front the day before, Stanley Heinricher saw an American insulting a wounded enemy soldier lying on a stretcher, calling him a dirty fascist and making threatening gestures. Stan, twenty-five, from Pittsburgh and a former vice-president of Local 1243 of the Steel Workers Organizing Committee, told the insulter in no uncertain terms to leave the wounded man alone and get on with the job of moving up to the front.[29]

The Lincolns assumed their assigned location, and then drove ahead for a mile to more defensible positions, chasing out the fascist troops who had begun to occupy them.[30]

8 How I was Captured

WHEN I AWOKE on April 1, 1938, it didn't occur to me that it was April Fool's Day. My muscles were aching from a long forced march the day before and I was cold from lying on the bare ground. Besides, I had been awakened by a hushed voice in Spanish. Was it an enemy, or one of our soldiers?

I was relieved when I saw Captain Ricardo Díaz, commander of the Mac Paps, a short distance away talking in low tones to several soldiers. A glance at the radium-painted dial of my wristwatch told me it was a quarter to four. I had slept almost three hours. The battlefront was quiet.

I went over to Captain Díaz. "Ricardo, did we make contact with the 11th Brigade yet."

"Not yet. The enemy has come very close to us along the road. Would you go back to Brigade and ask whether they have heard anything and what their plans are? And Carl, remind them that we haven't seen the food truck since yesterday morning."

I quickly made my way to the Gandesa-Calaceite road and then jogged up the road until a sentry challenged me. He directed me to a path off to the right that led me to the 15th Brigade command post, partially sunk into the ground and camouflaged with sod. On top of the eight-foot-high earthen mound I saw the brigade commander, Major Robert Merriman. He was looking intently down the road toward the fascist lines.

Before I could say more than his name, Major Merriman asked: "Did the 11th come in last night?"

"Not one of our patrols reported making contact with them." For a few moments we watched the headlights of a long line of enemy vehicles as they came down the road toward the Algas River some five kilometers away.

"If the 11th isn't holding those hills on our right, they'll outflank us in no time. Carl, whose company is on the right?"

"Johanchuk's 1st Company."

"Dan!" Merriman called to a runner. "Go to the MacPaps and tell Captain Díaz to send his 1st Company over to the right to hold those hills until the 11th gets in."

Merriman continued to scan the battlefront as the first glimmer of dawn appeared on our left. To my question of whether the food truck would be up today, he replied not unkindly, "Carl, I think we are going to be too busy to think about eating today."

A few minutes later he tried his binoculars, previously useless in the dark, then said: "They're getting ready to come up the road. We'd better not spread ourselves too thin."

I knew we had three infantry companies and one machine-gun company of the Mackenzie-Papineau Battalion, totaling about 450 Canadians and Americans, on the right side of the road. The left side was held by our Spanish 59th Battalion, and our right flank was to be protected by the legendary 11th International Brigade, manned by German and Austrian antifascists renowned for their fighting skill and bravery. We had no artillery and no tanks.

Without lowering his binoculars, Merriman commented: "We'll need all the strength we can muster along the road. Carl, I don't have any runners left. Can you go out and tell Johanchuck to send out only half of his 1st Company, and have the other half dig in to help cover the road?"

Dan had a fifteen-minute start on me, and even after stopping to see Captain Díaz, he reached Johanchuck's company ahead of me. The men were strapping on their gear.

Johanchuk quickly understood the situation and ordered half to remain behind to reinforce those along the road. I explained to the rest why it was important to occupy the adjoining hills on the right.

I had not come there with the intention of going out with the men. By this time the International Brigades had learned the hard way that putting officers in front was not a very effective way to fight a war. But political commissars are expected to lead by example. If it was so important to occupy these hills until the 11th Brigade came in, I should at least see the men to their new positions. So I finished my explanation with the announcement that I would go with them and then asked: "Any questions?"

"One. When do we eat?"

"I hope soon, because I am hungry."

The smiles of the men broke the tension. We set out in the direction in which I hoped to find the 11th. We had no maps and no compass. We split into two groups. Ed Hodge, whose family was among the first settlers in Kentucky, accompanied me along a ridge with a light machine gun and several riflemen. The rest, led by Sergeant Larry Cane from New York City, moved through the valley on the right side of the ridge.

The sun was rising in a cloudless sky on a fresh and lovely spring morning. Bushes and small tress along the ridge provided cover as we advanced rapidly. In less than ten minutes we came to a dip in the ridge. A faint odor of wood fires alerted me. I halted when I saw ahead of us several hundred soldiers preparing their breakfasts on a slope facing us. They seemed protected from fascist observation and fire by the ridge behind them.

An officer came alone to greet us, calling out in good English: "Come on over. Don't be afraid. We are your friends."

I thought, We got to our positions after dark last night, and the fascists would not know that we spoke English, but the 11th Brigade would expect us on their left flank. I was overjoyed, as was the rest of the patrol. We hurried forward happily to greet the officer. Less than fifty feet from him, I saw "23 de Marzo" on his jacket, the name of an Italian division.

I stopped. For the first time, I noticed crews behind three light machine guns on tripods in the background zeroed in on us. I carried a liberated Luger, for which I had been unable to obtain ammunition, and a hand grenade.

I looked back. Everyone had stopped. Hodge, carrying the light machine gun, had it resting in the crook of his arm. The riflemen were not prepared to fire. All were watching for my signal. It was painfully obvious that since we were out in the open we would all be shot down before we could open fire.

I knew all officers of the International Brigade were executed upon capture. I was not certain that the others would be. I gave a hand signal to hold fire.

The officer, now identifiable as a captain, after motioning to a squad of soldiers to come out, came up in a jubilant mood. "Welcome! Welcome, men of the 15th! Glad to see you! You won't be needing your guns, so my men will take care of them."

I was wearing a new officer's jacket, my first one, so new that I had not sewn on insignia. The captain, observing my jacket and seeing that I carried only a side arm, came directly up to me and with a smile asked: "May I take your pistol?"

Without answering, I allowed him to take it. Something caused him to break it open. He looked at me in astonishment. "Where's the ammo?"

"Sorry, I don't have any."

Recognizing it as a German Luger, he joked, "Oh, that's all right, I'll be able to get some."

Next he unhooked my grenade and gave it to a member of his squad, the rest of whom were disarming my comrades. "Now, let's see your military identification." My heart sank. I handed over the card showing my rank as battalion political commissar.

The captain's eyes lit up. "You're just the man I need. Step over there and call those men up here." He pointed toward the soldiers in the valley. They had halted, sensing trouble.

When I made no move to obey, he pulled out his pistol. "This one's got ammo in it. Now turn around!" Pushing the end of the barrel hard against my back, he ordered, "Forward march!"

Thirty steps brought us to a fifty-foot cliff, overlooking Cane's men. "Now, Commissar, call those men up here!"

Fall forward with a bullet in my back, or backward with a bullet in my chest? Since I could see that my comrades were already taking cover, I decided to face the captain. I turned slowly and told him, "As an officer, I will not call them up."

Scarcely had I finished when bullets started to whistle past our ears.

Sergeant Cane had ordered the group in the valley to open fire as close to us as possible without hitting me.

The captain and I looked each other in the eye as the bullets sang in our ears. If he pulled the trigger, those bullets would be directed at him. Motioning with his pistol, he quietly remarked, "OK, let's get out of here. You first!"

This time I obeyed willingly, and we soon joined the others in a slight hollow. Italian troops began to fire down on Cane's men to prevent them from coming to our rescue.

The captain's staff congratulated him on the way he had fooled us. I asked him where he had learned his English.

"Brooklyn. Lived there quite a few years. Sure came in handy, didn't it?"

"You speak it perfectly. But how did you know we spoke English?"

"Oh, a little pigeon told me."

This, plus the fact that we were not being questioned about our military strength, made me suspect that the fascist officers already knew how thin our line was.

The captain detailed a squad of six soldiers to escort us, and four MacPaps captured earlier, to the rear. He did not give my identification booklet to the sergeant in charge.

We climbed a hundred yards through masses of troops to the top of the ridge. The view on the other side, to the right and left, was sickening: it was filled with troops preparing for battle. At the next ridge, the scene was repeated. After picking our way to the left through troops for about ten minutes, we reached the road to Calaceite, much to my surprise.

We had to walk on the side of the road; it was filled with troops coming toward us. Long curving stretches below us on the road's descent to the Algas River were filled with military units. We passed battalion after battalion of infantry in close-order formation. We saw only regular Italian Army units. Between the infantry battalions were machine gun companies, their gun carriages strapped on mules, a luxury we did not enjoy. Whippet tanks noisily climbed the road, along with batteries of antitank guns. Always more infantry, all on foot. And only the MacPaps and the 59th were standing in their way.

The foot soldiers we met paid no attention to us as they toiled up the steep hill, sweating under the burden of their packs and rifles. At the bottom of the hill we saw to our left a walled enclosure with several one-story buildings. There our escorts directed us into an alley that led into a large courtyard, where they turned us over to another Italian squad.

The ten of us immediately gathered together in the center of the courtyard to decide on what we should say. We agreed that we would give our names and nationality and identify ourselves as part of the Mackenzie-Papineau Battalion. We would know nothing about the number of men, tanks, or amount of artillery.

Why had we come to Spain? To fight! Someone asked if it wouldn't be better to say we came to work or drive an ambulance to get out alive to fight again? To my relief, the rest realized that such an answer would disgrace the MacPaps and the 15th Brigade and slander the Republic, and would provide anti-Republican propaganda. We had come to fight, period.

What should one say when asked whether he was a Communist? This was a more ticklish question; we realized the probable consequences of declaring ourselves Communists.

"Look, we are all antifascists," said someone who I knew was not a Communist. "We all came to support the democratic government of Spain and to oppose a fascist takeover. So let's not let them divide us up. Let's all stick together. We are all antifascists, nothing more, nothing less."

All agreed on what seemed to me the right stand, not as a result of orders or exhortations but through a calm, collective consideration of our situation and our responsibilities. Democracy *can* work in a crisis.

Our guards, Italian soldiers in their early twenties, had become curious. Some approached in a friendly manner. We knew no Italian and they knew no English, but both could use Spanish.

"Where did you come from?" was the first question. One of us struck a responsive chord when he replied, "New York."

"Oh, I have an uncle there. I would like to go there."

Further questioning revealed about half of us were Canadians. One man replied: "From France."

This drew a quick exclamation: "*A Francia próximo!*"

"To France next? Why do you say that?"

"Before we left, Mussolini told us that although we are going to Spain by water, we will come back by land. How can we go back by land except through France?"

"Yeah, but the French are not going to let you go through."

"Well, we might have to do some fighting first. But maybe the French government will change."

"Talking about fighting, why aren't you up at the front?"

"Oh, we don't have to fight anymore. They promised to send us home months ago. Soon we'll be going home."

"Well, didn't you volunteer to come here?"

"Not us. Our unit was ordered here, so we came."

"Do you think it was right for the Italian Army to come and intervene in a civil war?"

"Mussolini said we had to help Spain fight the Reds, and I believe him, but I think I have done my share."

Our guards asked us our military rank. Most of us were *soldados*, equivalent to privates in the US Army. I was not anxious to advertise my rank, yet out of self-respect I thought it best to reply "battalion commissar" when they pointed at me.

The reaction was immediate: an expressive movement of the index finger from one side of the throat to the other. It was not an expression of hate or concern, just a statement of fact.

Our conversation drifted to the things every soldier complains about—food, tobacco, mail, leave. Here we struck a common chord of mutual understanding and sympathy.

Although we were hungry—our last meal had been breakfast the day before—we were fairly comfortable. But would we last out the day? I was sure my luck had run out when I heard an Italian runner calling "*El comisario!*" as he came toward us.

After my heart started again, I arose and acknowledged the call, *Un minuto, por favor."* Then I proceeded to distribute my earthly possessions to my comrades. There was my wristwatch, given to me at a bon-voyage party. Probably appreciated more was the pack of American cigarettes I carried for emergencies (I did not use them myself). There was also a pouch of Revelation pipe tobacco and my pipe. Then there was a photograph and a ring to be sent back to my wife.

I shook hands with each one and tried to find something to say to relieve the distress showing on their faces. Our guards watched attentively, and the runner waited patiently.

The runner and I had gone some fifty feet when we met Lieutenant Fuentes waving a document and shouting, "I don't have to worry about what's going to happen to me now!" Fuentes was a slim Portugese who had joined Franco's army as a volunteer, but had then deserted to the Republican side; he had recently been assigned to the MacPaps. We stopped to look at his paper. It was a pass stating that he was to be treated well in view of the valuable service he had rendered the Nationalist cause. I knew now that Fuentes was the captain's "pigeon."

The runner motioned me into a corridor on the right, where an Italian officer was standing eating his breakfast.

"Lieutenant, the commissar!"

The lieutenant dismissed the runner, then asked in Spanish, "Would you like something to eat?" pointing to the loaf of bread and slab of baked fish lying on a weather-beaten table.

My first impulse was to refuse. When I looked at the trim well-groomed officer, in his twenties, and saw that it was a friendly offer, I accepted.

He cut generous slices of bread and fish and handed them to me with a question: "What does a commissar do?"

Chewing my first bite gave me a moment to adjust to this unexpected situation. It seemed unlikely that this lieutenant was to be in charge of my execution. Nor would his knowledge of the role played by commissars hurt the Republic. I decided to answer him as clearly as I could.

"You're familiar with the role of chaplains?" He nodded. "Well, we perform many of the functions of a chaplain. Our main concern is with the soldiers' morale. We deal with everything that affects it. Not only the reasons why they are fighting, but also matters such as food, shoes, cigarettes, mail, and news. We also develop friendly relations between the soldiers and the civilian population. We provide instruction in reading and writing for those unable to read."

The lieutenant had listened patiently. He remarked with a smile, "I have no doubt that you are a commissar. Just what reasons do you give your men why they should fight?"

"Simply, that if fascism is not stopped here, it will have to be stopped someplace else, possibly closer to home. And in the meantime, fascism will have become stronger."

"Of course, and that is exactly why I am here. I am not a fascist myself but I support Mussolini because I think world fascism is preferable to world communism."

"But isn't there a third alternative, democracy?"

"Not really. Democracy always leads to communism. Communism is the bastard stepson of democracy." The lieutenant was speaking reflectively, not passionately. It was obvious he sincerely believed what he was saying.

"Then you must not believe that the people can be trusted to run a government democratically?"

"No, I do not. The majority are too poorly educated to understand how to run a government for their own good and that of the nation. Only the intelligent people in society, the better educated, the elite, are capable of building a strong nation and running an orderly society, and it is in the best interests of the rest to obey them. Only in that way can we have a strong and prosperous society."

"Does this not lead to rule by the wealthy and powerful who look after their own interests first? Only if you have democracy, rule by the majority, can you expect a government that looks after the interests of the people. Of course, in a democracy, the majority may make mistakes. But as long as they keep their democracy, they can correct mistakes."

The lieutenant smiled. "You are too much of an idealist and too naive. The end result of democracy is a communist takeover. That is why we must help Franco, and why we must help bring about fascist governments everywhere."

We went on to discuss the part the war in Spain was playing in the preparations for an eventual showdown between democracy and fascism. Spain provided a proving ground for weapons and military tactics, and an opportunity for officers and military staffs to gain battle experience. The war would determine which side would have access to Spain's iron ore, mercury, and agricultural products, and to Gibraltar.

We found ourselves in complete agreement in our analysis of the significance of the fighting in Spain. Except that I considered a fascist victory in Spain to be a severe setback for the democracies and humanity, while he considered it a crucial step toward the goal of a world fascist society. And I could not agree when he said. "The Spaniards do not have the understanding that we do. Therefore we Italians must help them organize their society and run their affairs."

The battlefront had been quiet. Exactly at eight o'clock the sudden booming of artillery and the rattle of machine guns announced the beginning of the attack on our lines.

"You saw the soldiers marching up the road toward Gandesa this morning?" I told the lieutenant that I had.

"We have 30,000 men headng for Gandesa this morning. On the road on our left there are another 30,000 coming down from Caspe, and another 30,000 on a parallel route on our right. We will take Gandesa by noon Tortosa tonight, and be down at the Mediterranean in two days. The war will be finished very soon. It has dragged on too long already."

I thought of the hungry men of the 15th International Brigade, not even numbering a thousand, who were trying to stop the 30,000 without artillery, and without tanks. Large numbers of bombers and fighters were flying overhead now, and they were not ours. The lovely spring morning had turned into an inferno of bursting bombs, flying shrapnel and steel, and death for our comrades along the road.

The lieutenant, saying he had work to do, expressed his appreciation for our frank conversation. Escorting me to the alley, he called an Italian guard to take me back to the other prisoners. At no time had he asked me any questions he knew I should not answer, nor had he at any time expressed the least personal animosity. I was certain, from the information he had given me and the free manner in which he had expressed his opinions, that he knew I was to be shot.

What troubled me most was that on their side, down to the level of lieutenant, it was clearly understood that the fascist leaders of the world were consciously preparing for a military showdown with the democracies. In the democracies, even the top leaders were either unaware of the fascist plans or, worse, were their willing accomplices. By refusing to the legitimate Republic the arms needed to defend itself while allowing Hitler and Mussolini to provide arms and manpower to the Spanish fascists, the democracies were helping the forces preparing to destroy them.

My comrades were astonished and delighted when I returned, and they crowded around to hear what had happened. They fell silent when I told them the size of the attacking force. Never had we faced odds of thirty to one.

Noting that Lieutenant Fuentes was absent, I asked about him. He had been called away. We knew then why there had been no attempt to obtain information from us. We knew he had betrayed us. Undoubtedly, the enemy was confident that they could walk right over the thousand men in front of them; then the road would be open to Gandesa, Tortosa, and the Mediterranean.

9 We Face a Firing Squad

A BOND of comaraderie had developed between the guards and ourselves through the discussion of common gripes and complaints. They were awed when they found among us not only workers but also professionals. None of the guards had ever held a steady job, and they did not know what they would do when they returned home.

Six more Internationals were now added to our ten. One was twenty-year-old Jules Paivio, from Thunder Bay in Canada. He had been in the first group to climb the Pyrenees in March 1937. Jules, and Leslie (Curly) Wilson, born in Kenora, Ontario, and four other Canadians in a forward position had been surrounded and captured shortly after the fighting began. I told them what we had agreed to say if questioned and what the Italian officer had said.[1,2]

The sounds of battle later that morning told us that despite all the men and materiel arrayed against them, the MacPaps and the 59th were holding on. And here we were, we thought, sitting comfortably and safely behind the fascist lines. But then a runner called out, "Bring the Internationals!"

Our guards marched us back up the alley. As we rounded the wall on our right, we saw a dozen soldiers with rifles standing about sixty feet from the wall, with a man with a Red Cross insigne on his arm,[3] and another wearing a long black gown.

Hodge commented to me, "This doesn't look so good."

We were ordered to stand arm's length apart with our backs against the wall. I was eighth in line, with seven on my right and eight on my left. We all stood quietly, showing no signs of fear. The firing squad was waiting for its commanding officer.

What does one think about while awaiting execution? My thoughts were not on the hereafter. Years earlier I had come to the conclusion that, contrary to what I had learned as a boy, there was no jealous ritual-loving God ready to deal out life everlasting in the fires of hell to those who did not honor him in the prescribed ways. Rather, for me, God was the well-being of humankind. I believed that the only way I would live on would be through the effects of my actions on humanity's future.

Nor did the knowledge that this belief had brought me into a situation where I would lose my life cause me to regret my dedication. I did not hate the men on the firing squad, for I understood that they too were victims of their environment.

Nevertheless, there *was* hatred in me, deep hatred. It arose out of my love for the fifteen fine men standing with me who had also dedicated their lives to the defense of democracy and who were about to die, and for those courageous men manning the thin line trying to stop the onrush of the fascist army. It sprang out of my love for the people of Spain who were so heroically and self-sacrificingly fighting and dying to stop fascism.

It was this love that fueled my hatred for those who were organizing and financing the forces of fascism and for their accomplices in the democracies who, under the guise of fighting communism, were betraying democracy and strengthening fascism. These men would, if successful, lead humanity into the worse period of suffering and destruction in history.

In a sense I was prepared to die. Though I had lived only twenty-seven years, I was satisfied with what I had done with my life. I believed I had made a contribution to humanity and had never consciously taken advantage of anyone. I had tried to follow the moral precepts I had learned as a boy at home, in school, and in Sunday school, later buttressed by strong philosophical beliefs.

And yet, I hated to die. It was not only because I would never again see my wife, my sisters and brother, and my many relatives and friends; it was knowing that I could no longer join them in making this a better world and that my death would not contribute to the benefit of humanity but rather to its harm and suffering—that was what made dying here so loathsome and foul.

Some who have faced sudden death say their past life flashed before them. I did not experience this. Others have reported feeling such terror that they lost control of bodily functions—shaking knees, tremors, abdominal pain, loss of bowel and bladder control. Imminent death places a severe strain on mind and body. For some it can lead to physical immobility, to collapse, and to mindless attempts to escape.

The fifteen men standing steadfastly beside me demonstrated that, given strong convictions, goals, and standards, one can keep one's physiological processes under control and remain primed for escape if the opportunity should arise.

What also enabled us to stand there quietly was our determination to do nothing that would disgrace the International Brigades or our country. If die we must, we would do it without begging for our lives, standing tall and proud.

Could we escape? The guards were on the other side of the wall. Automatic rifle fire made a concerted rush out either side or both suicidal. We saw no place where we could take cover.

And the priest? Would he ask if we wanted to be absolved of our sins before dying? Or would he merely insure that all the amenities of fascist culture were observed? Perhaps he too was a victim of evil forces? So far, he had not approached us, and was talking with the man wearing the Red Cross insigne.

Suddenly the firing squad was called to attention. Two officers ap proached the sergeant in charge. After a brief consultation, they approached the International nearest the road.

I could not hear the questions, but they did not appear to be presented in a threatening manner. After a half dozen questions, they moved to the next prisoners. When they were three men away from me, I could begin to hear the exchange.

"Nationality?"

"Canadian."

"Rank?"

"Private."

"Why did you come to Spain?"

I was proud of his quick reply, "To fight for the Republic."

"Are you a Communist?"

"I am an antifascist."

The unhesitating responses, the unflinching posture, the eyes fastened on them without fear, obviously impressed the officers. The next in line, an American, gave the same answers.

As they began to question the man next to me, I noticed two large black sedans. They were heading toward the front, and they braked as they passed out of sight. A moment later, they backed into view again. The officers ran over and saluted. After a brief conversation, the two cars disappeared.

The officers walked briskly over to the firing squad. I expected the executions to begin at once. But the priest and the Red Cross official were walking away! The firing squad was shouldering arms, preparing to march off! I looked at my comrades. Their facial expressions were a mixture of surprise, relief, and joy. I heard Hodge drawl, "Well, I'll be doggoned!"

A happy, excited, somewhat shaken group of men returned to the courtyard. Our guards were pleased too. They told us the men in the cars were high-ranking officers, and they had given orders that between April 1 and April 9 Internationals were to be taken alive. (Forty years later I would learn that the purpose was to obtain Internationals to exchange for the Italian prisoners the Republic had captured at Guadalajara.)

It was nearly eleven o'clock, and we could still hear the firing at the front. We were filled with admiration and pride for the fight our comrades were putting up. A little after noon, the firing began to drift away. We were elated; the MacPaps and the 59th had upset the fascist plan to take Gandesa by noon.

A few more MacPap prisoners were brought in. From them we learned they had held their positions until they ran out of ammunition and discovered they were surrounded. By mid-afternoon we heard only the booming of artillery and bombs. We knew the situation of the 59th and the MacPaps had to be desperate.

Late in the afternoon came that chilling call: "Bring the Internationals." This time we were relieved to see an empty truck. A bumpy hour brought us to Alcañiz, where we were unloaded in front of a large church having massive wooden doors. We were turned loose in a huge room with four large pillars supporting the ceiling. In the murkey light we saw it was filled with Spaniards, the first we had seen since our capture. They were prisoners too, both military and civilian.

The church had been used as a prisoner depot for a few days. Since no provision had been made for a latrine, an area behind the main altar was covered with human excrement and urine. The whole place stank. We made our way to the right side, where there were several empty coffins. There was much confusion and calling of names, with wild rumors circulating about executions. In the corner to the left of the entrance, officers were being registered, and a call came for all officers to report at once.

Undecided what to do, I gathered a group of Mac Paps in the semi-darkness and asked for their advice, and got it quickly.

"Don't be a fool! We need you to stay with us as long as you can, so you'd better become a private, or at most a corporal, and get rid of that damned jacket in a hurry."

The decision was unanimous and emphatic. I found a Spaniard who was happy to accept my jacket for his shabbier one.

Darkness was settling over the room, a flickering light coming from the registration area. We stayed as far away from there as we could, lost among the Spanish prisoners. Several managed to get inside the coffins along the wall and spent a more or less comfortable night in them. The rest crowded together on the marble floor to keep warm.

Lying there, hungry, exhausted and aching, I was extremely glad to be alive. Chance, which plays a fickle role for men in battle, had truly favored my companions and me today.

10 We Begin Our Retreat from Gandesa

A SUSPICION had arisen in a Lincoln outpost on the night of March 31 that they might already be behind the fascist lines. "In that case," Joe Young, twenty-five, born in Bellefonte, Pennsylvania, and a seaman, remarked to his squad, "You might have to travel at night, and to do that you'll have to read the stars."

Joe showed them how to use the Big Dipper to find the North Star. All paid close attention until one stood up, faced the North Star with arms extended, and exclaimed, "That's east, and that's west, and south is behind me. But where the hell's Gandesa?"

Before daylight, artillery on their right began shelling positions on the left. A rumor reached them: "Get out the best way you can." But where to go? As dawn broke, Joe noticed half a dozen Internationals moving toward the area where the shells were landing. That must be where the Republican lines were, and Joe fell in behind them. All carried only rifles and ammunition.

They followed a dusty wagon road. As they rounded a corner, they saw a truck, its tailgate down, both doors open. Hood and radiator had bullet holes. In the truck were sacks of shoes and boxes of archives. Identification folders, photos, personal belongings, even paper money, were scattered about on the road.

Now certain they were behind enemy lines, they destroyed their identification cards and removed rank and International Brigade insignia. They continued along the road until they heard voices calling: "*Brigada americana! Brigada americana!*" Joe knew they were fascists because they were calling out the wrong name. His companions waved their rifles, yelling, "*Aquí!*" Here, Bullets sang over their heads. All jumped into a field of wheat barely high enough to conceal them. Soon they heard soldiers. Joe describes his capture:

The voice I can never forget belonged to a boy wearing a red beret and a bayoneted rifle which he poked at me. He crowed like a rooster: "Arriba las manos! Viva Franco! Viva España! Viva Cristo! Viva el Rey!" If he had read it from a proclamation he could not have done it better. When I got up I arribaed los manos and looked at him, he was so young and appeared surprised. He asked if I was herido (wounded). After looking myself over I told him no, so he looked around apparently for instructions and started herding me over toward the road.

The rest were rounded up by these youthful soldiers wearing red berets or tasseled caps. Joe was struck by the white shirts and the suspenders

77

holding up their breeches. A black-uniformed sergeant came over, his chest covered with medals, a "potato masher" (a hand grenade with a long handle) in his belt, and a Luger in his hand. He ordered the prisoners taken to a terrace on the left. The boys used their rifle butts to hurry the prisoners along. The blow Joe got on the hip didn't bother him then, though he felt it for months afterwards. The sight of two bodies, one blond-haired, lying in their own blood, boots missing and faces shot off, numbed him to his own pain.

The sergeant lined the prisoners up next to the dead. Soldiers relieved the prisoners of their watches, rings, and cigarette lighters. The boy who had captured Joe searched him and found a Saint Christopher medal sent to him by Helen Mulholland. The boy took them to the sergeant. After some discussion, the sergeant approached Joe and asked if he was Catholic. Joe could see among the sergeant's medals a crucifix and a Sacred Heart medallion. He said, "Yes."

The sergeant stepped back. After more discussion, in which Joe heard *católico* and *americano,* the sergeant had a squad of four come forward and stand in front of the prisoners. The rest retired to the road to watch. The four soldiers grounded their rifles on order, and were listening to the sergeant when a bugle blew and someone yelled *Venga!* Come' here! The sergeant ordered the four soldiers to escort the prisoners to the road. The discussion about the religious medal had delayed their execution long enough for the bugle to save their lives.

The sergeant took his prisoners up to several officers having breakfast. One had a board across his knees, and an orderly with a napkin was serving him coffee and bread.

The seated officer asked, "Anybody speak English?"

Joe spoke up, "I do."

"Where are you from?"

"New York City."

"What the hell are you doing here? Are you crazy?"

The officer quickly issued an order, and a group of joyous young soldiers led by a proud sergeant marched the bedraggled and dispirited prisoners to Villalba de los Arcos. There a friendly clerk in the command post struggled to record their strange Dutch and French names and the un-Spanish Young.

Joe and his companions were taken to an evacuated house. The town appeared undamaged, and was empty except for Franco's soldiers. A guard gave them dried salted fish to chew on. All were suffering from thirst, but there was no water in the house, and the guard said none was available.

That evening they were moved to a barn large enough to hold thirty prisoners plus a cart and a mule that had missed the evacuation. A lantern was hung high above them. The need for water was now serious. Several prisoners investigated the cart. Beneath the farm implements and sacks of seeds were two large jugs. One held olive oil and the other a dark rich-smelling wine. They drank deeply of the fragrant wine.

Cries at the door silenced everyone. "Sons of whores! Shoot them! Kill them!" The guards were trying to restrain a drunken soldier holding a grenade, but he managed to throw it in a wide arc past the lantern. It came to rest near the mule's feet. The mule didn't move, but everyone else scrambled away as far as he could. Seconds passed in silence as the grenade lay beside the unconcerned mule. Finally the guards drove the drunken soldier away. Later some prisoners pronounced the grenade safe, but Joe kept his distance.

The next morning a tall, immaculately uniformed, and heavily decorated officer appeared at the doorway and asked whether anyone spoke English. A number pressed forward to be noticed.

"Where did the rest of your battalion go?"

Arms went out in several directions.

One prisoner asked, "What will happen to us?"

"You will get what you deserve," he replied as he left.

The discussion of what this statement meant was interrupted by the arrival of two empty trucks. The prisoners pointed out the grenade to the sergeant in charge. He nonchalantly picked it up and lobbed it across the road into a field. The prisoners were ordered to board the trucks. They clamored for water until several buckets were brought. The trip was delayed by the passage of battalion after battalion of soldiers, troops of cavalry, all sizes of artillery, tanks, fuel trucks antiaircraft guns, and ambulances. Fresh divisions were on their way to the front. To the prisoners they were a depressing sight.

That evening they passed the ruins of Belchite, reeking from the three-week-old dead buried beneath the toppled buildings. Early the next morning, April 3, the prisoners were dropped off in the enclosed parade grounds of San Gregorio Military Academy. Joe's sharpest memory of that morning is of a row of faucets sticking out of a wall, where they were able to get water. No basin, no drain, no soap, just delicious cold water.[1]

*   *   *   *   *

On the morning of April 1, Stanley Heinricher's squad of the Lincoln Battalion was stationed in an olive grove. Stan lay in the prone rifle position beside an olive tree, facing uphill, waiting for the expected enemy attack. Suddenly he felt something red-hot go through his body. When he regained consciousness, several comrades were at his side. A bullet had entered through his neck and exited from his lower back, close to his backbone. They thought it must have punctured his lung. An order came from Merriman to withdraw at once to avoid being surrounded. His comrades put a bandage on each hole, placed him on a stretcher and carried him twenty-five yards uphill to some bushes. After covering him with several blankets and camouflaging the stretcher with branches, they left hurriedly.

Stan heard machine-gun and rifle fire for several hours, then all became quiet. He lay there all day and through the night, staying warm under the extra blankets.[2]

The Lincoln battalion had been ordered to withdraw to defend the main road to Gandesa. Before they reached it, they learned the enemy had already occupied the road. Orders were changed to go through Batea to Villalba de los Arcos. News came that Batea had been taken by the fascists, so the Lincolns started over the hills to Villalba until word came that Villalba was already occupied. They then proceeded cross-country to Gandesa.[3]

Not all squads received the first order to withdraw. One squad, under fire for the first time, included members who had been among the eighty Cubans who had left Havana on February 5, 1938, on the SS *Oropesa*. They had received a week's training at the Lincoln base at Tarazona before the call came: "Everybody to the front!" They were part of the eight hundred who had joined the 15th Brigade when I did.

Evelio Aneiro Subirats was among those assigned to the Lincoln Battalion. On April 1 his squad, well dug in, survived shelling and bombing and held their positions well onto the afternoon, when they began to wonder if there was anyone else left. They sent José Real to find out. He didn't come back. Then they sent out Manuel Corcho Díaz. He didn't return. Juan Martínez Márquez went out next and didn't come back. Evelio was the next to go down the path the others had taken. Suddenly the enemy fired at him, and he dived into the adjoining bushes. There were the other three, unable to move without drawing fire.

They lay there, not certain what to do, until a scouting party with a red flag came along, calling, "Come here, comrades!" They came out, only to have the fascist patrol take them prisoner.

A member of the patrol warned them, "Say you are Spaniards. The order is to shoot the Internationals." They were taken to Santoña, on the northern coast near Santander, and held in the rubble of an unused factory along with hundreds of Spanish prisoners.[4]

The MacPaps and our Spanish 59th Battalion, instead of being bypassed like the Lincolns, had been hit head-on by the Italian troops whose numbers had so depressed me.

One of the MacPaps who held up their advance was Frank Blackman, from Valemount, British Columbia, a tiny village 175 miles west of Jasper. He was a blue-eyed, lean, six-foot-four twenty-four-year-old, slower in speech than in action, and an expert with the rifle. For the past few winters, he had packed his traps and gear and essential food supplies, such as salt, sugar, flour, and tea, and on snowshoes headed north into the Cariboo

Mountains, where he had six small cabins a day's travel apart. Several months later he would return with a load of furs, the fruits of his trapping and hunting, having lived off the game he caught.

On April 1, Frank formed part of the MacPap front line. He selected a spot with a clear view over a valley across which the enemy would have to infiltrate. He didn't have time to dig his foxhole very deep, so he positioned a large rock in front of him for protection and to make his rifle less visible. Enemy soldiers soon appeared across the valley and began to filter down a trail. Frank picked them off one by one, wasting no bullets. The infiltration halted while the MacPap line was peppered with mortar and artillery shells, killing one of Frank's buddies.

Another attempt to advance again ran into Frank's deadly fire. Frank heard his name called behind him. Thinking it was to check whether he was all right, he hollered back, "I'm OK," and stayed put. It was only when he ran out of ammunition that he discovered everyone had withdrawn and that Italian troops were on all sides. He was captured.[5]

Harry Kleiman, a cool 130-pound, twenty-three-year-old New Yorker, was fighting with the MacPaps under the name of Cohn Haber. On the afternoon of April 1 while helping to defend Brigade headquarters Harry had a bullet go through a knee, an extremely painful wound. Semiconscious, he opened his eyes when a *requeté*[6] pressed the muzzle of his gun against his head. Only the immediate intervention of an Italian sergeant saved Harry, and he was taken to a hospital.[7]

*　　*　　*　　*　　*

The trucks that had picked up the British and the three American prisoners took them to the large church in Alcañiz. Garry McCartney and Willie Collins sat down beside John Penman and Donald Carson, fellow Scots they knew to be members of the Communist Party. Expecting to be interrogated, they agreed they would urge all British prisoners to say, as they would, that they had come to Spain as trade unionists to fight for the Republic. They were alarmed when Frank Ryan was taken away, fearful that he would be shot.

The next day, April 2, *Diario de Burgos* carried a feature article, "Red International Forces Desert by the Hundreds," by its military expert, Tebib Arrumi (actualy Víctor Ruiz Albeniz, a doctor who had become acquainted with Franco in Morocco).

While I was amongst these hundred English prisoners, 480 more arrived at Alcañiz although these were deserters, having done so last night to the Legionary forces, stating they had had enough of war . . . are from the 15th Brigade, the celebrated 15th Brigade, in their majority French, English and Czechs. . . . We have taken care of them in such a way that they themselves have asked me to express their appreciation and joyfully posed for photographs for the foreign and national press.

Arrumi claimed he had interviewed the British, but none of the four I met with in 1981 who had been at Alcañiz that day could recall seeing him; he may have written his false propaganda article after a phone call. There were in fact, no French or Czechs in the 15th Brigade, and certainly no deserters to the fascist side. Some Americans did desert *from* the 15th Brigade, but I have found no record of anyone foolish enough to desert *to* the Franco side. If they did, they didn't live to tell about it. The deserters either went to the American consulates or headed for the French border. (State Department archives list fourteen who went to the consulates during the war.[8]) Some twenty captured Americans and Canadians, including myself, did arrive at Alcañiz late that afternoon, and Arrumi may have transformed us into 480 joyful deserters. But photographs were not taken of us: the church was too dark and crowded with prisoners.

Carney's dispatch in the *Times* on April 2 named the three Americans among the hundred British prisoners: Max Parker; Matthew Dykstra, a student of architectural engineering from Los Angeles; and John Logan, a sailor from New York.

11 International Brigaders Behind the Fascist Lines

STANLEY HEINRICHER was glad April 2 was a sunny day with mild breezes. The sounds of birds and insects were so much more pleasant than the dreadful sounds of aerial bombs and artillery far off in the distance. Lying on his stretcher for the second day, he tried not to think of the path the bullet had taken through his body, from his neck to below his ribs. "Let my body get on with its healing without interference from a worrying mind."

That afternoon Stanley wondered why he had to move his bowels when he had not eaten for three days. Better obey the call. Moving a few feet from his stretcher turned out to be not too difficult. He drank only a swallow of water in order to interfere as little as possible with any repairs his body might be making on his internal plumbing, then slept most of the rest of the day and night.[1]

During the night the Lincoln Battalion had gathered on the heights overlooking Gandesa. The rising sun on April 2 revealed Gandesa was under attack, and there were fascist troops on both sides of the battalion. Merriman and the battalion officers decided to break through the enemy lines to join the forces defending Gandesa, but the battalion ran into heavy enemy machine-gun fire. Melvin Offsink and Irving Keith were among those killed, and Fred Keller, the Lincoln Battalion commissar, had a bullet in the left hip.[2] The Lincolns were forced to return to the heights.

The daily operations log of the fascist 1st Navarrese Division, whose units were attacking Gandesa, reveals they had taken Villalba de los Arcos on April 1 without resistance, and by 3:30 A.M. on April 2 were within two kilometers of Gandesa. The division suffered heavy losses before it took Gandesa at 11:40 A.M. Its commander was concerned about the Republican forces in his rear, since he was short on munitions, needed reinforcements, and had lost contact with his division headquarters. Late that afternoon he received reinforcements.[3]

The Lincolns watched from the hilltop as Italian tank and troop convoys moved toward Gandesa. Sydney Harris, a twenty-one-year-old Chicagoan, and several others were detailed to cross a valley and set up a lookout on a hill to keep an eye on fascist forces moving toward Gandesa. They were above the tree line when fascist cavalry cut them off. Syd recalls:

Next think I knew I heard a sound behind me. I was reloading my rifle, and looking over my shoulder I see two guys on horses and they're screaming at me. I tried to cock the rifle and push in the bullet and pull the trigger at the same time—it doesn't work. Probably my quick turnabout frightened the horses, who reared up a little bit as they shot, and I got hit in the lower part of the leg here, and I just rolled head over heels down the hill right up to the tree line right up against a big rock, and scrambled behind the rock and pulled a grenade and took the pin out because I could hear them coming after me. I could look up and see them but they couldn't see me. They hung around a while and then left.

I spent an awful night where you think you hear all sorts of sounds, and you fall asleep and you hallucinate and in the morning there you are, all by yourself, a big hole in your leg and nobody around. And you're tired. And by this time I am thirsty as all hell although not hungry. And the bandages are soggy. And rolling down the hill I must have broken a collarbone because I couldn't lift this arm.

When Syd began to crawl down to the road, several women saw him and climbed up to help him. They said he would be safer hiding on the hill and with their help he climbed back a bit. They made a grass bed for him with a rock for a pillow. The youngest, Asunción, a pretty young woman about Syd's age, tore off part of her petticoat to bandage his leg. Then they left to get help. Asunción returned at dusk with some bread, an egg, and water and spent the night with Syd to keep him warm, then left to get help. (Asunción was alive and well in Gandesa in 1981.)

Syd waited until afternoon, then crawled down to the highway, only to see an enemy cleanup squad approaching. He was too weak to climb back up. He still had two grenades. Syd had heard stories about atrocities committed on Internationals. He put one grenade in a little hole and held his hand over it, so he could release its handle to kill himself if need be, and held the other ready to use on the enemy. They stopped a short distance away, pointed their rifles at him and called out, "*Ruso?*"

"*No, Americano!*"

"*No. Ruso, rojo.*"

"*No, Americano, yo vivo en Chicago.*"

"*Chicago! Al Capone! Al Capone!*"

They lowered their rifles and congratulated themselves on catching a guy from Chicago. Syd was carried on a stretcher into Gandesa, to a stable where there were more American prisoners, including Maurice Gurko, also from Chicago. A little later, the able-bodied men were taken away. Some Italian soldiers came in. One said, "Hey, I hear you come from Chicago. I'm from New York. The only difference between you and me, Buddy, is I picked the right side."

The New Yorker ordered water and a blanket for Syd and offered him a delicacy—chocolate. Syd slept for about an hour. He woke up with a start when someone started whacking him. Syd asked, "What, Comrade?"

"Don't call me 'comrade'!" The whacker now beat harder.

Fortunately, Syd's Italian friend came to his rescue and had him taken by ambulance to a large field hospital. Two Italian doctors who spoke English gave him a big drink of cognac and started sterilizing and cutting. The bullet had left a hole between the two leg bones, and had taken a small chip off one, a cause of trouble later. He was then taken to a hospital in Zaragoza.[4]

Pablo Valdes Laguardia, blackest of the eighty Cubans who had left Havana on February 5, 1938, had taken part in the Lincoln attack on April 2. Pablo was among the eight hundred who came up after Belchite, though he was having trouble breathing. A doctor had examined him on March 29, found he had pneumonia and a 104-degree fever and ordered him evacuated to a hospital. But Pablo, thinking he would get better, rejoined his company. His comrades put him in an ambulance going toward the front. It had gone barely a kilometer when the driver saw a village still burning from the bombs dropped on it. The ambulance was needed to carry back the injured, so Pablo started to walk.

Night fell, but the Lincolns continued on along a highway having many precipices and steep grades. Pablo, exhausted, slept under a pine tree. The next morning he stopped a truck coming up the hill by pointing his rifle at the driver. The driver, frightened and thinking Pablo was a Moor, was relieved to find he only wanted to ride up to the front.

His astonished comrades dosed him with cognac and hot milk. Pablo then experienced an artillery bombardment, followed by bombing and strafing and an infantry attack. He had fired his rifle for only a few hours before the order came to withdraw. Still suffering from pneumonia, he was among those captured and taken to Alcañiz and then to Zaragoza.[5]

Merriman and the Lincoln officers on the hilltop the evening of April 2 formed two columns to break out by traveling cross-country at night. The first was led by brigade officers Merriman, Doran, and a trim twenty-six-year-old Brooklyn union organizer, Leonard Lamb, and by Lincoln Commander Wolff and wounded Commissar Keller; the second by Commissars John Gates, George Watt, and Copernico, a Spaniard. The first column crossed the Villalba-Gandesa road just as an enemy convoy came along, and the two columns became separated.[6]

The first column of Lincolns scrambled up a bluff onto a heavily used dirt road. Following it, they heard men snoring. Moving quietly, they tried to pass the enemy encampment. Suddenly a hysterical voice cried out, *"Cabo de guardia! Rojos!"* Corporal of the guard! Reds! To escape the rifle fire, the members of the column scattered in all directions.

Merriman and Doran found themselves in the encampment occupied by part of the 1st Navarrese Division. They were killed either before or after capture; no record has been found, but the Navarrese Division's daily operations log for April 2 and 3 reports many Republican dead and prisoners, including the chiefs of the 11th and 13th International Brigades.[7] The 15th may have been mistaken for the 13th, which was not there.[8]

Leonard Lamb, Milton Wolff, and stocky twenty-nine-year-old Joe Brandt, from New York, struck out in different directions, and all reached the far shore of the Ebro. Leonard had had a problem; he couldn't swim. He tried to cross the collapsed bridge at Mora de Ebro at night, but found a twenty-five-foot gap in it, and drew fire from the Republican side besides. The next morning, at a small isolated farmhouse, Leonard was told to go up on a hill and wait. The farmer brought him a loaf of bread and an egg and suggested he remove his captain's bars. When he learned Leonard was in the International Brigade, the farmer said, "Then it doesn't make any difference. You'll be shot anyway."

The farmer told Leonard of a woman who lived with her two children in a cave near a cable that crossed the river. She would call for a boat for him. Leonard found her, and a boatload of armed Republican soldiers came over and picked him up.[9]

Fred Keller, with the bullet still in his hip, collected seventeen other Internationals along the way. Just as they came to the main road east of Gandesa, a fascist infantry column came along, flags flying, bands playing, and everyone marching in step, spic-and-span, with full equipment. Fred and his companions had seen nothing like it in this war.

They decided to go north. Near Fatarella they had to wait for nearly an hour while a column of cavalry passed by. After spending the night in a cave, they headed northeast, reaching the Ebro between Asco and Flix on the fourth day. Most of the men had doubts about swimming across the cold, swift river. Fully clothed, Fred swam across to show it could be done, but he wanted to be the last to cross, so he swam back to help the others.

At that moment a cavalry patrol opened fire on them. All who fled or tried to swim were shot. Fred, and Mark, a Canadian, gave themselves up. They were imprisoned in a house in Flix with some Spanish prisoners with one guard at the door. Several times Fred went up to him to ask questions. At dusk, he and Mark went up again, and as the guard turned to answer, Fred socked him hard. The guard collapsed, and Fred and Mark bolted for a wooded hill, where they were safe in the darkness. By sunup they were down at the river again. Mark wanted to wait until nightfall, but Fred plunged in and swam across. Firing broke out, and Mark ran back into an orchard, to an unknown fate.

Fred went to a hospital to have the bullet removed. He was eating four dishes of bean soup when news correspondents came to see him on April 11. Herbert Matthews awed by his feat, wrote in his dispatch that Fred was "young and strong as a bull and has all the courage in the world."[10]

Another member of the column, Fred Stanley, a twenty-one-year-old seaman born in Odem, Texas, scrambled away across country when he heard the firing up ahead. He ended up on a hill at dawn with a group that included another seaman, Fred Miller, thirty-three, from Detroit, Michigan; an ex-army man, Joseph Grigas, twenty-three, from Worcester, Massachusetts; and "Lucky" Roger Braley, thirty-five, from Newport, Rhode Island (lucky because he had been on leave when the submarine on which he was serving, the S-4, sank). That night, after sleeping all day, they could not agree whether they should head between two campfires or between a star and the moon. Spanish troops surprised them the next morning.

They had a thirsty eight-hour march back to Gandesa before they obtained water. Taken to a barnlike building, they were ordered to climb down a ladder into a wine storage cistern.[11]

The second column of Lincolns, led by George Watt, Copernico, and John Gates, hurried across the Villalba-Gandesa road after the enemy convoy had passed by. Unable to contact the first column, they moved ahead on their own, stopping occasionally to allow scouts time to check the best route.

One scout, Robert Steck, short and stocky, twenty-three years old, born in Rock Island, Illinois, had joined the Lincolns a few days before the eight hundred came up. At one stop Bob scouted ahead and heard snoring; there was an enemy encampment within twenty feet of the path. As he went back, the snoring of the Lincolns who had already dropped off into sleep sounded alarmingly loud. Quietly, he helped awaken them. Farther on, they heard a second enemy encampment snoring and gave it a wide berth.[12]

At dawn, as they entered a valley, a challenge rang out from a hilltop: "*Alto!*" Quick-thinking Copernico, the five-foot-one-inch Spanish commissar, repeated the challenge to halt.

The reply came back, "*Quién es?*" Copernico promptly demanded to know who they were.

Gates motioned for all to climb the hill on the other side while Copernico kept the dialogue going. The challenger insisted he come up to him. Copernico, waving a white hankerchief, slowly went up to the challenger, giving the rest time to hurry by.

A little later, they were hailed again in Spanish from a hilltop. Herman Lopez, born in Puerto Rico, volunteered to find out who was up there. When Herman saw they were fascists, he signaled to Gates. Seeing it was impossible to escape, Herman put up his hands and surrendered, saying he was a Spaniard.

Later, the column broke up into small groups. One group was headed by Gates and another by Watt. Both men reached the Ebro—Gates with Lewis Gayle, and Watt with six others. They met accidentally at the Ebro, where they plunged in before dawn. Only Gates, Watt, Gayle, and Joe Hecht reached the other bank. The others turned back or were drowned.[13]

Copernico had been taken prisoner. Six months later his comrades rejoiced when they read in the *Volunteer for Liberty* that he had escaped from a fascist concentration camp.

George Delich, forty, a metal worker born in Yugoslavia who had served in the US Army Reserves; Tommy Lloyd, a seaman; Ignatz Moskowitz, born in Hungary and an American seaman; Bob Steck; and several others stuck together. On the third day they were walking on the side of a road when they heard a convoy of motorcycles and trucks coming toward them. They quickly clawed their way up a very steep hill, where the group discussed how to proceed. Walking along the road would be faster and easier, but much more dangerous. Tommy decided to walk along the road; he made it to the Ebro and crossed it safely.

Bob, George, Ignatz, and two others decided to go cross-country. During the day they met other groups of Yanks and Canadians, but no one had maps or reliable knowledge about roads and towns. The terrain was very steep with many terraces. Almost all farmers lived in villages, and there were very few buildings elsewhere. There were no fruits, nuts, or vegetables to eat.

The nights were cold, and they spent the next one in a shallow rock cave. George had a spare sheepskin vest, which he gave to Bob; it proved to be his most valuable possession for the next year and a half. Deciding they would be less conspicuous if they traveled by twos and threes, they drew straws. Bob and Ignatz were paired, and spent the day climbing over terraces and the next night shivering in a rock crevice, with only a thin blanket to cover them.

The next morning Bob and Ignatz watched an isolated farmhouse at the edge of a wood and concluded it was occupied only by a woman and a boy. When they asked for something to eat, the woman invited them in and set the boy outside as a guard. Bob and Ignatz had just finished some fish, bread fried in olive oil, and goat's milk when they heard hoofbeats. The boy rushed in to announce, *"Enemigo."* The woman went to the front door to talk to the cavalrymen while Bob and Ignatz grabbed their rifles and scrambled out the back door after the boy. He led them into the woods and showed them the path to follow. The path, overgrown with brush and blocked by fallen trees, led to a fork, where Bob went to the right and Ignatz to the left. Later, Bob was unable to find Ignatz.

That evening Bob came upon a shack containing a string of garlic and a small cask of wine. He helped himself to both. Then he climbed up onto a narrow shelf and slept well into the next morning, and decided to stay there until that evening. Then, taking some garlic, some roots from the garden, and a bottle of water, Bob traveled through the moonlit night.

Bob found it more comfortable and safer to sleep during the day and travel by night and early morning. The experience he'd had leading moonlight hikes at Camp Unity—a vacation camp back in the States—served him well. Traveling alone cross-country at night, using the stars and enemy bonfires as guides, being startled by the braying of a burro, never knowing when you might run into an enemy sentry, not knowing where you are, is not for the faint-hearted.

After several very narrow escapes, one morning Bob found he was near a large culvert. There was no traffic on the road. He climbed the embankment and saw the Ebro River. On the other side was a marsh. Having been a lifeguard at Camp Unity, Bob was certain he could swim across, even though the water was still cold—it was April 10. He climbed back down and crawled through the culvert, taking no chances now that he was so near freedom. He took his rifle apart and buried the pieces in the mud. And just as he left the bushes to approach the Ebro, an Italian patrol captured him.

Taken to a base police unit, Bob found them

eating spaghetti. A soldier offered me a plate. I reached to take it but he threw it into my face. Another soldier rushed over and yelled at him. A hot argument ensued with several participating. One of the arguers brought me another plate. I was reluctant to take it. He put it on the ground. I grabbed it and wolfed it. He sat next to me and asked me about New York. Is there a possibility I would know his relatives on East 10th Street?

Later that day Bob was taken by jeep to a barn and left at the bottom of a deep cistern until the

ladder was replaced and I came out. Loaded into a small truck with two guards in the back. In poor Spanish we conversed, he in a mixture of Italian and Spanish, I in a mixture of Spanish and sign language. I learned that he had been in Ethiopia and after six months was to have returned to Rome but the ship came to Spain. He had been here nearly 18 months. In two months he expected to . . . rejoin his family.

As they approached Gandesa, Bob saw unburied bodies along the road. He was dropped off at a prison where he met two Dutch Internationals. The following day they were taken to Alcañiz and the next day to the military academy at Zaragoza.[14]

William Colfax Miller, a six-foot-four, twenty-seven-year-old volunteer from Hollywood, California, had been in the second column. He, Otto, and two others traveled north at night following the North Star as Bill had learned to do as a Boy Scout. During the day they slept in thick woods. By the fourth day they were quite hungry. Cautiously, they approached what appeared to be an abandoned farmhouse. Inside they found a pile of almonds. They were on their knees shelling and eating nuts when a shadow fell over them. Looking up, they saw a German officer with a pistol. *"Manos arriba!"* he ordered.

Hands rising slowly, they got to their feet. The officer waved the men toward the door with his pistol. Bill knew there must be a patrol nearby to serve as the firing squad. Better to take a chance with the one gun at his back than a half dozen in front, so he whirled suddenly and grabbed the pistol, while his companions wrestled the officer to the floor. Bill put a bullet into him and heard him scream in pain.

All four took off pell-mell down the mountainside, and an hour later they were staring at a swollen Ebro: the fascists had opened the dams. It looked as broad as the Missouri back home in South Dakota where Bill had grown up, but the four were good swimmers, and after shedding their clothing down to their shorts, they waded in and swam to safety on the far shore.[15]

Hy Wallach, twenty-four, teamed up with Charlie Keith, a powerful six-foot, ruddy-faced seaman from New York; Bill, a Canadian; and two others who soon left them—a Frenchman and a Spaniard. When the three men believed they were close to the river, Charlie said he could make the other shore if he tried to do so alone. This left Hy and Bill, but fascist cavalry on a nearby hill led to a scramble in which they became separated.

Hy found the river was farther away than he thought. After three days in wooded hills, he decided to go down for food. He came to a house where he found an old man who had two sons in the Republican army. He served Hy the best meal he has ever eaten—a raw egg, hot soup, bread, sausages, and wine. The old man also filled Hy's canteen with wine, even though anyone caught helping a Republican soldier faced a grim reprisal.

Unwittingly, Hy walked into an Italian encampment. Two officers called him. Hy had not shaved for six weeks and was wearing a blanket as a poncho, but his pretense of being a deaf farmer didn't work: the wind exposed his uniform. At the command post, Hy found the Italian soldiers were friendly and proud of the Italians in the International Brigades, saying, "Garibaldi and Matteoti good, eh?" A young Spanish prisoner had copies of speeches by La Pasionaria and José Díaz, leader of the Spanish Community Party. The Italian soldiers tore them up to protect the Spanish soldier.

Officers showed Hy a map and asked him where his unit was. Hy said he didn't know, it was all a bunch of hills to him.

Hy had an attractive watch he had bought in France, and two Italian soldiers tried to take it from him. One, a mobster from Chicago, told Hy he wouldn't need it after two o'clock. The other made it plainer, repeating, "He tella you—two o'clock—dead!" Finally a guard chased them away.

A distinguished-looking Italian captain who spoke English with a British accent interrogated Hy. He asked Hy what brigade he belonged to.

"American Brigade."

To the clerk recording the interrogation the captain said, "15th Brigade." Then to Hy: "What battalion were you with?"

"American Battalion."

To the clerk: "Lincoln-Washington Battalion." To Hy: "What is the name of your commander?"

"We call him Red."

"Put down Milton Wolff." Turning to Hy, he said, "We call him El Lobo."

Assured by the captain that he would be home soon, Hy was beginning to hope he might be lucky enough to survive. When Hy reached Zaragoza, he met Charlie Keith, Bob Steck, Claude Pringle—a forty-four-year-old Black who had once mined coal near Bellaire, Ohio—and four British. In spite of Keith's advice to say he had come to work, Hy told the authorities he had come to help the Spanish Republic fight against fascism.

The next morning they were put on a train to Burgos. They arrived at San Pedro de Cardeña concentration camp on April 14.[16]

Orlando Real Alvarez, another of the eighty Cubans who had left Havana on February 5, 1938, was assigned to our Spanish Battalion. On April 1, reluctant to retreat, Orlando and some Spaniards soon found themselves behind the fascist lines. Traveling over the hills in a small group, they came to an empty house with foodstuff. Starved, they started to prepare a meal. Four Italian cavalrymen surprised them. On the way to the cavalry's headquarters, an Italian captain spoke to Orlando in perfect Spanish and said he had orders to shoot Internationals. However, he had lived in Cuba, and because of the hospitable reception he had enjoyed there, he would respect Orlando's life. He invited Orlando to join his unit, but Orlando declined.

The next day Orlando was taken to Alcañiz where a Falangist told him he and an Italian International would be shot. The next morning four guards executed the Italian behind the altar and dragged out the body as a lesson to the prisoners. The four guards returned for Orlando, but they placed him in an armored car which took him to Zaragoza. There he was put in with other Internationals.[17]

Martin Maki, twenty-six, born in Newberry, Michigan, of Finnish parents, was an organizer and journalist. John Panaszewicz, twenty-six and powerful, born in Iron River, Michigan, had come from the Pennsylvania coal mines around Nanticoke. When the second column scattered on the morning of April 3, Martin and John joined together to reach the Ebro. They saw a horse alongside a road and thought they were in luck. As they were untying it, they heard the command, *"Manos arriba!"* from Italian Black Arrows.

An Italian lieutenant didn't get the information he wanted but did get a compliment on his English, to which he replied, "I used to live in New York."

Maki asked, "What are you doing in a fascist uniform?" He replied, "I wanted to be on the winning side."

Martin and John were told to wait under a tree; Herman Lopez was also waiting there. The three slept from exhaustion until trucked to a small village and placed in a barn with a half dozen other Americans. Next morning they were taken to Calaceite. There a group of Falangists, upon learning the prisoners were Americans, said, "Let us take care of them," but the Italian officer in charge refused their offer. The Americans spent that night in the Alcañiz church coffins, and the next day in Zaragoza listened to a priest slander President Roosevelt and boast about the fascist success at the front.[18]

Eugene Debs Poling, twenty-eight, born in Lone Wolf, Oklahoma, had left his cotton farm when cotton and pigs were being plowed under to come to Spain. Gene was retreating with a large group of Mac Paps when several trucks came along. There wasn't room for all, and Gene was among those who continued to walk. The next morning they learned the fascists were ahead of them. Debris from a barrage by antitank guns hit Gene in the back, flattening him. The rest, believing he had been killed, were disappearing over a ridge when Gene, in spite of a crippled left leg, tried to follow them.

From a mountaintop, Gene could see a road with guards below him. He left the mountain on the fourth day to evade a search patrol. Hungry, Gene went to an isolated farm house, where the farmer and his wife gave him a hot meal. Then they provided a blanket to hide his uniform and showed him the way to go. Gene walked through the night, only to run into a fascist patrol at dawn. They put him on a food truck, and it took him to Zaragoza.

That evening Gene's name was called, but he didn't answer. Several days later the prisoners were formed into two lines. The line behind Gene was to go to a work camp, and Gene managed to jump into that line without being seen by the sergeants. On the train, a prisoner helped him jerk half of a seat loose so he could squirm into the space below it. Several prisoners then sat on the seat. The car was emptied and filled twice before Gene crawled out the next day, surprising the new prisoners. He was brought to San Pedro de Cardeña concentration camp, starved, dirty, groggy, with a swollen leg and a ripped uniform.[19]

Stanley Henricher's fourth day on the stretcher started out peacefully, but early that afternoon an enemy cleanup squad noticed him. When they saw that Stan was helpless, they carried him down to the road.

There I saw the results of the fight three days before. The ditches on both sides . . . were filled with bodies, some . . . already bloated. A bright redhead lay there who had been with the English volunteers.

The cleanup soldiers let me lie there for about five minutes: they decided not to shoot me and dump me with the rest of the bodies. I assume that the senior soldier, for some reason or other, did not want to be responsible for my death. Four soldiers carried me on my stretcher to the center of the town of Gandesa, which must have been a mile or so away because they stopped several times to rest.

In Gandesa a large group of Franco's officers wanted to see what an International Volunteer looked like. They approached as a group and I'm sure that the central figure standing in that group was Franco himself. They all surrounded him as he looked down on me. They soon left and I was alone with one guard. . . .

I think we were outside a building that might have been a storehouse. They took me inside, where a hole in the floor led to a cellar. In the hole a ladder stood straight up and down. They made me stand up and go down that ladder. As I climbed down, hands reached up for me from below, and I realized these men were Internationals. I was so glad to see them. Two of them were with me when I was wounded.[20]

Fred Stanley was astonished when he saw Stan coming down the ladder. It was his group that had put him on the stretcher four days before without hope that he would survive. Sam Polansky, a twenty-two-year-old clerk from Newark, New Jersey, and a Lincoln first-aid man, redressed Stan's wounds.

* * * * *

The 11th International Brigade, holding a sector between Caspe and Maella, found itself surrounded on April 1 by an Italian Army corps and a unit of Spanish cavalry. The brigade, fighting its way out of the encirclement, assigned the task of protecting its rear to the 3rd Battalion—the Thaelmanns, named after the German Communist leader imprisoned by Hitler. Though they stayed off the roads and traveled at night, avoiding the numerous campfires of the fascists, the next morning some forty were detected and captured. They were locked in a barn.

A Spanish officer found a paper on Fritz Klein (Adam Erbach) identifying him as an officer. Klein said he spoke only German, so Hassan, a Turk, volunteered to interpret. Both were taken before General Rafael García Valiño, commander of two of Franco's Navarrese divisions.

General García asked, "How were you affected by our plane bombings?"

Klein, standing stiffly at attention, replied, "The planes bombed but did no harm."

"What caused your big losses?"

"The Italians."

"But what about the planes?"

"We knew how to take cover."

Hassan knew Klein was deliberately misleading García, but he translated Klein's answers exactly.

García ordered Klein returned to the barn, then turned to Hassan and spoke to him in German. Hassan, surprised, remarked, "But you speak German perfectly!"

"Yes, I was at Potsdam. I just wanted to check the accuracy of your translations."

When García found Hassan knew many languages, he asked, "How could you be part of this mob, you, a man of culture?"

Hassan spoke of the many writers, poets and cultured persons in the Republican Army, but the general's comment was, "Why didn't you stay in Turkey and fight your Atatürk?"

While Hassan explained that the struggle for democracy is the same everywhere, García brought out a bottle of cognac and offered, "Here, have some cognac."

Hassan refused.

"Well, have a cigarette."

Again Hassan refused.

"Does that mean you refuse to take anything from a fascist?"

Hassan asked diplomatically, "Do you have some coffee?"

While they were talking, the phone rang. García answered and then told Hassan he had just received an order from Franco "not to touch any foreign prisoner, not even one hair, and to send them to Zaragoza as soon as possible." He then added, "As one gentleman to another, I am glad you are not being killed."

Hassan was returned to the barn, where there were now some fifty prisoners. Most were Germans, with some Frenchmen and Scandinavians, all of them dirty and uncomfortable. It was dark in the barn, and neither food nor water was available. Even the fascists were hungry; their advance had been too rapid for their food supplies to keep up with them.

The next day a doctor, Miguel Rived, visited the prisoners. He was not unsympathetic and brought cigarettes. But he informed Hassan that he and the rest were to be executed at five the next morning. When Hassan mentioned García's phone call from Franco, the doctor said the general had just announced at dinner that the prisoners were to be killed.

Later, orderlies came in, including a Basque who told them to prepare for death. The wounded were taken away. The large number of guards made escape impossible. Five o'clock came, and hope arose that the execution had been called off. Hunger pangs were acute now, since this was the fourth day without food. Another two days passed, still without food. On April 6, they were loaded onto trucks and taken to Zaragoza, where they ate their first meal in six days, with wine and a dessert.

The next day they were interviewed by the Gestapo. Hassan served as translator for those who did not speak German.

"Were you forced to come to Spain?"

Each volunteer said, "No," but the Gestapo agent dictated for the record, "He says he came to kill Spaniards."[21]

*   *   *   *   *

When a call came about mid-forenoon on April 2 for the Internationals in the church at Alcañiz to report to the front door, we sixteen Americans and Canadians responded, glad to leave the pervasive stench, in spite of our fears about why they were calling us. We were surprised when we saw the 150 British. Frank Ryan was with them. Trucks took us to a railway station.

A few hours' ride in freight cars brought us to Zaragoza. Occasional three-pointed stars told the people as we marched through city streets we were International Brigaders. Some stopped to watch us, their faces sad, and some heads were scratched with fists, thus guardedly expressing solidarity with us. I did not see any signs of hostility.

As we marched north out of Zaragoza we saw an imposing building on a height, and a sharp left turn into the entrance road allowed us to read the sign over the gateway, San Gregorio Military Academy. A hundred yards brought us to a parade ground the size of a football field, with a wall in front and a building around the other three sides. We were marched through a doorway on the far right-hand corner and into a large room, which was for the *norteamericanos;* the British had a much larger room beyond it. A queue immediately formed for the toilet facilities.

We received a small ration of bread, and table wine for those who had cups. It was a pleasure to sleep on the bare floors without the foul Alcañiz stench.

The next morning the British were ordered to form lines at one side of their room by a Spanish officer. They were told that as prisoners of war they would be expected to salute in the same way and under the same conditions as their fascist soldiers saluted. After Max Parker had translated this into English, the officer described the salute.

"Stand at attention with your arms at your side with the fingers straight down. When I give the order '*Rompen filas*' [Dismiss], you shout 'Fran–' as you swing your arm straight in front of you to a vertical position, and then '–co' as you swing it back down to your side, always keeping your fingers straight.

No sooner had Max completed the translation than Frank Ryan said, "Sir, to give that salute would signify we pledge our loyalty to Franco. I call upon all my fellow prisoners to refuse to give this salute."

The officer angrily approached Frank. "You are now my prisoner and you will do as I say!"

Frank was adamant. "According to the Geneva Convention on the treatment of prisoners of war, we are expected to show the same respect to you as we would show to our own officers. I will therefore give you the British military salute, but I will not give the salute you described."[22]

Danny Gibbons and Lionel Jacobs spoke in support of Ryan's position, with Max kept busy translating. During this hubbub we Americans were brought in and lined up with the rest. We quickly learned what the problem was. A prisoner said, "Why make it hard for ourselves? Everybody will know we were forced to give it."

It was obvious a number shared this view and that some compromise was necessary to avoid splitting our ranks. A suggestion that we give the military salute and then the Franco salute seemed the best solution, especially after someone stage-whispered, "Let's show them what we think of Franco!"

Max informed the fascist officer that we were ready to salute. Immensely pleased, he formed us into straight ranks, making certain that each man would have enough room to swing his arm properly. Then he stepped in front of us, drew himself up to his full height, and barked, "*Rompen filas!*"

The number of creative ways nearly two hundred Internationals found to express their opinion of Franco was impressive. After giving the military

salute, arms went up in all directions, all out of synchronization and to al'
levels. Fingers drooped forward, even formed fists. Some were yelling "Fran-'
while others were yelling "–co."

The astonished expression on the officer's face told us we had scored
When he made the mistake of again shouting, "*Rompen filas!*" we attained
new heights of creativity.

The officer realized it was useless to continue, and with a show o:
disgust dismissed us. We were jubilant. What had threatened dangerously
to divide us had been converted into a morale-building victory. We were no'
asked to salute again.

That afternoon the British were assembled on the parade ground fo:
review by Spanish officials, among them Lt. Col. Martínez Fusset, Franco':
military juridical assessor in charge of the political cleansing of the popula
tion, and Alfonso Merry del Val, a Falangist diplomat. Jimmy Rutherford wa:
standing between Garry McCartney, a Scot, and Jules Paivio.[23]

Merry del Val stopped in front of Garry and asked where he had come
from. Garry said Glasgow, and del Val asked if he knew where Queen Stree'
was, but all the while he was staring at Jimmy. Del Val, about to walk on
suddenly stopped to ask Jimmy if he had been in Spain before. Upor
receiving a negative reply, he asked his name. Jimmy replied, "James
Small." Merry del Val did not seem satisfied, but went on.[24] Jimmy hac
returned to Spain several months earlier, believing his place was still in the
front line in the fight against fascism. Del Val had interrogated him the firs
time he had been taken prisoner.

That afternoon a group of reporters, including Carney from the *New
York Times* and Kim Philby of the *London Times,* wanted to meet ar
American. Max Parker described his meeting with them.

I asked if William Carney was among them and got no answer. One of them askec
why I wanted to know. I replied that according to everything I had heard or read c
Carney, he was a Franco propagandist. I later learned that one of these men wa
Carney and that he had written a completely distorted account of the interview. H
had also fabricated a story of 200 British volunteers who, he alleged, had surren
dered to the "Insurgents." There were one hundred and fifty British prisoners wh
had been captured and who were with me throughout this whole period and on int
San Pedro. He apparently got our names from the fascist records, and they were th
only accurate statements in his report.[25]

The next day Carney's dispatch to the *Times,* datelined Saragossa
Spain, April 3, included:

Lt. Colonel Martínez Fusset . . . explained that foreigners were treated exactly lik
Spanish prisoners. . . . "We have been bringing them all here at first," Col. Fusse
declared, "and after classifying them, we send them to one of our three big con
centration camps at Miranda de Ebro, San Pedro de Cardeña near Burgos, anc
Duess near Santoña."

Carney falsely reported that the American prisoners said the American Committee to Aid Spanish Democracy had recruited them, and that they believed there was little probability that the Lincoln and MacPap battalions would be reorganized.

The six Americans he named were Max Parker; John Logan, thirty-three, a seaman from Boston; Matthew Dykstra, twenty-seven, an architect from Los Angeles; Edward Hodge; Richard Thompson, twenty-one, a farmer from Newport, New Hampshire; and Morris Conway, thirty, a marine carpenter, born in Olympia, Washington.

Their relatives and friends pressed FALB and the State Department to ensure their safety. Carney's dispatch hurt the North American Committee to Aid Spanish Democracy, wrongfully accusing it of recruiting volunteers, something it had scrupulously avoided. And his report about the Lincoln and MacPap battalions tended to reduce the flow of volunteers.

Max Parker had explained to the reporters our fears that Frank Ryan would be executed. The next day the Irish minister to Spain sent a telegram to General Francisco Jordana, Franco's foreign minister, informing him of Ireland's deep concern for the welfare of Ryan and the other Irish prisoners. Lt. Colonel Martínez Fusset was immediately informed. General Jordana also heard from his agent in London that the Irish minister of foreign affairs had expressed Ireland's great interest in Frank Ryan.[26]

Both Franco and Hitler were courting Ireland because of its opposition to Britain. (Irish hatred for Britain can be seen in the Irish government's use of French in its diplomatic correspondence with Spain.) Franco was also indebted to Ireland for the six hundred "Blue Shirts" who had joined his army under General O'Duffy (even though they left in May 1937 after making a very small contribution).

At Zaragoza, Ryan was again separated from us. The presence of Martínez Fusset at Zaragoza may have led to a decision not to shoot Ryan until the matter had been discussed with Franco, since a day later he was sent along with us to San Pedro de Cardeña.

*   *   *   *   *

Most of us when we were captured expected that we would be killed at the point of capture or shortly thereafter. (I reserve "executed" for being put to death after a trial.) What was the real likelihood of our being killed? The accounts I have given come from those who survived; those who ordered the killing did not even count how many were shot.

On April 2, 1938, US Vice Consul Albert R. Goodman talked with Peter Kemp, an Englishman serving in Franco's Foreign Legion. Having been assured by General Quiepo de Llano that captured foreigners were not shot,

Consul Charles Bay was disturbed by what Goodman learned, and sent a "strictly confidential" telegram to Secretary of State Hull.

Peter Kemp . . . volunteered the following information regarding Americans who might be captured by Franco's forces:
    He said that, in general, any foreigners captured were executed by the troops taking them, without any kind of trial, and without their even being sent back to their Commander for disposition. . . .
    He seemed certain that any Americans captured would have been executed without their capture ever being reported to Headquarters. He has actually seen a few of such executions recently near Teruel and showed me part of a letter he had taken from one, showing clearly that he [the American] was an active Communist.
    He said that feeling against foreigners was very bitter on the part of the Spaniards he had fought with. . . . he tried to save an Englishman who he thought worthy, but was ordered to execute him himself.[27]

Ralph Hill, legal adviser to the State Department, attached the following note on May 4:

If as alleged in the enclosure, Americans serving with the Loyalist forces are summarily executed when captured by the Franco forces it is believed we should make the strongest possible representations against such barbarous practices.[28]

I have been unable to find any State Department instructions to its consular officials in Franco Spain instructing them to make such representations. Bay, Goodman, Hill, and Kemp were much more horrified by this "barbarous" practice than Secretary of State Hull. I cannot believe that Hull was under the illusion that Franco's forces were observing the rules of war in their treatment of prisoners. I am forced to conclude Hull deliberately chose not to use the powerful means at his command to prevent the killing of captured Americans in violation of the 1929 Geneva Convention. He could do this with impunity because he could keep pertinent information secret.

Bay in his covering letter to Hull gave the impression that the soldiers themselves wanted to kill captured prisoners. Our own experience showed that this was not true. Soldiers killed prisoners only when ordered to do so by their officers. Moroccan soldiers and Carlist troops recruited by the Navarrese Catholic hierarchy had standing orders from their officers to kill Internationals.[29] For Franco, the killing of Internationals was part of his *limpieze* (cleansing) policy; only by killing or jailing those who did not agree with him could Franco feel safe.

Franco, under pressure from Mussolini to take Internationals alive in order to exchange them for the Italians the Republic had captured at Guadalajara, ordered that done from April 1 to 9, 1938. Unfortunately, the order did not reach all units or reached them too late or was ignored. Of the 158 Americans captured during the first two weeks in April 1938, only 59, or 37 percent, survived. This is even less than the 40 percent who survived capture during the retreat from Belchite. Most of the prisoners were captured by Italian troops, who, even before Franco issued his order, had a policy of taking Internationals alive.

The names of the 173 killed, the 86 exchanged and the 20 freed after the war, the five who escaped (there were more, but their names are not known), the two who died in hospitals, and the one who was left in Spain when his American citizenship could not be verified, may be found on pages 259–267. All other Americans are accounted for either as killed in action or as returning to the United States.

12 Initiation to San Pedro de Cardeña

ON THE MORNING of our third day at the San Gregorio Military Academy in Zaragoza, all Internationals—including Frank Ryan—were trucked to the railroad station. The train took us to Franco's capitol, Burgos. We wondered why.

Night had fallen when we were marched to a row of waiting trucks. These carried us about eleven kilometers south and east to what looked in the dim light to be a long low barn.

Awaiting us were guards carrying rifles, commanded by a sergeant who carried a stick he was using as a cane. Our first impression was that he needed it because of his age. He ordered us to dismount and form several rows, and was not favorably impressed by some two hundred Internationals—ragged, dirty, unshaven, stumbling men slowly forming sloppy lines. He swung his stick sharply across the nearest prisoner's back. A growl from the others told him there was still some defiance left in us. Word passed to those who had not seen the blow: "Watch out for Sticky."

The guards directed most of the prisoners to proceed toward a stone building; some, including myself, were directed through the narrow doorway into the barn. Here we found ourselves in a fifteen-foot-wide gangway with haymows on both sides built over stalls for livestock. The guards, yelling, *"Arriba! Arriba!"* motioned that we were to climb up a wooden ladder into the haymow on the right side.

While others were crawling up the ladder, two guards pushed me into a corridor beneath the haymow and tried to take my wristwatch. I pulled my arm away and began yelling loudly. Alarmed, the guards allowed me to escape, and I wasted no time joining my comrades in the haymow.

Things were not going well there. The first ones up the ladder had immediately staked out sleeping space, leaving the rest milling about. "Why don't you try over there, they've got more room," the latecomers were told.

Then we heard a tapping sound. Hushing everyone, we listened quietly, and determined it must be on a floor board beneath us. We removed enough hay to expose the entire board. Someone below was trying to lift it. One end came up, and helping hands carefully lifted up the board and moved it aside. Up popped the head of a Spaniard wearing a black beret and a broad smile. *"Salud, Internacionales,"* he whispered.

His smile turned into a grin as the look of astonishment on our faces gave way to even huger grins when we softly greeted him in return. I could not imagine a finer welcome than the one he had given us.

Speaking in Spanish, he asked whether anyone was ill or injured. If so, he would try to get something to help him.

We thanked him heartily for his offer and informed him we were not in dire need of anything, but we would like to know where we were.

"In the concentration camp at San Pedro de Cardeña."

(San Pedro de Cardeña is on the site of the first Benedictine monastery in Spain, built in the fifth or sixth century. When the Republican government in northern Spain fell, Franco converted San Pedro de Cardeña, unused since 1922, into a concentration camp for the re-education and retraining of the male Basque and Asturian population, and organizing them into labor battalions to support his troops and provide labor power. Since it was not a punishment camp but a camp where an effort was being made to win the support of those taken there, the treatment and living conditions were better than at other concentration camps. Since we were to be exchanged, we were held at this camp[1])

Our friend with the black beret told us it held several thousand Basque and Asturian prisoners. With a broad wink, he informed us, "Here you are among friends as well as enemies."

We were overjoyed, and as many as possible shook the Basque's hand to express our friendship and appreciation for his brave act in welcoming us. Then we urged him not to risk his safety any longer for us.

After he had disappeared, we carefully put the board back and covered it so it looked undisturbed. His appearance was a great morale booster for all of us, and now the business of finding sleeping space for all went much smoother. Some who earlier had said, "I got here first," now said, "Let's see if we can make room for you here." The Basque's example in risking his safety to greet us made us all more considerate of one another. It gave us a wonderful feeling, strengthening us for the trials of the morrow. It could not make the night comfortable, but it did make it inspiring.

We were not the first Internationals to arrive at San Pedro. Those held at Caballería de la Reina had arrived earlier the same day. Included among them were those who had been held in the Soria Concentation Camp.[2] They had been herded into a large, barren room. After receiving their evening meal, they stretched out on the floor. Among them was Lou Ornitz.

I had slept only a few hours when I was awakened by the sound of many feet trampling the stone floor around me. . . . It occurred to me that the fascists had decided to take us out of the prison at night and shoot us. . . . In the dim light I saw a large number of men walking about the room or sitting on the stone floor. I . . . began to shout . . . "What's going on here?"

We could not see each other. The place was swarming with prisoners . . . tired and shifting about, hunting for a place to sleep. One . . . came near and shouted my name. "LOU ORNITZ!"

"Who is it? Who is it?" I called back anxiously. Then . . . I saw that it was a comrade of mine from the same outfit—Matthew Dykstra. We threw our arms around each other, bear-hugging for sheer joy. He told me everyone had insisted I was dead, that I could not have survived. He kept on feeling me to see if I was all in one piece with nothing missing. . . . When we were through bear-hugging and shoulder-slapping, another prisoner came over. He, too, was a friend of mine, one of my first instructors in Spain, Frank Ryan . . . and he told me that he had thought I was dead."3

Loud cries of *"Abajo! Abajo!"* the next morning called us down out of the haymow to line up in front of the barn. We now had our first clear view of San Pedro de Cardeña. Looking toward the sun, we saw a large gravel-covered assembly area. At its far end was a church, to which was joined on its left a massive three-story stone building.

Sticky motioned the guards to take us inside. Some forty feet from the building's entrance, which was on the left, the west end, Spanish prisoners had fires going under huge caldrons under the trees. What drew our attention was a sculpture above the entrance, a life-size rider astride a powerful and spirited horse, holding up his bent right arm as if giving the Popular Front salute. Even though we knew the missing fist must have held a banner or a sword, it cheered us as we passed beneath it.

Our guards led us through a twenty-five-foot-long archway, across a cobblestone inner courtyard open to the sky, to a narrow doorway on the left side of the far wall, then up a narrow stone stairway to the second floor on the building's north side, where we found Internationals brought there the previous day. Some were on the third floor, which had the same layout as the second floor.

There was a narrow room, twelve feet wide, that ran along the inside courtyard, which we could see through a half dozen evenly spaced windows. Parallel to this room was a larger one, twenty feet wide and one hundred feet long. From its eight windows we could see the fields and woods on the north side of the monastery. The outside walls were three feet thick with deep angled recesses at each two-by-three-foot window. The windows had no glass and no shutters, but there were vertical steel bars. Between the two rooms there were no doors, just two archways. A third room, at the west end, fifteen feet wide, extending from the courtyard to the outer wall, was reached through an archway from the large room.

The smallest room, six by fifteen feet, was the one that drew our immediate attention, since it contained the indoor plumbing, located in a protrusion of the north wall at the eastern end of the large room. There were three open stone cubicles, and in the center of each was an eight-inch hole in the stone floor. Beyond the cubicles were a stone urinal and a spigot attached to the end of a small pipe. Lines formed immediately.

Soon two sergeants arrived to drive us down the stairway and through the courtyard to one of the steaming caldrons we had seen earlier. As we filed past, a smiling Basque offered each of us a ladleful of a hot liquid.

Many of us, having lost our mess gear, had only small tin cans and could not accept a ladleful.

We were then directed into the assembly area in front of the church to savor our breakfast. None of us had ever tasted what the Basques call *ajo* soup, a mixture of water, olive oil, garlic, and bread crumbs. It was hot and had flavor, and no one turned it down. (When I returned to Spain in 1981, I ordered ajo soup for old time's sake. I was served a marvelous thick soup enriched with an egg and herbs, not at all like the watery solution I had received at San Pedro.) I wasted none of the soup, using my finger to wipe my cup clean. There were no facilities for washing our utensils.

About half of the three hundred International prisoners were British. Some fifty Americans made up the next largest group. There was much hugging and greeting of comrades before we were returned to our quarters.

Sticky asked for two volunteers to serve as his chiefs. Two prisoners volunteered—Joseph Weismayer, a tall, slender, blond Austrian with a narrow face, and David, a short Cuban.

At lunch time, Sticky came into our quarters and yelled, "A formar!"— the command for us to line up in a column four abreast. When he decided some were responding too slowly, he whacked them with his walking stick. While this was met with a growl and boos from the rest, it did speed up the falling into line.

Sticky believed in no loitering on the stairways, and again he used his stick to make us go down on the run. We were lined up to approach the same caldron as in the morning. First we passed a Basque with a sack, who handed each of us a *chusco*—a fist-sized roll. When I broke mine in half, I saw a gray, firm-textured bread.

The Basque at the caldron gave each of us a ladleful of boiled white navy beans. A fortunate few found a small chunk of pork fat among them. The prisoner cooks had done their best with the ingredients at their disposal, and our hunger was sharp enough to guarantee we would enjoy the beans. We cleaned our kit or tin with a piece of *chusco*.

One International, after eating the beans, decided he didn't like the camp, and walked north up a dirt pathway, having picked up a nearby garbage container as if to dump it. The guards allowed him to pass. When he was out of sight, he kept going. The prison authorities had not yet made a list of all the Internationals, so they didn't miss him. Several months later we received a card from him postmarked in France.

After returning upstairs at a smart pace, we had a few hours to ourselves. There was a guard at the door to the courtyard, but none on the second and third floors. We spent our time getting acquainted and exchanging experiences. Several of us discussed what our attitude should be toward Sticky's chiefs. A German told us Weismayer claimed he had ridden a white horse to the front to desert to the fascist side. While we were dubious about the white horse, it was clear he had decided to work for the fascists. The

Americans promptly dubbed him Rin-Tin-Tin, with apologies to the German police dog we had seen in many movies. There were rumors that David too was a deserter. We passed the word around that these two men were not to be trusted.

At 4:30 that afternoon, Sticky, with the aid of several sergeants and his stick, moved us back into the assembly area in front of the church. He lined us up in three rows along the wall of the monastery, facing a raised lawn. Then several thousand Basque and Asturian prisoners in civilian clothes, were herded into the area between us and the lawn, and formed into lines, with a ten-foot gap between them and us. Sergeants patrolled the gap, but they could not prevent our discreet greetings with the eyes.

A tall, lean priest appeared on the raised lawn, a Franciscan, wearing a long brown robe with a white sash. In a twenty-minute homily he explained why fascism was preferable to democracy and communism. Then a short, elderly, gray-haired major—the *comandante* of the camp—and several officers led the singing of the fascist anthem *"Cara al Sol"* (Face to the Sun). The ceremony concluded with an officer crying out *"España!"* to which the Spanish prisoners responded, *"Una!"* A second *"España!"* and the response *"Grande!"* A third *"España!"* and a resounding *"Libre!"* Then three weaker shouts of "Franco" synchronized with the raised and lowered arms. We took no part in this ritual, remaining silent and motionless—except for our two chiefs, who tried to imitate the Spaniards.

The Spanish prisoners were now directed over to the large caldrons for their evening meal. Finally it was our turn, and we found it was another ladleful of the beans we had received at noon. Hunger served as an effective appetizer as we ate our portions standing up. Since we were the last to eat, we were invited by the cooks to share what was left, quickly accepted by those among us who had taken up positions close to the caldrons.

Dusk was falling as we were driven back to our quarters. I was among the last to mount the stairway, and when I got to the second floor, all the floor space seemed to be staked out. But as I picked my way along the narrow room, I head the cheery and rough voice of John Panaszewicz, "Settle down, Carl, and make yourself at home here. Come on, we'll squeeze you in somehow."

Since I, like some of the others, had no knapsack, no blanket, no overcoat, no extra clothing or gear except my cup, I fitted snugly into the two-foot-wide space John made available.

John had left the coal mines of Pennsylvania to come to Spain and had fought with the Lincolns from Jarama until he was captured. He was twenty-six years old, strong, with a broad face, and I was relieved to receive his warm invitation. We had to lie on the floor, one row with heads against the wall separating the two rooms, another row with heads toward the inner courtyard; our feet overlapped. The large room had a wooden floor, but we were lying on a cracked stone floor.

As I settled in, I asked, "How do you feel, John?"

"Me? Oh, I'm fine, just fine. Glad to still be alive."

"So what do you think of this mess we are in?"

"Could be worse, Carl. Some of the fellows are a bit downhearted, but give them time, and they'll get over it."

"John, what do you think we ought to do?"

"Stick together, no fighting among ourselves, and get organized."

When I told him I was quite disturbed by the slanderous accusations some were making against our military and political leaders, he said, "Yeah, but you didn't see any of them give the fascist salute this evening. Carl, just remember that!"

"True, except for our chiefs. What do you think of them?"

"I'll tell you, Carl, I would sooner see you in that job. No, I'll take that back. We can't have you sticking your neck out, because you're going to have enough trouble staying with us as it is. But we need good guys in there, not rats."

"We may have made a mistake, John, in letting Rin-Tin-Tin take the job."

"Don't worry, we'll get him out of there. He doesn't know English, and Sticky will have to put in somebody who can get our cooperation. Here, I don't have to have a blanket under me. Let's use it to cover both of us or you'll freeze to death."

John's actions and words made the cold night and the stone floor more bearable. It never occurred to him to let up on his deeply ingrained anti-fascist commitment just because he was under Franco's thumb. He thought only of how to continue the struggle.

On the ground or in snow you can make small depressions for the buttocks and shoulders and a mound for the head when you lie down. You cannot do this on a stone or wooden floor, so by morning we were more than ready to get up. We could relieve our aches and pains, but could not change the reality that we were in a fascist concentration camp, nor could we abolish the fears of what the day might bring. One day my rank as battalion commissar would be uncovered, and that would be the end of me. Meantime, I would live from day to day doing whatever I could for my fellow prisoners.

Our meals the second day were exactly the same as on the first. Already these meals, with rest, had restored some of our physical strength. But our hunger was still keen, and the hungriest, quick to observe that sometimes there was a second portion available for a few, would crowd around the food caldrons trying to be among the first served and then join the tail of the line to get a second helping. Sticky didn't like crowding around the caldrons and would beat the laggards back in line. This created a nasty situation, because those already in line would then force the "hogs" back to the end.

The camp office needed to know who the prisoners were. So for each of us, name, nationality, birthplace and date, and the military unit in which we had served were recorded and an order was issued that we must remain on our respective floors.

It was during this registration of prisoners that I first met Alex de Seume. Tall, thin, stooped, with a long sad face, he seemed able to speak the language of each prisoner. A philologist, he had come to Spain from Holland to fight for the Republic. Later, I learned that his parents had belonged to the Russian nobility and his father had represented czarist Russia in Holland. The major appointed Alex as the chief interpreter, and he used that position to do all he could on our behalf.

Some prisoners had wounds that needed dressing. A few were so ill that they were barely able to stand in line, and the trip downstairs for meals completely exhausted them. Some needed blankets, others mess gear, but all needed something to sleep on. And all of us needed soap, though when everyone has a strong body odor you don't mind your own so much.

We needed someone to speak up for us, and it was obvious that David and Rin-Tin-Tin wouldn't. They considered it their duty only to pass the sergeants' orders down to us. We needed chiefs whom we could trust, who would serve our needs instead of the fascists.

Sticky also wanted prisoners to serve on each floor as *imaginarias*—guards, starting at 8 P.M., primarily to watch for fires. There had to be enough to fill two-hour shifts until 6 A.M. We agreed to supply them, because if a fire did break out we might not be allowed out of the building.

It was here that Rin-Tin-Tin ran into trouble. On my floor we pretended not to understand Sticky's Spanish and Rin-Tin-Tin's German, remaining silent when volunteers were called for. At the right moment, Herman Lopez offered to translate, and we responded. Sticky realized Herman could make his job easier and named him to take Rin-Tin-Tin's place.

Herman not only spoke Spanish and English fluently but also had the knack of always being where the action was. He was fearless, yet knew when and how to compromise to make the best of any situation. He knew how to bring our needs to Sticky's attention without antagonizing him, showing him how taking care of our needs would make things easier. An old soldier, Sticky wanted everything to go smoothly.

Not all problems could be solved by Herman and Alex. We still needed to "get organized." However, when I spoke to some Americans about a prisoner organization, I was taken aback by the strong negative reaction.

"Do you want somebody to get shot?"

"What do you want an organization for? We'll soon be out of here."

"Sticky will beat the daylights out of the committee if he finds out. Don't do it!"

I didn't tell them that we already had an informal International Committee made up of Canadian, English, French, German, and American representatives on our floor, in touch with Lou Ornitz and Max Parker on the third floor. By the fourth day we had already solved the problem of crowding around the food caldrons. We divided ourselves into seven groups, each centered on a large national section, with each group to take turns at being first in line. This was quickly accepted and enforced.

We had also discussed what could be done for the walking wounded and the ill. On our floor we agreed that the room at the far end would be our infirmary. Those not ill or wounded were asked to move out into the larger halls. Thus we provided twenty-two spaces, each only two and a half feet wide, even though one wounded Dane thought a patient was entitled to at least three feet.

Three prisoners were doctors. Roberto Luna Rubinos, a thirty-six-year-old Peruvian, had been physician for "El Campesino," a highly regarded Republican military leader; he had been captured several months earlier near Teruel.[4] Joseph Leitner, a twenty-nine-year-old Polish doctor, had been captured on March 14 when his ambulance ran into Italian troops between Híjar and Alcañiz.[5] Humberto Sinobas del Olmo, an energetic twenty-six-year-old Cuban, had been attending medical school in the North when the uprising began; he had joined the Republican army and was captured when the North fell.

What the doctors could do, without medicine or medical equipment, is illustrated by what Dr. Sinobas managed for wounded Stanley Heinricher. Stan, after his days on the hill before being captured and taken to Gandesa, had been called to climb out of the wine cistern the next morning. Internationals helped him climb the ladder, and he was placed on a stretcher in a waiting truck with other prisoners. The driver took care to position the stretcher so Stan would suffer least from the bouncing ride. Traveling day and night, the truck reached San Pedro the following morning.

Stan was made to stand at attention with the other prisoners in spite of their protests that he was wounded. When he reached the second floor, they helped him to a straw bag and laid him on it. Stan was having difficulty breathing, so Sinobas was called over. Through an interpreter, he learned how Stan had been wounded and immediately had him turned on his left side, through which the bullet had passed. Stan was able to breathe more easily, since his good right lung was now free to work without interference from his body's weight. Stan remembers to this day the relief he felt. Word was gotten to the camp commander about Stan's condition, and he was transferred to the infirmary in the church for Spanish prisoners.[6]

Herman informed Sticky that several Internationals were too sick to go down for meals but might recover if food could be brought up into our infirmary. Sticky agreed to see that a container would be available. Herman next asked for some blankets for those who had none, and Sticky said he could have twelve. When Herman asked permission to bring several prisoners along to carry the blankets, Sticky told him they would not be needed. When Herman got to the supply room, he understood why. The blankets were so thin and small that Herman, five feet four inches tall and 125 pounds, was able to carry the dozen himself.[7]

More prisoners were coming in, among them the group from the bullring at Logroño. They were assigned to the third floor. One of them, Max Shufer, annoyed by Sticky's free use of his stick, pushed Sticky aside in his haste to get into line. With one wallop across the top of the head, Sticky almost knocked Max out. Then he took Max down into the courtyard and went to work on him. After that he threw Max into what became known as the "black hole," because it had no light. It had a dirt floor and nothing else. Max was still suffering from the diarrhea he had caught at Logroño, and had to use the back of the hole for a latrine. He is not certain how long he was down there, but he says it was long enough to take some of the youthful cockiness out of him.[8]

Shortly after we returned from lunch on Herman's third day, he burst into our quarters with the announcement, "OK guys, get ready to be captured again."

Right behind him came the sergeants, yelling for everyone except those in the infirmary to rush downstairs. There was no time to consult, or to improve our appearance. Outside the main entrance, we were formed into a column four abreast, and guards armed with rifles took up positions on each side.

Sticky led us at a smart pace for about a quarter mile, and then circled behind a tall hedge. At an opening in the hedge, Sticky now took up his positon, stick ready, and ordered us to run through the opening with our hands stretched high in the air. With a little prodding from the guards and a couple of whacks from Sticky, we were soon lifting our arms and running two and three abreast through the hedge into a meadow. About a hundred feet from the gap, a newsreel cameraman was grinding away as we crowded through. Guards on our left motioned to us to go around the hedge again. Then Sticky ran us through the opening once more as the cameraman added to his footage.

The third time around the scenario was modified, and only a few of us were directed to go through, one at a time, again with hands held high. This time when we got through the opening, we saw a fascist officer about fifty feet away with a crate of oranges, offering one to each prisoner as he went by. The camera was focused on this scene, and did not take in the soldier fifty feet behind the officer who relieved each prisoner of his orange and returned it to another crate.

Back in our quarters, Fred kept smelling his hand and rolling his eyes in delight. His neighbor, watching him, asked, "What did you do, Fred squeeze that damn orange?"

Fred, continuing to smell his hand and roll his eyes, commented philosophically, "In this place you got to think fast if you want to enjoy the pleasures of life."

Herman had been our chief for about a week when we sensed there was something wrong with the count after supper. The sergeants had counted us more than the usual number of times and were now recounting quite excitedly. The toilets were checked again and the sick room count was repeated. The total was again short. Sticky was called. After listening to his sergeants' report that the count was two short, he angrily demanded of Herman, "Who is missing?"

Herman answered truthfully, "No one that I know of."

"Ask the prisoners who is missing!"

"Hey, any of you guys know of anybody who is missing?"

No one answered. Sticky was in a rage. He called Herman and David before him. Rin-Tin-Tin kept out of sight. After whacking the two, he berated them for failing to do their job and had them thrown into the *calabozo*.

Now Sticky had Alex call the roll to find out who the two were. Neither names nor nationality of the missing are known today, though it is known that they were not English-speaking.

The *calabozo* was a room about ten feet square directly beneath us. It had no light, no furnishings, no blankets, just four bare stone walls and a stone floor. Just below its ceiling was a narrow opening through which a little light filtered in from the courtyard. After pushing Herman and David through the door, the sergeants hit them with their rifle butts while shouting, "Two escape, two die! That's the rule here!" The sergeants left, promising they would be back later when it was time for the execution.

David, frantic with fear, beseeched Herman over and over, "What are we going to do, what are we going to do?"

"Take it easy, David. Calm down and rest. There is nothing else we can do. Sit down next to me and take it easy." And Herman sat on the floor with his back against the wall, and removed his shoes.

It was near midnight, Herman guessed, when the sergeants entered with candles and bayoneted rifles, announcing the time had come. Thinking he would have a better chance to make a run for it with his shoes on, Herman searched frantically and finally located them, but in all the excitement and with David hanging on to him, he had great difficulty getting his feet into them. As he finally got to his feet, a third sergeant came in and announced the execution had been postponed until morning. The three sergeants wished them a good night's sleep and left.

Herman tried to convince the frightened David that the best thing to do was to sleep until morning. But this time he did not take off his shoes.

An hour after daybreak, two sergeants entered with some ajo soup and asked Herman and David whether they had slept well. Herman admitted he had not and asked when the execution would be.

"What execution? We don't know anything about an execution."

"But last night they told us we'd be executed this morning."

"Oh, they were just having a bit of fun."[9]

Herman and David were put back with us about a week later, stripped of their status as chiefs. Herman's only memento of that memorable night is an enlarged joint on the stiff third finger of his left hand, the result of having it smashed between a rifle butt and a stone wall. He also earned the honor of being the first American to be thrown into the *calabozo,* Max Shufer having been the first to be thrown into the black hole.

13 Building Morale

WHILE every other word was an obscenity, let me extract from the profanity of some American prisoners at San Pedro de Cardeña the ideas they expressed with such bitterness and color.

- "We were sacrificed. Instead of letting us go home, they sent us out to be killed."
- Our Command didn't know what they were doing. They didn't even know what was going on."
- "There must have been fascists running the war on the Republican side. How else could they have made such a mess?"
- "And our Spanish 'comrades'! Ran like rabbits trying to catch up with their officers. And let the fascists outflank us every time."
- Well, the war is over. Bet they'll surrender in a couple of weeks. God, am I lucky I made it through this war."

As I had told John, I was shocked and alarmed. Only after listening to some describe the hell they had experienced from March 10 on[1] did I begin to understand why they were saying such things.

But others, like John Panaszewicz and the black volunteers Ed Johnson, a thirty-seven-year-old steelworker from Ohio, and Claude Pringle, would not join in the condemnation of the Republican leadership; their strong class instincts told them these statements were untrue and dangerous. I did not believe any American would have made such statements to a reporter. Nevertheless, such charges nourished an unhealthy atmosphere, so I discussed with Norman Dorland how we might restore morale.

Norman—twenty-five, five feet nine inches, trim, blond, born in St. Paul, Minnesota—had worked as a stevedore and a seaman. Arriving in Spain in March 1937, he had risen to a lieutenant. I had met Norman early in 1938 at our Tarazona base, where he was training recruits. He returned to the Lincolns with the volunteers from Tarazona at the end of February, just in time to take part in the retreat from Belchite. On March 12, Norman ran into a fascist patrol while searching for headquarters.

He too was concerned about the demoralized state of some of the Americans, but he said, "Carl, it's important to keep in mind that these guys are still antifascists, regardless of what they say about treason, incompetence, and bad leadership. It would be a serious mistake to isolate them in any way or to attack them personally for what they are saying."

"I agree, Norman. I don't think we have a single rat like Rin-Tin-Tin among us. But how do we get everyone to realize that we are here not

111

because of incompetence and betrayal, but because of the arms and men Hitler and Mussolini supplied."

"Carl, how about translating the fascist newspaper? When you read it to the fellows, you'll have a chance to discuss things in an objective way without getting anyone's dander up."

"All I need, Norm, is a copy of their paper."

"Leave that to me. We also need something besides bitching and spreading rumors to pass the time away."

"How about making a chess set? Say, out of that bread we get. Moisten it a bit, mold it into shape and let it dry a day, it'll probably get as hard as a rock."

While experimenting with the remains of our *chuscos*, we also agreed to talk individually with those most vociferous in their condemnation of the Republic. After agreeing with them that the fascists had given us a bad beating, we would ask how they thought we ought to continue our fight against fascism here. We would be letting them know we had faith in their antifascist convictions while encouraging more positive thinking.

Two days later, Norman handed me a copy of *El Diario de Burgos,* an eight-page newspaper, obtained through a friendly guard. A circle of listeners immediately gathered around me, including a skeptic who, after feeling the paper's texture, said, "Even though it'll dirty your mind, it'll clean your behind! How about dividing it up after you are finished and we'll get some benefit out of it, seeing as how there's no toilet paper in this joint?"

"Great idea, George. I'll give it to you when we're finished, and you can be in charge of dividing it up."

"Now, just a minute! Can't a guy make a decent suggestion without getting saddled with a lot of responsibility?"

"OK, George, we'll have a vote. All those in favor of making George the minister of toilet paper say aye!"

George listened to the chorus of ayes and then smiled. "OK, guys, I want to see what each one of you is going to do with one square inch of newsprint."

When the laughter subsided, I announced, "We'll start with the "Parte de Guerra" [the daily military communiqué] with news hot off the front."

Again I was interrupted, "Pure propaganda! All lies!"

But as I translated, it became clear that the fascists had not yet reached the Mediterranean. My listeners were amazed. "How is that possible?" "Who in the world stopped them?"

I told them what the Italian lieutenant had told me shortly after my capture on April 1: the 90,000 fascist troops then on the move were scheduled to take Gandesa by noon, Tortosa by evening, and be at the Mediterranean in two days. Now, ten days later, they still hadn't reached the sea!

A listener said, "Somebody is putting up a helluva fight, that's for sure.

It can't be the Internationals, because we got wiped out the first couple of days. It has to be the Spanish troops who are holding them up."

"Yeah, but we helped!" someone else commented. I could feel pride in the Republican forces and in ourselves surfacing again. The "Parte de Guerra" was listened to carefully each day, and when, on April 15, a big headline announced that the fascists had reached the sea, the prisoners showed their growing respect for the fight our Spanish comrades had put up. A belittling remark about the Republic was usually met with a spirited defense of the courage and fighting spirit of the Spanish troops.

An early problem we had was the occasional swiping of a *chusco*. Unless we wanted to carry the *chusco* with us, our only alternative was to leave it at our sleeping spot along with whatever other possessions we had. Several Americans set up a continuous watch and succeeded in catching the thief red-handed. Then they came to our informal committee, wanting to know what we were going to do about it.

Our committee of British, Canadians, and Yanks (as the rest called us) discussed the alternatives. The men themselves could dispense quick justice, but that would weaken our unity and might give the fascist authorities an opportunity to recruit an informer. Because of our principled opposition to the use of the bodily violence the fascists used so freely on us, we rejected roughing up the thief. And there were dangers if the prison officials were to get wind of a kangaroo court. Nevertheless, that appeared to be the best alternative.

Frank Ryan was the unanimous choice to head the court. We didn't follow the norms of English jurisprudence too closely. The defendant represented himself, and the complainants served as the prosecution. No jury was sworn in; everyone was free to offer his opinion. Lookouts were posted to provide a warning if Rin-Tin-Tin or a sergeant approached, in which case the court would instantly transform itself into a group of lounging prisoners.

Frank Ryan opened the proceedings with a statement that stealing a small piece of bread might seem a trivial matter, and if it had happened in Dublin, he could see himself as the defense attorney, but never as the prosecutor or judge.

"Our circumstances here make it necessary for us to take a different attitude toward stealing. We are in the hands of the fascists and what they have in store for us we do not know. But we do know that it is important that we stand together, fully united. And to be united, we must be able to trust each other, and we must look out for each other. It is because stealing a small piece of bread threatens this all-important unity we treasure so highly that this court has been convened. The object is not so much to punish the guilty as it is to preserve and strengthen our unity as we face our fascist jailers."

The proceedings were calm and businesslike. The aggrieved presented their evidence; and the defendant admitted his guilt, giving as his only excuse that he was very hungry and did not realize he was endangering the welfare of all. He apologized for his conduct and vowed he would not do it again. The court sentenced him to turn over a part of his *chusco* each day until he had made restitution. He agreed to do this, and the court adjourned.

But shortly thereafter, Herman Lopez reported someone was stealing his *chusco*, which he always hung up on the wall above his head with a piece of string. Herman set a watch, and caught the thief red-handed—a mouse that climbed straight up the wall to the *chusco*, much to Herman's amazement and everyone else's merriment.[2]

Late one afternoon two Frenchmen suffering from abdominal pains were helped up our stairway: Louis Fornet and Victor Sulot, both thirty-eight years old and from Romainville (Seine). Fournet was born in Rosières-en-Santerre and Sulot in Paris.[3] Their pains grew more severe as the night wore on, causing them to moan constantly and cry out occasionally. Our doctors suspected they had appendicitis but had nothing to help them.[4]

The next morning they were transferred to the infirmary in the church. Stanley Heinricher, who was there too, remembers: "Their last days were awful. They screamed continuously. I don't think the nuns could have done anything to relieve their pain; there was little or no medicine."[4]

When it was certain they were going to die, a priest offered them the last sacraments. Only Sulot accepted them. They died on April 17, and we were asked to take up a collection to purchase coffins for them. We had only Republican pesetas, which were worthless, and could do nothing. They were buried side by side outside the eastern wall of the monastery.

That both had developed appendicitis at the same time is unlikely. The two were truck drivers who had come to Spain to buy oranges, and were then caught by fascist troops and sent to San Pedro because they were foreigners. They were friends and may have developed food poisoning from a shared meal, thus becoming ill together. In any case, our "wits" passed the word around: "Don't get appendicitis."

After a week's steady diet of white navy beans, one evening we were served a ladleful of red kidney beans. Everyone was pleased, but a week of kidney beans twice a day was more than anyone cared for. One evening, next to the beans there was a huge black pan about six inches deep and at least four feet in diameter, filled with small, dark, fishy-looking objects. To our questions our grinning chefs replied, *"Sardinas fritas,"* while piling one, complete with head and tail, on top of our beans.

The more vitamin-conscious went back to scrounge some of the black oil in the bottom of the pan, sopping it up with their *chuscos*. The next time sardines were served, many tried to collect the black oil.

Keeping clean was a serious problem. We had no washcloths or towels, no soap and no toilet paper, and many suffered from diarrhea. The water supply was an erratic trickle. What clothes we had, we wore twenty-four hours a day. We all stank more or less. Toward the end of April, each man received a two-inch cube of green and gray marbled material. Optimists insisted that though it produced little in the way of suds, it did help, and some gathered together pieces from disappointed users and carved chess sets, putting our bread sets to shame.

More annoying were the fleas and the lice. Lice can suck much more blood, but flea bites are painful. You try to grab a flea through your clothes; it moves a short distance and bites again. This goes on until it has had enough, and you—more than enough. Our only defense against these pests was murder. Fleas, although tiny, have a very hard shell; we found the best way to deal with them was to pop them between our two thumbnails. Every morning we would roll up our blankets quickly to prevent the fleas from hopping off. Then at a window, we would slowly unroll the blankets and pop fleas.

To get the vermin out of our clothes, we had to remove one garment at a time and carefully check the seams, where we would find both fleas and lice. We easily disposed of the lice, but of course their eggs went undetected, and new generations were always coming on the scene. One had to be quick to catch fleas, since cloth provided a more solid launching pad for them than the surface of a blanket. But we could not win this battle; the fleas and lice always counterattacked the next night.

Listening to and passing on rumors was the major occupation the first month. Sources cited were guards, a sergeant, or the camp office. By the time it got back to the originator, he accepted it as a new rumor. Three hundred men with nothing to do but talk can keep a rumor mill in full production.

Circulating constantly were stories that we would be court-martialed, officers and Communists shot, and the rest given lengthy sentences. Since no one knew we had been captured, the fascists could dispose of us without the outside world being any the wiser. Those interviewed at Zaragoza did not know if their names had been printed. According to a rumor, two French officers had been taken away and shot.

The rumors that this or that nationality was going to be freed traveled fastest and received the greatest amount of elaboration. Everyone hoped there might be a grain of truth in them. We did not think in terms of exchange since we did not know that the Republic had hundreds of Italian prisoners.

In 1983, Prior Marcos García, head of the Cistercian Order at San Pedro, kindly permitted me to see a copy of the death records of Carcedo de Burgos, a small village a few kilometers from San Pedro. Until the end of 1937, Spaniards who died at San Pedro were buried either in Burgos or in the Carcedo Cemetery. After 1937 and until May 20, 1939, they and the Internationals were buried outside San Pedro's eastern wall.[5] Of the sixty-six Spaniards buried during this period, thirteen were between the ages of nineteen and twenty-two.[6] (My impression had been that the great majority of the Spanish prisoners were well over thirty.) The cause of death was listed in only one instance, a suicide.

My search for the civilian death records in the village of Carcedo took me back into the Middle Ages. Tom Entwistle located Carcedo's secretary, who serves six villages, and brought him to Carcedo. The mayor was supervising the threshing of his wheat by a circling pair of black oxen pulling a flat-bottomed sled over a two-inch-high mound of heads of wheat. On the sled sat a Spaniard equipped with a long pole to drive the oxen and a pail to catch anything they might drop.

The mayor led us to an old stone building, through a dark corridor, up a rickety stairway, through what may have been a classroom, over creaking floor boards, into a small room with several ancient wooden cabinets. After opening a huge lock, the secretary selected one of a number of volumes such as I found were common in Spanish archives, loose sheets bound between two heavy cardboard covers tied together with two red ribbons. This volume contained the death certificates for this century.

I examined the few covering the years from 1936 to 1940. All were inhabitants of Carcedo and included a doctor's statement of the cause of death. It did not include any of the seventy-six who had died at San Pedro. If any records were kept of those killed in the *limpieza,* I was unable to find them. *Diario de Burgos* during those years did not report any executions.

The orchard adjoining the eastern side of the monastery was pointed out to me as the place where San Pedro prisoners had been shot. I believe that many of the sixty-six Spaniards buried outside the wall had met that fate.

That Spaniards were executed at San Pedro is documented in José María Bereciartua's *San Pedro de Cardeña: El Monasterio del Cid,* which reports a Spaniard at San Pedro had escaped and was recaptured. A court-martial in Burgos condemned him to death. A priest at San Pedro, P. Víctor Gondra Muruaga, known as Aita Patxi, a member of the Passionist Order, offered the prisoner last rites. When he refused them, the priest said to Commander Don Emeterio García Guárez, "This one has not prepared his soul before God. Therefore I offer myself to be shot in his place, and also because he has children."

The commander said he would have to consult with his superiors. Aita Patxi went to his monk's cell. A few hours later four helmeted soldiers with fixed bayonets informed him his offer had been accepted. He was placed in front of a firing squad in a clearing at San Pedro. The commander gave the usual orders, "Get ready! Aim!" but when he saw Aita Patxi standing calmly prepared to die, he dismissed the firing squad. At dawn the next morning the priest heard the shots executing the prisoner. Aita Patxi died in Deusto at the age of sixty-four. The Diocese of Bilbao had begun the process of canonizing him for this and other virtuous deeds.[7]

Spaniards were executed at the edge of a ravine near San Pedro. Ernest Amatniek, a Lincoln veteran, with the help of Tom Entwistle met a brave woman who took them to it.[8]

Diario de Burgos on April 16 reported a fascist pilot had fought twelve Republican fighters and twelve bombers single-handedly and shot down one of each. This was matched the next day by a story of how their pilots had celebrated the Virgin of Pilar's Saint's Day on October 12, 1937, by shooting down half a hundred Marxist planes, and then duplicated the feat two months later, on the Virgin of Lareto's Saint's Day, December 11.

"Do they think people are stupid enough to believe such lies?" someone asked.

"People may not believe them, but they are not stupid enough to say so to the fascists, because they don't want to stand in front of a firing squad; so the fascists think they believe it. It's the fascists who get fooled, not the people," is the way Fred Stanley had it figured.

*   *   *   *   *

In spite of Carney's prediction on April 17 in the *Times* that the Republic would collapse within two weeks, it became stronger. France briefly allowed Soviet war materiel to cross to Spain. Negrín's call to resist and his reorganization of his cabinet on April 6, without Prieto but with representatives of the two main trade unions, had heartened the men at the front, who fought courageously. Líster's men stopped the fascists at Tortosa. Campesino's 46th Division, together with the Durruti Anarchist 26th Division, led the forces that stopped Franco's drive toward Lérida. Franco exhausted several army corps in a drive toward Valencia, making only small gains against the determined armies under General Vicente Rojo. These failures strained Franco's relations with the Germans and Italians.

Premier Negrín's "Thirteen Point" program, subscribed to by all sectors of the People's Front, was received enthusiastically.[9] Abroad, massive pro-Republican rallies were held all over England and France, protesting Hitler's seizure of Austria and Chamberlain's pact with Mussolini, which provided for the withdrawal of Italian troops from Spain after the war was over. In the United States, the New York District of the American Student Union dedicated its Peace Ball on April 29 to George Watt, its former executive secretary, and all teachers and students who had gone to Spain.[10]

The primary goal in the USA was the lifting of the embargo. Fraternal, ethnic, religious, and sports organizations as well as students and labor unions lobbied their legislators. With FDR's blessing, Senator Gerald P. Nye and Representative Byron Scott introduced resolutions to end the embargo, Arthur Krock, a *New York Times* columnist whose son was fighting in Franco's army, reported on May 5 that FDR planned to lift the embargo. The resulting furor organized by the Catholic hierarchy against aiding "bolshevists and atheists" caused Democratic big-city congressmen to fear they might be defeated in the 1938 election. Roosevelt, needing their votes to carry out his economic recovery plans, decided not to lift the embargo.[11]

On April 26, Merry del Val reported that Ryan was being held at San Pedro de Cardeña for having served on a Republican execution squad. Sir Robert Hodgson, the British agent at Burgos, said he would make a verbal request on Ryan's behalf, but without interest.

A letter was sent to Franco on May 2 signed by the heads of eleven Irish organizations, including the Irish Academy of Art, the National Union of Newspapermen, and the 12,000-member Irish National Organization of Teachers. Ryan's integrity and self-sacrificing struggle for Irish national goals, they said, had won respect for him even among those who did not agree with him. Any consideration shown Captain Ryan would be appreciated by the people in Ireland and by Ryan's friends in the United States.

By May 7, Franco's Foreign Affairs Ministry had decided, if Ryan were to be pardoned, "to give out the news through the British Government, in this way destroying Ryan's reputation in his country by publishing the fact that he owes his life to the intervention of a Government against which he had always fought obstinately."[12]

An example of fascist deception is a feature article by L. Villena Aharez which appeared in *Diario de Burgos* on April 1, 1938. It described his visit to the concentration camp at San Pedro de Cardeña.

The brown mass of the monastery can be seen from afar with its innumerable narrow monastic windows, in whose glass the rays of the sun show its happy smile.

We have arrived. . . . We pass under an arch of arms which salute tremulously, with the profoundly felt emotion of the new Spain. Very old faces alternate with faces of men almost childlike, filled with an infantile joy, whose eyes fill with emotion at the sight of the red and gold flag which waves over the monastery.

It is necessary to ask them to lower their arms in order to halt their greetings of peace, of liberation.

Men from all provinces, from all regions, fraternize, anxious to be able to contribute in their small way, from their heart, to the realization of the new Spain which protects them and smiles upon them in that concentration camp. . . . In passing by, we ask one a question, "Are you contented here?"

"Contented, no, most contented. If those who are still in the red zone knew the treatment we have received. . . . This is not a prison, it's a rest home." . . . arms are raised in a fraternal greeting, the hand well open.

We arrive at the infirmary, under repair. It is a large room, well ventilated. In the background, an altar, decorated by the prisoners themselves: at the side two rows of painted beds, immaculately white and protecting, equal to those in the best hospitals. . . . And while our coach carries us away from the Monastery, a low murmur, very low, rises toward Heaven. It is the voice of that multitude of men saying the rosary with that same profound and appreciative faith which in remote times were said by the devout who lived behind those holy stone walls.

On April 20, I translated from *Diario de Burgos* Tebib Arrumi's heart-rending story of how the Reds shot a father in front of a mother and their two small children, then ordered the children to dig a grave with their bare hands, threatening them that if they didn't dig it fast enough they would have to make it large enough to bury their mother also. I could see in the faces around me the strong feelings of disgust for fascism and its spokesmen who made up such foul lies.

14 We Get Organized

HALF A DOZEN Basque barbers entered our floor early in May, each armed with hair clippers, shaving brush and straight razor and carrying a pail of water. Assignment: remove all hair from our faces and heads. My barber had a piece of mirror in which I could view myself before and after. I was astonished to see a bushy red beard, in contrast to my brown hair. Grinning at my surprised look, the barber quickly removed all hair. He used my green soap to lather my face before he shaved it. Now I saw in the mirror a pale face and head set on a neck with a ring around it.

On April 25, 1938, H. de Pourtales, from the International Red Cross visited San Pedro.[1] He did not see us, but he did obtain for us the right to send a printed message form to a relative. British nationals, on May 6, received the forms,[2] headed Cruz Roja Española, with space for the sender's and the receiver's address, and four lines for the message. On the back, lines marked where a reply could be written. All, including the ill and the wounded, were instructed to write these and only these words: *Notificandoles que me encuentro bien.* Two months later some relatives were rushing around frantically to find someone who could tell them it meant "Notifying you that I am well."

Nine days later each American received the same form and had to write the same message. I sent mine to my wife, who received it on July 28, ten weeks later. It had had to pass the camp censor, then go to the Spanish Red Cross at Burgos, then to the IRC in Geneva, and then to the American Red Cross in Washington, DC. It was forwarded to my wife with a kind letter.[3]

Undoubtedly, the fascists monitored Radio Madrid's shortwave broadcasts in English. On April 28, they must have heard that Jimmy Rutherford and several other prisoners had returned to fight again.[4] The announcer, of course, was unaware that Jimmy had been captured a second time. But three weeks later, on May 18, we had a most unwelcome visitor, Alfonso Merry del Val. He peered at each face on the third floor, where most of the English were, stopped before Jimmy, spoke to him, and then left.[5]

An hour later in the assembly area we saw the food truck arrive. Sacks of beans were unloaded. Frank Blackman recalls,

they called him [Jimmy Rutherford] out. Put him in the back of the food truck with two guards. Before he disappeared from our view he gave us the clenched-fist salute. A thousand arms returned his gesture. England and the world lost a worthy member.[6]

Frank's estimate of the number of arms was a bit high (our numbers had grown to about 650), but we had no doubt that Jimmy would be executed. Court-martialed in Burgos, he was sentenced to death, and executed on May 24, 1938.[7] Jimmy was the only volunteer captured and taken alive twice. During the six weeks he'd been with us, we had learned to appreciate his strong antifascist beliefs and his calm courage.

On May 23, the day before Rutherford's execution, Consul Bay let Hull know (in a strictly confidential dispatch we would find years later in the US Archives) that the director of General Motors had told him he had arranged the sale of 3500 Chevrolet and GMC trucks to the Burgos government. He also reported that a British official had told him British prisoners were being exchanged for Italians and Germans through the IRC.[8]

The English-speaking members of our informal committee sought ways the prisoners could spend their time usefully and maintain morale. The activities could not require money and had to be acceptable to the camp authorities. Playing chess, including the making of the boards and shaping pieces out of wood and stone, was such an activity. Lectures would be helpful, if we could get Rin-Tin-Tin to consider them harmless.

We passed the word around that the next afternoon there would be a lecture on our floor on "Hiking in the Adirondacks." When I got up to speak, some thirty to forty prisoners formed a semicircle around me. From first-hand experience, I described trails and mountain ranges, the equipment and food needed, and how to deal with black flies. Rin-Tin-Tin immediately wanted to know what was going on. We invited him to learn about hiking in the Adirondacks, but he soon left, since he knew no English.

Our next lecturer described hunting chinchillas in the Andes. Arthur Grey, a Briton, then told us how animals were fed and cared for in the London Zoo. I reserved May 30 for a lecture on the meaning of Decoration Day in the United States.

We had over a hundred English-speaking prisoners on our floor, mainly workers, with a few students and professionals. We did not lack lecturers; mention a place or a skill, and someone was familiar with it. As Tex said, "The working class is everywhere." Rin-Tin-Tin soon disregarded the lectures.

The most popular American on our floor was Matthew Dykstra, because he had brought a book into San Pedro. We were avid readers and sorely missed printed material. Matthew's book, Willa Cather's *Death Comes for the Archbishop*, was popular because of the vivid picture Cather painted of life in the Southwest. Sticky saw the book and asked about the *arzobispo*. When the title was translated, he confiscated the book and, suspecting a plot against the priests, took it to them. We informed Alex about the book's sympathetic treatment of the *arzobispo*. Fortunately, one of the priests could read some English, and Alex was able to persuade him that the book would have a beneficial effect. Within a week, we were happily reading it again.

Our British comrades had brought in two books. One was a Wodehouse novel relating the antics of Bertie and Jeeves. Taking turns reading it aloud, we spent pleasant hours. It provided merriment and opportunity for kibitzing.

The second book, *Lawrence of Arabia,* spent most of its time on the floor above us, where many British slept. They formed groups of fifteen, and each group was allotted one hour a day to listen while someone read it aloud.[9] It led to much serious discussion of the role of Britain and Germany in the Near East, and of the role of the individual in history.

Our English-speaking committee decided to hold classes in the forenoon. The first subjects were Spanish and English. I began a class on the principles of electricity, glad to use for the first time my college education in electrical engineering. We had no paper or blackboards, few pencils, and no textbooks. I borrowed a pencil and wrote lesson outlines on the white wall where I slept. Students could review them at their leisure. The language instructors were making our walls language textbooks.

Sidney Rosenblatt, Bob Steck, and Hy Wallach decided San Pedro needed a newspaper for reliable news and to promote morale, discipline, and self-respect. To keep it out of Sticky's hands, they made only one copy of the *The Jaily News.*

With Alex's help, they obtained several eight and one half by fourteen sheets of white paper. A day later the first issue was circulating, and it was received enthusiastically. The second issue followed shortly, illustrated by a twenty-two-year-old London artist, Jimmy Moon. His sketches were usually humorous comments on our life at San Pedro. A British comrade loosened a floorboard and hid them under it.

Decoration Day, May 30, 1938, was a lovely, warm, and sunny day. I had decided to center my talk on Lincoln's Gettysburg Address, which I had memorized in elementary school. I looked out the window and hungered for the right to walk freely over the green fields and through the woods, to enjoy the feel of the sun and the scent of flowers and the sprouting earth. I could sense that the men who were forming a semicircle around me were longing to walk the face of the earth as free men. Because of their devotion to the cause for which Lincoln had spoken so eloquently, they faced an unpleasant and uncertain future.

Facing me were Richard Browne, a twenty-three-year-old from America's heartland, Kansas City; Homer Chase, a rugged twenty-three-year-old whose ancestors were among the first to settle New England; John Hollis Jenkins, a sociology instructor from Seattle; Charles Hall, a tall twenty-three-year-old from South Dakota; Sidney Rosenblatt, a cheerful twenty-four-year-old from the East Side tenements of New York City; Claude Pringle, the tall and slender black forty-four-year-old coal miner from Ohio; and Fred Stanley, twenty-two, who gave the National Maritime Union as his home address. Among the Canadians were six-foot-four Frank Blackman and Jules Paivio, barely twenty, from Ontario. Among the other fifty prisoners were Jack Jones, a prominent labor leader from London, and Kearney Cassels, a dapper young Englishman from Liverpool who knew the score.

"Seventy-five years ago on a November day, a large multitude gathered in Gettysburg, Pennsylvania, to dedicate a national cemetery where a bloody and crucial battle had taken place in our Civil War a few months earlier. Out of 150,000 men engaged, 50,000 were killed, wounded, or missing.

"A great orator, Senator Edward Everett, had held the audience spellbound for two hours. Then a tall, gaunt man, whose name we have chosen to honor, spoke for two minutes.

"During the intervening years, more people have become familiar with Lincoln's speech than any other in our history. No speech is better known world-wide. Much of the high regard the people of the world have for our country arises from Lincoln's opening remark, which millions can quote: 'Fourscore and seven years ago our fathers brought forth, on this continent, a new nation, conceived in Liberty, and dedicated to the proposition that all men are created equal.'

"His next sentence provides a most appropriate description of the situation today, seventy-five years later, here in Spain. 'Now we are engaged in a great civil war, testing whether that nation, or any nation so conceived and so dedicated, can long endure.'

"Never before in the world's history have such powerful forces joined together to erase the concept that all men are created equal, the basic premise for democratic government. Those evil forces have taken over much of the world, destroying democratic governments, outlawing labor unions and people's organizations and political parties, jailing and murdering their leaders. Some form of fascism now rules Italy, Poland, Yugoslavia, Hungary, Roumania, and Germany. Powerful profascist forces in our country, ranging from Father Coughlin to the Nazi Bund, loudly proclaim that democracy no longer works, that we need an all-powerful leader to solve our country's problems.

"During this period the people of only one nation have been able to break free from a dictatorship—the people of Spain, in 1931. And only the people of Spain have taken up arms to prevent the return of a dictatorship. They would have been successful had it not been for German and Italian intervention, and the hypocrisy of Non-Intervention.

"The brave fight of the people of Spain has kindled the admiration of the people of the world who believe in democracy. You and I became the living expression of that admiration when we took our places in the front lines of the fight for democracy. If Lincoln were alive today, he would be greatly pleased that we have chosen to fight under his name in Spain today.

"But why are the governments of the democratic countries such as England, France and the United States helping the antidemocratic forces? Is it not because individuals in positions of power fear that their privileges and wealth will be endangered if the people are allowed to govern? Is it not because these people deceive many others by telling them that the issue is Communism? This lie will cost the people they have deceived dearly.

"It is fitting that we should on this day remember both the Spaniards and the International Volunteers who lie buried in Spanish soil. All of us knew many of them well, shared their dreams and their fears. They are worthy of the tribute Lincoln paid those who had given their lives at Gettysburg.

We are met here on a great battle-field of that war. We have come to dedicate a portion of that field, as a final resting place for those who here gave their lives that that nation might live. It is altogether fitting and proper that we should do this.

But, in a larger sense, we can not dedicate—we can not consecrate—we can not hallow this ground. The brave men, living and dead, who struggled here, have consecrated it, far above our poor power to add or detract. The world will little note, nor long remember what we say here, but it can never forget what they did here. It is for us the living, rather, to be dedicated here to the unfinished work which they who fought here have thus far so nobly advanced. It is rather for us to be here dedicated to the great task remaining before us—that from these honored dead we take increased devotion to that cause for which they gave the last full measure of devotion—that we here highly resolve that these dead shall not have died in vain—that this nation, under God, shall have a new birth of freedom—and that government of the people, by the people, for the people, shall not perish from the earth.

"Let us stand and honor our dead by renewing our own dedication to that goal."

No salvo of artillery, no firing of muskets, no blowing of bugles, only the silent consecration of whese ragged men to their fallen comrades and to the ideal for which they had given their lives. Nearly forty-one years later Fred Stanley recalled, "Every word had more meaning than any other lecture I had ever heard."[10]

*   *   *   *   *

There were no significant changes in the front in May. The 15th Brigade was rebuilt with new volunteers, Spaniards, and the return of the wounded. The International Brigades and medical services were now based primarily in the Catalonian half of Spain. The People's Front organizations had rallied enthusiastically to Negrín's call to put the entire country on a war footing. Soviet arms, including three hundred planes, crossed the border from France,[11] until British pressure caused France to close its border again on June 13.

On May 11, Alvarez Del Vayo, the Republic's minister of foreign affairs, presented irrefutable proof of German and Italian intervention to the Council of the League of Nations.[12] The Soviet Union and Spain voted for a motion to reconsider the Council's support of non-intervention. Britain, France, and fascist Poland and Roumania voted against the motion; nine abstained.[13]

The first negotations for an exchange of the prisoners at San Pedro began on May 19, when the Marquis de Rialp, representing Franco, presented a proposal to Ambassador Bowers. The Republic held 29 fascist pilots—23 Italian, 1 Portuguese, and 5 Spanish; Franco held 15 Republicans—3 Russian and 12 Spanish. Rialp proposed to make up the difference with 14 Americans from San Pedro de Cardeña. Bowers obtained permission from Hull to act as an intermediary only. Bowers passed Rialp's proposal on to the Republic.

During the third week in June, Alvarez del Vayo informed Bowers that the Republic could not exchange Franco aviators for government privates.

In the case of the Americans who fought on our side, with a courage to which I desire to pay homage, and because of your highly esteemed intervention, my Government would be disposed to exchange the 14 Americans in the list for the same number of rebel or foreign prisoners belonging to the military force not being of aviation.

The result was an exchange of fifteen pilots.[14]

President Eamonn De Valera of Ireland, through the papal nuncio in Ireland, asked the Catholic archbishop in San Sebastian to use his influence to secure clemency for Frank Ryan. A partial listing of the vice-presidents of the Frank Ryan Release Committee included Cu Uladh, president of the Gaelic League; Miss M. Pearse, sister of the first president of the Irish Republic; and P. T. Daley, secretary of the Irish Trades Union Council.

On June 1, Thomas Gunning, a journalist, told Franco authorities that Ryan should be shot because he had assassinated seven people before going to Spain, but by June 3, the Irish minister to Spain had informed them that the accusations were false.[15] At San Pedro, Frank Ryan and we were unaware of the false charge, and of the efforts being made to save Ryan's life.

Meanwhile at one o'clock Sunday afternoon on May 29, Hull sent a rush telegram to Bay informing him that the *New York Times* was carrying a dispatch from Carney at Burgos reporting rumors that captured Americans had been executed without trial. What worried Hull was not the executions, but a quotation attributed to Bay: "When Americans enlist and fight under a foreign flag they cannot expect our government to worry about what happens to them thereafter."

Bay telegraphed a denial: he had met Carney at a social affair in Burgos, and asked whether he knew of any American prisoners nearby (about eighty of us were eleven kilometers away). Carney had said there were a few. "At that time he mentioned a rumor about the execution of prisoners and I made no comment whatever." On Tuesday morning, the *Times* published a complete retraction of Carney's statement.[16]

*   *   *   *   *

Paul Wanzel, a twenty-one-year-old volunteer from Vienna, Austria, died in the infirmary on June 4. A group of Internationals, including Norman Dorland, Hassan, and me, attended the funeral services at the grave. A priest conducted a service assisted by a small Basque choir. In my farewell I said that since Paul's family was not here we would take their place, and I spoke of his steadfast and disciplined adherence to our ideals.

Without preplanning, the Internationals marched back from the funeral with such precision that the authorities became uneasy. We were not permitted to attend subsequent funeral services, if any were held,[17] and were unaware that four Spanirds, eighteen, twenty-one, twenty-eight and forty-three years old, were buried in June.

The second International to die was Frank Papp, a thirty-nine-year-old, born in Balasagyarmal, Hungary, who had emigrated to Windsor, Canada. He died of pneumonia on June 27.[18]

John Smith (Nagfeur Hudar) from India described in a lecture some of the skills developed by yogis and fakirs. Asked if he had any skills, John said, "Yes. For example, I can tell by looking at your hand how many sisters and brothers you have."

I was the firstborn in a large family which would have been even larger had my father not died in the flu epidemic after the end of World War I. I had told no one how many sisters and brothers I had. After John had studied my hand for a moment, he said, "You have one brother and four sisters."

I was flabbergasted. He had hit it exactly. But I noticed his face was solemn as he looked more closely at my hand.

"Do I have a short lifeline?"

"Oh, no! On the contrary, you will live a long time."

I insisted he tell me what he saw that he did not like. "Carl, in your old age you will have an affliction. Exactly what it will be I do not know. But don't worry about it."

"John, if I thought there was something to your prediction, I would be very happy, for it means I get out of here alive."

(John's prediction came true. In my early sixties I began to notice a quiver which made it difficult to write legibly. It slowly became more noticeable, and was finally diagnosed as intention tremor, which has a genetic origin. There is no pain, but it is a real nuisance. Drugs can attenuate its affects, but it steadily becomes more bothersome. My uncle, who died recently, at ninety-one, could have attested to that.)

We began to add lectures on sociology, history, economics, and philosophy. John Hollis Jenkins, who had taught in the Sociology Department at the University of Washington, gave us several lectures on social problems. Jack Jones, a leader in the British labor movement, talked on ths history of the British working class. John Smith reported on the struggle for independence from Britain of the people of India under the leadership of Mahatma Gandhi and Jawaharlal Nehru.

Several fascist officers, while watching from a balcony above our assembly area, flipped cigarette butts over the railing, setting off a scramble among the Internationals below to retrieve them. The officers, enjoying the scene, broke cigarettes in half and tossed them down.

When the same scene occurred the next day, Tex, a smoker, worked his way to the center of the crowd and stamped on the butts, telling the others their behavior was a disgrace. Most of them moved away, and the officers soon tired of throwing butts for Tex to trample into the ground.[19]

We now had about 175 British nationals, including some 30 Canadians, and about 75 Yanks at San Pedro. The remaining Internationals totaled about 450, the largest groups being French, Portuguese, Argentinians, Germans, Cubans, Poles, and Slavs.

Our dignity and self-respect were assaulted daily. We were clubbed for unintentional infractions of petty rules; we couldn't keep clean; our food was poor and the conditions under which we ate were miserable, some having only sardine cans as mess plates, with spoons they had carved of wood; we were vermin-infested; and we had only short, straw-filled burlap bags to sleep on; and we lacked reading material.

Our International Committee, now known as the House Committee, set up the San Pedro Institute of Higher Learning (SPIHL). I headed a committee for the English-speaking to find out what additional courses were desired and to find instructors. We encouraged individuals who had expertise in a subject or activity to gather together a group of interested prisoners. Class format was up to the group, whether it would be a lecture by the instructor, or class members alternating in discussing a topic, or just a "bull session" on a subject. Classes could be formed and discontinued at any time. Each instructor was given wall space for his class notes. Three hour-long class periods were arranged between nine and twelve in the morning. A prisoner with a watch beat his spoon on his food dish when it was time to start or change classes. A few classes were held in the afternoon.

Students soon had a choice of beginner's math through geometry, algebra, trigonometry and calculus. There were classes in radio circuitry, labor history, music, and art. Jenkins elaborated on his lectures in a popular course in sociology, as did Jones in an excellent course on British labor history.

But it was the language classes that drew the most students and lasted the longest. Spanish, French, German, Russian, Esperanto, and English, for beginners and for advanced students, were offered, as well as considerable private tutoring. Hassan taught several languages for non-English-speaking nationalities.

Courses were set up by other nationalities. Karl Spannbauer taught history and dialectics; Rudolph Berger taught military tactics; Arthur Karlsson taught engine maintenance; Karl Kormes translated *El Diario de Burgos* into German and led a current events discussion; Rudi Kampf, a twenty-year-old musician from Dresden, taught courses in the history of music and in music composition; and Alberto Abinum, from Sarajevo, Yugoslavia, taught a course in agricultural technology.[20]

Sticky was alarmed when he noticed so many semicircles of prisoners sitting on the floor around individuals who were instructing them. But Alex was able to convince the major they kept the prisoners occupied. No other activity we engaged in was as important as these classes in resisting the dehumanizing and degrading atmosphere of the concentration camp.

There was much excitement at San Pedro on Saturday, June 11. Colonel E.C. Martin, the British military attaché in Burgos, had come to see the British prisoners; he was the first foreigner to visit the Internationals at San Pedro. He asked the British to sign a contract to repay the British government four pounds for the cost of repatriating themselves. All but one refused. Then they learned that one hundred would be sent to another prison camp.

The next morning, Sunday, with no classes, Maurice Levitas, a twenty-year-old Dubliner, engaged a twenty-three-year-old Briton, David Goodman, in a chess game. They heard someone in the narrow corridor start to read the names of the British to be transferred. Both prided themselves on looking at such a matter in a purely rational way and continued to play, certain they would be told if their names were called. Levitas recalled that after some minutes "we looked at each other and decided that listening was more important than playing chess. So we . . . went to listen to the list, and found our names were not on it."[21]

Those fortunate enough to be called were loaded onto three trucks. One of them, Clive Branson, left a substantial sum of money with the House Committee for tobacco and paper. The committee asked Alex to obtain permission of the camp commander to give out tobacco on the next four Saturdays. When the major agreed, we gained his recognition of the House Committee.

That Sunday, Frank Ryan was taken away in handcuffs by three guards.[22] Several weeks later the grapevine reported he had been sentenced to death—a grim warning to us.

On June 15, we received new Red Cross forms, with the same warning; write only "Notifying you that I am well" in Spanish.

June had brought a new sergeant to San Pedro. Below medium height and not very heavy, he was the most vicious sergeant we had. He had been in a tank that had met the British Battalion at dawn on March 31, and he had received a painful knee wound. Judged unfit for front-line duty, he was assigned to San Pedro. Sticky made him his right-hand man for imposing discipline on us. It was the job he wanted. His opinion of the ancestry of the Internationals was low, and of the British lower still. We dubbed him "Tanky."

Sergeants carried wooden sticks about five feet long, one half to two inches in diameter, to beat both soldiers and prisoners. Officers carried pistols, and privates carried rifles.

The camp commander, who had his office near the barn, did not want to see prisoners beaten, so when we were in the assembly area, Tanky did not dare use his stick too freely. But inside the courtyard he could use it without being seen. He would stand beside the small door through which he had to pass when we left our quarters. Yelling *"Venga!"* Come on! Tanky would apply his stick to the backs of as many as he could. We would dash out as fast as possible, so he could hit only one in every four or five. Occasionally he would catch someone off balance, causing him to stumble, or even fall prostrate, his tin plate clattering on ahead of him. As a result, those who were ill or not too hungry would not come down, and on occasion Tanky come up with his stick to drive down all except those in the sick room.

Within a week Tanky had splintered several sticks, so he had a pizzle made from a dried bull penis, with a leather cup at one end for a lead slug, and a leather grip on the other end. Although it was a bit short and not very rigid, Tanky was able to raise welts on many a back without damaging his weapon.

"I have bad news," Alex said with his perpetually gloomy air. "You are going to be forced to give the Franco salute. There will be a training session this afternoon. All the sergeants will be there with their sticks."

Our House Committee met immediately. Could we get everyone to refuse? We were uncertain about the thirty prisoners who had come to Spain many years ago from France, the United States, and Portugal and had not served in the Republican Army. Even in our own ranks, there were some who would not refuse to salute.

One of the cooler heads said we should consider, not our feelings, but the consequences. To refuse would cause disunity in our ranks. And all, except the rats, would join us in refusing to salute if a foreign dignitary were present.

Reluctantly, we decided to swallow our pride and offer only token resistance. We passed the word along that everyone was free to salute, but that those who wished first to take a whack or two from the sergeants could do so. Some did take a few blows before raising their hands. The sergeants ignored sloppy salutes as long as the fist was not closed.

When Stanley Heinricher walked back into our quarters, Tex said he was the closest thing to a ghost that he ever would see. Tex vividly remembered the bleeding hole in Stanley's neck where a bullet had entered between his collarbone and the spinal column, and the hole where the bullet had exited from his back below the rib cage. Now Stan was back from the infirmary. In 1978, Stanley recalled his treatment:

I was placed on a clean white bed with a pillow. All the beds were metal—good and sturdy, painted white. It felt so good—excellent medicine. This infirmary was light and roomy and was inside the church. The front end contained the nave, and a priest came every Sunday and said Mass. It was very old and the walls were whitewashed. The infirmary was very clean. My bed was just beneath one of those large windows, which were filled with plain glass—nothing ornate. . . .

Our bandages were washed every day. I marveled at how white they were kept. The nuns did a wonderful job. Sister Esperanza Bajo Bajo was the Mother Superior. She was very kind to me and always came to me to make sure I was comfortable. Sister Inez was her helper. She was young and beautiful. Sister Inez was there only a short while and then was sent away somewhere. Another nun, whose name I don't remember because she never attented us Internationals, was a real workhorse. She was in charge of the people who washed the bandages and did general housecleaning.

The official Spanish doctor was a military man and he made his rounds once a week. He went by each bed quickly, at the same time talking with the Mother Superior. The times when other officials accompanied him, he never failed to stop at my bed and explain how I was wounded. He always marveled that I was still alive.

I was healing very rapidly when one day Mother Superior detected I was running a fever. She felt the wound in my back, which had gotten hot. She squeezed it, and suddenly it burst open, disgorging pus. There was almost instant relief. . . . Mother Superior was good to me. On Easter Sunday, 1938, she gave each patient about an ounce of sweet liqueur. She went around to each bed, and then came back to me with another ounce.

About the food we received in the infirmary: what little we got was well prepared and was nourishing. I do remember getting some meat on Fridays, and I was always puzzled, since I thought that Catholics did not eat meat on Fridays. Later I found out that the Spanish people were exempted from having to eat fish on Fridays by a medieval Pope because Spain supplied so many troops for the Crusades.[23]

We held the imprisoned nuns in high esteem; we had learned they had been at Guernica when it was bombed and had refused to sign a statement that it had been destroyed by the Reds.

Our sick room always had patients suffering from flu and diarrhea. Aside from occasional small supplies of aspirin, rest was the only medicine. When Tony Gilbert ran a very high fever with severe abdominal pains, Dr. Sinobas burned wood to make charcoal, ground it, and had Tony swallow large quantities. His fever came down and shortly he was able to walk about again.[24]

*   *   *   *   *

Acting Secretary of State Sumner Welles had noted the discrepancy between Carney's report on March 16 that he had talked with Babsky, Ecker, Neafus, and Ticer after their capture and the statement by Franco's inspector of prison camps on May 30 that they were not prisoners. On June 4, during Hull's absence, Welles sent a telegram to Consul Bay asking for an explanation. Bay did not respond to Welles, but replied to Hull on June 14 that he had been asked to assure him again that Franco observed the rules of war in regard to prisoners. There was no further discussion of the fate of the four men.

In the response to Hull Bay also mentioned an invitation to visit the concentration camp at San Pedro de Cardeña. Hull then gave Bay permission to visit us.

On June 24 two officers took Bay to San Pedro. Bay reported he had found about six hundred foreign prisoners basking on a grassy hillside, and had interviewed twenty Americans with complete freedom. Their chief concern was to obtain money to buy small personal needs, such as tobacco. They complained they could not send letters to their relatives. Bay reported he had obtained a promise from the warden that we would be allowed to write, subject to consorship.[25]

The result was that on July 15 we received another Red Cross form. Now I was allowed to write in Spanish: "I am well. I need five dollars a month. Write letters to me." My wife received the form on December 3.[26]

Bay noted, "In general appearance, they were healthy and strong. The prison doctor said all had gained weight since their arrival." This was true for many who had lost considerable weight before their arrival at San Pedro. But Bay had not visited those in our sick room. He also reported there were two doctors on the premises—false—and five others among the prisoners— there were three—and did not mention that we had no medical supplies.

Bay observed that some three thousand prisoners were given a fifteen-minute address by a priest. "The address was political and pled for a united Spain with a strong government, freedom of the laborer and better social conditions." In fact, not even a priest would have dared to speak out for freedom of the laborer; the men standing before him were living witness to the fate of those who believed in that. The priest's formula for better social conditions required the laborers to obey without question the regulations laid down by Franco, their employers, and the landowners.

According to Bay our dinner consisted of "white bread, lentils and a meat stew of very appetizing appearance." We agree only on the lentils. We had received our *chusco* at lunchtime, but what meat stew? How could we have missed it? Once or twice a week there was potato stew, with a piece of pork fat in it if we were lucky, but then the stew took the place of the beans. I recall being quite pleased with a square-inch chunk I got in my stew one noon meal, until I turned it over and found it had a split copper ring through it. It was from the snout of a hog, and the coppper ring had been put there to keep it from rooting up the ground. I knew the nose had to be clean after having been boiled in that big kettle of stew, so I chewed whatever was edible and saved the copper. Later one of the prisoners fashioned it into an attractive ring.

Bay did observe that our latrine and washing facilities were "distinctly insufficient," but said that others were being provided in new construction. (They were never completed.) He added that prison conditions were passable in the summer, but "the rigors of winter would impose great discomfort and perhaps suffering."

According to Bay, both he and the prison doctor were concerned about the deterioration of Barr's remaining eye, but decided nothing could be done even if funds were available. Fortunately, American doctors later not only saved the remaining eye but also provided Barr with an excellent glass eye.

Bay reported, "Estimates of the number of Spanish prisoners now on hand are generally given as 160,000 in confinement, and some 90,000 on probation or on qualified liberty, distributed in some 30 concentration camps."

Bay attached the names, some badly misspelled, the addresses, and the age and occupation of seventy-seven Americans, with eight more to come. The average age was twenty-seven.[27]

The camp authorities thought close-order drill in the assembly area would be beneficial. The sergeants formed us into twenty rows of thirty; this allowed us to march about fifteen steps in one direction and twenty in the other. The sergeant constantly had to bellow out orders to keep us from marching into a wall or out of the area. Part of the time he would have us stand still and while he repeated "At ease!" we were supposed to yell "Franco" while raising and lowering our arms. But then Alex obtained permission for Max Shufer to lead us in calisthennics. Within a few weeks we had quite a snappy routine worked out.

Sticky decided that one of his sergeants ought to lead the calisthenics. The sergeant had not mastered the routine, and invented some of his own, such as holding out the hands and rotating them from the palms-up to the palms-down position. Within a week the sergeant gave up, and Max then led us in calisthenics whenever we were allowed out in the meadow.

*   *   *   *   *

When the one hundred British left San Pedro on Sunday, June 12, they were taken about a hundred kilometers southwest of Burgos to a prison camp near Palencia run by Italians. First they bathed in a nearby canal and put on clean Italian uniforms. In low brick buildings inside a barbed-wire compound, they found beds with straw mattresses. Food was served in a courtyard from large caldrons, but they could eat sitting down in the courtyard or on their beds. No one was threatened with a stick. The British were asked to work with the Spanish prisoners in an Italian auto park in return for a ration of cigarettes and additional food, but only one accepted. They did dig a trench latrine.[28]

Carney in a dispatch to the *New York Times* had reported on May 29 that Frank Ryan was charged with commanding squads of Internationals who had executed prisoners without trial during the Brunete offensive, and with having shot some who had surrendered.

These charges were completely false, said seven Americans who had fought in the Irish unit under Ryan at Brunete: Paul Burns; the three Flaherty brothers, Charles, Edward, and Frank; Philip Haydock; James Murphy; and Joseph Whelan. The *Times* printed their letter to the editor on June 1, 1938.

The stage was now set for Frank Ryan's trial. On June 15, he was brought before a military court consisting of three officers, a prosecutor, and a defending officer. The proceedings were in Spanish, which Frank, partly deaf, understood poorly. Serious charges about his activities in Ireland had been made by letter, and Ryan said they were false.

Frank was not told the court's decision. He suspected he had received a death sentence (which was true, but without an execution date). Frank wrote to his sister Eilis in French, telling her he had been tried and asking her to send money and clothing. He ended the letter with "Best regards to all my friends and especially Deviele, Baolbais and Silim. I thank each one." The censor didn't know that in Gaelic, Deviele referred to De Valera, Baolbais to "danger of death," and Silim to "I think." Eilis lost no time letting Frank's friends know he was in Burgos Central Prison and in danger of being executed.[29]

Frank's friends never ceased their efforts on his behalf. Appeals were made in Parliament for his freedom, and RELEASE FRANK RYAN OR ELSE was painted in huge letters on the stone breastworks of the Thames.[30]

15 Visitors

"GET YOUR SOAP and dirty clothes! We're taking you to the river to wash and bathe! Quick!"

The order came right after lunch, early in July. Getting our dirty clothes together was easy; most of us were wearing everything we had. Only one floor at a time would make the trip. Armed soldiers were lined up along the dirt lane running north. A sergeant started up the lane, motioning us to follow him; we did so in a loose column, and the soldiers fell in alongside us.

I enjoyed the walk along a lane bordered by bushes and trees and open fields with stone fences. The odors in the hot sun brought back memories of hard but pleasant labor on my grandmother's farm, of many hikes I had made through wooded areas. The many-hued flowers, the humming insects, the calling birds—all made me aware again of the rich life that goes on regardless of humanity's struggles for riches, or for freedom.

On our way we passed a small village of some thirty houses. The children and women going about their everyday affairs also reminded me of my life as a youth. Within an hour we reached the "river," a good-sized creek by mid-American standards. Knee-deep pools and longer stretches of narrow rivulets running over a rocky bed provided places to do our washing and bathing. In a short time we were soaping and pounding our underwear, if we had any. Then we pounded our shirts and pants, without pity for their many soft-and hard-shelled occupants. Finally, best of all, we washed ourselves. The little soap we had was ineffective in the stream's hard water, but we scrubbed energetically. The guards took delight in our pleasure and enjoyment. In a short time the banks were covered with clothes drying in the sun while we continued to splash and play in the water. All too soon a whistle signaled time to dress. On the walk back, with clean clothes and a clean body, I felt even more in tune with nature.

Our diet was improved on some Catholic Saints' days by the addition of a chunk of tuna, aged a bit, but well prepared. It was a welcome addition to our diet, when it was free of maggots.

Though warmer weather had made our life less miserable, we remained subject to arbitrary beatings. Severe beatings were administered in a cellar room known as *la Sala de Tortura*. There was no printed or announced list of infractions for which one could be beaten, nor any consistency in punishment. For instance, we always ate standing up, but one day early in July, Bob Doyle, an Irish seaman from Dublin, Jack Flior from South Africa, and Bob Steck sat down to eat their lunch. Steck recalls:

134

Tanky pointed to Jack and two soldados motioned with their rifles for him to get up. They did the same to me and to Bob.

We were marched into the Monastery, down to the cellar and ordered to face the outside wall of the Sala de Tortura with our hands on the wall.

Tanky left. The two soldiers guarded us. Tanky returned with five soldiers, some of whom carried tree limbs. They entered La Sala. Tanky came out and struck Jack with his club made from a bull's penis. Jack was closest to the entry door. He was ordered into the room followed by Tanky and one of the two guards. Yelling erupted in La Sala—"Rojo, rojo!" We heard the blows, the dull thuds. There was a scream and then silence occasionally interrupted by groans.

Fear has a way of creeping under one's skin. As I stood against the wall I tried to visualize the scene inside. In my imagination I felt the blows. My brain told me that my fear was rational. I realized that the more detailed I visualized the blows and the reactions taking place, the more ready I would be with the reactions I wanted to make. It was like practicing going over the top. For a moment it was a nightmarish unreality. Jack groaned.

I recalled at the age of six or seven I was tied to a clothesline and strapped. My father later took pride in that I did not cry out nor own up to the charge against me.

Another cry. I was apprehensive and fearful. I pictured what was going on. I lived it. I was determined not to cry out, not to react their desired way. I was not obsessed by fear, my fear was rational. My reactions, too, must be rational—how to preserve a decent conduct. I remembered all the Westerns I had read where the cowboy fighting for his water rights withstood the fists and kicks of the predator until the day of judgment came.

The door opened. Jack was pushed out and led away. I was next. The room was small. No more than eight by eight. Windowless. Nothing in it, not even a stool.

Two of the soldiers were removing their tunics. A short sturdy fellow, could have been a farmer, looked at me. He held a heavy limb. Another with a limb had the look of an old nag. One with crinkled skin had a heavy strap. A surly fellow had a club. The two who had removed their tunics picked up their limbs. Tanky, of course, held his bull's penis.

The soldier who had escorted Jack returned. Tanky closed the door. They were in a circle. The air was close. I smelled their sweat. I was struck. Instinctively I crouched and my head ducked, my forearms covering my ears and my head. The blows stormed on by back. I realized I had screamed. No more of that, I told myself. There had been no questions, no interrogation. Why beat me? Were they evil or just doing a job. Occasionally one shouted, "The Reds will not win." My teeth were clenched and yet a partial groan passed through them as I felt the buckle circle my back and strike my ribs. What information did they want? I kept telling myself— think of other things—the Westerns. After all I was here because of what I had been and, perhaps, would be. My teeth clenched harder. My knees buckled. I was crouched on the floor, my knees touching my chin. I was a ball. There was pain but not as much as I had anticipated. My shirt and the sheepskin vest underneath had not been removed.

They stopped. They were panting and sweating. My tongue licked my lips and tasted wet perspiration but it was salty. I was fighting tears of hurt, tears of rage, but mostly tears of humiliation. Tanky opened the door. I was escorted back to quarters. I sat on my straw mattress and then lay on my belly. Curly Wilson and Bill Stone raised my shirt and vest carefully and looked at my back. Curly asked: "Why did they beat you?" I shook my had, having no answer.[1]

News of the death of a friend at the front, or a propaganda atrocity story in a newspaper, rather than our behavior, probably triggered the beatings. It didn't take much to set Tanky off.

A London dispatch in *Diario de Burgos* caught our eye on July 7. The Non-Intervention Committee had approved a plan for withdrawal of foreign volunteers. "Hey, that means we go home soon, for they wouldn't keep us after all volunteers have left."

But Tex had a more sober estimate. "Franco can't win without German and Italian manpower. So you can bet your bottom dollar they're not going to be withdrawn. This is just some kind of game they are playing."

The next day the *Diario de Burgos* reported that Jacques Doriot was visiting Franco Spain, protesting the Soviet Union's support of the Republic, and would have International Brigaders appear with him who "had fled from red Spain in rebellion against their criminal communist betrayers." We knew Doriot had been a Communist deputy in the French Parliament, and had flirted briefly with followers of Leon Trotsky before forming the PPF (Peoples Party of France), with avowed fascist goals.

Doriot came to San Pedro to recruit rebellious Brigaders and was taken to the major's office while the Frenchmen were lined up in the assembly areas. The sergeants tried to find someone to meet with Doriot, explaining that he had come to help them. An elderly truck driver, who had come to Spain to buy oranges, said he would speak to Doriot, but only if he could remain in the ranks. But when the tall well-dressed Doriot stood in front of him, the Frenchman

was so flustered and excited he could hardly talk. And when he finally did get started, he said the wrong things. He complained that he was always hungry, that he was covered with lice and filth, that he was beaten every day, and that he was in fear of his life all the time. He pointed out in a torrent of words that he had never been a soldier, that he was a peaceful citizen of France, going about his business when he had been taken prisoner and thrown into this awful place. He begged and pleaded with Doriot to help him get back home again to his wife and family. As one Frenchman to another he trusted that something could be done in his case.[2]

This was not what Doriot had expected. When he said he would see what he could do, a second truck driver spoke up with the same story. No others would talk with Doriot. Accounts in *Diario de Burgos* of Doriot's subsequent activites made no mention of rebellious International Brigaders.

We had learned on Saturday morning, July 9, that William Carney would visit us that afternoon. We chose two spokesmen, Lou Ornitz and Edgar Acken. A member of the American Newspaper Guild, Acken had been on the staff of the Newark *Ledger.* He and Ornitz would be assisted by Bob Steck and Bob Doyle, Charles Barr, Stanley Heinricher, Andy de la Casa, Howard Earl (who had participated in the sit-in strike at Douglas Aircraft Company in Santa Monica, California), and Hy Wallach.

Carney talked with the major before we were brought into the assembly area for his inspecton. Carney brought eighteen packages of cigarettes—under the impression, he said, there were only eighteen of us. Did he think the rest of the hundreds he had reported captured were killed?

After handing over the cigarettes, he asked that sheets of paper be passed around so each prisoner could write down his name, home town, and date and place of capture. Carney collected 75 signatures and thought he had all but five, which accounted for the figure of 80 mentioned in the *Times.* Actually, he had the names of 74 and missed eleven who had not signed the sheet.[3]

We learned from Carney that while the British had started negotiations to exchange their nationals for Italians held by the Republic, the State Department would neither take the initiative in arranging our exchange nor pay our repatriation costs.

When Ornitz and Acken told Carney we wanted to return to the Republic (in an exchange for an equal number of prisoners held by the Republic), Carney said the Non-Intervention Committee wanted all foreigners withdrawn from Spain.

After assuring the committee, "You know me, boys, I'm an American and I'm here to help you," Carney wanted to know who had supplied the funds to send us to Spain. Ornitz and Acken told him that they did not know who had paid for our passage. Carney then claimed that we would be required by any consulate in Europe where we would apply for passports to state under oath who had "sent" us to Spain. (When we were exchanged, we were asked no such questions.) Ornitz and Acken explained that none of us had been sent, that we all wanted to come.[4] Carney also wanted to know how many of the Americans belonged to the Communist Party. Ornitz and Acken replied all were antifascists and they did not not know how many were CP members. Did we have our passports? No, we had left them at the International Brigade base so they would not fall into the hands of the fascists.

It was obvious that Carney wanted information that would besmirch our reputation, but Ornitz and Acken insisted on describing our living conditions to him. When he seemed skeptical about our being beaten, the others turned Bob Steck and Bob Doyle around and pulled up their shirts, revealing long red welts across their backs.[5] Carney was visibly taken aback.

Invited to come up to our quarters to see where we were living and sleeping, Carney begged off. Acken informed him that we were very worried about Frank Ryan and Jimmy Rutherford. He was also told that those who had written a little more on their Red Cross forms had had them returned by the censor. We had almost no reading material. We knew our relatives would send us some if they had our address.

The committee and others asked Carney about events in the United States. Had John L. Lewis, Mayor Fiorello La Guardia and Senator Robert La Follette formed a third party yet? Which team was leading the American League? Who would Joe Louis fight next?

Ornitz ended the interview by telling Carney that if he wanted to help us, he would tell the State Department: "As prisoners of war, we are entitled to adequate medical care and decent sanitary facilities and should not be forced to salute the fascist flag." Ornitz soon found out who got the message.

That same evening as we were filing out to salute the facist flag the prison commander pulled me out of the line. He repeated . . . the statements that I had made to Carney. . . . That night I was severely beaten by the fascist guards and put on half rations for several days.[6]

Three weeks later the first letters arrived for Americans. One had a clipping from the July 11 *New York Times* of a 6500 word dispatch by Carney. The front-page two-column headline blared: WRITER SEES 80 AMERICANS HELD IN SPANISH REBEL CAMP. The subhead read: "They Complain to Correspondent About Food and Quarters—Say Communists or Allied Groups Paid Their Fares from U.S."

But we were delighted to read the names and home towns of seventy-four prisoners, for now we knew that the FALB and friends and relatives knew where we were. Much of the dispatch was false. Here is Carney's dishonest description of us:

Then the eighty shuffled out into the courtyard, and the prison officials all withdrew, leaving me to converse with the men as long as I liked. Having previously interviewed about a dozen Americans soon after their capture, I was not prepared for the rought aspect of the ragged, dirty, mostly unshaven crew confronting me.

We were ragged, but not dirty; we had washed in the river only a few days earlier. All had beards of the same length, since no one was allowed to have a razor and we were shaven by the Spanish barbers at intervals of several weeks.

After some landscaping—converting an odorous ditch, sometimes almost dry, into a river where men bathed and washed their clothes—Carney said he "saw a group of healthy looking men going in for athletics in a large field" on the other side. He claimed that he

was told by a prison official that they were French, British and Scandinavian Internationals who from the time of their capture had not only conducted themselves with exemplary discipline but had asked to be put to work immediately. Some were helping in the kitchens, while others had turned out to be good barbers and gardeners.

We were not on the field because we were being held in our quarters awaiting Carney's arrival. None of the Internationals asked to be put to work, nor were any of them cooks, barbers, or gardeners. The work of policing our quarters and standing night watches was shared equally by all able-bodied prisoners.

Carney claimed that the major had complained about our "sulky rebelliousness against all discipline with a personal inclination to complain" about our sanitary conditions, lack of exercise, and the lice and fleas, and had said most of us had to be forced to bathe and wash clothes in the river, and refused to join other nationalities in simple sports. All objected to church service on Sunday morning "because not one is a Catholic."

There were a number of Catholics in our ranks who were highly incensed by the profascist sermons of the priests. They as well as the rest of us believed in everyone's right to worship God in the way he chose, or not to worship any God at all. At San Pedro, anyone who did not kneel at the proper time was beaten into a kneeling position.

Carney did reveal later in the article that Bob Steck had shown him "several red welts on his bare back," but said he had received them for "not giving the Fascist salute to their flag and always refusing to kneel in church."

Carney also wrote that the major had prepared him for our complaints about the food, and had showed him fish being fried and red beans being stewed with *chorizo* (sausage). Of course, a visitor meant a better meal, and on that day we did get *chorizo* with our kidney beans. Carney further added that he was told the guards received the same rations. In 1982 Efrén Manzilla, a former guard, assured me they had a separate and better mess.[7]

After Lillian Hellman read Carney's article, she wrote, in the "Lyon's Den" in the *New York Post* of July 22:

Remember that Mr. Carney is an American. Remember that even a Fascist can have manliness enough to admire bravery in the enemy. Well here goes our little gentleman to see his fallen foes. First he has an interview with a Fascist major who warns him that the Americans, infinitely less well behaved than the French or British, will complain about the filth and the food and the treatment because most of them, although Carney is a little confused on the figures, are Communists and it seems only Communists like cleanliness and decent food and humane treatment. . . .

But the words I am carrying next to my heart come from one who should not die unknown. Carney was wishing his compatriots good-by and good luck. One of them said: "I do not want any of your good luck." Standing there, a guy who might die . . . said "I do not want any of your good luck." Those are words of great and good contempt, and, honey, I send love and kisses.

The editors of the *Jaily News* devoted a whole page to *An Open Letter to the Comandante* headed with Jimmy Moon's illustration, "As Mr. Carney Saw Us":

Dear Comandante:

It is only after reading Mr. Carney's report in the *N.Y. Times* of his interview with you, and incidentally, with us, that we realized how our disgraceful actions here have affected you. This letter is, therfore, in the nature of an apology and a promise of better things to come.

In the past, not content with having thrust ourselves upon España U.G.L. [Una, Grande y Libre] we have not cooperated with you, our host. No longer shall this be so—we have undergone a spiritual change!

If you will restore to the grounds of San Pedro the flowing stream and the athletic field which Mr. Carney described, we will bathe and exercise freely.

Give us the opportunity and we will join the Scandinavians. French, etc., in cooking, gardening, woodcutting and other labor for the common welfare. If you only knew how we long to join them as they go valiantly forth every morning!

We realize that we are never beaten, no matter how much we provoke it, but to spare your feelings we will cease taunting the guards.

We acknowledge our quarters are as commodious as Mr. Carney observed in his careful inspection. We pledge to welcome the medical surgeon upon his arrival. We promise no longer to spread the Red Virus among our fellows.

And most of all, if given the chance, we propose to seek in the Catholic Church that gentle, tolerant, Christ-like spirit which characterizes Fascism and its sergeants.

The Americans.[8]

On July 14, the British received permission to write letters to their families. Jimmy Moon sent his letter to his mother, asking for magazines and a pound note. The letter reached his parents on August 18.[9]

Diario de Burgos amazed us on July 18, not with its headline—SPAIN COMMEMORATES THE SECOND ANNIVERSARY OF THE GLORIOUS NATIONAL UPRISING WITH GREAT REJOICING—but because its lead story praising Franco's national and Catholic movement was a paean to the contribution the Moors had made against "those without God and without country."

Africa occupies the most prominent place because in the present Crusade their sons came to demonstrate, once more, their love for Spain with the maximum offering, their lives, which they joyfully give for her and for Franco.

The front page carried no mention of Italian and German support fo the "glorious national uprising."

I had expected that our captors would flood us with written propaganda extolling the virtues of Franco and his brand of fascism. But our initial re-education, aside from that administered with sticks, was limited to lectures. Two priests who lived at San Pedro lectured three to four times a week to prepare the Spaniards for life under Franco. Men from Asturias, Vizcaya, and Santander spent about six weeks at San Pedro before leaving in labor battalions, so the priests' talks had a six-week cycle.

We named the two priests "Hermanos Mios" and "Señores" because this was the way they began their talks. Hermanos Mios (My Brothers) was the short and chunky member of the Passionist Order, Aita Patxi, who had offered his life for that of a condemned Spaniard. Señores (Sirs) was a tall Franciscan.

Early in the series came the "electricity" lecture. Dramatically, the priest would ask, "Señores, do you know what electricity is?" Some were illiterate, and electrical phenomena were a great mystery to all.

But you know how to push a switch to make a light come on. But do you know how to make electricity? Would you try to make it yourself? Of course not! So what do you do? You very wisely leave it to the experts, to those who know how.

It is the same way with everything else in life. In matters of religion and God, you must listen to your priest and your bishop. And in matters of government, you must listen to the leaders of your government and do what they tell you to do. For they know, they understand, they are the experts. You must leave government to Franco and the Falange, for they know what is good for you and for Spain. Now, if you don't do what they ask you to do because you don't understand, is it not right that they should do whatever is necessary to make you do the right thing, for your own good? Of course, it is! But it is even better if you do understand, and do obey your leaders willingly without being forced to do so.

Then there was the "democracy" lecture:

Señores, today we will discuss the root cause of Spain's problems. It can be described with one word, democracy. How can democracy work if the people do not understand the problems of government and do not know what must be done. The people will only fight amongst themselves, only create disunity in the nation, only weaken Spain. Democracy can only lead to that terrible scourge of mankind, Communism, for it allows demagogues to lead the people astray.

It is the doctrine of democracy, based on the false concept of sovereignty of the people which led to Spain's downfall. If Spain had not adopted this slogan, she would still be reigning in all her imperial glory. And it is only by rooting out this false and dangerous idea that Spain can regain her strength and greatness, and once more assume her rightful position as the spiritual leader of the Americas.

Fortunately for you, it is not your task to concern yourselves with how to solve your country's problems. Your task is much simpler. You need only listen to Spain's great leader, Generalissimo Francisco Franco y Bahamonde, and do what he asks you to do. If you do it with an eager and willing heart, Spain will become great again.

The first pamphlet we received for our education was written by a former member of the British Battalion. He told of his bitter disillusionment with the International Brigade and the Republican leadership. But several Englishmen had known him. A great braggart about what he was going to do when he got to the front, he tried to evade it, and drank so much that he had been judged useless and sent back to England. The British thought he had written it for pay. The paper was appreciated.

When we received another bundle of pamphlets, we all gathered around in anticipation. The first American to receive one yelled, "Hey, guys, we're in luck. They're in English." We sat down to read. The pamphlet was an attack on the leadership of the Communist Party and the Communist

International, claiming they were responsible for the victory of fascism in Germany.

The first thing that struck me was the name of the author, Maria Reese. I had heard of her. A leading member of the German Communist Party, she had left it to join a Trotskyite faction, and Germans told me she had now joined the Nazi Party.[10] What struck me most was the frontispiece, a picture of a Red Front Fighters' parade in Hamburg. The Red Front Fighters League had been organized by the Communist Party and trade unions to protect their offices and meetings from attacks by Hitler's Brown Shirts. The man leading the parade was a fellow prisoner, Arthur Karlsson. The picture would expose him. I said nothing to anyone, but confirmed it with Arthur.

Within a few days the pamphlets were gone. The green covers had been converted with considerable artistry into playing cards. The paper, in spite of its glossy surface, was being put to good use. Jimmy Moon was besieged by prisoners who wanted a "Moon" set of cards. He agreed to make face cards.

A week later, word came that next day, in the assembly area, a volunteer would be asked to read the pamphlet out loud because the camp authorities thought we had not read them. Our House Committee was amused by the report since all who knew English had read the pamphlet, and we were quite certain no one would volunteer. Then Sticky would ask me as chief of the English-speaking group to select someone. So we found a husky Welsh volunteer who agreed to do the reading.

An hour after lunch, all Internationals were lined up in rows in the assembly area. Sticky and one of the priests holding the green pamphlet stood on the platform facing us. Sticky called us to attention and announced through an interpreter, "We have an interesting pamphlet here in English. Who will volunteer to read it out loud?"

As we expected, no one volunteered. Sticky then ordered Tanky to find someone who could read English. Tanky started with the prisoner closest to him. "*Qué nacionalidad?*"

"*Ungaro.*"

"*Hablas inglés?*"

"*No.*"

To show that he knew who spoke English, Tanky concentrated on finding an Englishman or an American. If he heard a man say Canadian or Oklahoman, Irish or Scot, he passed immediately to the next in line, looking for his Englishman or American.

The Internationals could no longer hide their surprise and amusement that Tanky did not know that Canadians, Scots, and Irish spoke English, though he could be excused for not knowing that an Oklahoman spoke it. Tanky suspected that prisoners were lying; when a Pole answered "*Polaco,*" he shouted, "You're lying! Get up there!" and hurried him along with his stick.

The priest handed over the pamphlet, but the Pole protested he could read only Polish. Finally, Sticky ordered me to select someone, and I picked our young Welshman, who was standing nearby. As befitted the man of the hour, he walked very deliberately onto the platform, took the pamphlet, and in a delightful brogue began to read.

The Internationals who knew English were all smiles as they listened, enraptured. Sticky and the priest, seeing this and suspecting he might be doing a little editing as he went along, looked over his shoulder. The Welshman now added gestures so those Internationals who did not understand English might also enjoy the occasion.

The performance proceeded smoothly, our Welshman enjoying his role, and the priest and Sticky wondering why we were getting so much pleasure out of the reading. When we applauded at the end of the fine reading, Sticky and the priest may have been uncertain why, but in any case they were pleased that we requested additional copies. Unfortunately, they didn't have any.

An unbelievable rumor circulated on July 27. Republican forces had recrossed the Ebro River! Many were quite skeptical and some said it was impossible, but all were convinced of its truth the next morning when we ran past Tanky: standing at the doorway, he swung madly at us as we dashed by. Friendly guards and Hassan confirmed the rumor, and the news did more to spruce up our ranks and appearance in one day than Sticky had been able to accomplish in three months. Nor could our sergeants prevent the proud exchange of glances between the Spaniards and ourselves during the assembly before our evening meal.

In the *Diario de Burgos* of the twenty-ninth, we learned that the Red offensive had been paralyzed. Tex said, "That means we only advanced ten kilometers instead of 20." We laughed when we read Para Bellum, the paper's "real" military expert. He proved with his "in-depth" analysis that "one of the characteristics of the Reds has been not to recognize our superiority."

The British prisoners held at Palencia meanwhile were waiting impatiently to return to England, even though they had prisoner H. Jackson in the kitchen helping prepare meals to the British taste. Moreover, the British were beginning to feel about macaroni the way we felt about beans.

The Italian commander had a shortwave radio set. He invited Ed Konigsberg who knew Italian well, to his quarters daily to translate the BBC news broadcast.

When the prisoners learned from Ed about the recrossing of the Ebro, they staged a demonstration alongside the canal, singing the Republican anthem and "Bandiera Rossa." Girls in groups of two and three who were strolling on the other side of canal waved to them.

The Falangist leaders in Palencia heard about this and demanded that the commander punish the prisoners, or they would come in and do so. Informed by the commander of this threat, the British agreed that a half dozen could be tied to the barbed wire fence long enough for photographs to be taken to prove to the Falangists that they had been properly punished.[11]

* * * * *

"The Gestapo is coming! The Gestapo is coming!" The news that we were to be interrogated by the much feared German State Police, set up by Hitler to silence or "neutralize" all who opposed fascism, alarmed us. Today we consider it an honor to have had a dossier in that organization's records of the leading antifascists of the world, but then it was another matter.

The Gestapo had visited San Pedro in April to interrogate the Germans and Austrians. This time they would interrogate all, searching for officers and commissars, and for Communists, whom Hitler rightly regarded as his most dangerous enemies.

A few Americans had special reasons to worry. Lieutenant Norman Dorland had been attached to the 15th Brigade Staff and was our ranking military officer. Samuel Grant, small in size but a very cool and determined fighter, had received a 35th Division Award in March 1938 "for outstanding courage and meritorious service in the face of the enemy." Many had been members of the Communist Party or the Young Communist League. Sidney Rosenblatt was the Lincoln Battalion clerk when captured. I had been elected to the National Council of the YCL shortly before I came to Spain, and had served as battalion commissar for both the Lincoln and MacPap battalions.

But none of us confronted danger comparable to that facing tall, slim, white-haired Arthur Karlsson, who had appeared in the frontispiece of the Reese pamphlet. When Hitler came to power and outlawed the German CP, Karlsson worked underground in Nazi Germany. Ordered to leave by the CP, he escaped a jump ahead of the Gestapo. He worked in the Soviet Union until the fascist uprising, when he came to Spain as a tank commander. Captured along with a score more on the Madrid front, the beatings and torture, of which he was the sole survivor, had turned his hair white. Assuming the name Arthur Karlsson, he claimed to be a Swede. When brought to San Pedro, he polished up his Swedish background with the help of the Swedish prisoners.[12] We knew he faced death if his identity was discovered by the Gestapo.

Each of us had to decide what he would say. Almost all of us were in our twenties, and we valued our lives highly, wanting to return to our families and our communities to continue our fight against fascism and for democracy. Yet we did not want to harm the Republic, the International Brigades, or our fellow prisoners.

The House Committee proposed guidelines: Assume the rank of private, name only dead officers, deny Communist affiliation, express antifascist convictions, and make no derogatory statements about the Republic or the International Brigades. Answer questions about yourself innocuously; give no information about anyone else. Our freedom depended on the support of the antifascist people of the world. Any aid to the fascists would weaken that support and be unfaithful to our dead.

Each member of the House Committee passed this information verbally to the leaders of his nationality, and they in turn passed it on to key people. We issued no orders; nevertheless, our instructions were followed because they made sense and were what the prisoners themselves considered desirable. And knowing what fellow prisoners would say made it easier for all to do the same.

The Gestapo agents on their arrival briefed Alex on their plans. Several knew English well. Each German and Austrian (and each prisoner suspected of being either) would be interrogated for a half day, while the rest would be questioned for an hour. Each nationality would be called out alphabetically.

Alex immediately briefed our House Committee, which circulated the facts to curb the wild rumors. The committee thought it unlikely that the Gestapo would use force against prisoners from democratic countries. Violence might be tried on the weaker individuals, so our best course was to be firm and unflinching, without being impudent.

The Germans were questioned in small rooms near the guards' quarters, while the English-speaking were questioned in a small room close to the major's quarters. The chief interrogator sat behind a small wooden table with a chair in front for the prisoner. A second interrogator stood, or sat in another chair. Both wore civilian clothes.

No physical violence was reported the first day. The agents questioning the English-speaking prisoners were well enough informed about the USA and England to be able to trip up anyone who falsely claimed British or American citizenship. Their main concern was to find German and Slav antifascist leaders.

Czechs and Hungarians and prisoners from the Balkan region were shown pictures of underground leaders in those countries and asked if they knew them and if they had come to Spain. Martin Maki was asked what he thought about "Rosenfeld," the Jewish President of the United States, and whether he would like to finish his education in Berlin. During World War II, when Martin was in the 166th Infantry Battalion patrolling Florida beaches to watch for German agents coming ashore in rubber rafts, he took his work seriously.

We were all shown photos of devastated towns and villages, and were asked whether we thought it right that the Republican government should cause such suffering and destruction. In some we recognized damage inflicted by fascist bombing and artillery, which led to spirited exchanges between Gestapo and prisoner. Asked to identify photos of Marx, Lenin, Stalin, and Trotsky, most prisoners said they did not know them or gave wrong answers.

Finally we were taken to a field on the north side of the monastery. There we were ordered to strip, tie on a breech cloth and form a line in front of a table on which lay several calipers. Behind the table sat a Gestapo agent with a ledger. As each prisoner was identified, an assistant using the calipers called out the length, breadth, and depth of his skull, the distance between his eyes, the length of his nose, and described skin color, body type, wound scars, and any disability.

Next, each prisoner was instructed to stand in front of a camera for a front and side view and a closeup of the face. We were now "scientifically" classified.

As group chief, I was the last to leave. As I walked back, the photographer walked close to me, close enough that I could smell the alcohol on his breath. Catching my eye, he smiled, reached out his hand, and in Spanish said, "Here, take this for the boys. My son is a Red too." With a wink he handed me a twenty-peseta note. It made a nice addition to our house treasury.

When Arthur Karlsson didn't return for several hours, we feared the worst. When he did come back, he told us his white hair had helped convince them he was Swedish; and besides, "They are not very intelligent."

The interrogation of some of the German prisoners was brutal. Karl Loesch, a five-foot-six, slim twenty-three-year-old, had been hit in the head by a bullet at Teruel. When the call came to the hospital for all who could to go back to the front, Karl returned to the German 11th Brigade with his bandaged head. Placed in charge of a fortifications battalion, he had found himself behind the enemy lines. He evaded the fascists for six days and came within three kilometers of the Ebro before falling into the hands of an Italian division and being sent to Zaragoza.

There he told a fascist captain that the maltreated Spanish prisoners ought to be treated as prisoners of war. The angered captain threw him into a cell for the condemned. Mornings there might be a half-dozen Spanish prisoners in the cell. Another fifteen or so would be added during the day, but about that number would be taken out to be shot that night, and the process would start over the next day. Karl waited for his name to be called each morning until late April, when he was sent to San Pedro.

On his second day there he was called before the Gestapo. He gave Karl Schneider as his name, with a false birthplace, but refused to give any further information, except that when asked if he was a Communist, he said yes. They called in two Spanish sergeants who tried unsuccessfully with their sticks to beat him into talking, then threw him into the *calabozo*, where he was tended by a tall, blond Englishman. After several days of interrogation, the Gestapo informed him they would check on him in Germany. Karl used his spare time to learn some English.

Several weeks later, Karl was moved across the hall to a similar calabozo that held several Spanish Republican officers. Karl was appalled when he saw them taken out each day and returned with bloody fingers. He had the impression that they were ashamed that he should see the way fellow Spaniards were torturing them. Eventually he was returned to our quarters.[13]

Hermann Streit, a twenty-eight-year-old veteran in the fight against fascism, only five feet eight inches tall, but powerfully built with broad shoulders, had been battalion commissar in a German battalion in January 1937, until wounded. He was captured with part of the 3rd Company of the Thaelmanns on April 2, 1938, but he did not reach San Pedro until early summer of 1938, having served as a laborer in the interim. With the help of Czechs at San Pedro, Hermann had carefully prepared an alias, Hermann Strumm, born in the German part of Czechoslovakia.

When brought before the Gestapo for interrogation, he coolly gave them his alias. The reaction was immediate and loud. "You are a liar. You are Hermann Streit. Give him a beating and throw him in the *calabozo!*"

Hermann now knew one of the prisoners had betrayed him. He was held in the *calabozo* until the agents left to check their data against their master file of two million names. Herman was then returned to our quarters.[14]

*　　*　　*　　*　　*

On July 25, the unexpected happened. At 1 A.M., troops commanded by Líster, El Campesino, and Modesto crossed the Ebro on a forty-kilometer front. They advanced twenty-five kilometers toward Gandesa in three days, with no air or artillery support for the first two. Snow would be falling in November before Franco could retake the ground he lost in those three days.

All five International Brigades took part in the crossing, though by this time 75 percent of their soldiers were Spaniards.[15] So impetuous was the advance of the Lincoln battalion that several Americans were captured. Jack Cooper, an auto worker from Cleveland, Ohio, adjutant of the brigade machine-gun company, was out ahead with eight of his men when they were surrounded on the afternoon of the second day. Four Moors among the fascists would have executed Cooper had not young Spaniards intervened. He was brought before their commanding officer. The *Volunteer for Liberty* reported Cooper told him

we had Gandesa, and that by tomorrow [July 27th] we'd be in Calaceite. When they asked where our forces were, I answered, "Way ahead" pointing to the west.

"How many?" they questioned.

Without hesitation, I answered, "Five army corps."

Although worried, the fascists went on, hoping to break through the Republican lines, and picked up five more prisoners. Cooper and his fellow prisoners talked with their captors about conditions on both sides; two of the officers had relatives or friends in the United States. They spent the night on a hill, which was attacked by Republican forces. But the fascists didn't return fire, so the Republicans went on, believing no one was up here. Next morning observers reported Republican troops on adjacent hills. When planes came, Cooper told his captors, "Don't worry, they're ours."

The fascist troops were exhausted from lack of food and fear. Their officers conferred, and decided to turn themselves over to Cooper and his men.

It was dark most of the time we were with them, and they were pretty well scattered. It was not until we marched them to Brigade headquarters that I discovered there were 208 of them. Among them were six officers and 19 sergeants.[16]

Lieutenant Howard Goddard, from Los Angeles, and chief of brigade operations, also on the second day of the offensive, wanted to locate the Lincoln Battalion. Since his car wasn't available, he hopped on a motorcycle driven by Minuto, a Spaniard. They spotted a platoon of soldiers who fired at them.

Over the roar of the motorcycle, Goddard yelled to Minuto, "Go like hell!"

Instead, Minuto stopped in front of the soldiers and scolded them, "What's the idea of shooting at us? We're comrades!"

"We're not comrades, we're soldiers of Franco. *Manos arriba!*"

Goddard and Minuto were escorted up the side of a mountain. Goddard noticed their captors were all young and appeared uncertain what to do. A part of the Mora de Ebro garrison, they had been told to withdraw to Fatarella, where a stand was to be made. Goddard informed them we had already taken Fatarella. When they then decided to head for Corbera, he said that it was already ours.

Goddard pointed out to them that our soldiers were all around and they would be captured, but they need have no fear, for our prisoners of war were not harmed.

While we argued back and forth, with their spirits perceptibly drooping, we marched along. Presently we ran up against the spots where the Lincolns were fighting some fascists. By that time we had established better relations with the group of 15. They were all very curious and very friendly. The cabos [corporals] finally decided to talk it over with the men. When the conference was over, they decided to stack up their rifles and make a pile of their hand grenades, which they did. Then they returned my pistol, and turned themselves over to us as prisoners. . . .

After surrendering, they were happy for the first time since we had encountered them. They sang songs, and explained that all of them—except one—had relatives on our side, whom they were very anxious to see.[17]

* * * * *

The State Department could have made an accurate list of prisoners at San Pedro de Cardeña by comparing William Carney's list of seventy-five of July 11 with the seventy-seven in Charles Bay's letter of June 24,[18] using the home towns on both lists. But the Department did not, so there were long delays in answering queries, while unnecessary telegrams were sent to consuls for information. It sent telegrams to Barcelona, Valencia, and Seville inquiring about John Hollis Jenkins and Ignatz Moscowitz, although Carney had reported both were at San Pedro.[19]

To inquiries about names spelled exactly as on Bay's list, letters went out between July 21 and 23 reporting that they were at San Pedro. An information sheet was enclosed saying that an American consul had found us well and healthy, that we had filled out Red Cross forms, which were being forwarded, and that we needed money to buy tobacco, clothes, and toilet articles. (We needed them, all right, but clothes and toilet articles could not be purchased.) Our relatives could send money through the American Red Cross, and a mailing address for letters was included.[20]

On July 13, two days after Carney's article appeared, Friends of the Abraham Lincoln Brigade sent a letter to Hull confirming its offer to provide the money necessary to bring back Americans now held captive by Franco. David McKelvy White, who had returned from Spain to become national chairman of FALB, urged that a US representative visit all camps where Americans were held, with authority not only to ask that the men receive reasonably good care, including medical attention, but also to make inquiries about their release or exchange.

Hull telegraphed Bay on July 16 "to proceed to Burgos at the earliest practicable moment and endeavor informally to ascertain the reaction of the authorities to the proposal. Report results by telegraph. Transportation and per diem authorized."[21]

A copy went to Ambassador Bowers, who replied two days later that he had had no prior indication from the State Department that it was interested in securing the prisoners' release; he could long ago have had negotiations going on between De Rialp, representing Franco, and Del Vayo for the Republic. Hull telegraphed that the State Department couldn't act until FALB had made the offer to pay the costs.[22]

Why *was* a decision made at this point to look into our release or exchange? Undoubtedly, pressure from families and organizations contributed. And with the British government negotiating for the exchange of their nationals for Italians, there would be questions as to why the United States couldn't do the same.

James Clement Dunn, adviser on political relations in the State Department, informed FALB that steps would be taken to find out under what conditions Franco would release us, making no mention of the Department's success in obtaining Guy Castle's release under much more difficult circumstances.[23]

Ambassador Bowers, negotiating at last, was able by July 23 to announce that the Republic had informed him the latest proposal from Burgos was on the whole satisfactory, with a few details to be adjusted before the exchange could occur. Fourteen Americans were to be exchanged for fourteen Italian soldiers held by the Republic. Bowers thought the Republic had selected those seriously wounded and imprisoned the longest for exchange.[24] Fifteen Spanish and foreign aviators also were to be exchanged.

Three days later Hull received a telegram from Bay that he had seen Señor Vidal, a functionary in the Ministry of Foreign Affairs, who would take up an exchange with the foreign minister. Vidal had stated *release was impossible,* but exchange of some or all was quite possible and the conditions for an exchange would be given to Bay shortly.[25] Apparently, neither Bay nor Vidal knew what Bowers had already arranged.

The FALB officers were very pleased to read about the impending exchange of American prisoners, even though it presented them with a severe financial problem. White took advantage of his trip to the State Department on July 13 to see Ernest Swift, vice chairman of the American Red Cross, to inquire unofficially whether they could make funds available to bring back American prisoners. Swift's reply unofficially but firmly was no. But the Red Cross would forward funds to the prisoners, and would consider buying clothing and tobacco abroad to be distributed to them. White told Swift that FALB would provide five hundred dollars for that purpose.[26]

Numerous communications came to the State Department urging that it help us. All received similar replies. Josephine Wood, corresponding secretary of the Interprofessional Association at San Diego, wrote to Hull on July 23 on behalf of Marshall Garcia, Samuel Grant, Matthew Dykstra, and Henry Megquier of Los Angeles, and Howard Earl of Santa Monica, California. Pierrepont Moffat, chief, Division of European Affairs, answered for Hull, in the standard format: The men were at San Pedro, and with reference to

obtaining the release of these men, I regret to inform you that there appears to be no action which this Department can appropriately take at this time in this regard. . . . It is understood that negotiations are in progress between the two sides in Spain looking toward an exchange of prisoners, which may possibly include a number of Americans captured by the forces of Franco.[27]

The State Department received two lists on July 29. One was from Bay, correcting the spelling on his original list and adding seven names.[28] The second list came from David McKelvy White; the Carney names had been matched up against Bay's, and White had also added nineteen he believed were prisoners although they were not on Bay's list.[29] But while the State Department was working on our names, it was Ambassador Bowers who was working to get us back home.

16 Fourteen Americans Leave San Pedro

THE HOUSE COMMITTEE, worried about a return visit by the Gestapo, decided that officers and Communist leaders from fascist countries should be helped to escape. The rest would be urged to endure willingly any resulting hardships.

Alfred Richter, alias Robertus Van Dregt, a German Communist leader, together with Johannes Roselle from Holland and two others, escaped at the end of July.[1] We were in the meadow playing soccer with a ball we had made of old clothing. Yelling drew the attention of the guards, allowing the four to slip behind a hedge.

We stood in our columns of four a long time that evening as the count was repeated several times. Alex had to call the roll, over six hundred names, before the four missing Internationals were identified. Tanky and Sticky were furious and asked how the four had escaped. No one answered. Rin-Tin-Tin did not know.

That night a few men picked at random were taken downstairs and beaten. We were held in our quarters the next few days except for meals. The four escapees were back during the first week in August, badly beaten. They had been caught in Seville trying to board a foreign ship.[2]

The camp authorities, embarrassed that visitors had seen our ragged appearance, gave us grey smocks with half sleeves to cover our exposed areas. We received them just in time to make a fine appearance before our next visitor, a Spanish archbishop.

The second week of August we enjoyed another trip to the river. John Blair and Martin Maki were sitting under a tree when Tanky came to say it was time to return. He picked up an empty cigarette case. Written on it in Spanish was, "Victory for the Republic is certain—time will bear witness." Tanky accused John and Martin of having written the message and had them brought back under separate guard.

Martin reports they were taken before a tall black-booted lieutenant. He read the message, "then gave me a damn good boot in the rear," and ordered them held in the *calabozo*. John and Martin sat down to wait for their beating. But Ben, a six-foot 180-pound Dutch prisoner who was Alex's assistant, came instead. John and Martin asked that their handwriting be compared with the strange script on the paper. Tanky showed up with two sheets of paper and pencils and ordered them to write a sentence he dictated. Martin was then returned to our quarters, but John was held in the *calabozo* and within a week was taken away, for a rumored court-martial.[3]

Isaac Matson, born in Sweden in 1897, had come to Spain from Canada. A short, slender man, unassuming and uncomplaining, he had been losing weight and becoming steadily weaker. We did not know what ailed him. Finally, we got permission to transfer him to the infirmary. I picked him up in my arms and carried him down the stairs. There I said good-by to him, each of us knowing we would never see the other again. A Spanish prisoner carried him to the infirmary, were he died on August 18. Five Spaniards between eighteen and twenty-six were buried at San Pedro in August.[4] Of our six hundred Internationals, only one under the age of thirty died in eleven months.

On August 12, Jimmy Moon got back the Red Cross form he had sent on May 10. It was his first family news. Now Jimmy wrote a letter containing the address of Gloria Gonzalez in New York and asking that she be informed her brother was at San Pedro, and he enclosed a letter from Jack Mail, to be sent to a friend in San Francisco.[5] Although the censor held up the letter for two weeks, it reached Jimmy's parents on August 30. They immediately did as he had requested.

Jimmy sent another letter on August 21 telling his mother that letters, money, and a book had come through to some of the English prisoners. He added, "The more letters from home, the better. I don't think people understand the real significance of a letter, no matter how short and sweet it is." To gladden his mother's heart, Jimmy asked for a toothbrush.

A day later, through the IRC, Jimmy received 143 pesetas (two pounds) from his father. After he and his American neighbor had feasted on Nestlé's tinned milk, a coarse chocolate, biscuits, grapes, and bananas, Jimmy wrote to thank his father for the money and the book *Tarka, the Otter*. He noted that copies of the *Manchester Guardian*, the *Times*, and the *Observer* had arrived, and asked for a French novel or a newspaper to help him master French.[6]

Almost all, like myself, had no money and had been unaware of the canteen. Now those who received money faced ethical problems. "How and with whom shall I share this precious wealth? To whom shall I give tobacco? How much shall I give to a comrade in the sick room? Or to close friends?[11]

The House Committee discussed asking everyone to throw the funds they received into one pot to be shared with all. "But the parents sent in funds for their son, not for all the prisoners."

"That may be true, but he can then do whatever he wishes. We need aspirin and supplemental food for the ill and wounded, paper and pencils so that those who have no money can write letters home—and a ration of tobacco once in a while would be great. And we need funds for emergencies. Let's ask everyone who receives money to kick in a certain percentage to a House Fund."

"Fine. How much?"

That was a difficult question. Prisoners from fascist countries said this should be decided by those expecting to receive funds. The final decision was a not too generous 10 percent, which all gave. Responsibility for administering the fund was given to the representatives of nationalities who had no hope of receiving any. Kurt Scheffler, a German, became the treasurer.

Two German sociologists came to San Pedro to find out what kind of human being had enlisted in the International Brigades. They had a two hundred-item questionnaire, in English, German, French, and Spanish. It began with name, race and nationality, education, skills, jobs held, criminal record, family income, names and addresses of relatives. Then came political and social questions: Are you a Communist? What do you think of your government? What do you think of Russia, of the Spanish Republic and its policies, of the International Brigade and its leaders? Then ethical questions, including religious affiliation and beliefs. Finally, our views on free love, and the questions: "When did you first have sexual intercourse? With whom? How often? How often have you visited a house of prostitution? Are you a homosexual?"

The House Committee sent out word to present ourselves as paragons of virtue with strong democratic and antifascist beliefs. No information was to be given that would demean the International Brigades or the Republic. Give simple answers, such as: "What do you think of Russia?" "It's a big country."

Most Americans followed these guidelines. Our leading anarchist later boasted of his defiance, having painted himself as a sexual giant who had begun his exploits as a child with his mother. But his defiance had been limited; we learned that he had written that he had come to Spain to work!

I was frightened one afternoon a few days later when Sticky told me I was wanted at once. Without giving me an opportunity to say good-by, he escorted me downstairs to a small table placed in the shade of a tree. Behind it sat Hermanos Mios. He invited me to sit opposite him.

After gravely confirming my name, he asked: "How many wives do you have?"

This was not a question I was expecting, but after a moment I realized why it had been asked. In the box for "Religion" I had written "Mennonite," the religious denomination of my father's family. Hermanos Mios had confused Mennonite with Mormon. He was quite disappointed when I explained the difference.

Hermanos Mios then turned to a stack of photographs, views of badly damaged churches, and asked if I thought it was right for the Reds to destroy churches. I told him that the deadliest fire I had experienced had come from a church tower; it would not be necessary to fire at churches if the fascists did not use them as their principal fortifications. When he showed me the bombed and burned remains of Guernica, with only walls and chimneys standing, I asked him if he didn't know that Guernica had been destroyed by the German Condor Legion.

"How do you know that?"

"Someone who was at Guernica described it to me."

"What is his name?"

"I cannot tell you that. But I did not expect you to claim we destroyed Guernica when you must know that it is not true."

Hermanos Mios looked uncomfortable and dismissed me.

Tanky had a playful habit, after he had given his evening orders to our four group chiefs in an anteroom at the head of the stairway, of guessing the rank each of us had held in the Republican Army. When he turned to me, he always made the same remark. "And you, Carlos, you must have been a commissar."

We always laughed for the sergeant. One I tried a reply. "You are flattering me, Sergeant. Besides, you know that all commissars were shot when captured."

"I know they were supposed to be, but in your case somebody must have slipped up."

I don't know if my laughter fooled him. I had not forgotten that the Republic had given me the rank and responsibilities of a battalion commissar, and I did not lose them when captured. My concern was how best to carry them out under the circumstances. Sooner or later my rank would be uncovered by the fascist authorities but worrying about this did not seem to be of any use. Besides, one tends to make more of one's life if one lives each day as if it could be the last.

The major inspected our quarters and was struck by the writing on the walls—it was a disgrace. He called the group chiefs together and told us that the walls would be whitewashed and there would be no more writing on them. The next day a block and tackle was set up at a courtyard window, and huge pails of whitewash were hoisted up to obliterate our laboriously written study outlines. Fortunately, some students and instructors now had money to purchase pencils and small notebooks in the canteen, and the House Fund helped the others.

Sticky had several sergeants helping him, and he answered to a lieutenant, whom we seldom saw. The total military guard was approximately a hundred, responsible for some six hundred International and approximately three thousand Spanish prisoners. We were never told the sergeants' names so we made up our own; Navarro because he came from Navarre, Porky because of his appearance, Stinky because of his perfume, and Mad Moor because of the vicious way he hit us.

I still had the wristwatch I had received as a going-away present. One day I noticed a sergeant eyeing it. I asked Alex to sell it for me. I don't remember how much money I got, but I used some of it to buy a supply of paper and pencils for our school. I did splurge on one item, a hardcover copy of Cervante's *Don Quijote*, only to find its sixteenth-century Spanish quite difficult to read. Still, I spent many pleasant hours poring over it, as did others.

On the thirty-first we again enjoyed a trip to the river. The water was clear even though a storm on the twenty-ninth, with a particularly brilliant display of lightning, had raised the water level several inches. Some gathered watercress to add to their evening rations.

On August 27, 1938, *Diario de Burgos* carried a dispatch from Paris, reporting that the fascists had collected documents from more than a thousand dead foreigners, the majority of whom had arrived between May and July of 1938 to obtain high wages promised by the Communist International. The dispatch also claimed all officers and 80 percent of the soldiers of the 45th Brigade as well as the majority in the 11th, 13th, and 15th Brigades were French. We knew there were a few in the 13th and none in the others. The 14th was the French Brigade.

The dispatch also made General Walter an American. Not only was Walter a Pole, but he had left Spain before the recrossing of the Ebro. Another article from Paris reported that about two hundred Americans had just come to France as stowaways on the SS *Normandie*, on their way to Spain. Our seamen guffawed at that.

*   *   *   *   *

On July 25, 1938, David Amariglio, FALB's agent in Paris, asked US Ambassador Robert Murphy how cigarettes, chocolates, clothing, and medical supplies might be sent to the prisoners. Murphy suggested the International Red Cross,[7] and four days later, the IRC at Geneva received $500 from FALB.[8]

A week later an IRC delegate, Count Horace de Pourtales, was in Burgos to find out how supplies could be distributed to us. Pourtales recommended that small amounts of cash be given each prisoner to buy tobacco, food, and necessities and that clothing, including heavy overalls and good quality sneakers, be purchased in England and shipped to San Pedro.[9] On August 27, FALB sent an additional $635 to the IRC to provide each prisoner with $5 and to buy the clothing.[10]

On August 9, the *New York Times* reported Ambassador Bowers had arranged the exchange of fourteen American prisoners for fourteen Italian soldiers, and gave their names. Five names were badly spelled, but they were decipherable. FALB was puzzled only by one, John Berkley. It had no record of a volunteer by that name, let alone a prisoner.

John Berkley was a fiction, the creation of an intended act of kindness. Leo Berman was on the list of fourteen to leave. Well recovered from his leg wounds, he thought it was wrong that he should leave when his close friend, John O'Beirne (in his forties and suffering badly from arthritis), had to stay in San Pedro. John's slow movements had earned him many a blow from the sergeants. Leo proposed that John assume the name John Berkley and take his place on the list. He hoped that once John crossed the border into France, he would be able to return to Ireland. The ruse was discovered, but not before John Berkley had been placed on the exchange list sent to Ambassador Bowers.

On the twentieth, a dispatch from Carney carried the correctly spelled names, plus the mysterious Berkley. Carney also reported that French officials were puzzled why the US government would not take responsibility for repatriation of its nationals.

On August 1 the State Department completed another list of the American POWs at the San Pedro de Cardeña—this one numbering eighty-four. Most significant, however, was what it revealed about the Brigaders' occupations, forty in all. There were twelve seamen; five each of clerks, laborers, and salesmen; four each of chauffeurs, cooks, miners, and students; three each of journalists, mechanics, and steelworkers; two each of accountants, artists, and machinists; and one each of activities director, architect, assistant librarian, baker, bartender, brewery worker, circus roustabout, clothing-worker, construction worker, electrical engineer, furniture worker, glazier, interpreter, iron worker, labor organizer, locksmith, medical student, merchant, printer, realtor, roofer, sheet metal worker, stonecutter, teacher, telegrapher, upholsterer.[11]

Many individuals and organizations were sending letters and telegrams to the State Department on our behalf. The Finnish Workers Federation received a typical reply to its request to bring back Martin Maki: There was no action the Department could take toward the release of American volunteers. It enclosed the standard information sheet about San Pedro.[12]

Two attempts to exchange Frank Ryan went awry. The first was a proposal to exchange him for an Italian sergeant, turned down by the Italians on August 10. The second was to exchange him for José López Pinto. But López was to be exchanged for Felix Miaja Isaac, the son of General José Miaja. More fortunate were eight Soviet sailors, captured when their ship was sunk by a submarine. They were exchanged on August 18 for eight German civilians held by the Republic.[13]

*   *   *   *   *

A handwritten notice was circulated among all English-speaking prisoners during the first week of September.[14]

SAN PEDRO INSTITUTE OF HIGHER LEARNING
Free and Non-Sectarian
FALL SCHEDULE OF CLASSES

Second term will begin September 22 for three months with Advanced and New courses.

Unpopular courses have been dropped.
Any course desired will be given if instructor can be found.
Have Reference Library of 6 texts, a dictionary, more than a
ream of paper plus miscellaneous supplies and 160 pesetas in cash from
voluntary donations.

NEW COURSES (*Tentative*)

Plane and Descriptive Geometry—3 p.m.
Spanish History—to be arranged.
Dramatics—4 p.m.
Analytical Mathematics—9:45 a.m.

Other nationalities organized courses, but no other group had such a large number to draw from. About 160 spoke English, 100 Spanish, and 100 German. Some 60 spoke French and another 60 Portuguese.

Al Ziegler, a poet of sorts, taught analytical mathematics. Captured on March 10, Al now wrote a "Prayer from Jail."

> Dear God, I've never prayed to you to do
> the things I want you to
> I've figured that you're always just
> When things go wrong I guess they must
> I've realized in your great domains
> Sometimes time lacks for human pains.
>
> And so I've lived—not perfect, true
> But all my faults I've left for you
> To punish or grant mercy 'cause
> I know you've sympathetic laws.
>
> I promise not to whine again
> Down in this world of little men
> But six months now have passed away
> A second in your infinite play
> But in this little world dear God
> Six months in jail is very hard
> So I let out this little whine
> to hope you get around sometime. [15]

But Al also believed in helping himself, and got a British prisoner to include in his letter one to Al's family.

After all these months of silence I suddenly receive three inquiries [on Red Cross forms] and three letters in about three days plus an anonymous fourteen pesetas which I suspect is from Mrs. Spitzer, not to mention seventy-two more from Daddy Ziegler.

Arthur Oehlke, one of the three letter writers, had sent Al

three swell pictures of Grace. A Slav here weaved me a handsome frame out of old cement bag paper. I hope I get a chance to show you this remarkable sample of prison art some day—some day soon.

Some unknown female philanthropist has been sending the American prisoners newspapers and magazines from Boston, and we have been getting periodicals from England.[16]

On September 6, death came suddenly to Erling Nordstrom, a Norwegian volunteer.[17] Born in Trondheim, Norway, Erling was thirty-one and in good health. We suspected he had caught a blow on the head, but it was not until I was doing research in the archives of the ministry of Foreign Affairs in Madrid in 1981 that I learned he had died of a cerebral hemorrhage.[18]

The first week in September all prisoners received a summer-weight khaki shirt, a pair of breeches that buttoned up the calf, and *alpargatas*— canvas shoes with soles of braided cord.[19] The new clothes arrived just in time for the British prisoners to show them off to visitors.

The widow of Austen Chamberlain, former foreign minister and brother of Neville Chamberlain, the British prime minister, was the first accompanied by a gentleman with monocle, cane, and spats.[20] Kearney Cassells, who slept next to me at the time, gave me a first-hand account of her inspection of the British prisoners.

The fifty-two British and fifteen Irish were lined up in our assembly area, and Sticky rehearsed *"Rompen filas!"* several times to make sure no one had forgotten the "Fran–co" salute with uplifted arm. Then a heavy shower soaked them.

As Lady Chamberlain and her escort came out of the major's office after the shower, Sticky barked, snapping the bedraggled to attention. Then came *"Rompen Filas!"* Everyone stood at ease, but not a single arm was raised and no one cried out "Fran-co." Sticky was furious, but he was too cold a hand to repeat the order.

Now milady boldly went up to the first prisoner. She asked a few questions, then went on to the next. Soon she started to skip some. When she came close to Kearney, he could hear she was asking where the prisoner had come from and why he had come to Spain. All said they had come to stop fascism before it came to England. This was not the answer she had been led to expect by Franco's propaganda, which was that they had come to look for work. As she approached Kearney, she turned to her escort and said, "All right, you ask an intelligent one."

The escort moved in front of Kearney, who was wearing his black-and-white checked cap for the occasion, hemmed and hawed, fussed with his cravat, and then asked: "Rawther ghastly, wot?"

Kearny, not to be outdone, came back with "Raaawtherr."

We appreciated her visit, for that evening we each received three small lettuce leaves with our beans, the first fresh vegetable in six months.

The next day's visitor was a reporter for the *Weekly Review,* a British magazine. It was raining, so he visited indoors; the British were able to show him our sleeping quarters and the toilet and washing facilities. He agreed they stank.

Colonel C. C. Martin, the British military attaché in Burgos, came the next day, Saturday September 10, with the news that negotiations for an exchange of prisoners were under way.[21] We had prepared a list of names of the American prisoners to give to the colonel, including two who had just arrived: Tom Brown, a black from St. Louis captured across the Ebro River, and Eulogio Caricedo Martínez, a nineteen-year-old born in Morenci, Arizona, and brought to Spain as a child. We asked the colonel to tell Consul Bay that we still were not allowed to write letters and that scurvy had made its appearance.[22]

The next day, a quiet Sunday afternoon, we were in our quarters waiting for the bugle to call us for our evening sermon and meal. A loud explosion and a thud beneath us drew us to the patio windows. Both archway guards were sprawled on the ground. The first guard who ran over fainted. Others came running, yelling for the stretcher: but when it was brought, they didn't know who to carry away. One guard obviously was dead, but they were unable to see anything wrong with the other two.

We learned from Alex that one of the archway guards had been standing with his head over the end of the barrel of his rifle. It discharged accidentally and had lifted the top of his skull, his brains spilling out as he fell. His companion had fainted at the sight, as had the first guard who had run over.

No game occupied so much of our time as chess. Among the English-speaking, Hy Wallach was undisputed champion. When attending Jefferson High in Brooklyn, he had won the New York interscholatic chess championship. Only two could test his mettle: Radavoy Nicolitch, a Yugoslav, and Marco Sinaglia, an Argentinian. After having learned the fundamentals and gained some skill, everyone's ambition was to beat Hy at least once.

We had about thirty sets and boards. Hy made a sporting offer—he would play all simultaneously. One afternoon we set up our boards and told ourselves, "Today I am going to beat Hy!"

Hy took his place in the center. He barely stopped long enough to move his piece for the first half-dozen rounds. Then he began to spend a few more seconds at each board, giving us more time to think. No one spoke, the only sound that of lost pieces being dropped into receptacles.

We were concentrating on our middle game when in came Tanky. Suspicious that we were up to some subversive activity, he demanded to know what was going on. When we explained that Hy was playing against all of us, Tanky was dumbfounded. He had never heard of such a thing. As he watched Hy, stopping only a few moments in front of each board and then going on to the next, Tanky slapped his thighs, unabashedly showing his astonishment. I must give him credit for being human enough not to break up our chess games that day. Hy won all but two matches, and they were draws. I was one of the losers.

Sergeant "Blue Boy" (because he usually wore a blue coverall) did not as a rule carry a stick, and he treated us decently. Through Hassan he informed us that if we obeyed his orders, we had nothing to fear from him. We did ask the Americans to obey him at least as promptly as we did a stick-toting sergeant, but there were a few who responded slowly, muttering taunts.

Blue Boy was replaced on September 18 by sergeants Díaz and Navarro, who made it plain that their sticks were meant to be used.[23] I suspect they were brought in not for our failure to respect Blue Boy but as a retribution for the British refusal to salute and because of a general increase in our defiance, especially noticeable in sloppy saluting and the shouting of obscene versions of "Fran–co."

Díaz, Navarro, and Tanky, under Sticky, now went to work on us. Tanky swung more viciously as we left our quarters. Anyone slow to respond to an order was sure to get several whacks. Failure to salute properly could mean a stretch in the *calabozo*, after a painful beating. Also, the British were no longer allowed to send letters home, and we were no longer permitted to sing folk songs in the evening. There was some change in our behavior, but what the sergeants did not see was that their violence was making us stronger antifascists.

When I called Tex's attention to the headline in *Diario de Burgos* of September 21, 1938, "Franco Is Defending Civilization," his reply was brief. "Yeah, with a club."

Five more Americans joined us in September: Ray Anderson, from Los Angeles, but born in Lake City, Minnesota; Sydney Harris; and Otto Lemke, Marzo Lionetti, and Fred Salvini from New York. Syd and Otto had been in a hospital since April; the others had been captured during the fighting across the Ebro.

The fourteen prisoners who were being exchanged left San Pedro on September 23.[24] The next day there was pandemonium in our quarters; the remaining Americans each received 54.10 pesetas from the Friends of the Lincoln Brigade through the IRC.[25] Reactions ranged from quiet contemplation to joyous babbling about what could be done with so much money. Even the House Committee had a problem; what to do with nearly four hundred pesetas. Some who wanted to go right down to the canteen found it was now off limits. The major knew if he were to let us loose there, nothing would be left for the guards and the Spanish prisoners. So now we had money, and no place to spend it!

Someone suggested we ask the major to send a truck to Burgos to buy the things we wanted. The major insisted on a single order for each item. This proved to be quite a task: keeping records and combining orders for seventy-one individuals, who had numerous excited questions and requests for changes, sorely trying the order-takers' patience.

The most popular items were tobacco, cigarette papers, rope cigarette lighters, canned sweetened milk, chocolate, biscuits, and sausage. Fresh vegetables and fruits we hoped to get from the farmer's wife and daughter. We also ordered notebooks, pencils, a Spanish-English dictionary, aspirin, and first-aid materials.

A few of the more foresighted bought a braided string of large Spanish onions from the farmer's wife, and hung it up on the wall above their mattresses. One enterprising American, Ed Hodge, even opened up a small store.

The euphoria generated by our sudden wealth made us tend to ignore the sergeants' blows for a few days while we relished foods and tobacco we had not tasted in seven months.

Late in September, I was one of several Americans who went to the assembly area to talk with Merwin K. Hart, head of a group of anti-New Deal businessmen, and a Franco supporter. His questions surprised me. He was genuinely interested in learning why we had come to Spain rather than how, and what our life was like in the camp. He listened carefully to what we had to say as we described the unsanitary conditions and lack of medical care, the free use of sticks by the sergeants and the refusal to let us write to our families.

He offered to communicate with our families, if the major consented. We gave him names and addresses and asked him to tell them we were well, would like letters from them, clothing, tobacco, and a small monthly stipend. Remembering what had happened to Ornitz after he had talked with Carney, we wondered if the same thing would happen to us. It did not. Hart had not labeled those who spoke to him as troublemakers, as Carney had.

Three weeks later my wife was surprised by a letter from the president of the New York State Economic Council, Merwin K. Hart.

I write to say that I found your husband in apparently good health and as well satisfied perhaps as one could be under similar circumstances. It is not a very satisfactory life from the standpoint of those who are in the camp; but I do not see how it could be so. War is a serious business. All of the men stated they would like to have money, clothing and tobacco sent them. It would be particularly useful to send them clothing because some kinds of clothes are hard to obtain in Nationalist Spain.[26]

Hart was sympathetic to Franco's cause, but he was a decent American in his relations with us.

*   *   *   *   *

I spent May and June of 1981 in Spain doing research, and I asked scores of officials, from officers of the Association of Ex-Prisoners to heads of archives where I could find the records of the concentration camps. No one knew. Then in the archives of the Ministry of Foreign Affairs in Madrid, in a file of foreign-office correspondence, I found a letter from the Italian ambassador thanking Marquës de Rialp for a list of prisoners at San Pedro. But I could not find the list.

I had a fifteen-day Eurail pass and was to leave Madrid on Saturday, July 11, for Geneva to visit the IRC archives, interview former Swiss and German prisoners, and end at Erfurt, East Germany, where I had a room reservation for the twenty-fifth.

Twenty minutes before closing time on my last day in Madrid, Friday, July 10, I found the list of foreign prisoners held at San Pedro, issued on September 10, 1938, by Franco's General Staff. It had the names of 653 prisoners, with places and dates of birth and military units. I quickly filled out and handed in the required form.

The supervisor informed me that the copying facilities were closed and refused to have a copy made. I knew who made the copies, an elderly, tall, gaunt Spaniard. When the supervisor was not looking, I showed him my name, number 208 on the list. He looked at me in astonishment. "You were at San Pedro?"

"For eleven months."

"I was at León for eighteen months, where there were eighteen thousand prisoners. Where were you captured?"

"Between Gandesa and Calaceite on April 1."

"I was captured on the same front in April. I was with the Campesinos. "May I have a copy of these names to take with me today?"

"Of course. I'll make it right now."

The sixteen pages cost me eighty cents. In my excitement I failed to note the reference number for the list, but the survivors of San Pedro in Switzerland, Germany, England, Canada, and Cuba did not question its authenticity when I showed them their names.

The 653 prisoners were born in thirty-eight countries and the Free City of Danzig and the Saar. The 100 British and an unknown number of Italians had left San Pedro before the list was made. Of the 653, forty-two reported they had not fought for the Republic and were listed as farmers or businessman. (See Appendix 2.)

The large number of nationalities presented more of a problem to our captors than to us. We had a strong common bond that helped us to see each other as equals and to stand together.

The officers in charge of us knew only Spanish, and relied on Alex, Hassan, and the group chiefs for communication. But Sticky amazed us one day when he spoke Tagalog with Servando Acevedo, the fifty-two-year-old Filipino. Over sixty years old, Sticky had spent some forty years in the

Spanish Army, and before the United States took the Philippines from Spain, he had served there.

Half the prisoners came from countries having some form of dictatorship, and they could not communicate with their families or receive any help from them. To go back to their countries would mean imprisonment in notoriously cruel jails.

In mid-September ten German prisoners were suddenly taken away.[27] This was a warning to the remaining Germans. Preparations began in earnest for six to escape.

$$* \quad * \quad * \quad * \quad *$$

The Lincoln 3rd Company had seventy men on the morning of September 7, 1938, but only eight that evening. The day before, the 15th Brigade had been sent into the Sierra Caballs to prevent a threatened breach. Manuel Aznar, a Franco historian, explained the importance of the Sierra Caballs:

it was not possible to exploit the initial success if at the flank the formidable position of Sierra Caballs was not taken, a stupendous observatory from which the reds dominated the whole plain of Gandesa.[28]

Captain Milton Wolff had led the Lincolns back into the lines at night, with the 3rd Company occupying a hill on the left flank. During the night they saw the fascists capture a hill on their left rear, so Larry Lustgarten was sent back to Wolff to get an order to abandon their now untenable position, though meanwhile they would try to hold it. Before Larry could return, the fascists had attacked from the front and the rear.[29]

Some forty Lincolns were captured. When their captors heard a foreign language, they halted the march to the rear and ordered all foreigners to step to one side. About twenty did so, and a machine gun opened up on them. Juan, a Lincoln Spaniard, was thirty feet away and cannot forget the sight of men falling and blood flowing.[30] (The names of fourteen of the Americans are on the list of those killed on September 7, 1938 on page 266–267.[31])

Between July 25 and September 24, when the Lincolns left the front for the last time, only seven Americans survived capture, other than those who talked their captors into surrendering to them. Four more Americans were killed after capture. The names of the survivors are on page 260–263 and of those killed on 263–267.

M. V. Miller, of the British Foreign Office, trying to locate missing British volunteers at the end of the war, reported:

I am informed confidentially that any International Brigader taken in the Ebro offensive was asked one question, "When did you come to Spain?" If he replied after the 19th July 1936 he was shot *sin formación de causa* [without trial].[32]

The British Commission for the Exchange of Prisoners held its first meeting on September 1, 1938. The Republic proposed that both sides suspend death sentences for one month to give the commission time to get its work started, and invited the chairman, Field Marshal Sir Philip Chetwode, to visit the Republic.

Chetwode accepted, and the Republic sent cars and an escort to bring him to Barcelona, where he met President Manuel Azaña; Premier Negrín, who provided a house for him; Minister of State Del Vayo, and José Giral, the cabinet minister in charge of prisoner negotiations. Chetwode reported to Lord Halifax, the British foreign secretary, that the Republic genuinely wanted to exchange prisoners. The only untoward incident occurred when, invited

to a dinner, he assumed from what he had heard in London that the "reds" would appear without coats and in jeans and dressed accordingly. He was horribly embarrassed to find the guests, mostly of the government, in evening dress, and the scene quite like one in London.[33]

At the Franco border, Chetwode was kept waiting five days and then had to hire a cab to go to Burgos. Franco was at the front, and Count Jordana explained to Chetwode that they could not suspend executions; they executed only those who had committed abominable crimes and had been convicted after a fair trial.[34] Two weeks later Chetwode returned to England. Bowers learned from the British embassy that it had little hope anything would be accomplished.[35]

*   *   *   *   *

A very modest young man with a strong belief in democracy had joined the International Brigades in April 1938. James P. Lardner, son of Ring Lardner, America's beloved short-story writer, had come to Spain as a correspondent for the Paris edition of the *Herald Tribune*. His friends Herbert Matthews and Ernest Hemingway were unable to dissuade him from joining up.

Brigade officers assigned Jim to a safe job with a unit in the rear, in charge of malcontents and misfits. He didn't stay there long. Early in May he was at the Lincoln headquarters with his horn-rimmed glasses and a knapsack loaded with books. Milton Wolff felt he could do more good behind the lines than at the front, but reluctantly assigned him to a company.

The grousing and bitter complaints of the men did not discourage Jim. Rather, as he learned of their horrible experiences during the March and April retreats and watched them training recruits, his admiration for them grew. Jim quickly gained the respect of the men in his company. His mild appearance and manner fooled some larger men. He agreed to wrestle them, and promptly flopped them on their backs, for he was a skilled wrestler. His generosity, his dry sense of humor, his uncomplaining accept-ance of poor food, exhausting marches, fleas and lice marked him as a good soldier.

He crossed the Ebro with his unit, and on the third day his squad helped escort some prisoners back to the river. On the way back, Jim climbed a tree near the river to pick some fruit. Bombers struck at the bridge and missed, instead getting Jim in the buttock. The wound was not serious and in a short time he was receiving good-natured ribbing and being asked why he didn't have sense enough not to come back.

Jim now survived the worst shelling and bombing the Lincolns had experienced, losing only his glasses in the process. His value as a soldier can be judged by the reply George Watt, the Lincoln commissar, gave Alvah Bessie when he asked to have Jim fill an opening on the Brigade bulletin. This would have taken Jim out of the lines most of the time, but Watt said Jim was one of his best men and a fine squad leader. Wolff also did not want to let him go because of his value to the battalion.[36]

Late on September 22, Jim came back from the rear, where he had had a tooth pulled. The Lincolns had just taken new positions. Elman Service, a close buddy of Jim's who was in a hospital that day recuperating from a wound, later received a letter from Jim's mother asking him to find out what had happened to Jim. Service questioned everyone at Ripoll, where the Americans had been assembled to await repatriation.

Some Loyalist outfit was supposed to be on an adjacent hill. Someone was sent out to contact this outfit and returned without any success (somebody told me scouts were sent out more than once). I forget who was company commander then, but he evidently thought the adjacent hill truly was occupied by our people and that our scout(s) had lacked the guts to go far enough, and this was probably true: I remember several people said, "Sure, how in hell are you going to go up a hill occupied by any Spaniards (many of whom were about 16 years old then) and not get killed?" Anyway, the commander finally sent Jim (in charge, as he was a cabo then), Nowakowski, and a Spanish kid. Jim left them at the bottom of the hill and went up alone, according to Nowakowski. Guns went off and grenades exploded and I would suppose this is what killed him. He probably just walked right up confidently to introduce himself. He had a kind of total guts and determination. But he had no experience and was practically blind at night. His vision was only 20/200 (same as mine) and we both busted our glasses. He wouldn't have said anything to the C.O. about this.[37]

Whether Jim was killed as he approached the enemy position, or was taken alive and then killed, is not known. Several weeks later, Hemingway told Ring Lardner Jr., Jim's brother, that a correspondent on the fascist side had informed him a corpse with press credentials had been found on that battlefield.

Jim undoubtedly would have said he did no more than many another

Lincoln volunteer. I do not agree. In devotion to the cause of democracy, and in willingness to make personal sacrifices on its behalf, there were few, if any, who ranked above James P. Lardner.

Twenty-four hours after Jim was killed, the Lincoln Battalion left the front lines to be sent home.

17 The Big Escape

THE GESTAPO returned the first week in October to interrogate the Germans once more. Olaf Domnauer, a tall, blond, Aryan-appearing Jew from Berlin, recalls that he was questioned for three hours, only to be told that they were not interested in him, only in Aryans. Later he learned that he had been deprived of German citizenship two weeks earlier. [1]

The camp authorities at the same time renewed their efforts to get prisoners to name officers and communist leaders. A Cuban told me he had overheard two "rats" discussing letting the authorities know that I was a battalion commander.

I lost no time in getting the House Committee together. One rat openly claimed to have deserted to the fascist side, and the other made no secret of his fascist sympathies. Would moral and ethical arguments affect their behavior?

George Delich, a forty-year-old Yugoslav, was the Balkan representative on our committee. He had lived for many years in the United States and was a veteran of many labor struggles. After listening to our discussion, George said, "We don't want to take a chance on losing Carl, because of the kind of person he is, and because we need him here. I know those rats. There is only one way to deal with them, and it is not by reasoning with them. We have to let them know in no uncertain terms that if Carl is taken away, there will be two dead rats in San Pedro."

The others agreed. But how would we do it?

"Let me tell them," said George, "I think they will believe me."

The others smiled; George, though not quite six feet tall, was tough, with powerful hands and a very rugged long face. If anyone could strike fear in the rats, it would be George. I favor persuasion over violence or threats of violence when dealing with a fellow human being, assuming he does not have a weapon in his hand and is not trying to kill me. But in this case, I was willing to make an exception.

That evening, George came over to me and said, "Carl, I don't think those two rats are going to sleep too well tonight."

"Why is that?"

"They are worrying that somebody else might turn you in and they'll get the blame."

Colder weather kept us in our quarters, and attendance at the San Pedro Institute of Higher Learning reached its peak in October. Syd Harris described one of the new classes:

We had all these Portuguese who couldn't read or write, so Herman Lopez started a class . . . for them. And you could see them with their wooden slates and a hunk of glass they found somewhere, a pencil or so, and they're erasing their slates every day and writing ma–madre and pa–padre and in a few weeks they're handwriting letters back to their wives or their mothers in those little villages in Portugal and writing real postcards. Lopez did a fantastic job. . . . I remember sitting down with him and he is going over the letters . . . they're short, but because of the flowery language and the idiomatic expressions—they were beautiful.[2]

Maurice Levitas, a bit slow to respond to an order, was given "a bit of a bashing" by Tanky and thrown into the *calabozo*. The day he came back, the English were brought into the assembly area to listen to the reading of a new pamphlet. The call for a volunteer to read brought no response. Tanky asked the first one in line if he was English. He said he was Scotch. The next one claimed to be Irish. The sergeant was puzzled; all were supposed to be English. Then he spotted Maurice and called on him.

Maurice had to read aloud a pamphlet written by the Catholic bishop of Bilbao claiming the Republic had destroyed Guernica and calling for support of Franco. Returning to his quarters, he found a large supply of them in English, French, and German had been distributed and were being used for personal hygiene. The French had been called down two days earlier, and had taken a bit of clubbing before one of them read it. The Germans had been spared the beating when one volunteered.[3]

Looking through Jimmy Moon's library, I picked up *Cloud Howe* by Lewis Grassic Gibbons. I was immediately taken by the lilting and cadenced language, and borrowed it. The author wrote sympathetically of the problems faced by a young woman growing up in an impoverished area of the Scottish highlands and how this experience had shaped her character. It was the first volume of a trilogy and Jimmy had the other two, *Sunset Song* and *Grey Granite*. For a while I could forget San Pedro as I followed the life of the central character, described in a lovely prose.

We received our second typhoid shots on October 31, having received the first a few days earlier. They were administered mercilessly in the buttock.[4] These shots gave rise to a host of rumors, ranging from typhoid epidemics among the Spaniards to preparations to send us home.

On October 13, Bowers telegraphed Hull that "all Franco papers are running almost hysterical articles in large black type and in 'boxes,' and editorials with interviews denouncing the idea of mediation" (ending the war through negotiation) as treason. Bowers also said visitors from Franco Spain reported the people were war-weary and discouraged over the three months' failure on the Ebro. The object of the press campaign was "to intimidate growing desire for mediation among the people."[5]

*   *   *   *   *

At least half the American prisoners had been members of the Communist Party or the Young Communist League before they left for Spain, the majority for less than two years. Some had been in factory groups, and would have been dismissed had their membership become known to management. In San Pedro, the consequences could be far worse.

The Scottish and English Communist groups that had formed at Alcañiz and Zaragoza quickly merged into one at San Pedro. Among the Americans, however, there was no organization until the second half of April 1938. Instead, we worked together to raise prisoner morale without inquiring about party membership. No one thought it wise to ask, "Are you a member of the CP or YCL?"

Few of the prisoners knew who was on our International Committee, later known as the House Committee, yet its recommendations, passed on by word of mouth, were widely accepted. The party groups served as advisers to the committee and supported its decisions. Within two months, at the initiative of the English-speaking groups, the House Committee was formally set up with a representative for each large national section and for each group of nationalities with few members.

A small American CP group (no YCL group was ever formed) developed around the middle of April. Its first task was to lift morale and to convince all to declare themselves antifascists who had come to fight for the Republic and to avoid statements that could harm the Republic or our reputation.[6]

Early in May the group discussed how to provide maximum participation of members in decision making while maintaining security. It was agreed to set up groups of three. One from each group would meet with two other representatives of their respective groups of three to form the next higher body and so on up to the top. A requirement for admission to a CP group was a desire to rejoin the International Brigades.

But problems arose that required decisions within an hour, barely giving the top committee time to consider what to do. Consequently, the groups of three would be left out of the decision-making process. When there was time, and problems were considered first by the groups of three, conflicting decisions usually came back. Whatever the top committee decided, some groups had to be convinced of its correctness, frequently by someone who might himself have favored a different decision. Also it was difficult to find safe places and times for serious discussions. And the small groups didn't always have adequate information, resulting in poorly considered suggestions.

This procedure seriously slowed up the decision-making process and weakened the top committee's authority, leading eventually to attacks on the leadership as incapable because it did not function well. The British had a top committee of five, all experienced CP members, and its decisions were passed down through chains of individuals to be carried out; there was little complaint about their good and timely decisions.

As former members of the American CP and YCL became aware that a CP organization existed, more wanted to join and were accepted gladly. However, one applicant, a powerful ruddy volunteer noted for his rank-and-file union militancy back home, had carried that militancy over into the ranks of the Lincoln battalion, and had been stripped of his company commissar's insignia when he put the interests of his company above that of the battalion and the brigade.

When captured, he had stated he had come to Spain to work. At San Pedro, he agreed to say he had come to fight, but for a time he went along with those who attributed our capture to mistakes in Republican leadership rather than the overwhelming manpower and material thrown against us. This man's experience at leading rank-and-file union groups had taught him he could gain recognition by defying the bosses. But in San Pedro unorganized acts of defiance led only to retribution without any gain for us.

He was admitted, but whenever a decision came down to his group that was not in agreement with his ideas, he found it difficult to go along with it. After the fourteen Americans had left, he came to me with serious charges, including cowardice, against some of the top committee members. He proposed a meeting of all CP members to elect a new top committee. I told him I thought holding such a meeting would be dangerous. Shortly after this a newspaper, *Undercrust,* appeared with an attack on the "Secret Six," whose names it revealed. While it did not directly say they were CP leaders, most Americans were alarmed by the danger to which those named had been exposed.

This brought matters to a head. The *Undercrust* staff were close friends of the defiant member. He was asked to come to a meeting of representatives of the British and American top committees. The British recommended we use their form of organization—choose a top committee of three in our case, with power to make decisions without prior discussion below. This recommendation was accepted. In view of the serious accusations that had been made, a meeting would be held to elect the American top committee of three. Only nine members attended that meeting (I was not there), and they elected three of the "Secret Six."

As chief of the English-speaking prisoners on my floor, I worked very closely with the new committee, and in my opinion, the CP from then on worked more effectively. *Undercrust* was discontinued. A campaign for more democracy had brought about a less democratic form of organization, but one that provided better leadership.

*   *   *   *   *

On October 5, 1938, Consul Bay telegraphed Hull that "[Vidal at Burgos] stated it was *wholly impossible to consider the release* of American prisoners but he would be glad to receive any concrete proposal for their exchange" (emphasis added.)[7]

Three days later fourteen American prisoners crossed the bridge to Hendaye in France. Ambassador Bowers, who had arranged the exchange, noted in his telegram to Hull that this was the first exchange of army personnel since the war began. The fourteen Americans had waited two weeks in Ondarreta Prison in San Sebastian, until fourteen Italian prisoners had been picked up by a British warship. Hull had refused to allow a US naval vessel to pick them up.

It was noon on October 8 before the exchange formalities were completed at the bridge. The prisoners were instructed to walk across as their names were called. Fourteen names were called, including John Berkley. This left Leo Berman standing there. The IRC representative asked Leo his name.

"Berman, but my name was skipped."

"Son, you are the fourteenth. Hurry up and cross."[8]

Leo hurried, thankful that the representative was not a stickler for names. Bowers, who waited at the other end of the bridge, described those first few minutes to Hull:

after their first question as to who had won the World Series, they plied me with questions about the international situation, asking questions that were more intelligent than the average. When I suggested to one of their leaders, a former newspaper man, that they refrain from giving out any bitter interviews on their treatment, since it might operate against their friends still in prison, I was told that they had . . . decided on that course. I was most favorably impressed with their gentlemanly conduct, the absence of bitterness in their talk, their courtesy to everyone who approached them. Carney, of the *New York Times,* whom they heartily dislike, was treated in a friendly manner to my surprise.[9]

Bowers turned the fourteen men over to David Amariglio of the FALB, who had come from Paris with travel money for them. The first step was vaccination, then a shower with hot water, real soap, and a towel. Ah, civilization!

The French police commissioner said that the Americans could not go on the train in their worn uniforms. Amariglio purchased blue denim coveralls, shorts, and socks for them. Properly attired, they had lunch, on a plate with a cup and saucer, a fork, a knife and a spoon, on a white tablecloth. Fresh bread, wine, ham and eggs—all were things to wonder at and to enjoy. After lunch they went to a barber shop for a shave and trim.

Sam Romer, a prisoner and a socialist journalist, later wrote in an article that

we met Mr. Carney again, on the French side of the international bridge. We accused him of outright lying, and he blandly admitted it. Shamelessly he told us that he lied because "it was the only way to get the story out"—another falsehood, since he could have sent it from France. His unqualified statement that we all admitted having been recruited by the Communist Party or the North American Committee was preposterous; the subject was never mentioned in the interview, and the facts were otherwise.[10]

Carney's dispatch on the exchange at the bridge falsely quoted Amariglio as having said FALB was an auxiliary of the Communist Party and that the Communist Party had provided most of the money necessary to send the volunteers to Spain.[11]

At seven that evening the fourteen left on a sleeper for Paris. They were going to sleep between sheets—"Oh boy, smell how clean they are! And on a mattress. And no fleas and no lice—what more could you ask for?" And as each one thought of all that had passed since he had last slept between sheets, of the many times death had barely missed him, and remembered his comrades whom death had not missed, he felt the burden fascism was placing upon the world. But now he would sleep without worrying about what Franco's minions might do to him on the morrow.

Before they boarded the *Queen Mary* at Le Havre, each was outfitted with a new suit, shirt, overcoat, hat, and shoes.

As they approached New York on October 18, they received a greeting from Albert Einstein. At the dock they were met by a band and several hundred veterans and relatives for a parade up Broadway.[12] That evening Norman Dorland spoke at a dinner at the Hotel Commodore, launching a drive for $150,000 to bring back the remaining Americans who had fought in Spain. Stephen Vincent Benét presided, and among the speakers was Lillian Hellman. Part of the program was broadcast over the radio.[13]

The official reception for the prisoners was held on October 26 at Mecca Temple under the joint auspices of FALB and its New York post. The principal speaker was the Honorable Stanley M. Isaacs, president of the Borough of Manhattan. Dave White also spoke, as did Robert Raven, who had lost both eyes in the fighting at Jarama. The former prisoners gave short talks.

Now the fourteen scattered to their home towns. But first, Charles Barr looked up Charles Youngblood's family, and then joined Norman Dorland, Sam Romer, and seven other VALB members in a visit to Immigration Commissioner James V. Houghteling on October 28 in Washington, DC, on behalf of seventeen foreign-born veterans who had lived in the United States. They had been refused re-entry papers, even though some had families and had lived here up to twenty years. Desperate, they had managed to get on ships as stowaways, but had been caught and were being held on Ellis Island, awaiting deportation. Among them were Mirko Markovitch, born in Yugoslavia and the commander of the George Washington Battalion, and Herman Engert, born in Germany and commander of its machine-gun company. All faced jail and probable death if returned to their native countries, now dominated by fascist governments.

Houghteling refused to make an exception for them or grant them asylum. At most, he would allow some time to make arrangements for them to go to a friendly country.[14]

At Palencia life for the British went smoothly again after their "punishment" for celebrating the recrossing of the Ebro. Dougal Eggar, to obtain money that had arrived for him, had to go to Palencia with an Italian brigadier (a rank between sergeant and lieutenant) and an interpreter. On the way back, they stopped at a café in which the brigadier had an interest. Doug felt obligated to treat. He noticed that when Spanish soldiers and officers passed by, the brigadier took no notice of them. The interpreter asked, "Don't you salute the Spanish officers?"

"No, we don't salute them and they don't salute us."[15]

On October 18, the British cruiser *Hood* took 97 instead of 100 Italian prisoners from Gandia to Majorca; three had decided they preferred to stay in Republican Spain.[16]

On Saturday, October 22, the one hundred British prisoners were taken to Ondarreta, a very unpleasant prison as Doug recalls it, even though the Spaniards who shared their food with them said they were in the best part of it. There were sixteen in Doug's cell. The adjoining cell held fourteen women. On Monday, forty prisoners, including Doug, crossed the International Bridge to Hendaye and freedom. Still wearing their prison clothes, they took a train to Dieppe, a boat across the Channel, and a train to London, arriving at Victoria Station at 6:30 P.M. on October 25.

That evening Thomas Moon, worried because he had not received a letter from son Jimmy for a month, saw the sister of a prisoner as he was passing the barrier of Platform 15 at Victoria Station, decided to wait with her, and noted there

were lots of police about, Inspectors, Sergeants, Constables and doubtless numerous detectives. From their subsequent behavior, it was plain that for political reasons they had been instructed tactfully to prevent any demonstration which might be unpleasantly misconstrued by their High and Mightiness the Dictators of Germany and Italy.

When the British arrived, they made a picturesque appearance in their khaki shirts, knee breeches, and berets. Mr. Moon, "midst fervent reunions, the flash of cameramen's apparatus and the excited questions of journalists," talked with several who knew Jimmy (still at San Pedro) and recalled his sketches in this *Jaily News*.[17] The remaining sixty British prisoners at Ondarreta returned to Britain during the next few days.

* * * * *

At San Pedro a bar in a second-floor window was being cut with a saw fashioned from a knife blade. It took nearly two months to do the job. Work was done in the evening while a group sang songs so the saw's screeching would not be heard. The prisoner peering out the window would saw surreptiously back and forth, with several others standing around him so his actions could not be seen.

I knew an escape was being organized because the House Committee had authorized a large sum to purchase bread and chocolate and provide funds for the escapees. The six Germans who would leave were Heinz Hauser, alias Wilhelm Polians; Walter Kutschkau; Herbert Ney; Wilhelm Reitz, alias Joop de Kat; Alfred Richter, alias Kornelius Hubertus; and Hermann Streit.[18]

Once they had cut the bar and made the rope, they waited for a moonlit night with clouds. A chess match was going on between our European and American players. Hy Wallach recalls a German player had made arrangements to play the next day, but to Hy's surprise, he was missing the next morning.

Sunday, November 13, after the midnight patrol had passed, the first man went out, feet first. Before he had dropped to the ground, the second man was already partway out of the window, and as soon as the tension on the rope eased, he started down. Wisely, they had chosen Herbert Ney, who was heaviest, to be the last, for the rope parted and dropped him, shaken up but uninjured. The six men ran to the stone wall. The first boosted the next five up, and in turn was pulled up and over. In the meantime, confederates had pulled in the rope and bent the bar back into place.

Next morning we were lined up four abreast after breakfast, as usual, to be counted. The count came up six short. Sticky and Tanky, certain they had made an error, counted again. Still six short! Cursing, they checked the toilets and the floor for malingerers, and found no one. Sticky demanded to know who was missing. No one spoke up.

"If you won't tell me who is missing, then you'll stand at attention while we call the roll!" Sticky called Alex to read off the names. Alex went through the list methodically and unhurriedly; every minute that the search was delayed helped those who had escaped. Finally, he came to the last name. Every prisoner on the list had answered! Sticky realized that some had answered twice.

Now each prisoner had to step to the other side of the room when his name was called. It wasn't long before a name was called and no one stepped forward. Sticky held up his stick, menacingly. "Now, who answered for him before?"

There was no response, and Sticky glared at us, but contented himself with some profanity. This time when Alex was finished, Sticky had six names without bodies.

To have one prisoner escape would have been bad enough. But six! At one time! The sergeants were now really alarmed. The major was in Burgos. If they could find out how the escape had been carried out, they might partially redeem themselves. Since most of the missing Germans slept on the second floor, Sticky now proceeded to question us, with Alex interpreting.

"Who knows how they escaped?" No one answered.

"But six can't escape without some of you knowing about it!" Still no answer.

Rin-Tin-Tin was called upon to explain. He knew nothing. Then Sticky called for the chief of the German group, but he was among the missing. "Who was night guard between eight and ten o'clock?"

A small, elderly Polish volunteer quietly stepped out.

Sticky sneered, "Now, you tell me how the six escaped!"

"I don't know."

"What, six men escape and you saw nothing! Were you asleep?"

"I did not sleep, and I did not see them escape."

Sticky hesitated only a moment. "Out into the yard, both floors! Quick!"

With Sticky and Tanky whacking us across our backs, we rushed down the stairs pell-mell. Navarro had stationed himself at the door and was swinging with all his might. Fred Stanley managed to feint and then dash through unscathed as Navarro fanned the air. As Fred glanced back, he saw Peter Raacke, next behind him, catch a heavy blow that almost knocked him down.

We cleared both floors and assembled in the yard in record time. Sticky mounted the platform while the sergeants and guards arranged us in straight rows facing him. "Attention! And stand at attention until you tell me how the six escaped. Bring the night guard up here!"

The Pole was hustled up beside Sticky. "Look at this man! At eleven o'clock he will be shot unless someone tells us how the escape was made. Now, let's see. Does anyone care enough about this comrade's life to say anything?"

No one moved or said a word.

"Guards, see that these prisoners remain at attention, and that this one stands there!" With that Sticky and Tanky left.

I knew that a few others besides myself were debating what to do. Our innocent Polish comrade stood there, looking helplessly at us. I could not let him die, but to say anything would be to admit I had known an escape was planned and had not informed the authorities. Such an admission would lead to quite nasty consequences, especially since Sticky had entrusted me with responsibility as a chief. I had no doubt he would try to beat information out of me; the prospect was very unpleasant. It was impossible to consult with anyone, it was now nine o'clock, and I had two hours to decide.

Barely twenty minutes had passed when a sergeant approached and yelled an order to go back to our quarters. The guards drove us, including the Polish volunteer, back up almost as fast as we had come down. On the second floor, Sticky and Tanky were waiting at the window. The cut bar had been bent to one side.

Sticky looked around angrily. "Now, who slept here last night?"

Rin-Tin-Tin knew who they were. Those who had slept right in front of the window had escaped. The first to admit they slept near the window were two Americans. Georg Heinzmann and another German joined them. [19]

Sticky now seemed satisfied. "Take them downstairs! And the rest of you, stay away from that window if you don't want a bullet through your head!"

We remained silent for a moment after the four had been taken away, thinking of the beating they faced. Then we admired the opening in the window, from a safe distance. A "God, I hope they make it!" expressed our common thought.

The four were taken across the patio into a hallway. Georg was pushed through a doorway. Those outside soon heard the thuds of sticks against flesh and the groans of pain. When the groans stopped, the door opened and Georg, half conscious, bleeding from head and body, was dragged out into the hallway.

The sergeant motioned to an American. When he entered the room, he saw four sergeants waiting with clubs. "Take off your shirt so you won't get it bloody."

The American obeyed. Another then asked, "What nationality?

"American."

The sergeants exchanged glances. Then one said, "Get out!"

Expressionless, the American picked up his shirt and stepped outside. The second American was called in, and ordered out.

It was the second German's turn. Again the thuds and muffled cries could be heard. Meanwhile the two Americans were trying to staunch the flow of blood from Georg. When the sergeants were done, they ordered the two Americans to assist the other two across the patio and into the black hole. There in the semidarkness, without straw sacks or furnishings of any kind, the Americans tried to relieve the pain of their two beaten comrades.

When Alex learned what had happened, he immediately asked Sticky for permission to bring the men blankets, water, and food. "Let them die," was Sticky's reponse.

As soon as the major was notified, he had the Guardia Civil search for the six escapees, but it was afternoon before the major returned to San Pedro and Alex was able to call the plight of the two beaten men to his attention. The major, in serious trouble because of the escape, realized his troubles would be even greater if these prisoners died from their beatings. He ordered blankets, water, and food taken to them, and a week later he ordered them released from the black hole.

As the days went by without word from the six, our hopes rose that the escapees had reached France. Three weeks passed before we learned from Alex that three had been caught in the Pyrenees. They were badly beaten and thrown into the black hole. A few days later the other three were also brought back, beaten, and thrown in with the first three.

Eventually we learned what had happened. When the six reached the river we bathed in, they split into two groups. Streit, Kutschkau, and Reitz, to throw off dogs sent after them, waded a long distance in the river and then continued north twenty kilometers that night. Sleeping during the day, they walked only at night.

Then came the day when they would reach the French border and freedom that night. But early that evening they came upon a herd of cows. The cows started walking, their bells ringing. A border patrol investigated, and suddenly Streit and his two comrades found themselves surrounded. The border patrol, warned that prisoners had escaped from San Pedro, refused to believe their instantly composed story that they were Italian farm workers trying to get back to Italy. They were sent to Zaragoza, where they were held with Spanish prisoners.

The next morning the guards took out some Spaniards to be shot and said the Internationals would be next. But when the guards came back, it was to send the three Germans to San Pedro. There the guards who had been on patrol duty when the six had escaped, and who had been beaten because of the escape, were now allowed to beat the three.

Thrown in the black hole, they were soon joined by the other three, also beaten by the guards. When days passed by without food, the six shouted and pounded on the door. The sergeants took them out and beat them again, but did provide food after that.

It is a tribute to the Germans' dedication and self-discipline that they lived without friction in semidarkness and close quarters for over a month. Herman Streit lived in that cell for ninety-nine days, some of the time alone. The only object in the cell was a stick tied to a bundle of small branches, for sweeping. They shaped a wedge out of the end of the handle by rubbing it against the stone wall, and then began to dig a hole under the wall, to have something to do.[20]

As a child I spoke a Swiss dialect of German before I learned English. I had not forgotten my German, so I offered to serve as chief for the German-speaking on our floor. The Germans accepted, and Sticky agreed.

Life was never dull at San Pedro. On November 1, Colonel Martin told the British that the first one hundred had left Palencia and some had arrived in London. He said the rest at San Pedro would soon be sent to Palencia for repatriation. Jimmy Moon wrote to his mother that evening, "I may yet be home for Christmas."[21]

We spent most of our time indoors, since the weather was cold and we had only summer clothing. For exercise we played various games. Howard Earl and Fred Stanley, using prearranged movements and holds, put on wrestling exhibitions. Bridge teams began a contest for a million points. Fred Stanley was the undisputed checkers champ after Harry Kleiman had been taken away without warning or reason. Hy Wallach was invited to the major's quarters to play chess with an officer, once.

US Consul Bay had visited us on November 12, the day before the six Germans escaped. For each of the seventy-eight Americans, he wanted the correct spelling of his name, the place and date of birth, and the name and address of his closest relative. We told Bay that we lacked medical care and facilities for washing, that we were still not allowed to write letters to our families, and that beatings continued to be given capriciously. We had no winter coats, some had only rope-soled sandals, and our quarters were unheated and without windows. Bay promised that he would try to stop the beatings and get us the right to mail letters to our families, and said we should receive some warm clothing soon.[22]

One morning I awoke to find a pant leg stuck to dried pus exuding from a round sore about the size of a dime. Our doctors told me it was nothing to worry about. It was scurvy and would go away when I ate some fresh vegetables and fruit.

"And what will happen in the meantime?"

"Oh, you'll get more sores and they'll get larger," was the cheerful reply. "They are showing up on quite a few."

More serious was the loosening of teeth, though that only bothered us when we ate bread. Fred Stanley woke up one morning with his throat swollen on one side. Our doctors diagnosed mumps and suggested he take it easy for a few days to avoid serious consequences. This was not hard for Fred to do, and he recovered. Two more cases developed, without complications. Most, like myself, had had mumps in our first few years of school, when you were expected to get them along with measles and whooping cough.

While I was still chief of the English-speaking group on our floor, a "literary" magazine called *The Parader* appeared. It was put out by Ed Hodge, who published anything submitted to him. Only two issues appeared. Charles Hall recalled:

It had illustrations and it had dirty jokes and it was rather clever. . . . Some of the stuff in it was antifascist and some of it was caricatures of Franco and so forth, but it was semi-pornographic. I remember . . . Geiser saying, "I don't mind going into solitary for a political newspaper, but I don't want to go into solitary for pornography."[23]

*   *   *   *   *

Ambassador Bowers, FALB, the fourteen who had returned, and our relatives and friends were trying to get us out of Franco Spain before winter set in. But Secretary of State Hull wanted to keep us there until Franco had won. James Douglas Little, in *Malevolent Neutrality,* examines the activities of the State Department during the war and documents how Hull opposed the Republic and aided Franco. Hull could not stop the return of the volunteers from Republican Spain, but he did keep us imprisoned while pretending he was trying to obtain our release.

On October 10 Bowers had concluded his report to Hull: "If the reaction in Franco quarters to the exchange of these prisoners is not bad, I am convinced that we should make an effort to exchange the remainder of the Americans for Italians."[24]

In the communications between Hull, Consul Bay, and Bowers during October, we find Hull asking Bowers how the approach to the Franco authorities should be made.[25] Since Rialp, Franco's exchange commissioner, came to the embassy once or twice a week, Bowers replied on the twenty-fifth that he should make the first approach, and Hull in a coded cable authorized Bowers to do so informally. FALB would bear the cost, and Bay was preparing a complete list of all prisoners.[26]

On October 31, Bowers notified Hull that he was ready to approach Rialp and that Del Vayo had already agreed to an exchange. Hull's cabled order, B-464, came immediately. "I do not want you to approach the Burgos authorities with any proposal for exchange of Americans for equal number of Italians, as any proposal for exchange of prisoners must come from one side or the other and cannot be initiated by us." Hull then instructed Bowers to take up informally only the release of the prisoners.

In his telegraphed reply on November 3 Bowers said:

There has never been a release of prisoners except through an exchange since war began and am positive impossible now. Pressure by Italians on Franco for exchange of Italian prisoners makes acceptance improbable. However, I shall, if . . . so directed, act on your B-464. . . .

Since Del Vayo in a personal letter to me said that he would do anything to aid in getting the Americans out and home I suggest that I ask him personally, not officially, to submit to me as acting intermediary selected by both sides a proposal for exchange of the Americans for an equal number of Italians. . . . If authorized I can thus arrange for the proposal to "come from one side or the other" and assure you this plan is infinitely more promising than the other. Will take no action until I get your reactions and instructions.[27]

Instructions came the next day: Bowers was to take up only a release, because the Italians might go back to fight again for Franco. Bowers cabled right back that a condition for the exchange was that they fight no more. Hull again insisted that Bowers must not in any way initiate an exchange.[28]

In a lengthy letter, "Confidential for the Secretary and the Under-Secretary," Bowers discussed how we might be freed:

any such thing as the release of prisoners by General Franco on any other basis than an exchange has been utterly impossible, and I have known of no attempt that has been made by any nation.

In fact, up until the time I secured the exchange of the Americans for Italians it had been utterly impossible during the entire length of the war to persuade the rebels to even an exchange of military prisoners.

It may seem incredible that both sides would not be glad to escape the burden of feeding and guarding military prisoners providing an exchange can be effected: but incredible to those only who are not in contact with the illogical, unreasoning hatred that is involved.

Since I am in contact with Franco's Commissioner on exchange, the Marquis de Rialp, it seemed to me, since I have acted as intermediary on the request of Franco, I was in position to suggest to Rialp that all the Americans be exchanged for the Italians, the request coming from one side or the other. This would be in the course of conversation and not formally presented.

Your suggestion that you do not wish me to propose such an exchange does not take into consideration the fact that the proposal would come from either Barcelona or Burgos. If we are free to ask for a plain release, we should be able with equal propriety to suggest a release through an exchange such as has already been effected.

. . . I am convinced that it is too much to expect that Franco will release any of his prisoners without the release of a corresponding number of prisoners held by the other side. I know he would be severely criticized by his allies.

Of one thing I am positive—that having secured the release of some of the American prisoners we should make an effort to secure the release of all. The British have just effected an exchange of British for Italians. The British are as convinced as I am that there is no other way that is practical. However, of course, I shall follow whatever final instructions are sent after the receipt of my telegram No. 553, November 5, 1 P.M., calling attention to the fact that the Italians exchanged do not return to the fighting but are immediately sent to Italy.[29]

My brother Bennet and my uncle, John J. Schmid, sent letters to the State Department (as did many prisoners' friends and relatives) asking why the British could get their prisoners back and we could not. They received the stock reply that there was little the Department could do.[30] In "I Was Franco's Prisoner," an article Sam Romer wrote for *The Nation,* he noted that we would not be released unless the State Department "drops its disinterested attitude and demands their freedom."[31]

Bowers cabled Hull on November 18 that Rialp had proposed exchanging the remaining Americans for the fascists who had taken refuge in Madrid embassies. Again Hull replied that Bowers was to ask only for the prisoners' release.[32] In view of Bay's telegram of October 5 that Vidal, who spoke for Franco, had said "it was wholly impossible to consider the release of American prisoners,"[33] and Bowers's strong statements, Hull's insistence on asking only for a release when he knew an exchange was possible can only be interpreted to mean that he wanted to keep us imprisoned.

Negotiations were going on for the exchange of 100 Frenchmen, about 60 Swedes, Cubans and Swiss, and 120 British. The Republic refused an exchange for the Frenchmen, but was negotiating the exchange of the others for the 180 Italians it had. Since a British ship would take off the Italians, the British Foreign Office said priority should be given to their nationals.[34] That meant there would be no Italians left to exchange for Americans.[35]

Bowers referred to this in a telegram to Hull, pointing out that other nations would be certain

to seek exchange of their nationals for Italians and unless we show equal interest we may find ourselves without any one to exchange . . . it would be a serious mistake for us not to act. There is no possibility of securing any release except on the basis of an exchange.[36]

Hull may have been alarmed by Bowers telegram on the nineteenth:

A pro-Franco member Diplomatic Corps just returned, unofficial observer rebel territory, assures me that conditions behind the lines are quite serious because of bitterness of factional dissensions and the physical combats between factions in Burgos last week. From another completely dependable source told that one more reverse for Franco would be fatal.[37]

(Franco's losses in driving the Republican army back across the Ebro River were 100,000 according to a German colonel, and 145,000 according to an Italian journalist, or 15 to 25 percent of his infantry.[38])

At San Pedro, Americans without shoes were wearing either *alpargatas* or a sneaker the prisoners made by unraveling a burlap sack and then weaving a cloth to be sewed to a piece of discarded tire casing. The packages sent by the IRC for the Americans and the Swiss prisoners had been received by the inspector of concentration camps at Burgos, but some of the clothing had been stolen en route from San Sebastian. The items remaining ranged from sixty pairs of socks to eighty blankets. The packing lists showed that eighty-seven blankets, pullovers, shirts, underpants, socks, and bars of soap had been shipped.

There were 78 Americans and 13 Swiss. Bay suggested to the inspector that when cold weather set in, the clothing be given out as far as it would go. He noted that the prisoners had no underwear or socks, and many were without shoes, and he reported having been promised that we would be allowed to write every two weeks and that the beatings would stop. Bay also noted that although we appeared healthy,

With the approach of winter many discomforts are certain to be experienced and this despite adequate clothing, since the winters are bitterly cold and men in confinement without an occupation may be expected to fall victims of minor disabilities and many discomforts. If their release by exchange can be effected before midwinter arrives, it would seem to be a most desirable situation.[39]

*　　*　　*　　*　　*

An exchange of 147 inmates of the Cuban embassy in Madrid for 147 prisoners held by Franco had been arranged by the Chetwode Commission for November 5. The 147 from the Cuban embassy, under the supervision of the IRC, were embarked on the British battleship *Hood* on that day and taken to Marseilles. But the 147 from Franco's side did not appear at Hendaye as scheduled—nor on the twelfth, nor on the fifteenth. Bowers reported the media correspondents did not believe the fascist charges about spies and anarchists having been included among the 147 from the Cuban Embassy. Bowers added that Marshal Chetwode, not favorably impressed by the rebels, had even been charged with saying the Republican infantry was superior to that of the rebels.[40]

Franco had not suspended executions when the Republic did on September 11. At the request of the Chetwode Commission, the Republic extended its suspension until the end of October, and then until November 20, to give the commission more time to get Franco to agree. "Absolute assurance" had been given that no executions had been carried out on Franco's side, but the commission had unimpeachable evidence that there had been fifty-five in September and October in Burgos and Bilbao, including that of Lieutenant Colonel Federico de Angulo.[41] There is no evidence that the practice of killing thousands each month in Franco Spain was affected in the least by the negotiations and promises.

18 A Cold Month at San Pedro

THE WIND blew cold at San Pedro in December. We wore our blankets draped over our shoulders as we ran out the door to ward off the cold and Tanky's blows. Those who wore *alpargatas* danced to avoid frozen toes. The covering on our heads ranged from none to Mark Fajardo's leather cap with fur-lined earmuffs. Those ill with diarrhea or flu were permitted to remain upstairs, and we brought them food in pails. Our unheated rooms had only makeshift coverings over the paneless windows; it was our body heat that kept the temperature above freezing.

Early in December, the IRC clothing packages arrived for the Americans and the Swiss. Since there were not enough to go around, those in least need took only one or two items. Those who had army boots left the socks for those with *alpargatas*. Especially welcome were the blankets, which we frequently wore twenty-four hours a day.

The Germans, Austrians, Slavs, Poles, and Italians had no one to send them clothing or money. The blankets and shirts we passed on to them could not begin to fill their needs. Our few tailors, having obtained needles and thread, repaired clothing—charging those who could afford it, and bartering with those who had no money. A sergeant asked one tailor if he could make a coat.

"If you can supply the cloth, buttons, and thread."

The sergeant could. A fee was agreed upon, and within a few weeks he had his coat. Some prisoners thought their comrade should not have made the coat. Others felt the sergeants now had more respect for us, while the tailor had some needed money. A Portuguese shoemaker had managed to fashion a last, an awl, a knife, and a small hammer, and to obtain some heavy thread and nails. His handiwork was greatly admired and he was kept busy—until a sergeant spotted the last and confiscated his equipment.

One day Fred Stanley was looking into the courtyard, watching three sergeants beating three Spanish prisoners. Just then Señores, the tall priest, entered the yard through the main door. He walked right by without a glance.[1] After all, the sergeants were practicing what the priest had preached: "If you don't do what the authorities tell you, it is right for them to force you to do it, for your own good."

Not long after the last of the six Germans had been brought back, we learned Alex and his Cuban aide, Pedro, had escaped. Everyone wondered why. It wasn't like Alex to walk away from a position where he could help us. The only logical explanation was that the authorities had placed such severe restraints on him after the Germans' escape that he could be of little help to us. Alex and Pedro were returned within a week. Of all the beatings given at San Pedro, none caused as many sad faces as Alex's.

Hassan was the only prisoner capable of taking Alex's place as interpreter, but when the major asked him to do so, Hassan asked for two days to think it over. He discussed the offer with Robert Weinand, a thirty-five-year-old Communist from Essen, Germany, and Karl Kormes, who would become chief of the German-speaking group after I left. They asked Hassan to accept. When he told the major he was willing to take Alex's place, the major asked, "Why did you wait? Did you consult others?"

"Yes."

"So, then, you'll work for them?"

"No, I'll need to find a way to express loyalty to you and to them simultaneously."

"But will you tell us of plans to escape?"

"Certainly not. They, of course, won't tell me. You wouldn't do so if you were a prisoner of the Reds. Why should I be less decent? Your guards are responsible to you regarding escape attempts. I will assume responsibility for internal order and for encouraging self-discipline."

The major found Hassan an excellent choice. Hassan, Kormes, and Weinand set up groups of five, called "soup communities," for mutual self-help and education, enabling the prisoners to run their own affairs and avoid unnecessarily antagonizing the authorities. Hassan's success in getting concessions from the camp authorities and in gaining tolerance for prisoner self-help activities earned him the title "Elder Statesman."[2]

The San Pedro Institute of Higher Learning continued, students sitting around their instructors, all wrapped in blankets to keep warm. With the blanket forming a peak over each head, they looked like a group of medieval monks.

Class attendance had dropped at the end of November when a large shipment of Pelican and Penguin paperbacks arrived. Jimmy Moon had written about our need for books to a young woman he knew in the Fulham Library in southwest London. She passed on the request to the board of directors, one of whose members was Harold Laski, an important Socialist leader. The library then sent us a large collection of paperbacks.[3]

The cold weather led groups to pool resources and ingenuity to build stoves, using candles or sardine oil to heat liquids. Heating a can of sweetened evaporated milk to obtain a brown caramel-flavored paste to smear on a chusco, or of diluted milk with coarse Spanish chocolate to make hot chocolate, could keep four men busy a whole afternoon.

December 20 was a great day for me: five letters with three photos, a package of magazines, and two dollars. Two days later I received the glasses I had requested in July. I had been able to read without difficulty, but I needed glasses for distant vision.

Christmas Day supper included a treat—a small can of fruit to take to our quarters. But how to open a can? One man placed his on the floor, bent over it, and carefully put his weight on a pointed tool. When the tool pierced the can, a stream of fermented fruit juice decorated his face. We now examined our cans more closely; some, including mine, had bowed-out ends.

Word spread quickly: "Look out for the fizz bombs!" By this time several others had come up with pointed tools, and I borrowed one. With my face safely to one side, I came up with a gusher. Some thought that if the fruit had fermented, it must contain alcohol, but one taste was enough to deter them. It was an hour before the hilarity subsided, though the odor hung on.

The cans were appreciated. Those who had sardine can mess kits now used the fruit cans. Some made stoves. The artisans among us converted the cans into one rectangular and two circular pieces of tin, with which they fashioned ingenious devices.

Late on December 23, C. B. Jerram, the acting British agent at Burgos, received a telegram authorizing him to use forty pounds supplied by the British Dependants' Aid Committee to purchase gifts for the seventy-six British prisoners. The next day the women employees of the British agency found the shops had little left. They were able to buy one case of 150 oranges and a case of apples, 240 packets of chocolate, 33 pounds of mixed sweets, and 9 tins of biscuits. They also obtained 360 packets of cigarettes. Because of the escape from San Pedro, no one was allowed to visit the prisoners, but Colonel Miracles, in charge of concentration camps, promised to see that the gifts were delivered; the prisoners would be told they came from their relatives.[4]

When the packages arrived, some had been opened, but whether this was the result of rough handling or pilfering is not known. Danny Gibbons, George Ives, and Lionel Jacobs made an inventory. Some gifts were set aside for the prisoners in the Spanish infirmary, and the rest were divided equally among the British, who were urged to share generously with the other nationalities.[5]

*   *   *   *   *

Ambassador Bowers cabled Hull on December 15 that plans for release of the Americans had been accepted by both sides and were practically complete.[6] The main problem was how to take off the Italian prisoners held by the Republic. Hull would not permit the use of US naval vessels which were in the area. On December 31, 110 Italian prisoners were at the Gandia port to be exchanged for 77 British and 33 Canadians, and no ship was available for them.[7]

Our families organized the "Relatives of the American Prisoners in

Franco Spain." One of its first actions was to suggest that its members and friends send Christmas cards to President and Eleanor Roosevelt. My wife wrote on hers:

This is a greeting and a plea: a greeting for the fine work you both have performed and to the inspiration you have been to millions of Americans; a plea that you give your invaluable aid to the American Boys now suffering in the Concentration Camps of Franco.[8]

The outstanding event in our life in the concentration camp at San Pedro de Cardeña was our Christmas Eve performance.[9] Bob Steck, a member of the Workers Laboratory Theater in New York and of the staff of *New Theatre Magazine*, arranged the program; Rudy Kampf, a graduate of the Heidelberg Conservatory of Music, provided the music and developed a large chorus.

Singing had been banned, but the major agreed to lift the ban if no "revolutionary" songs were sung. We invited him to attend the concert with his officers and soldiers, for we hoped the performance would improve our image in their eyes. We did not know if he would attend, or how many he might bring with him. But he came cross the courtyard with about thirty men and officers, including Sticky and Tanky—without sticks or arms.

I welcomed them at the doorway. The major, leading his officers and soldiers, followed me up the dark stairway, through the poorly lit narrow corridor to the last archway, and then into the larger room, since we had filled all except that end with seats made of doubled-up sleeping sacks.

I showed our guests to the two front rows. "We are sorry we cannot offer you chairs. We hope you will find our straw sack seats comfortable." Then I squeezed in behind the major, where I could watch his reactions.

Three weak, unshaded light bulbs hanging from the ceiling, one near each end of the room and one in the center, dimly revealed the many rows of wall-to-wall prisoners seated on similar straw sacks. However, I could see that our guests' main interest was not in the prisoners behind them but in the curtain immediately in front of them. I knew that all except one were wondering where we had obtained the wire over which we had hung four of the blankets we had received recently from FALB.

When all were seated, Bob, master of ceremonies, rose to greet our guests in Spanish. "Major, officers, and soldiers, we are happy that you have joined us to celebrate this Christmas Eve, which unfortunately both you and we must spend here. To make this evening a pleasant one for all, we have prepared a program appropriate to the season. We will begin with Christmas and folk songs from Germany, Poland, Italy, the Slavic countries, Cuba, England, and the United States. After that we shall present a short adaptation of *The Barber of Seville*, followed by short skits. Our concert will conclude with a bell song especially adapted for this occasion."

The curtain parted in the middle and was drawn magically to each side.

Eight German prisoners faced us, about to sing. But what drew the attention of the major and Sticky was the charcoal mural on the wall just behind the prisoners. We remembered that the major had angrily ordered all walls whitewashed to blot out our class outlines, and had warned us there had better be no further desecration of the walls. Now one whole wall had been used to depict a winter scene in a small village in the Austrian Alps. One looked down past a church belfry upon a street lined with two- and three-story houses nestled in a valley between the mountains on both sides. One could almost hear the bell's joyous peal this Christmas Eve.

I caught a *"Bonita"* from the major to Sticky as a soft tenor "aaaaa" preceded the opening bar of "Stille Nacht." The perfect harmony of the eight separate voices, ranging from a deep bass to a high tenor, startled the seated soldiers and prisoners into absolute silence. Stone walls three feet thick, with deeply indented alcoves every ten feet, carried even the softest tones to the last row and produced no echo from even the loudest passages. Forgotten were the straw sacks and the concentration camp; there was no reality except the song and the chorus.

Tears came to my eyes as I listened, exulting in the artistry of our German comrades, for whom our jailers had always reserved the most brutal treatment. I could also sense the elation of the prisoners behind me, and see the astonishment in the faces of our guests saying. "These are our prisoners? They can sing like this?"

"Tannenbaum" was next. The strong plaintive voices aroused a deep feeling of nostalgia as we thought of our families and our faraway homelands, and the happier surroundings in which we had sung this favorite. This was reflected in all our voices as, six hundred strong, we joined in on the choruses, flooding the room with emotion-packed harmony.

The Poles and the Slavs, inspired and challenged, each made their unique contribution to a varied program. The superb quality of all these voices was due, I was told, to the large role group singing plays in the culture of their native lands.

The British chorus favored us with several old ballads, including "The Twelve Days of Christmas" and "What will I do if I be an old maid in a garret." The blending of Scotch, Irish, Welsh, and English accents, each expressed clearly in short solos, provided a pleasing effect. Even Tanky applauded.

The Ukrainian Canadians with their powerful voices sang the "Volga Boatmen" while slowly pulling on a rope cleverly made from tightly rolled blankets. The Cubans were especially well received by our guests since they sang Spanish songs.

While as a whole Americans could not sing as well as the Europeans, Max Parker did get up a respectable quartet in which he was joined by John Hollis Jenkins, Henry Megguier, and Eugene Poling.[10] They presented a very creditable rendition of two labor ballads, "Joe Hill" and "Casey Jones."

"We should have an intermission at this point," announced Bob, "but since our refreshment and promenade areas are still to be constructed, we shall continue our program as soon as we can arrange the scenery for *The Barber of Seville*. Rossini's opera was first performed in Rome in 1816. One of our operatic experts has undertaken to modernize it for our times, and to adapt it to our stage. So with apologies to Rossini, and for your entertainment, we present a modern-day *Barber of Seville*."

This brief introduction had provided enough time to prepare the scenery—four stools in a row facing us. Against the wall on each side stood a man, waiting. For a long moment nothing moved. Then a man came through the archway and was motioned to a stool. Another wait, and a second man entered, to be motioned to a stool. Absolute silence.

A third man entered and was motioned to a stool. Only when the fourth man had entered and sat on the remaining stool did the two men leave the wall and spring into action. Each took one end of a two-foot-wide sheet, goose-stepped backward, then side-stepped two steps to align themselves with the four men. With one quick flourish, the sheet was raised and lowered, and four heads were sticking above four holes in the sheet.

The head barber now stepped forward, while his assistant grabbed a pail of suds and a wide brush. At the head barber's command, "*Ojos a la derecha!*" the four heads looked to the right and the assistant with one sweep of his brush lathered one side of all four faces. "*Ojos a la izquierda!*" and another pass of the brush lathered the other side. "*Ojos a la derecha!*" and one pass with a large wooden razor shaved one side. "*Ojos a la izquierda!*" and the job was done. All that remained was to wipe the faces, and that was quickly accomplished, each barber grabbing one end of the sheet and lifting it with a seesaw motion. The four men stood up as one, bowed stiffly to the barbers, and marched out as the curtain was drawn. The prisoners applauded this satire uproariously, but the major and his officers applauded politely and briefly.

Next the Cubans put on a parody of a nightclub. Several were dressed as women; we all wondered how they had obtained the clothes. The dancing and singing were hilarious, and drew much laughter and applause from our guests and ourselves.[11]

The French skit overcame all language barriers. It depicted in pantomine the life of a tramp, keeping the audience laughing without a word being said. Then there was a juggler, and finally two Polish Ukrainians performed an acrobatic Russian dance that amazed us all.[12]

A large number of Internationals had unobtrusively moved out of the audience into the corridor. Bob now announced, "May I take advantage of the few moments required to prepare for the next number to tell you something about it. Rudy Kampf has prepared a special adaptation for a chorus of eighty male voices of the Russian song 'Evening Bells.' It is with great pride and pleasure we present to you Rudi Kampf and the Bell Singers."

The curtain was drawn back slowly and steadily, revealing Rudi in front of eighty men standing shoulder to shoulder in four rows. After a small bow to the audience, Rudi turned and faced the men. As he raised his hands, audience and performers observed absolute silence. A momentary wait, a slight motion of the hand, and somewhere from the depths of the group came a slow steady "ding, dong, ding, dong" followed by the opening theme sung by the entire chorus. The purity of the voices and the perfect coordination between the various groups of voices were thrilling even to the least musically educated listener. The smallness of the room in relation to the size of the chorus brought a tremendous range of intensities to the listeners' ears. The softer passages, where one again became aware of the "ding, dong" background, alternated with full-throated passages, providing a second level of counterpoint in addition to that developed between the groups of voices.

I stole a glance at our guests. All were frozen motionless. Tanky's face was a study in astonishment; a pleasant smile of appreciation played on the major's face. And I knew the men behind me, who listened to the low-voiced rehearsals of groups in dark corners, were as astonished as I was by the stunning effect of the complete chorus in full voice. And the men on the stage? It was as if each, rebelling against the dehumanization of life in the concentration camp, was pouring out his soul, creating beauty with his fellowmen, for his fellowmen.

Gradually the voices became more subdued, and more and more joined in the "ding, dong" background. Finally, only the background could be heard. Its quiet regularity bred an air of expectancy. Suddenly a high sweet tenor rang out from the midst of the chorus, carrying a haunting melody. My spine tingled and tears again came to my eyes. The unwavering clarity of the high notes called out an emotional response that electrified the room. Every man, both in the audience and in the chorus, was thrilled by the sureness and purity of the tenor voice. It brought to my mind a line from Shelley's ode "To a Skylark": *And Heaven is overflowed.*

All followed the melodious rise and fall of the song, now quickening, now hauntingly slow, always perfectly joined to the muted "ding, dong" in the background. Slowly voices began leaving the background and resuming their usual role, and gradually the tenor blended in with the full chorus. The performance of the chorus, as if inspired by the tenor voice, was yet more precise, more harmonious, and rang out more firmly. How long the song lasted I cannot judge, for the beauty of it made keeping track of time impossible. At the closing "ding dong," there was complete silence for a brief moment. Then the entire audience rose to its feet, clapping vigorously and shouting, *"Olé! Olé!"* the distinction between prisoner and jailer lost in the wild applause. It was a performance we all knew we would never hear equaled, an evening no one would forget. Two days later we received a request to repeat the program on New Year's Eve. The major wanted to bring several of his fellow officers from Burgos. We gladly complied, for we ourselves wanted to see and hear it again. The second performance was more polished, and delivered in a more professional manner than the first; it may not have had the excitement of surprise that the first performance had, but it was still the most memorable New Year's show I have seen.

The exhilarating effect of the performances lasted for many days. Those suffering from ailments were much improved. The bond of international solidarity was greatly strengthened as we congratulated each other on the contributions made to the evening. And there was no doubt our jailers now looked at us with new eyes: they used their sticks less when giving orders or reprimanding "offenders." Even Tanky, for a few weeks, stood at the doorway without swinging his stick. Bob Steck and Rudi Kampf, modest in manner, must have obtained much satisfaction out of the evening, as did all the others who had played a part. And to the inner amusement of all prisoners, at each performance, some of the fleas in our straw sacks left us and established new residence with our guests.

19 We Leave San Pedro

TEX DECIDED to start the New Year off with an encouraging rumor. "Hey fellows, this is the year we go home." Hy Wallach decided to be more specific, and prophesied we would leave San Pedro on or before February 28. Since Hy had accurately predicted when the first fourteen would leave, word went around quickly: "We are leaving here by Febraury 28. Hy said so."

January was so cold that we wore our blankets continuously, for days on end. Many of the other nationalities, who had thin clothing and blankets and wore *alpargatas*, suffered severely. A few days were so cold that the sergeants allowed some of us to manhandle the food caldrons up the stairs, a difficult feat, so that the rest would not have to go outside for their meals. The cold weather also eliminated, or at least shortened, the priests' lectures.

We experienced less illness than we had expected. The standing joke was that bacteria and viruses couldn't survive under our conditions. While some had colds and diarrhea, the worst hit were the older men who suffered from arthritis. No treatment was available, and some of them endured pain day and night.

By this time all of us had quarter-sized scurvy sores, especially on the legs. Loose and sore teeth were becoming more of a problem. Tony Gilbert had a front tooth become painful enough that he yanked it out by hand.[1] Lice and fleas seemed to be more ravenous than ever, multiplying as rapidly as in warm weather.

We still could not write letters to our relatives. Al Ziegler got around the restriction by purchasing postal cards. On these he wrote in Spanish, with *Viva España* written on the card's front in order to get it past the military censor.[2]

We completely forgot our cold and hunger on January 23, when the remaining British, Canadian, and Swiss volunteers left San Pedro to go home.[3] But the news from the battlefront was depressing. The copies of fascist newspapers that we were able to obtain predicted Catalonia would soon fall. We knew the Republican forces in the southern half of Spain were much larger, and their failure to relieve the pressure on Catalonia left us with a sinking feeling. And the democratic nations—would they allow the Republic to fall? We knew pro-Franco forces wielded positions of great power in the democracies, yet we hoped the antifascist millions might force their governments to realize the dangers inherent in a fascist victory.

We did suffer the loss of a comrade, Candido Curti, a forty-year-old single Italian volunteer. Born in Campos, Italy, he had lived in exile in Paris. He died on January 30.[4]

Funds and messages sent through the ARC and the IRC took many months to reach us. Murray Young, an English instructor at Brooklyn College and a close friend of David White, sent me $15, to which my wife had added $5.[5] At the end of January I received 274 pesetas in exchange for the $20. After contributing 28 pesetas, the usual 10 percent to the house fund, I gave 175 to the German and Austrian comrades.[6] I thought I was being generous, but some eighty comrades had had to share that 175 pesetas.

*   *   *   *   *

"The Americans are already receiving too much money," the major had commented a few days before Christmas as he accepted $30 for us from M. d'Amman, the IRC delegate. One peseta a day (equivalent to seven cents) was enough, the major thought; he had already withheld from us the last amount he had received, but promised he would give the Americans more later.

Then a letter came to the ARC that an American had given a Russian 500 pesetas, with which he had made his escape, as he had confessed when caught four days later. No more funds should be sent until an IRC delegate could give them the amounts already received. The overalls and sneakers that had passed through customs and were reported lost had been found.[7]

The "Russian" was Alex de Seume, who had tried to escape in December. The story that an American had given him 500 pesetas was a pure invention. And we received neither the funds nor the overalls and sneakers.

On January 6, the British Admiralty was ready to take 110 Italian prisoners from Gandia to the Italian base at Palma in exchange for 110 British and Canadians. The Canadian government refused to assume the repatriation cost, so the Foreign Office tried to arrange the release of the British without the Canadians. But Franco refused to modify the arrangements, and the French would not let the Canadians enter France without identification papers.[8]

Barcelona fell on the twenty-sixth, so all ships were being used to evacuate embassy staff and refugees from Catalonia; the Italian prisoners would have to wait.[9] On the twenty-eighth, funds had been made available for the Canadians.[10] The end of the month found the British and the Canadians waiting very impatiently at Ondarreta Prison, wondering what was going on.

*   *   *   *   *

Fred Keller led a delegation of seven relatives and friends into the State Department on Tuesday, January 9, 1939, to see Pierrepont Moffat and Eric C. Wendelin. Asked what the Department was doing to bring us home, Moffat claimed that because the United States did not recognize Franco, it could not propose that the Americans be released or exchanged for Italian prisoners. Fred did not know that Hull had instructed Bowers to ask only for the release of American prisoners, not what he had done for Guy Castle.

Fred told Moffat that the lack of winter clothing and the ill-treatment were worse than reported by Consul Bay and that the prisoners were still not allowed to write home. Moffat said the clothing had reached Burgos and that Bay had reported the Americans would be allowed to write every two weeks.

When Fred suggested the prison camp be visited more often, Moffat claimed lack of personnel made that difficult. Fred offered to send a representative of FALB, but Moffat didn't think Franco would grant permission. When Fred asked what was being done to locate the missing Americans, Moffat assured the delegation that every effort was being made to locate these men.[11]

The single most important plea to lift the embargo was made by Hull's predecessor, Henry L. Stimson. In a letter to Hull on January 18, Stimson called on the United States to "Take decisive action and that by doing so this country may well be able to ward off serious consequences to the whole world."[12] Five days later the *New York Times* printed a letter from Stimson saying that Roosevelt had a legal right to lift the embargo on the grounds that it constituted a danger to the United States. He also quoted Thomas Jefferson on a fundamental rule of international relations:

We certainly cannot deny to other nations that principle whereon our own Government is founded, that every nation has a right to govern itself internally under whatever form it pleases and to change these forms at its own will; and externally to transact business with other nations through whatever organ it chooses whether that be a king, conventions, assembly, committee, president or whatever it may be. (Jefferson to Pinckney, *Works,* vol. III, p. 500.)

A Catholic lay leader replied, and was rebutted by a prominent lawyer and a Columbia University professor of international law. These three letters constitute an excellent summary of the legal and moral arguments advanced by opponents and proponents of the embargo.[13]

Harold Ickes noted in his diary that at Roosevelt's Cabinet meeting on January 27, 1939,

The President also brought up the question of the Spanish embargo. He very frankly stated, and this for the first time, that the embargo had been a grave mistake. . . . I gathered from what he said that the State Department had been back of this embargo from the beginning. . . . The President said we would never do such a thing again, but I am afraid that will not help us very much. He agreed that this embargo controverted old American principles and invalidated established international law.[14]

The Gallup Poll asked people, "Which side do you sympathize with in the Spanish Civil War—the Loyalists or Franco?" Of those who had a decided preference, 76 percent favored the Loyalists.[15]

*   *   *   *   *

On February 1, we learned that we could write one letter in English to a relative, and would be allowed to write another on the fifteenth. We wrote in an optimistic tone not only to pass the censor but also to avoid worrying our relatives. Al Ziegler wrote to his mother about the San Pedro Institute of Higher Learning and the Barcelona City Band.

A fresh supply of paper came in from Burgos and our school has started its spring term. I am teaching Descriptive Geometry. A recent attack of nostalgia has sent me back to Calculus.
. . . The Barcelona City Band dressed in blue capes with a red lining . . . returned from France . . . at Mass after the death of the *Papa* [Pope Pius XI] we had a choir and Schubert's serenade on a violin by the newcomers.[16]

Al did not mention that when we looked out the windows the first frosty morning when we heard the band playing the fascist hymn, what disturbed us most were the shouts of "Death to Negrín" from some Spaniards in the courtyard below.

February was just as cold as January, but worse for those suffering from arthritis. Pop Jenkins was suffering badly; but wrapped in a blanket, he still taught his classes. Sidney Rosenblatt wrote to his parents:

Today I am wearing an additional garment, a trench coat. One of the boys had it, and wasn't using it because it was very dirty, lousy, torn and buttonless. Well, I spent about two hours scrubbing it with grease soap, on the front I sewed four big buttons (which I got in exchange for a pack of tobacco) and sewed a lining in it from an old blouse I had. This took me three days to sew, and I am very proud of the job I made. So now, I am warmer, and look rather snappy besides.
Bill told me in a letter that Sol sent some money home for you and for me. Please, if this is so, use my share for whatever you need.[17]

Many suffered from diarrhea. From a Spanish-American, I learned the best defense was a cloth wrapped around the waist. This was why Spanish farmers in cold weather wore black scarves around their midsections rather than around their neck.

The main topics of conversation, walking or sitting, were "When do we got out of here?" and "What's holding us up?" We speculated: Could the Valencia-Madrid area hold out? Would the armies in Catalonia move there? We did not know that France was putting the Republican troops into concentration camps.

Rumors increase as reliable news decreases. A persistent rumor that alarmed us was that we were being held to be court-martialed. Sergio Sanjenis Cabarrocas, a Cuban, was taken away on February 13. He had worked as a correspondent in Paris before joining the Lincoln battalion, and had been captured on April 4, 1938. Our alarm in this instance was not justified; he was freed and turned over to the Cuban Red Cross.[18]

Valentine's Day was a great day—the French suddenly got orders to pack and leave. With the English, Canadians, Swiss, and now the French gone, shouldn't our turn come soon? Why did Hy have to pick the twenty-eighth? That was still two weeks away!

On February 27, a rumor spread that we would be leaving the next day. Hope and wishful thinking fed on each other, making us forget our pains and ills. Pop Jenkins's arthritis improved remarkably as he walked around visiting the excited groups of Americans discussing the rumor, by this time attributed to the major himself. Only Peter Raacke, our fastidious St. Louis tavern owner, appeared oblivious to the rising excitement. The more optimistic were already giving away what they thought they could spare. How many times can you rehash a rumor? Until sleep overtakes you late at night. And then you can dream about it.

Next morning, breakfast as usual—well, almost as usual. Then back up to our quarters. Hy was calmly preparing to leave. Lopez had put a copy of the *Jaily News* in his shoes, just in case. Others looked out the windows, watching the archway into our court. Soon the cry arose, "Here come Sticky!"

Sticky had never enjoyed so attentive and quiet an audience. The eager look on our faces brought a smile before he announced, "All Americans, Chileans, Cubans, Danes, and Swedes, downstairs in five minutes, ready to leave." A cheer went up, which told those on the floor above us that we were really going home. Sticky broke into the widest grin we had ever seen on his face as he went upstairs to repeat the announcement.

Five minutes to give away spare items and say good-by to dozens of close friends, to collect last-minute addresses and messages to take out, to gather together whatever possessions we wanted to take with us. We were wearing the only clothes we had, and many of us left our blankets with friends, taking only our eating utensils. When Sticky reappeared, we were ready to go.

Down in the assembly area, Hassan called the roll for each nationality to make sure we were all there, with no extras. Then on to waiting trucks, and good-by to San Pedro de Cardeña as our drivers headed for Burgos. There we were loaded into freight cars for the 250-kilometer trip to San Sebastian, which we reached that evening. Again we mounted trucks, only to find we had no place to go—all prisons were badly overcrowded and had no room for us. After an hour's wait, the Basque prisoners at Zapatari Prison made room for us.

Zapatari was a makeshift prison in a three-story brick factory building on the south side of San Sebastian. As we settled into our small bare rooms, which the Basque prisoners had swept clean, we found we were going to have to pack ourselves in pretty tight. We would have to lie on our sides, our feet sandwiched between those of the two persons opposite us. But we felt we could tolerate the tight quarters for one night.

Turning over, when our bones ached too much, was most easily accomplished if we all got up at once to make the change. I had never seen such crowded rooms, and we all laughed when someone said, "It's a good thing we didn't get anything to eat since breakfast." I wondered how tightly the Basques had had to pack themselves in to make room for their "guests."

*   *   *   *   *

The British, Canadian, and Swiss prisoners who had left us on January 23 were delighted by the reception they received as they marched through the streets from the San Sebastian railroad station. Frank West, a London carpenter captured on the last day the British were in action, recalls that people marched along with the prisoners to give them cigarettes and chocolates.[19] Jules Paivio, the young Canadian from Thunder Bay who had faced the firing squad with me ten months earlier, remembers the guards allowed young people, including girls, to walk along with them. "What a wonderful human feeling it was, and it showed the mood of the Basque people and their solidarity with the Republic."[20]

But then they were marched into the basement of Ondarreta Prison. There was a strong stench from open sewers that overflowed at high tide. In the exercise yard Jimmy Moon could see men through narrow windows at ground level—Basques awaiting execution. Jimmy, who had not complained at San Pedro, classified Ondarreta as "bloody rotten."[21]

The Basques called the basement the "punishment floor." The cell doors were open, and the prisoners were free to wander about in the muck. Some Basques had been there since the fall of Bilbao almost twenty months before. The Internationals hoped each day would be their last at Ondarreta. But no one came to see them, and they were unable to contact the British authorities; for two weeks they received no letters or funds.

Several officials came on February 6, read off the names of sixty-seven British prisoners in alphabetical order and ordered them out to waiting buses. This left ten British, including Frank West, thirty-one Canadians and eleven Swiss, with no explanation.

We now know only sixty-seven were released, even though seventy Italians had been taken to Palma, because three more British than Italians were released in the first exchange.[22]

The Foreign Office received the name of the battalion or artillery unit for each Italian taken to Palma along with the date it had arrived in Spain. The first to arrive had been the 1st Artillery Battery, on September 23, 1936. The Indomito, Aquila, Carocco, and the 524b Battalions had arrived in December 1936.[23] When the sixty-seven reached the border, it was a quick walk over the bridge to Hendaye and freedom. After a welcome shower, an inoculation, new clothes, and a meal, they headed for London. Three Irishmen—Bob Doyle, John Lennon, and Dublin-born Maurice Levitas—went to Paris to see the Irish ambassador. Maurice's real purpose was to seek help for some Germans at San Pedro who had friends in Paris. When Maurice knocked on one such friend's door, a woman opened it, took one look at the shaved head, cracked eyeglasses, blue pullover, and dungarees and slammed the door. But Maurice shouted the name of the German prisoner, and the door then opened for a very warm welcome.

The three arrived in London about six the next morning. They had only French currency, and no exchange was open. A cafe used by cab drivers refused to serve them breakfast for French money. But the cab drivers, who noticed their resemblance to the prisoners who had arrived the day before, provided them with magnificent breakfasts, as well as change for the telephone.

Jack Flior, born in Latvia, had become a British citizen in South Africa (then a British colony), and spoke Latvian, Yiddish, Russian, and English. He had memorized the names of several Soviet citizens at San Pedro, some of whom were pretending to be Poles. He was very warmly received at the Soviet embassy in London, where the information was gratefully accepted.[24]

Thomas and Connie Moon's last letter from their son was dated November 1. Their worries ended on February 7, when Thomas Moon could enter into his diary:

JIM IS HOME AGAIN! . . . Donald, Stuart, Connie and I went to Victoria Station to meet him. . . . When the train arrived at 6:15, it was heartbreaking to watch the pathetic reunions. There was Jim, tall and manly with a Republic Army cap set jauntily on his head, apparently unaltered in appearance. When Connie discovered him she went completely to pieces for five minutes or so and became hysterical. It was difficult to pacify her. At such times her emotions overcome her. . . .

On February 9, Mr. Moon made the following entry:

Yesterday morning Jim went to the Dependants and Wounded Aid Committee of the International Brigade at Litchfield St., Charing Cross Road, as requested. They fitted him out (and his companions) with a new suit, boots, shirt, underclothes, etc.[25]

By February 16, Consul Goodden at Valencia had arranged for forty-five more Italians to be exchanged for thirty-four British and eleven Swiss. Then an order came from the Spanish Council of Ministers, incensed by British assistance in the fascist takeover of the island of Minorca and the news that Britain was ready to recognize the Franco government, suspending all exchanges. Britain and France recognized the Franco government the next day.

Goodden hadn't given the whole story. Before the fall of Catalonia, Negrín had arranged with France that he would turn over to them six hundred important fascist supporters of Franco held in Catalonian prisons, some under a death sentence, on the condition that France would hold them in concentration camps until Franco had released the Internationals. The Republic carried out its part of the agreement under very trying circumstances. By February 20 Franco had released eighty-two French prisoners and promised to release the rest. But then the French foreign minister, Georges Bonnet, released the six hundred "respectable supporters of General Franco" without the release of the remaining International prisoners, or even all of the French.[26]

The British, Canadians and Swiss left at Ondarreta were continuing their education in Franco's "pure justice" flowing from his honor as a "gentleman." A Catholic priest who had been in Ireland when San Sebastian was captured returned to Spain. He was asked to read a statement over the radio, prepared by the fascist authorities. After looking at it, he told them, "I will tell the truth, but I will not say this." He had since spent nearly twenty months in Ondarreta. A Basque explained to Frank West why there were two rows of bullet marks on the wall. The lower one showed where the bullets had hit when prisoners had been forced to kneel so young fascists twelve and fourteen years old, could shoot them, encouraged by their mothers standing behind them.[27]

In Janaury 1939 FALB asked the Spanish ambassador to the United States, Fernando de los Rios, to start negotiations for our exchange. On February 8, he informed Hull that the Spanish government was willing that the US government initiate the negotiations. When Hull asked Bowers whether anything practical could be done, Bowers replied that Del Vayo had assured him months ago that they would be glad to exchange Italians for Americans. He added:

When the Italian Ambassador wrote me he was urging our exchange I informed De Rialp. . . . He promised to act. After many days he came here and said he had been so swamped he had not yet taken the matter up but would at once. Since then I have reminded him and asked a report. Have been expecting to see him any minute.[28]

On February 28 Rialp informed Bowers he was ready to deliver the Americans at the border as soon as the Republic agreed to an exchange; Bowers immediately cabled this news to Hull and asked Del Vayo to take the exchange up with Negrín. That very evening we were stuffed into Zapatari Prison. Two days later, the exchange was approved, and Del Vayo asked when an American ship could pick up the Italians. But the archives reveal that Hull insisted no US naval vessel be used.[29] This meant we would spend seven weeks in Zapatari, and with Hull able to keep all this secret, there was no outcry from FALB or our relatives, beyond collecting signatures on petitions to free us and writing letters and collecting funds on our behalf.

At a meeting of the Relatives of the American Prisoners in Spain on February 9, cheers had greeted the announcement that fifty thousand signatures had already been collected. Gates described a nationwide appeal to raise funds for the rehabilitation of returning veterans and aid to the prisoners. Among those who signed the appeal were Columbia University anthropologist Franz Boas, actors Franchot Tone and Orson Welles, sculptor William Zorach, poet William Rose Benet, and Manhattan Borough President Stanley Isaacs. Tom Mooney sent a letter supporting aid for us. Irene Soames reported the Prisoners' Fund had grown from minus sixty cents to over $200. A Prisoners' Ball featuring Frances Farmer would be held on March 3. Several relatives had sold hundred-ticket blocks to organizations.[30]

Both pro-Republic and pro-Franco agitation were intense nationwide. In New York City alone, on Sunday, February 19, eleven thousand supporters of Franco gathered in the 107th Regiment Armory. They cheered Mervin K. Hart's call for immediate recognition of Franco. They applauded enthusiastically when a picture of Father Charles E. Coughlin was carried down the aisle. Several speakers praised Franco, Hitler, and Mussolini for their suppression of Communists.

And that evening, the Grand Exalted Ruler of the Elks at their 71st Anniversary Dinner at the Biltmore Hotel denounced "some 25,000 Italian Blackshirts" who were "galloping around our country."[31] Raymond Massey, Lionel Stander, Supreme Court Justice William Black, Jean Muir, Rockwell Kent, and Lillian Hellman were auctioning off manuscripts, letters, and books at the Delmonico Hotel for the benefit of exiled anti-Nazi writers and FALB's rehabilitation fund. The auction netted $8000.[32]

At the February 23 meeting of the Relatives organization, members learned that the IRC could supply each prisoner monthly with a package containing 500 grams of chocolate, 1 box of cheese, 6 Maggi cubes, 1 kilo of sugar, 2 tins of condensed milk, 1 piece of soap, 1 bottle of concentrated cod liver oil, for $1.50 per prisoner. A motion was passed unanimously to fund eighty-seven parcels, plus $25 a month for cigarettes, scientific magazines, and books. But the IRC on February 25 said food packages could not be forwarded to the American prisoners at San Pedro or Zaragoza; all transport was required for food distribution in Catalonia, now occupied by Franco's troops.[33]

*   *   *   *   *

Leo Hecht, a Lincoln Brigade veteran, was arrested on his return February 4, 1939, for fraudulent use of a passport, having used the name Seymour Rosenberg. The Brooklyn grand jury heard the case on February 14, 1939, and refused to indict him.[34] That set an important precedent. There were no further attempts to prosecute veterans on charges involving passports.

20 Zapatari

FEW SLEPT WELL that first night at Zapatari. The excitement of fantasizing what life would be like as free men, plus the crowded sleeping arrangements, kept most of us awake a good part of the night. We rose early, ready to go home.

Even the skimpy, thin ajo soup we had for breakfast did not dampen our spirits. We could tolerate anything once, if it led to freedom. As we stood around speculating on the how and when of our release, we were told we could go up on the flat roof above us for fresh air. The sunshine was pleasant and it was a lovely spring day, the vegetation greener than at San Pedro. A dozen rats scavenging through refuse in the rear provided diversion.

The day passed, interrupted only by our meals, each consisting of a small portion of a thin bean soup with a small chunk of bread. Both the quality and quantity of food were inferior to what we'd had at San Pedro. However, our high hopes to be out of there within a day or so made that quite bearable.

After a second day like the first, the Communist Party Committee of Three suggested that all Americans meet that evening and elect a chief. Max Shufer was chosen by acclamation. Two days later, the Swedes and Danes elected Arthur Karlsson, while the Cubans and Chileans chose Evaristo Rodríguez Oliva. Max, Arthur, and Evaristo arranged fair distribution of any seconds at mealtime, and the distribution of gifts of food and tobacco received from the Basques. We were free to mingle with them, and a very cordial relationship quickly developed.

After it appeared we might be in Zapatari for a while, the Committee of Three arranged several classes. We had fifteen who either had been born in the United States and taken to Spain when young or had lived in Puerto Rico or the Canal Zone. One had fought in the 15th Brigade, and five had fought in the northern part of Spain. They knew little or no English and had little knowledge of our country, so we organized crash courses in English for them, and arranged lectures in Spanish about trade unions, people's organizations, the principal political parties, and their rights as American citizens.

For the English-speaking Americans, we provided courses in Spanish and in conversational French. We also found that lectures about various trades and professions were very popular.[1]

Practice was making our going-to-bed procedures smoother. Our main complaint was about the lack of food. I had not lost weight at San Pedro, but I did here. Tex complained that he wasn't able to feed his lice and fleas in their accustomed style.

During our third week at Zapatari, Red Cross packages arrived for twenty-three Americans. The Committee of Three decided it was essential that they be shared with all Internationals and Basques. The twenty-three were called together and told about the packages.[2]

Then a prisoner alerted by the committee said, "The only problem is I can't enjoy all this with hungry guys watching me eat. I don't know why my name is on that list instead of somebody else's. Maybe the Red Cross can only send in packages to individuals, so they picked out twenty-three of our names. Besides, you know the Basques squeezed themselves together in order to make room for us, and deprived themselves of food in order to share with us. I say it is about time we did something to show them our appreciation and solidarity. Let's take all the coffee and sugar, half the condensed milk, and all the soup cubes, and turn them over to the kitchen, so everyone, including the Basques, can enjoy them. Then let's divide the rest equally among all the Americans, including our Spanish-American comrades, after making a donation to the Chileans, Cubans, Danes, and Swedes."

Several more agreed with this proposal, no one spoke against it, and a motion to share everything as proposed was passed without opposition. The thanks from the Basques were profuse, and our ties with the Chileans, Cubans, Danes, and Swedes were strengthened. While the twenty-three received less, they enjoyed it more.

Some may say this is an example of how Communists force some to do what they might not have done were it not for peer pressure that they had mobilized, that the freedom of some individuals to do as they wished had been curbed. Others will see it as an example of fine leadership, calling out the best in all prisoners, and strengthening our morale and solidarity.

Eugene Poling, a thirty-year-old from Lone Wolf, Oklahoma, was the first prisoner to receive money from home. He gave the $5 to Shufer, saying, "Here, use it for the benefit of everybody."[3]

The Committee then had a problem. "What do we do with the $5?" Their solution was to form an International Co-op with three sections—American, Cuban-Chilean, and Scandinavian—with two rules: (1) Each member was entitled to share equally in the Co-op's benefits; (2) The only qualification for membership was a willingness to turn over to the Co-op any money received.

All the American CP members, now numbering about twenty-five, joined. The last week of March the Americans met to set up the Co-op's American Section. About two-thirds of the Americans joined the Co-op immediately. Hy Wallach was elected treasurer; Herman Lopez, secretary; and I, chairman.[4] Cuban-Chilean and Scandinavian sections were set up. Each section shared in proportion to the number of its members. The prison had no canteen, but purchases were made with the help of the Basques, who had warned us not to trust the daytime *comandante* of the prison.

Everyone did not join. Some, certain they would not receive money, felt they could not, with a clear conscience, join the Co-op. We tried to persuade them to join, as long as they were willing to put in any funds received. A few still stayed out.

We were not permitted to mail letters, and we received no packages through the mail. No visitors came to see us. At first these restrictions did not bother us, since we expected each day to be our last in Franco Spain. But by the end of March we were becoming quite worried about the negotiations for our release.

*   *   *   *   *

In New York, fifteen hundred people attended the Prisoners Ball at the Center Hotel on Friday, March 3. My wife was alarmed the next morning when my name was not listed in the *Times* among the seventy-eight to be exchanged.[5]

Ambassador Bowers boarded the *Queen Mary* on March 4 after Hull had wired Roosevelt, then at sea, suggesting Bowers "be ordered home for consultation in order to free our hands for establishing relations with the Franco Government."[6] On March 5, the phony National Defense Council seized power in the Republic.

Federic Jacosta di Lorenzo, the tall slim Frenchman who knew eight languages and had been a source of strength for prisoners at San Pedro, Zaragoza, Burgos, and Valdenoceda, was released the first part of March along with sixteen other Frenchmen.[7]

The rest of us, though we did not know it, awaited the repatriation of the Italians for whom we were to be exchanged. But on March 7, Sir Robert Hodgson, now British ambassador to Spain, reported that Franco had stopped prisoner exchanges. Hodgson shortly reported that Colonel Martin had not been allowed to see the quarters where the British were held at Ondarreta, or their food, on the ground that it was a civilian prison. Martin had left soap and money from the British Dependants' Aid Committee, and had obtained the names of thirty-one Canadians and ten English prisoners, including the John O'Beirne whom Leo Berman tried to help.[8]

On the fourteenth, Sumner Welles, acting secretary of state, cabled Walter G. Thurston, who had taken Bowers' place, about plans for the exchange of American prisoners. Thurston replied on the eighteenth that an "arrangement" existed, but that he saw no way to take off the Italians. He concluded, "The alternative is to wait the end of hostilities, following which it is to be assumed that Franco will be disposed to relinquish the Americans."[9]

On the sixteenth, British Consul Abington Goodden in Valencia wired the Foreign Office that permission to evacuate about two hundred Italian prisoners at Gandia was expected shortly.[10] But when Britain recognized

Franco, Goodden lost his authority as British consul. However, on March 28, using a telegram obtained by the IRC and Denys Cowan in Madrid just before it fell, Gooden was able to get the local documents needed to embark the Italians. HMS *Sussex* and HMS *Nubian* arrived at Gandia the next morning. The harbor was crowded with Spaniards desperate to leave. With the help of the prison authorities and the police, Goodden had 167 Italians taken to Palma on the *Sussex* on March 29.[11]

The thirty-one Canadians, ten British and eleven Swiss spent the month of March at Ondarreta learning how to cope with their "bloody rotten" conditions. If they didn't keep a cover on the toilet bowl, rats would use it to get into the cell, providing considerable excitement before they were caught. At the end of the month, a group of Spaniards entered the basement. Frank West, in the first cell, found out they had just come from the refugee camps in France. He told them, "We are members of the International Brigade." Seeing the Spaniards' fright, Frank suggested they go upstairs where there was a Republican artillery captain. Soon Frank heard the captain and his companions shouting with appropriate profanity: "You were in France and you came back here! You deserve what you'll get here! Get out!"[12]

Frank didn't know military refugees in France had been held in concentration camps with brutal guards, without shelter, with little or no food, without water fit to drink, and with no medical services. They found Ondarreta nicer—if they didn't get shot.[13]

*   *   *   *   *

"Uh-oh, the war is over! The guards have their guns upside down," Joe Young commented April 1 as he looked down from the roof of Zapatari. That day's war communiqué read, "Today, the red army captured and disarmed, the national troops have reached their final military objectives. THE WAR HAS ENDED."

We were a sober group of prisoners as we discussed what it meant. We had lost the cause for which we had come to Spain and for which friends had sacrificed their lives. Now the repression and executions would spread over the rest of Spain as military and civilian leaders of the Republic were captured. Would Franco now let us go, or would he try to trade us off, perhaps for recognition or for some commercial advantage?

We continued our classes and lectures. Arthur Karlsson gave a select group a fascinating account of his experiences in the underground in Germany after Hitler took power. When the Gestapo was on his heels, he had slipped across the border into Poland, and then went on to the Soviet Union. Hitler's treatment of antifascists was brutal then and had grown worse by 1939.

We selected Max Shufer to tell the prison's night commanding officer that we wanted to contact the American consul about obtaining more food. Just then, on April 5, we received a second shipment of fifty food parcels from FALB through the International Red Cross.[14] The contents of the parcels were distributed in the same way as the first shipment, except that the Cubans decided to exclude six who had expressed pro-Franco opinions.

Our maverick CP member was dissatisfied with the Cubans' action, and at a meeting of the American Co-op, said they had joined the International Co-op only to obtain some of the money we were receiving. Several Americans objected strongly to his statement as a slander against the Cubans. Furthermore, denying them the right to decide with whom they wanted to share the food smelled of "Yankee superiority." A motion was passed that we censure members guilty of slander against the Cubans, and further, that the American Section apologize to the Cubans for the slanderous statements. I was selected to make the apology.

The night commanding officer listened very sympathetically to our complaints about the food. He would let our consul or the IRC know that we wanted to see them, and he informed Max, not for quotation, that the day officer was pocketing food money.

A few days later I met a very angry young Basque who had been an officer in the Republican Army. The officers of his unit had been told to choose between trying to hide in their home towns or going to Alicante, where British ships would take them into exile. Since he would have had to cross enemy lines to reach his home, he had gone to Alicante, where he found some ten thousand people waiting. They saw the British ships on the horizon, but none came in, and on March 30 they were surrounded by fascist troops. He was convinced the ships had just been a ruse to help Franco trap them. He cursed Chamberlain. Later I learned that fifty thousand Republican military and civilian leaders had been captured at the ports, saving Franco the trouble of hunting for them.

At the next meeting of the American Co-op, on Tuesday, April 18, Max Shufer reported an IRC representative had told him that we might be leaving that week. This news made it easier to put up with Zapatari's discomforts a little longer. I reported that I had extended our apology to the Cuban Executive Committee. Hy Wallach's motion to send our remaining funds to San Pedro was approved.[15]

On April 21, the first packet of mail arrived. I received three letters from my wife, but the censor had kept five-sixths of one page of the February 24 letter.[16] I hoped there had been nothing in it that might cause me to spend more time in Spain.

On April 5, 1939, thirty-one Canadian and eleven Swiss were exchanged for forty-two of the 167 Italians who had been freed a week earlier. The past ten weeks at Ondarreta had been wretched. But ten English prisoners, including Syd Harris, were not included in the exchange. Those freed traveled by bus to the border, waited to be checked off, and then walked across the bridge to freedom.

The Canadian representative, with much understanding, first offered them cigarettes; then he took them for a bath, vaccination, a change of clothes, and a meal before starting them on their way to Le Havre.[17] The Swiss representative made clear his opinion that the Swiss prisoners had fought for the wrong side and refused to buy them new clothes. Only when the Canadian offered to buy them did the Swiss representative pay for the clothes, a meal and rooms in a hotel for the night.

When the Swiss volunteers returned home, they were jailed, tried, and sentenced by a military court to five months' imprisonment, to be followed by compulsory military service. The Swiss volunteers who had not been captured received the same treatment; Switzerland was the only democratic country to imprison its nationals when they returned from Spain.[18]

The names, place and date of birth, and military unit of the thirty-one Canadians are listed in Appendix 3.

*   *   *   *   *

Cheers had broken out on Friday, March 31, in FALB's office when a cable arrived from Paris: AMERICAN EMBASSY SPANISH BORDER INFORMS US 70 AMERICANS ENROUTE FRANCE TOMORROW.

But David White's heart sank. FALB did not have the money to bring us back. Funds were constantly being raised, but there were always more needs than money, for the care of disabled returnees, for support of over one hundred veterans in Le Havre held up for "unacceptable documentation," and for associated costly legal expenses (even though the lawyers were serving with little or no pay), as well as the cost of an office. Sam Bard, in charge of raising funds, immediately sent out an appeal signed by Vincent Sheean and Dave White. Bill Rosenblatt called the relatives together Saturday afternoon, and they pledged to raise $3000.

Sunday's newspapers reported that US had recognized the Franco government, but said nothing about our release. Monday morning White received a new cable from Paris. DESPITE PROMISES EMBASSY AMERICAN PRISONERS NOT YET LIBERATED NO DEFINITE DATE RELEASE KNOWN AT BORDER STOP ASTOUNDED RECOGNITION FRANCO WITHOUT EVEN PREVIOUS RELEASE AMERICAN PRISONERS STOP URGE CAMPAIGN PROTEST PRESSURE WASHINGTON OBTAIN IMMEDIATE RELEASE.

Anger led to action. That evening Bill Rosenblatt, Bob Steck's father, and my wife left for Washington, carrying with them petitions with 57,000 signatures calling for our release. The next day, aided by veteran Leonard Levenson, they spoke to senators and congressmen, and presented the petitions to Pierrepont Moffat in the State Department. Moffat's advice was just to wait, and the delegation felt it had accomplished very little. But former Congressman Vito Marcantonio spoke that same afternoon to Sumner Welles, the Under Secretary of State, in "quite a vigorous manner," and fifteen minutes later learned that H. Freeman Matthews, the embassy chargé d'affaires, had been instructed to make the release of the prisoners his first priority. So the delegation saw Moffat again, and he then said that the State Department would do all it could to free us.

The delegation left after visiting the Lincoln Memorial, aware of the effort required to achieve the goal "that government of the people, for the people, by the people, shall not perish from this earth."[19]

A "Bring Bob Back" studio party—admission fifty cents—was organized by Bob Steck's friends at the New Theatre School in New York on April 15. The Good Neighbors of Hamilton Heights in Upper Manhattan advertised: "Leave your Pots and Pans Behind, Come to the FIRST ANNUAL SPRING DINNER. . . . Proceeds to Friends of the American Boys in Franco's Spain. . . ." Since a dinner was included, the cost was higher, seventy cents.[20] Relatives and friends walked through the subway trains with collection cans, obtaining donations from people on their way to and from work. Many spoke at union meetings. Irene Soames received a $250 contribution from one union and several hundred dollars more from others.

On April 16, Hull sent Matthews a telegram marked "Urgent":

We are under extreme pressure from relatives and interested persons and organizations in this country who are concerned because of the delay in releasing these Americans. Please report result of your conversations with Spanish authorities on this matter.

Matthews replied the next day that Rialp had assured him that morning that eighty-one Americans and fifteen Swedes, eight Danes and five Cubans have been taken to San Sebastian to be exchanged that week. The State Department phoned this information to Levenson and Rosenblatt.[21] We had arrived there seven weeks earlier, with forty-five Cubans and four Chileans as well as the Danes and Swedes.[22]

On April 20, Ambassador Bowers informed Hull that release of the Americans was blocked by Rialp's insistence on a simultaneous release of all nationalities.[23] Thanks to Bowers' energetic intervention, arrangements were made to receive each nationality.

But the next day Robert D. Murphy, the American consul in Paris, telephoned Moffatt that the FALB agent had just informed him FALB was "broke." This meant the French would refuse to admit the eighty-one Americans who were to be released and that they might have to stay in Spanish prisons for an additional three or four months.

Moffat had James Dunn phone FALB. John Gates answered that FALB could obtain the funds that he would call back later that afternoon. At four, White called Dunn to tell him we had enough funds, provided the men were not delayed in France by documentation difficulties. The Passport Division reported the documents of sixty-eight of the eighty-one were in order, but those of thirteen, mostly Puerto Ricans, were in doubt.[24] In fact, only three were Puerto Ricans, and there were no sailing records for two of them, Herman Lopez and Ferdinand Ribera Vasquez, because they had gone to Spain as stowaways.

Chargé d'affaires Matthews cabled Hull that Rialp had

stated that in view of British insistence and the fact that it was the British who actually took off the Italian prisoners and in view of the further fact that the exchange agreed upon was strictly on a man-for-man basis, the number of other nationalities must be reduced. He said therefore the number of Americans who will be permitted to leave is 71 instead of 81 . . . while he personally believed . . . foreign prisoners would be released in the relatively near future he could get no guarantee with respect to the remaining 10 Americans.

Rather than delay the departure of the seventy-one, Matthews had insisted they be released immediately. Rialp had promised they would be taken to the border at ten the next morning.[25]

21 Freedom

A RUMOR SPREAD early Saturday, April 22, 1939, that we were leaving. Herman put his *Jaily News* in his shoes and hid his Co-op minute book. Henry Giler hid his green-pamphlet deck of cards. We were thanking our Basque friends for their wonderful hospitality when the commander came in with an aide, who then called out the names of the four Chileans. They were escorted down into a waiting bus. Next he called out the names of seven Cubans[1] and, without explanation, ordered the remaining thirty-eight to go up on the roof. Then he called out the names of the eight Danes and all fifteen Swedes, including, to our great joy, Arthur Karlsson.

Now the clerk began to call out in alphabetical order the Americans, in lots of ten.[2] Where he had difficulty with pronunciation, Max Shufer helped him. When he called Richard Chompson, Max signaled to Dick Thompson.[3] The list was long, but each name meant the world to an individual. The seventh lot consisted of eleven, ending with Fred Stanley. "Only seventy-one, not one more!" was the aide's only explanation as he ordered the ten remaining Americans up on the roof. When the last eleven boarded the buses, they told the rest of us about the ten being left behind, now waving to us from the roof. We could do no more than wave back as the buses took off. Had "Chompson" been Thompson, Bob Steck, next on the list, would have been among those freed.

Actually, Franco should have released 21 more. The British had taken off 167 Italian prisoners from Gandia on March 29.[4] Then Franco had released 31 Canadians and 11 Swiss on April 5, and 4 Chileans, 7 Cubans, 8 Danes, 15 Swedes, and 71 Americans—making a total of only 146.

The Franco authorities had held back the British at Ondarreta and ten Americans because, they claimed twenty Italian prisoners had not been taken off from Valencia before that port fell. Whether the twenty at Valencia had been trucked the 67 kilometers to Gandia or had simply been released when Valencia fell is not known.

The ten left behind were all Lincoln volunteers. Among those released, fifteen had come to Spain before 1936.[5] Yet there was no thought that the ten Lincoln veterans should have had priority. If Franco had found the others enough of a threat to arrest them and throw them in with us, then we would give them full rights in our group. Many of them were very young; one had just turned nineteen. They might well have been in greater danger than the ten veterans, had they remained in Spain.

The buses took us through Irún to the 300-foot-long stone bridge over the Bidassoa River. Once across that, we would be free. Roll calls, and conferences between Civil Guards and IRC officials, took until 2 P.M. Then everything was ready. Each nationality, crossing in a body, would be received by the appropriate authority on the other side.

Finally, our great moment: we marched silently and smiling. The first person I saw was Angela Guest, sister of David Guest, a brilliant British mathematician and Marxist philosopher killed in 1938 in the fighting across the Ebro. I had last seen Angela in a small valley near Brunete after having been bombed and strafed. A petite blonde, she had come trotting along wearing a smile and no helmet, having left her ambulance nearby to look for wounded.

Now representing FALB, she smiled at our excited faces, and told us that French officials would see to it that we took a shower, were vaccinated, and got clean clothes. Then two embassy attachés would take care of us. I wanted to give Angela a hug but decided it would be more comradely to take the shower first. Carney's article in the *New York Times* the next morning said that no representative of FALB had met us.

The shower water was hot and we lathered away the winter's grime. And then towels!—an amenity we had missed for more than a year. Next, an attendant handed each of us a bundle—underclothes, shirt, pants, and a jacket. The vaccination was done quickly, and then, sockless, tieless, and hatless, we were ready to enjoy the free world.

The IRC surprised us with pocket money from FALB, 140 francs each (about $7). We immediately took up a collection for those left behind and asked the attachés to forward it to them.

Since we had had a skimpy breakfast and no lunch, we enjoyed an early dinner, reveling in our freedom while sitting at tables with white tablecloths, with knives, forks, and spoons, and drinking wine with our meal. The braised lamb, green peas, and potatoes were delicious.[6]

We didn't sleep much in our coach seats on the overnight train to Paris as we discussed our plans. It felt too good to be free to spend time sleeping.[7]

FALB learned on Monday morning, April 24, 1939, that seventy-one American prisoners had arrived in France, and that money had to be provided at once to maintain them and bring them back.[8] That afternoon Dave White telephoned Eric Wendelin at the State Department to tell him that $2500 for transportation had been cabled to Peter Rhodes, FALB's agent in Paris. Wendelin promised that Matthews would do all he could to obtain the release of the ten still held.

White expressed his fear that some prisoners would be held back because they could not prove American citizenship. Wendelin said the citizenship of all but twelve had already been established. In that case, White asked, why was Consul Samuel H. Wiley at Le Havre demanding birth certificates, not previously required, thus detaining fifty-five volunteers for whom evidence of legal entry had been provided, especially twenty-five for whom affidavits of support and employment had also been obtained. Wendelin defended a "most able and conscientious officer, entirely familiar with our immigration laws."[9] But two days later Wiley asked the State Department to

please instruct on the legal aspects of following points: (one) payment of passage by the Friends of the Abraham Lincoln Battalion; (two) membership of applicant in Spanish Branch of "International Red Aid" or similar organization; (three) maximum period of time which may be reasonably construed as temporary visit abroad in view of circumstances common to practically all of these cases; (four) value of affidavits of support executed by representative of the Friends of the Abraham Lincoln Battalion?[10]

It took the Department ten weeks to answer those questions, forcing FALB to exhaust its resources supporting the veterans, now more than a hundred, waiting in France. Finally, on July 7, the Department replied, basing its answers on a twenty-page analysis by the Department of Justice. It was illegal for FALB to pay the fare of an alien, either directly or indirectly; the International Red Aid was "the international counterpart of the American Civil Liberties Union"; and anyone who was a member of it must be excluded from the United States.

Each alien who had left to fight in Spain had (1) To present proof of previous legal admission to the United States. (Ellis Island was about 60,000 cases behind in certifying lawful admissions.) His case was not to receive priority. (2) To present proof he had intended to return. (This might be difficult even for those who had left families behind, for they might have intended to "become little commissars" in Spain and move their families there if they had won.) (3) To prove he had an established domicile in the United States while in Spain. (The fact that he was returning to a job was not considered proof.) (4) To prove that "his stay, if protracted, was caused by justifiable reasons over which he had little or no control." Visitors to the United States may come as tourists, or for business or pleasure, and it was assumed that an alien could go abroad for the same reasons; but these men had not gone to Spain for such reasons, so they could not meet this requirement. (5) The State Department could not accept affidavits of support by FALB because affidavits from organizations such as "the Jewish Relief Committees throughout the country" would then have to be accepted.[11] These requirements made it impossible for any of the noncitizen volunteers to return to the US legally.

We knew nothing of FALB's financial and legal problems as we traveled happily toward Le Havre. We were delighted to see the long craggy face of Art Shields, the veteran correspondent for the *Daily Worker,* who joined us at Paris. Later, I learned of his own narrow escape from a firing squad when Madrid was taken over by Colonel Segismundo Casado.[12]

In Le Havre, we and the thirty-one Canadians from Ondarreta were quartered in one-story brick barracks in the Parc de la Hève. We ate at long tables in a mess room in military fashion. And long rows of cots provided us with a luxury we, unless wounded, had not known for up to two years—a bed.

Monday morning, April 24, we bought personal items—razor, toothbrush, comb, handkerchief, and socks. We also had to catch up on the news of what had really happened during the past year. Wiley's attaché came to clear up discrepancies. Those who had been using a nom de guerre now reverted to their true names, but they were detained until the new information was checked.

The Canadians had bad news for us. The nuns in Guernica who had survived the Condor Legion's bombing had had to choose between signing a statement that Guernica had been destroyed by the Reds and imprisonment. Most who had chosen imprisonment were now, two years later, still in Ondarreta, and some were ill with tuberculosis; it was probable all there would die.

My high point that Monday was a visit by Helen Simon, a lovely, tall young woman, who was representing American students at the World Student Federation. She described the world-wide efforts students were making on behalf of peace and against fascism. Helen also brought me news of my wife and her work with students at Evander Childs High School.

FALB was pleased that fourteen who had been in Spain before 1936 had escaped from Franco Spain, but it informed Peter Rhodes that he should not assume financial responsibility for them. Since fifty-one volunteers were now free to return, he used the $2,500 to buy thirty third-class tickets on the SS *President Harding* at $81.75 each. The next day Rhodes obtained $1800 from Louis Fischer to buy tickets for the remaining twenty-one.[13]

That night, April 25, the closest relative of each of the seventy prisoners at Le Havre answered a knock on the door and found a Postal Telegraph messenger boy seeking to collect for a night letter. The letter sent to my wife read:

TELEGRAM FROM AMERICAN CONSUL HAVRE REPORTS ARRIVAL THERE FROM PARIS OF CARL GEISER RELEASED AMERICAN PRISONER FROM SPAIN AWAITING ARRANGEMENTS BY FRIENDS OF THE ABRAHAM LINCOLN BRIGADE

CORDELL HULL   SECRETARY OF STATE[14]

*   *   *   *   *

On Thursday morning, April 27, the two Canadians and eight British from Ondarreta joined us.[15] Thirty-one of us didn't have much time to talk with the newcomers, for we sailed that same day on the *President Harding*. (Juan Perez's passage had been paid by the ARC.) We traveled light: our worldly possessions were in our pockets or our hands. I shared Cabin 306 with Fred Borer and Tom Brown. The trip across the Atlantic was enjoyable, especially the eating part. I could already see my scurvy sores drying up, but my teeth handicapped me at mealtimes.

While we were at sea, the State Department received the list of names of those of us, due in New York on May 6 or 7 and of the fifteen on the *Ile de France* due May 10. Mrs. R. B. Shipley, head of the Passport Division, issued instructions to check our "identity with the person described in the appropriate passport file and that arrangements be made for the examination of the baggage and persons of the men to determine whether they may be in possession of passports."[16]

It was Western Union's turn to bring my wife the good news; I would be arriving on the *President Harding* on May 6.[17] A photographer came aboard in time to take a picture of us with the Statue of Liberty in the background.[18] Before the ship docked, we were informed that we and our baggage had to be searched. On our way to the examining lounge we passed reporters and gave them things like the Zapatari Co-op Minute Book, copies of the *Jaily News*, and radical literature.

The search did not take long. Most of us had no baggage, and the body-patting search was quickly done. Then there was a check of our identity against their files and we were free to go. Of course, we retrieved our "valuables" from the kind reporters. (It was only while doing research for this history that I learned the search was for passports and none had been found.)

As the *President Harding* was eased along Pier 59 at the foot of West 18th Street in Manhattan, we saw a large crowd waving and cheering. We wondered what celebrity had come back with us, but when we got close enough to recognize relatives and friends, we realized the crowd had come to greet us. Soon we were on the dock, being hugged and kissed and welcomed home. FALB had made arrangements for the weekend for those whose relatives or friends were not there.

At a "Welcome Home" party for me in our apartment that night, I was warmly greeted by many old friends, especially Dave White. I must confess that the question, "Well, how was it?" grew a bit tiresome, even though I knew it was difficult for friends to ask specific questions. Some two hours after the party started I found Sylvia, my wife, in an easy chair, sound asleep, worn out by the stress and strain she had been under during the past several months, always fearful that something might go wrong, and by her work to prepare the apartment and the homecoming. I did not awaken her.

Sunday evening, at a celebration for our return, the ex-prisoners were on the dais at the Hotel Roosevelt, and were introduced to the large audience. Dave White spoke about the work that had to be done to bring the rest of the prisoners safely home. Ralph Bates, the British author and early member of the 15th Brigade staff, predicted that Hitler's and Mussolini's victory in Spain would set the stage for a second world war.

I related incidents from our life at San Pedro, showing how the fascists used force and violence against us and the Spanish people to maintain their rule, and described their attempts to blame democracy for the world's ills. I told about my talk with the Italian lieutenant after my capture, calling to their attention that even that level of command understood the fascist powers were preparing for war with the democratic countries.

The *Times* did not think it fit to inform its readers of the large audience that had welcomed the prisoners, nor of the evidence Bates and I presented that Hitler and Mussolini were preparing for a war against us. However, the paper devoted five inches to Father Coughlin's weekly radio address and its lies. As proof that England, the press, and Hollywood had a plan to propagandize us into the next war, Coughlin cited Warner Brothers' movie *Confessions of a Nazi Spy.*

When the ex-prisoners came to the FALB office on Monday, some just to thank FALB for the help given them, all were urged to have a medical examination; there were about five hundred doctors, including well-known specialists, and dentists who were donating their services to veterans.[19] Several whose scurvy sores were particularly bad were sent to a dermatologist; he assured them that a diet rich in citrus fruits and vegetables would soon make the sores disappear. Mine, to my amazement, were gone within a month.

There had been concern that we would need considerable medical care and rest. Adjustment to prison life had been a trying experience, but adjustment to the freedom and amenities of life at home was easy and pleasant. Important contributing factors were the splendid receptions we received from relatives and friends and the pleasure of being a local celebrity for a few days.

I was invited to attend the National Convention of the YCL, as were all former prisoners. From the reports and discussions, I learned what had happened during the past year on college campuses, and in the workshops and unemployment lines.

On Wednesday evening, May 10, the second group of fifteen was also welcomed by a crowd of relatives and friends. The leader of the group, Stanley Heinricher, told reporters, "We'd do it again if we had to," and he called for freeing all Americans and Internationals remaining in Spain.

22   The Americans Left Behind

ON APRIL 26, two Civil Guards escorted the ten Americans to the San Sebastian railroad station, where they met two other *Americanos,* a former deported inmate of San Quentin and a Puerto Rican engineer.[1]

The twelve traveled in style—third class—with a loaf of bread each, and tobacco provided by their Civil Guard escort. Arriving at San Pedro too late for the evening meal, they spent the night in the hay mow. The next morning they were greeted by a new officer, an *alfarez,* equivalent to our second lieutenant. Calling them "poor little ones," he escorted them back to their old haunts.[2] Radavoy Nicolich, the Yugoslav chess master, had prepared a place for Hy Wallach at his side.[3]

The day the Americans returned, Lieto Madjez Levi was buried outside San Pedro's east wall.[4] His nationality is not known, and he does not appear on the September 10, 1938, list.

The Americans welcomed the accumulated letters and money, but not the weather; it snowed on May 6. More chilling was the news that the Gestapo had returned and was taking away six Germans.[5] Bob Steck was grilled on why he had not been exchanged, and about the disappearance of a Civil Guard at Alcañiz.[6] But there was a welcome change at San Pedro. The new *alfarez,* named "the Soother" by the Americans, did not use a stick and saw to it that the sergeants used theirs rarely.

The *Diario de Burgos* editorial on May 5 questioned why the United States was rearming at an unheard-of rate in the interests of International Judaism. On May 9, *Diario* claimed the greatest event in this era was the rebirth of the Roman Empire under the aegis of Mussolini. A chill went down the prisoners' backs a day later when they read of how Franco administered justice—ten judges sitting in Madrid were conducting two hundred courts-martial a day!

"Why have they been sent back to San Pedro?" was the burden of phone calls to the FALB office by prisoners' relatives and friends after reading Carney's May 3 dispatch in the *Times.* The State Department explained that the ten had been held back because the Republic had not freed an equal number of foreign prisoners before the end of the war; as for the return to San Pedro, they were fed better there; and the Department would forward funds to them by telegraph at FALB's expense, or free by mail.[7] The last was a welcome change on State Department policy.

Apparently the Department was not aware that the Republic had released 167 and Franco only 156. Nor was Amabassador Bowers aware of this when, as one of his last official acts, he asked Under Secretary of State Barcenas at Burgos for their release.[8]

On Monday morning, May 15, a tall, distinguished-looking visitor, with a square jaw and a high forehead, accompanied by a very attractive wife, asked to see the American prisoners at San Pedro. Earl T. Crain had no permit to see them, but he used his credentials as the third secretary of the US embassy, fluent Spanish, and diplomatic tact to have the American prisoners called to his car. Thirteen showed up. The new prisoner was Bernardo Alvarez y González, born in Tampa, Florida, August 26, 1913. He had gone to Spain in 1931 and was a soldier when captured in Catalonia on February 11, 1939.

To Crain all of them appeared to be in reasonably good health and spirits, though they reported their diet consisted principally of beans and soup, poor in quality and insufficient in quantity. Their treatment was fairly good, but there were occasional punishments for relatively minor offenses. One had been beaten so badly that he was hospitalized. (A Chilean had washed his pants, and while they were drying he wore a smock. Accused of indecent exposure by a sergeant, he was strung up in the barn and struck with belts so severely that he had to be placed in the infirmary.[9])

The major pressed Crain to make his visit short. Crain nonetheless took the time to ask each prisoner his name and place and date of birth, how and when he had come to Spain, the name and address of his nearest relative, and whether the relative could pay for his return fare. He asked Leon Tenor to write down information about their situation and the whereabouts of other American prisoners; Leon wrote that Alf Andreasen, Cohen Haber, Clarence Blair, and Conrad Hendricks [Stojewa] were reported to be in Zaragoza and that Destruye Iglesias had been taken to Gijón and sentenced to death (later commuted to thirty years). Joe Young also added a note that a Gestapo agent had asked the Americans if they "would support American government against Fascist uprisings. We told him yes. Were asked if we would support American Government in case Germany declared war on the United States. We also told him we would."

Joe and Leon slipped their notes into Crain's pocket when the major wasn't looking, along with another asking that letters be sent to Canadian addresses informing relatives that Paul Szusko, E. Zdananskas, and Charles Scanlon were at San Pedro.

Crain received permission to distribute twenty packages of cigarettes contributed by Chargé d'Affaires H. Freeman Matthews. An American offered the major a pack. He politely refused, saying, "I smoke Spanish tobacco."

Crain also arranged canteen privileges for soap and cigarettes and for the treatment of Toole's trench mouth. He assured the prisoners that the embassy was trying to free them.[10]

For the first time the prisoners felt they had been in contact with a capable, trustworthy American who treated them as fellow Americans. Crain, from Quincy, Illinois, had served in Cuba, Costa Rica, Nicaragua, Mexico, and Chile;[11] he had arrived at the embassy in Spain only five days before. His first task was to find and return to the United States all Americans—POWs or not—who wanted to leave Spain.

Many of the Americans expected to be in San Pedro for quite a while. To raise their spirits, Hy Wallach bet Bob Steck that they would leave San Pedro not later than August 15. If they did not leave then, he would push a coin across the floor with his nose. If he was right, Bob's nose would do the pushing.[12]

Al Ziegler received letters from his mother, his sister Flora, and a girl friend on May 26, his twenty-fourth birthday. Early in June he received a package from Sol Lerner containing E. B. Wilson's *Advanced Calculus* and Lancelot Hogben's *Mathematics for the Millions*.[13,14] Al, who enjoyed books on mathematics as others enjoy romantic novels or science fiction, wrote in thanks:

Honest, if you never write again, I'm more than happy. I have enough mathematical problems to keep me pleasantly dazed forever. . . . Sure am glad the ring fit. . . . [Al had sent a prisoner-made ring for Natali, Sol's fiancée.—CG]
There, that's another novel finished. Back to the Math books.
Your friend to the Nth power.[15]

The articles in *Diario de Burgos* were alarming. May 16: Mussolini announced, "We shall always march with Germany to reach Peace with Justice." May 20: Franco announced, " 'Our Empire' is not an Empty Phrase!" May 24: "Germany and Italy are not thinking of using force to solve Europe's problems." June 13: Rome: "Pope Pius XII blesses 3000 Spanish Legionnaires."

*   *   *   *   *

Once back in the United States, I wanted to tell the State Department about the fascist plans to overthrow democratic governments, including ours. David White made the appointment; Fletcher Warren, an assistant to the assistant secretary of state was assigned to meet with us on June 13. I told him about my interview with the Italian lieutenant an hour after I was captured and the fascist propaganda I had seen that painted our country as an evil and degenerate state.

Warren listened courteously and, when I was finished, patted me on the back, saying, "We know what is going on, so don't worry about it. You've done your share, so go home and take it easy." Dave and I left with the impression that opposing fascism had a low priority in the State Department.

On June 12 Matthews was authorized to spend $25, received from

William Rosenblatt, to purchase whatever the American prisoners at Burgos needed, a further change in State Department policy. A week later, Rosenblatt sent another $25 for all American POWS.[16] In the middle of June, Crain left some letters at San Pedro, plus the 225 pesetas we had collected when freed.[17]

That the embassy in Spain now felt free to make a stronger effort to gain our freedom can be seen in Ambassador Alexander Weddell's statement to Franco's minister of foreign affairs on June 22. In it the new ambassador pointed out that the number of Americans imprisoned was small and that their continued detention

meant continuous pressure from relatives and others in the United States and offered a fruitful cause of irritation, and from this latter standpoint gave the matter an importance in the relations of the two countries which a problem so easily solved did not merit.

On July 1, Weddell submitted to Hull a list of all Americans in Spanish prisons and information about each one. It included twenty-eight citizens, of whom eleven were POWs (in addition to the eleven at San Pedro). The list also included four whose citizenship was doubtful and twelve who had dual citizenship.[18]

Al Ziegler continued his use of postal cards:

Dear Florence and Herman:

Your four packages (including Young's) more or less arrived, and I'm dressed up like a million dollars . . . with no place to go.

The surveying and arithmetic courses arrived (thanks from Steck) and we're practicing up to do some field work.

Your kid brother Al

Dear Sis:

We received a letter from John H. Morgan, 2nd Secretary of the Embassy; and he has promised to deliver all the money this week no less. (The money from the Relatives, I mean.) The same day the Red Cross showed up with 25 pesetas a head. (Also from the Relatives, I guess.) Two of the "Internationals" here who claim to be Americans are not on Mr. Morgan's list, after investigation. So now eleven here instead of my lucky 13. New "Internationals" arrive slowly but regularly however. The other nite they even rounded up a citizen of the tiny Republic of Andorra the which is balanced up in those Pyrenees where I once went hiking. Since exchange of prisoners has officially ceased, practically all Spanish prisoners (not "Internationals") here have been liquidated. Among us, two trips totaling 12 Hessians have since been accomplished. . . .

In a letter to his father, Al said he was

studying the I.C.S. course in surveying, some calculus, "La Dama de Camelia" (in Spanish) by Dumas, the younger. Tell Florence I am now sporting the latest style in berets, *boina blance,* by our San Pedro tailor—large and made out of white toweling including the nib: especially startling when you take the hat off, it's worn on bald heads. . . . See from Ida's letter they run dances for us back there: hope you will go because somebody ought to enjoy this. Like an Irish Wake. . . . believe it or not, the Internacionales are scheduled to play [baseball] the local soldiery this coming Saint's Day in a regular field and the Pueblo is invited! Fritebol (a kind of Soccer) and wrestling are also on the programme. The "Mass" part of the Saint's Day is optional.[19]

Bob Steck wrote that

conditions have changed a lot. H_2O is more plentiful, but swinging lead [Tanky] has disappeared. Beans and lentils still fight for supremacy. Mainstay [bread] has dwindled to less than ¼ of the issue we received when you were here. Best news of all is that cold showers twice a week till snow falls have been promised. [They were never put in operation.—CG] . . . We spend half of the morning in the field rather consistently—baseball and soccer are the popular summer sports . . . we've turned the place, insofar as possible, into a study and workshop making shoes and all kinds of souvenirs. Insofar as the studies are concerned, they're about the same as those you remember. I'm a veritable Spaniard—pretty good in French, and Russian is coming along.[20]

The parish death records of Carcedo de Burgos report that Peter Tisma, while in a punishment cell, committed suicide on July 1, 1939, by strangling himself with a strip made from his mattress. Extreme unction was administered because of signs of insanity, and he was buried in Burgos. Peter Tisma, born in Yugoslavia in 1897, fought with the 129th Brigade.[21]

*   *   *   *   *

Ambassador Weddell was trying to get the American prisoners out of Spain and to get Colonel Sosthenes Behn in. Behn was the head of the International Telephone and Telegraph Company, which owned the National Telephone Company in Spain. It was worth $125,000,000.[22]

Three months of negotiations had brought no results: the prisoners were at San Pedro, and Colonel Behn was waiting in France. On July 17, Robert M. Scotten, the embassy counsellor, aware that the Spanish government needed cotton credits, let them know that "he felt that should permission be granted for Behn to return to Spain it could not help but facilitate the granting of the cotton credits." Three days later Under Secretary Barcenas, the Franco representative, told him: "I think I can say that if you can arrange for the cotton credits, the Generalissimo will not only agree for Behn to return but will authorize the release of your prisoners."[23]

Upon being informed of this, Secretary of State Hull sent instructions at once. A careful reading will show how fine a line he drew—some might even call it an imaginary line.

You should, of course, make it clear that this Government cannot consent, directly or indirectly, to bargain for the release of the American prisoners, for the entrance of Colonel Behn into Spain, nor for the fair and equitable treatment of American interests in Spain on the basis of a conclusion of the cotton credits requested by the Spanish Government, or any other basis. You should say that when this government was approached by representatives of the Spanish Government with a view to obtaining credits for the purchase of American cotton, this Government expressed its willingness to give favorable consideration to the proposal because of the fact that normal and friendly relations existed between the two Governments and because of its belief that if an agreement were found possible, such agreement would be of value to the commercial interests of the two nations. It assumed that the Spanish Government was animated by the same desire and that the Spanish Government would be willing to signify this desire in a practical manner by expediting the release of the American prisoners still under the jurisdiction of the Spanish authorities, by granting Colonel Behn permission without further delay to enter Spain to attend to legitimate interests of his company, and finally, that the Spanish Government would be willing to give assurances that fair and equitable treatment would be accorded all American interests in Spain in accordance with the generally accepted principles of international law.

The cotton involved was 250,000 bales to be delivered in equal monthly installments during one year, and to be paid for over a period of 27 months. The interest rate was 3.5 percent.[24]

On July 24, Franco received Ambassador Weddell cordially and said both matters would be settled favorably in a day or so, and arranged an immediate appointment for Weddell to see Jordana, his foreign minister. When Weddell met Jordana and began to speak, Jordana interrupted to say, "The American prisoners are at your disposition; where do you wish them delivered?" Weddell said he would let him know. As for Behn, Weddell was told that evening that Behn could get his visa at Hendaye in three days.[25]

Wednesday, July 26, the State Department phoned David White that the eleven Americans at San Pedro and possibly the rest of the prisoners could be released as soon as we could provide $150 for each one. Dave, with barely enough money to pay for one prisoner, said we would provide the funds in a few days.

I was now the national executive secretary of FALB. My memory of those days is of constant hectic scrambling for funds to support veterans still waiting for visas at Le Havre, to aid the disabled who had come back, and to pay our rent and office expenses. Neither Dave nor I drew a salary, and the wages paid our clerical staff were minimal. Much of our office work was performed by volunteers. Lawyers, doctors, and dentists provided free services, even covering some of their material costs themselves.

We knew there were eleven prisoners at San Pedro and six others under thirty-year sentences elsewhere. That meant we neded $2550, and that afternoon we organized a letter and telegram campaign.[26]

VALB posts provided a large part of the money. Milt Cohen sent in $300 from Chicago, Ben Gardner in Philadelphia and Dave Thompson in San Francisco sent in $200 each, and Carl Bradley in Baltimore and Howard Goddard in Los Angeles sent $100 each.[27] The following week, we sent the State Department $1725 (roughly equivalent to $17,000 today). In addition, relatives had put up $125 for Morris Tobman and $150 for Cohn Haber. A confidential note from Welles to Ambassador William Bullitt in Paris said that the American Red Cross had made up to $2500 available for repatriation of American prisoners for whom VALB or relatives could not pay.[28] On August 9, Weddell asked Jordana to take the prisoners to the bridge at Hendaye.[29]

In our desperate effort to raise the $2550, we sent a letter to Eleanor Roosevelt asking for her help. She sent a note to Sumner Welles, the acting secretary of state, asking whether the government could bring "the American boys home." She was told no funds were available, but that all except about twenty had been released, and FALB and relatives had deposited $2650, which should be sufficient.[30] (By then we had scraped together another $600.)

*   *   *   *   *

At 8:15 A.M. on August 15, the day Hy had predicted the Americans would leave San Pedro, an American died in the infirmary there.[31] Gustave Listhaeghe, twenty-four years old, was born in East Moline, Illinois, on September 28, 1914. His father was a naturalized American citizen from Belgium, and his mother, Elise Cocker, was a native American. The family had moved to Belgium in 1928, and Gustave came to Spain in 1937 and served in the 11th Brigade. He was listed as an American at an "unknown prison" on Weddell's July 1 list. At San Pedro, Gustave had stayed with the other four Belgians and was considered a Belgian; he had not been called out when Crain visited. The other Americans did not know he was a US citizen. The cause of his death is unknown.

That same morning Al Ziegler wrote another postal card.[32] Bob Steck was going to tease Hy about his bet, when the call came for the Americans to leave. Bob was astounded. Hy had guessed the date right on the nose! What luck! No time to make good on his bet. He hid two copies of the *Jaily News* on his body, and gave his many International comrades a strong embrace.

On the way, the military escort showed them the Burgos Cathedral, and bought wine for them on the train to San Sebastian. The well-fed, well-dressed civilians summering at this famous resort watched as the Americans were marched to the seaside and into a building grim outside and fearsome inside, Ondarreta Prison.

The reception room was the center between two rows of cells, all with iron-plated doors. This was the condemned area, packed with men. . . . When we told them that we were Americans from the International Brigades, we could hear the buzzing and excited comments. When they told us who they were, the men awaiting execution, we could only reflect on the ferocity of this regime, which was taking revenge on these men who had defended their popularly elected government.

A special area had been reserved for us in the cellar. In Spain when you talk of cellars in jails you mean dungeons and that is what it was. Badly lit, cage-like cells, cobbled floors, dampness and a smell of brine and excreta. . . . A trench running through the center of the floor would fill up twice a day with seawater . . . and there were a dozen Spaniards there who were to be our companions. . . . "We are not politicals so we get better treatment. We are not locked up and we may buy things from the outside." Their clothing was clean and they had plenty to smoke. They also had a fancy youth who wore lipstick and rouge and he lisped and pranced about. These men were criminals.[33]

Ambassador Weddell, his wife, and his private secretary, Murat W. Williams, went to Bayonne on August 17 to buy clothes the prisoners would need after their delousing.[34] When Weddell was finally informed on August 21 that eleven Americans had been brought to Ondarreta, he expressed his expectation that eight others would also be brought there for release, as promised by Franco. The eight were Andreasen and Barr, from Saragoza; Doran, Kerlicker, and Opara, from Central Prison, Burgos; Blair and Haber, from Valdenoceda; and Dahl, from Salamanca.[35]

Weddell sent Earl Crain and Murat Williams on August 23 to tell the Americans at Ondarreta that they wanted to get them out of Spain; war was likely to break out shortly. Hy recalls:

They also told us that they understood we have pent-up feelings and would like to express them. But they counseled us not to demonstrate but to walk quietly across the bridge. For the situation is very tense in the world today and France is not the same as it was when we crossed that country on our way to Spain. But they reassured us that everything would be all right.[36]

The Americans and Frenchmen were to leave at 10 A.M. on August 25. Woodruff Wallner, American vice consul at Paris, arrived at the French side of the bridge at 10:30 A.M. and was joined by Robert Scotten and Murat Williams. Crain was on the other side to sign the receipt for the Americans. The French representative was so late that it was 12:30 P.M. before the Americans walked quietly across the bridge and were directed to the commissariat at the Hendaye railroad station.

After a shower and vaccination, they received their new clothes from Williams. Wallner had arranged for lunch at the *buvette* in the station, where they also received cigarettes donated by the commercial attaché in San Sebastian. Each one also received 128 French francs, the remainder of the FALB funds given to the IRC to be distributed to prisoners when they were released.[37] The prisoners immediately took up a collection for their comrades at San Pedro. Wallner not only offered to get it to them but also matched their gift. The Americans reveled in walking about freely, and bought French pastry, newspapers, and post cards. Al Ziegler wrote to Herman Cohen:

August 25. It happened. Waiting for the nine o'clock train to Paris. Been here since lunch. Everyone talking war. Treatment by State Department swell. Practicing up on knife and fork.[38]

Twenty-one French prisoners who were being freed followed the Americans across the bridge. The French authorities handcuffed them and treated them as criminals, much to the amazement and anger of the Americans. They had the impression that France was already semifascist.[39]

At the station *buvette*, the prisoners, who for sixteen months had been eating poor food standing up, leisurely enjoyed their dinner with a good table wine, topped off with dessert and real coffee. That evening the eleven Americans boarded the Paris train. After breakfast in Paris, Wallner escorted them to the 10:15 train for Le Havre. In his memorandum on his trip, Wallner wrote:

I found the prisoners in good physical condition. They had been confined since March or April 1938, and while they were hardly enthusiastic about the treatment they had received, they agreed that on the whole it was better than that accorded Spanish Republican prisoners of war. They were full of praise for the efforts of the State Department and its officers abroad to make life more bearable during their confinement and to have effected their release. Their own esprit de corps was excellent. I found them most cooperative.[40]

At breakfast Wallner had told the men that they would all be right back, since war was about to break out. "However, you'll probably all be generals."

One of the prisoners asked, "Do you think they'd trust us?"

"It would be foolish not to use your experience," was his rejoinder.[41] Unfortunately, for the most part those who made military policy were not as close to the enemy as Wallner was, and they allowed us to contribute in World War II only a small portion of what we wanted to contribute and could have given.

There was much confusion at Le Havre when the eleven Americans arrived on August 26. Fearful that France would be at war the next day, thousands wanted to leave. Those with third-class tickets found it difficult to get on a ship. But the *President Roosevelt* needed workaways, and it was leaving that day; William Stone, Leon Tenor, Sam Toole, and Al Ziegler shipped out on it.[42]

The remaining seven found rooms in a hot garret over a grocery store. Joe Young knew that sailors always helped sailors, but he got a cold shoulder on the two US ships in port, even being told, "You guys are all Commies." Then he learned they were Nazi crewmen on the Hamburg run. People were desperate for identification papers; for the one Joe carried—no photo, no fingerprint, just a statement that he was an American in transit—he could have had his throat slit if he were careless.

Five days passed and Joe tired of watching trawlers unload fish and barge people hang out their wash. True, there was the Rue de Galion, with its dozens of houses featuring girls of all sizes, shapes, and ages, and music—usually a saxophone player and a drummer. When evening came, pleasure-seekers crowded in—some to dance, others to fight or to make love. But on his fifteen-franc daily allowance Joe could do little more than enjoy the tunes.

Newspapers were stale by the time they hit the vendors; the latest news was written with whitewash on store windows. Crowds watched anxiously as the eleven o'clock news was replaced by the 11:15 announcement. Hitler invaded Poland on September 1. Would France and England keep their promise to come to its aid? Would we be at war that day?

The next morning the seven Americans were asked to help dig air raid shelters to provide good publicity. Joe argued it was a lousy idea; France had not helped us when it closed its borders with Spain. "Some bureaucrat would get the credit and somebody else would get any money that might be allocated. All we would get is blisters." But finding he was a disgruntled minority, Joe said he had some matters to attend to and left. Bob Steck joined him on the way to the American consulate. Joe recalls that

on entering the office, one of the staff recognized us by our bald heads. He called out to us: "If you two guys run over to the Compagnie General Transatlantique, you might get a passage." He gave us two chits saying that passage payment was guaranteed by the U.S. Consul. We ran.

The offices of the C.G.T. were packed with people waving their arms and shouting trying to get the attention of the hard-pressed clerks. I felt we didn't have a chance unless we took some bold action, justified by the fact that we had sacrificed much more than any of these people. So I led, pushing and elbowing ourselves all the way to the counter where we thrust our papers in the hands of one of the men. I guess the words "U.S. Consul" on the slips worked like magic for we soon had our tickets to board the *Ile de France*.

Boarding was easy since they had no luggage. They shared a room with two men. For the passengers fleeing Europe, cots were put up in the gymnasium, swimming pool, and ballroom; and three settings were required for each meal. News came after one day at sea that France had declared war on Germany; that meant the *Ile de France* was now fair game for Nazi submarines. Joe, not impressed with the braggarts and self-important snobs at the lounge bar, took delight in telling them to make sure they knew where their life jackets were, and that being out in the Atlantic in the summer was like being in a rowboat in Central Park, except for the sharks.

Joe and Bob were out on deck when they passed the Statue of Liberty; looking at it brought a lump to their throats. When their turn came to clear customs and immigration, they were told to step over to the other side of the room because their papers were not in order. So they stepped over—and kept stepping until they saw the crew gangway. It was manned by a petty officer who thought they were French; they confused him enough by speaking English so that by the time he had gathered his wits together, they were on the dock and headed for the street.[43]

In Le Havre, when the remaining Americans sat down to dinner on September 2, Bob and Joe were missing. Having heard from tall Alwyn Stevenson about a Paramount News-Reel of the crossing at the International Bridge, they went to the movies and watched themselves cross into France. Afterward, Joe and Bob were still missing. Alarmed, Hy Wallach and Morris Tobman scoured the town and especially the "nightclubs" on the Rue de Galion, which were unaffected by the blackout. The next morning they learned from a consular agent, Biddle, that Joe and Bob had sailed on the *Ile de France.*

A few days later Biddle offered workaway positions to the remaining five. Wallach said that going as workaways was against the rules of the National Maritime Union; they would be glad to work if signed on as seamen and paid.

Biddle angrily burst out, "Don't speak of unions to me!"

Wallach told him he was sorry that he felt that way, but they were working people and respected unions.

A few days later Biddle informed them that freighters were being turned into emergency passenger ships and the five could be part of such a crew. And before Wallach could say anything, Biddle continued, "You'll be paid." So Alvarez, Steinberg, Stevenson, Tobman, and Wallach shipped as crew of the *Schodack* on September 10. It took the freighter thirteen days to make its way to Hoboken, but they arrived back home with money in their pockets.[44]

Since all but two of the eleven had worked their way across, FALB asked the State Department to set aside $900 to bring back the remaining prisoners, and to refund the rest. FALB received the balance of $915.64 on October 23, 1939.[45]

23 Americans in Other Prisons

THE LAST AMERICANS to be captured during the retreat from Gandesa were Lawrance Fant Doran, twenty-five, from Los Angeles; six-foot Sergeant Anthony Kerhlicker, thirty-one, born in Polk County, Iowa; and Rudolph Opara, twenty-three, from Cleveland, Ohio. All had fought with the Lincoln Battalion, Lawrence having joined it only two weeks earlier. The three, heading east through the mountains, evaded fascist patrols for nearly three weeks. Then, on April 19, 1938, soldiers from the Italian Black Arrow Division captured them near San Carlos de Rápita on the Mediterranean. The Italians not only beat them but didn't feed them for the first four days, with the excuse that they were going to be shot anyway.

Taken to Vinaroz, they were court-martialed on May 16, charged with being Communist propagandists behind the lines and members of the International Brigades. The sentence was death. A week later, they were surprised by a second court-martial and death sentences. Then Franco, during a visit to the area, commuted their sentences to thirty years' imprisonment.

On July 3, 1938, they were moved to the Central Prison in Zaragoza. On September 5, they were taken to the Central Prison two miles outside of Burgos.[1] They remained there for eighteen months.

In July 1938, Kerhlicker's parents had their senator and congressman make inquiries. On November 29 the State Department replied that their son was not on any prisoner list. It had not checked on FALB's report that he was in the Burgos Central Prison, even though it had received a petition on his behalf signed by the members of the city council of Moline, Illinois.[2]

Opara's sister Olga was informed by the State Department on November 3 that Rudolph was at San Pedro de Cardeña; on January 13, 1939, at Burgos Central; and February 9 at Zaragoza.

On April 20, 1939, Bay telegraphed Hull that he had received a postcard from Kerhlicker in the Central Prison at Burgos asking for clothing, and that Opara had a life sentence, place unknown.[3] Six weeks later, June 14, Earl Crain arrived at Central Prison to see Kerhlicker and Doran. He carried two packages and fifty pesetas from the IRC and one hundred pesetas from H. Freeman Matthews through three sets of locked gates and a deserted courtyard into an inner building. To Crain's surprise, Rudolph Opara was there too.

The packages contained sugar, chocolate, coffee, condensed milk, soap, a khaki short, woolen underdrawers, woolen pullover sweater, and a pair of woolen socks. Crain was permitted to give the prisoners only the clothing and soap.

Crain interviewed the prisoners in a private office, one at a time. Doran wouldn't talk until he saw Crain's credentials. Doran said they were being treated humanely compared with the way the Black Arrows had treated them. He was suffering from sarna (itch), rheumatism, and stomach trouble and was in an infirmary brigade. Meals consisted primarily of rice or beans or occasional servings of macaroni. No meats or green vegetables were served. Because he was ill, he was given milk.

Opara was pale and thin, with a very bad case of sarna. His hands were covered with scabs, and he had two boils on his body that had never been treated. An official promised treatment that day. Kerhlicker was cheerful and in good condition. The money had to be left with the prison official. Crain was not allowed to see Frank Ryan and Tom Jones, who were in the same prison.[4]

When Crain again visited Burgos Central Prison on October 31, he found a fourth American—Destruye Igleslas Pardo, twenty-eight, born in Tampa, Florida. Because his father was Spanish and had taken him to Spain before World War I, he was also a Spanish citizen. Iglesias had been at San Pedro from April to November of 1938. When the State Department refused him diplomatic protection, he was court-martialed in Gijón on January 20, 1939, for having been a member of the "Young Socialists" and the Republican Army. His death sentence was commuted to thirty years.[5]

On December 12, 1939, Crain returned to Burgos Central Prison with packages prepared by Ambassador Weddell's wife. Each package contained a blanket, two pairs of socks, two undershirts, two handkerchiefs, two towels, a pair of gloves and a knitted shirt, as well as fifteen cans of condensed milk, two pounds of lump sugar, canned sardines, a carton of cigarettes, magazines, and soap, as well as shoes and trousers of the size given to Crain to October 31. He also brought Destruye Iglesias a package from his sister in Madrid.

The shoes and clothing were especially appreciated by the men since they had to spend ten hours a day outside in the open inner courtyard, where they had to walk vigorously to keep warm. All four asked Crain to tell Mrs. Weddell that they would never forget their kindness. Doran had an additional request, an English-Spanish dictionary for his use as the prison English teacher.[6]

Frederic Jacosta, a tall, slim Frenchman; John Blair; and Harry Kleiman had been taken from San Pedro to the Provincial Prison at Zaragoza in August and September of 1938. Three Americans were already there—Al Andreasen, Reuben Barr, and Peter Matas.[7] And the prison held some ten other Internationals, including Roberto Vega González, a nineteen-year-old Mexican; James Cameron, a Canadian; Randulf Dalland, a Norwegian; and a Dane.

Inspired by the recrossing of the Ebro in July, the prisoner's planned a revolt in Zaragoza to coincide with a public uprising. But a stool pigeon warned the fascists the day before, and Jacosta, Vega, and six other Internationals were called out that evening, expecting to be shot. Instead, they were sent to Burgos Provincial Prison. On December 24, Blair, Matas, Kleiman, and Cameron were also sent there, because—it was rumored—the authorities were fearful of an officers' uprising.

Burgos Provincial Prison, an ancient two-story building a short distance behind the cathedral, was very crowded. Nevertheless, the Spanish prisoners welcomed the Internationals and shared their Christmas food baskets with them.

Three weeks later, all Internationals, hands and feet tied, were hauled seventy kilometers north as cargo in a freight car, in freezing weather, to Valdenoceda Prison, six kilometers from Villarcayo. They were assigned to a basement room for "undesirables." The large room was filled with Spaniards, with a toilet over an excavation. A coarse cloth sack served as a mattress and blanket at night and as a shawl during the day.

Breakfast was a cup of warm unsweetened black water misnamed coffee and a small piece of bread. The other two meals were a small ration of boiled potatoes. Consequently, food was the main topic of conversation. Bread could be bought, but the Internationals had no money. Then came an announcement from Franco: "Spanish fishermen have caught large quantities of codfish for the humble classes." As the cod, caught off the coast of Africa, neared Valdenoceda, the stench preceded them. Huge maggots were cooked and served with the cod, but those who wanted to live ate, for the bread ration had been cut.

Soon the potatoes were replaced with *titos*, a fodder pea. The *titos*, infested with weevils and not fit for cattle, were cooked in large cauldrons. The top black layer consisted of weevils from broken beans. Jack Firmin, a Canadian remembers:

The first thing you did . . . was to pick off the bugs. Then you opened each bean, one at a time. . . . I have taken as many as five bugs from one bean. One day we piled up the beans in a corner as a protest. The only result was that we had to clean them up.[8]

The prison chaplain offered inmates the "most perfect food" and was displeased that they would not accept it. On Sundays and Saints' Days, he spoke of the beauties of heaven, of how happy they would be when they reached it. "What is life on earth but a vale of tears?" In preparation for Easter, the chaplain, determined to prepare each prisoner for his death, cited cases where prisoners had confessed their sins and had been given absolution before facing the firing squad.

He announced that twenty-five "fishers for souls" were coming to hear their confessions, and next day the prisoners saw twenty-five black figures bicycling downhill and toward the prison. The inmates were called into a large assembly area, where the twenty-five fishers were lined up in front of them. The chaplain again explained the advantages of confession and asked the prisoners to form lines in front of the confessors. Not one responded. After a half hour's pleading, the chaplain in exasperation said that anyone who did not wish to confess would leave, whereupon all began to leave.

The wardens clubbed the prisoners as they left. The black-robed fishers followed the prisoners to their rooms. There the prisoners explained that they were not the rebels; it was their captors who had rebelled against their government; they were not criminals; their captors had committed so many crimes that few families in Spain had not suffered from them; they were not traitors to Spain; it was Franco who had brought in the Italians and Germans.[9]

Prisoners at Valdenoceda were allowed to communicate only with their families in Spain. The Americans were not allowed to send letters or receive them from abroad, or communicate with the embassy in Spain. Blair, Kleiman, and Matas often wondered whether death would come first from disease, starvation, a warden's club, or a firing squad.

*   *   *   *   *

Earl Crain made his first trip to Valdenoceda on Saturday, May 27, 1939. The director, because some inmate attempted a jail break a few days earlier, insisted on being present and that all conversations be in Spanish.

Valdenoceda had 1583 prisoners. Crain was conducted through two sets of locked doors to an inside room, and all prisoners claiming American citizenship were brought in—Cohn Haber (Harry Kleiman), Clarence Alvie Blair (John Blair), and Pietr Madis (Peter Matas). Crain reported that all looked to be in reasonably good health and were immensely pleased to see him. They said they were reasonably well treated, though there was little food, and that was bad.

Crain then gave each one an IRC package, which the director insisted had to be opened in front of him. Each contained a shirt, woolen shorts, woolen pullover, woolen socks, a kilogram of sugar, some chocolate and coffee, a tin of condensed milk, and a large cake of soap. The 150 pesetas he had brought for them (75 from the Red Cross, 50 from Matthews and 25 from himself) could only be given to them as credit at the canteen. Crain also gave them a carton of American cigarettes. Harry Kleiman expressed the prisoners' feelings: "This will save our lives."

The director confirmed that the prisoners were not allowed to send or receive letters. From the prison records, Crain found they were at the disposition of the prosecutor of the Sixth Military Region, but there was no information about why they were being held. He also gave the Canadian Jim Cameron three Red Cross packages from the British embassy. As Crain left, he passed seventy-five prisoners coming in, roped together.[10]

The Americans and Cameron had the pleasure of sharing their sudden wealth with the rest of the Internationals and their Spanish friends, providing a bright moment at Valdenoceda.

On June 1, 1939, the State Department informed Naomi Blair, John's sister, that it would forward money to him. She sent $60 from August to November. How much John received is not known.[11]

The State Department did not inform those who had written on Kleiman's behalf that he had been located until Congressman Vito Marcantonio intervened. Harry's father immediately sent a $5 money order, and David Zisselman sent a check for $150 to cover the cost of bringing Harry back to New York.[12]

Crain paid his second visit to Valdenoceda on December 12, 1939, arriving at 7 P.M. after a slow fifty-mile drive through heavy fog from Burgos. He reported Valdenoceda now had a more enlightened director and that Blair and Kleiman were in good spirits and good physical condition; funds received from their families and the clothing Mrs. Weddell had obtained for them had made their life easier. Crain did not ask to see Peter Matas because the State Department said he was not a citizen.[13] FALB would learn Matas was a prisoner when Blair and Kleiman returned, but by that time Peter would be in a labor battalion at Belchite. Crain reached Madrid long after midnight.

The Friends and the Veterans of the Abraham Lincoln Brigade held their conventions during the 1939 Christmas holidays. FALB disbanded and VALB immediately set up a Committee for the Release of the International Prisoners in Spain, under the chairmanship of Bob Steck. VALB received a letter from the US embassy in Madrid that "it will be pleased to forward to citizens of the United States who are prisoners of war in Spain any letters, packages or money that may be received in its care." The embassy added that duties and import restrictions usually made the sending of packages impractical.[14]

Negotiations had been going on. The Spanish minister for foreign affairs had told Ambassador Weddell early in November: "We have some eighty thousand prisoners of war to be tried for offences; there is frightful congestion in the military tribunals. I beg you to be patient."[15]

On November 7, 1939, Sumner Welles in Washington called in Ambassador Cardenas to review the Franco government's many broken promises. He told him

what harm it would do to relations between our two countries if these facts were ventilated in the American press, and such a possibility was of course great. . . . it

[was] consequently indispensable to good relations between the two countries that the Spanish Government immediately make good the assurances previously given and turn over these remaining eight prisoners to our Ambassador on the French frontier.[16]

Milton Wolff, representing VALB, visited the State Department on January 5, 1940, and authorized it to use the remaining FALB funds to repatriate eight prisoners: Cohn Haber, Clarence Blair, Alf Andreasen, Conrad Henry Stojewa, Rudolph Opara, Anthony Kerhlicker, Lawrence Fant Doran, and Raymond Epailly. Subsequently, the Department was informed of Raymond Epailly's death of pulmonary tuberculosis on December 15, 1939, by the medical director of the military hospital at Guernica.[17]

On the nineteenth, the Department forwarded evidence that Reuben Barr had received 121.70 pesetas on October 14, 1939, and 189.60 pesetas on December 11. This was for the $10 given on September 5 and $15 on October 4.[18]

One midnight in mid-February, 1940, John Blair and Harry Kleiman were awakened at Valdenoceda, taken to a railway junction, and locked up in the local jail. The next day they were taken by train to Burgos Provincial Prison. The following day John and Harry was taken to Salamanca, where they spent the night in the baggage room. The next night they spent at Cáceres, on a second-floor stair landing in what they took to be an apartment building converted into a prison. They spoke through a keyhole with some prisoners, who said executions were continuing as they had during the war.

The next night they spent in a holding cell at Seville, where they met Doran, Kerhlicker, Opara, and Dahl. The cell was crowded, and they slept sitting up with their arms around their drawn-up knees. Three days later, on February 22, their Spanish escorts took them to a World War I freighter, the *Exiria* and turned them over to a representative of the US consulate. They were free at last. He had brought some clothing for them, including leather jackets and some US sailors from the cruiser *Trenton* who were buying beer from the *Eixira's* canteen provided them with a beer treat.

The *Exiria* reached New York on March 17, 1940.[19] A group from VALB greeted all prisoners except Dahl. Dahl's passage was paid by the American Red Cross, not VALB, and he was shunned at the time because the VALB believed he had harmed the reputation of the Republic by statements he made while a prisoner. (This was unjust: Dahl proved to be a strong antifascist.)

Before he was released, Reuben Barr was called before a military court and asked to sign a statement that he would not return to Spain, and warned that if he did return he would be executed.[20] He and Andreasen arrived at Seville too late to catch the *Exiria,* and had to wait for the American Export freighter *Exford* which arrived on March 24. Then the last two American volunteers were on their way home.[21]

24 The Fate of the Other Nationalities

TOM JONES, a short, stocky coal miner from Wales, fighting in the Sierra Caballs, was in a desperate situation on September 17, 1938. Enemy fire had killed all but three in his machine-gun crew. A tall Spanish corporal, dazed, stood up and said to him, "We'd better get out of here." Glancing down, he saw his intestines hanging out and fainted, never to regain consciousness.

Tom said to Joseph Kleiman, an American with blood flowing out of a chest wound, "You've been hit bad."

"Yeah. You got a handkerchief?"

Tom gave him one and Joe shoved it into the hole in his chest before asking, "You got a cigarette?"

"No, but I'll get one." Tom, who had been hit in the arm, legs, and thumb, salvaged a cigarette from the dead, lit it, and gave it to Joe.

After taking a few puffs, Joe asked, "Tell me, sir, I haven't done a bad job of it?" Assured that he had fought well, he said, "I think we are going to win it, one way or other."

A few moments later, he said, "So long," and died.

Fortunately, the shelling and firing had died down, for Tom had diarrhea. As he was squatting in the trench with his pants down, a fascist patrol pointed their rifles at him.

Tom, who knew Spanish well, coolly told them to wait a minute. "You can't shoot me in this position," he said, and added,"I'm an International Brigader. I'm English actually."

Tom heard one of them say, "Ah, he's the first one we got. Let's shoot the bugger." Another said, "No, no, we have orders to take him to headquarters." When one asked Tom, "What are you doing here?" he replied, "Fighting fascism." From the look on their faces, Tom realized they didn't know what that meant.

A corporal robbed Tom of his pants before they reached the fascist brigade headquarters. There he was interrogated. Tom knew the trick was to answer very quickly, giving misleading or no information. The officers gave him some coffee and ordered him taken to the first-aid post at the far end of a large drill yard. Hundreds of young soldiers were taking a short break as Tom was lead through them. Hair matted with blood, his arm a mess, his hands bloody, his legs oozing blood, he walked erect. The stunned soldiers made no sound as Tom marched through them.

The paper bandages applied at the first-aid station disintegrated before Tom reached a hospital, and that led to serious infections. After several months in a hospital at Bilbao, Tom was returned to Zaragoza. On January 2, 1939, he was tried and sentenced to death. While waiting, Tom saw men called out to go to their deaths, only to be replaced by others who would follow them. To his surprise, he was called out on January 30, and court-martialed again, again sentenced to death, and returned to the death cell.

Called out again early in April, Tom was told his sentence had been commuted to thirty years' imprisonment. He was moved to the Central Prison at Burgos. Looking for a place in this crowded jail, Tom saw Frank Ryan, who made room for him. They slept on a concrete floor, and the food was as bad as at Zaragoza.[1]

Leopold Kerney, the Irish minister to Spain, visited Ryan on October 14, 1938. Kerney used his influence to provide Frank with books, food parcels, and cigarettes, which Frank shared with Tom and Basque friends. An Irish priest, Father J. J. Mulrean, also visited Frank. As a result, Frank and Tom were treated well by the warden and the guards. They organized English classes for the prisoners, and Frank taught Gaelic to some.[2]

Tom learned that the Masonic Order membership list had been found when Madrid fell, and the professionals and intellectuals who were Masons had been imprisoned. Doctors and others were taken out temporarily as needed, even to perform operations. The doctor attending the prisoners, when it was learned he was a Mason, became a prisoner.

Mass was compulsory. Above the altar was a picture of Franco, below that a picture of the Virgin Mary, on the right a photo of Hitler, and on the left a photo of Mussolini. During mass, machine guns in the corners were aimed at the prisoners.

One Sunday the senior priest, who carried a revolver on his hip, called the prisoners rapists and murderers. When they began to protest, the guards drew their guns and the machine gunners prepared to fire. The priest ordered the prison commander to select two hundred men and put them in solitary confinement on half rations for two months. Frank Ryan spoke to Father Mulrean, who got the priest replaced; even the prison staff were relieved to see him go. Tom's family sent him a Bible, but he was not allowed to have it because it didn't have a cross on the cover.

Frank suffered frequently from chest pains and rheumatism. The prison doctor occasionally provided him with dried milk and once in a while with some fish. Frank did not want to alarm his family and always wrote that he was well, and even asked Tom when he left to tell them that he was in good health.

After he was freed in the spring of 1940, Tom spoke at numerous meetings in England on behalf of Ryan, and in spite of wartime restrictions, visited Frank's parents in Ireland.[3]

In the meantime, negotiations were going on, directed by Admiral Wilhelm Canaris, head of German Intelligence, for Ryan's "escape"; the Germans hoped to use Ryan for propaganda broadcasts. Near midnight on

July 14, 1940, Frank Ryan was escorted across the border to France, and on August 4 to Berlin.

Sean Russell, leader of a faction of the Irish Republican Army that believed Ireland could only be united by military means, and that ideology was unimportant, was in Berlin, having had discussions with the Nazis. Russell was to return to Ireland in a U-boat and Ryan was sent with him, though he did not agree with Russell's views. In the submarine, Russell became very ill (probably from a perforated duodenal ulcer) and died in Ryan's arms on August 14. Russell was buried at sea, and the U-boat returned Ryan to Germany.

Ryan spent over three years in Germany, neither a prisoner nor a guest—a stranger. The fact that he was a sick man, almost completely deaf, helped him avoid being used by the Nazis for propaganda purposes. He suffered a stroke on January 15, 1943, after which he was in and out of hospitals, spending part of the time in a Dresden sanitarium. Wartime conditions, aggravated by Allied bombing, made life difficult. On June 10, 1944, he died and was buried in Loschwitz Cemetery. A friend marked the grave with a small wooden cross bearing the name that Ryan used in Germany—Frank Richard—and his Irish name, Proinsias O Riain.[4]

Vacationing in the German Democratic Republic in 1978, Tony Gilbert learned that Ryan was buried in Dresden and spent two days looking through cemeteries before he found the grave.[5] Although Ireland and the German Democratic Republic did not have diplomatic relations, the GDR exhumed the body and sent it to Dublin. Six people had attended his original burial, but thirty-five years later thousands attended the mass at the Whitefriars Street Carmelite Church and marched in the funeral procession past places rich in Ireland's struggle for independence to the cemetery in Glasvenin.[6]

Tom Jones became regional director of the Transport Union in Wales, vice chairman of the Council of Wales, and was decorated twice by the Queen of England, first in 1962 as Ordinary Officer and then in 1974 as Ordinary Commander of the Excellent Order of the British Empire. But Tom still considers the year he spent with Frank Ryan at the Central Prison at Burgos one of the richest of his life. In Tom's words, "Frank Ryan was a great Irish patriot and a Socialist. He was a brave man, highly cultured, and his honor, integrity and kindness were of the highest level."[7]

Jim Cameron was a Scotch-Canadian and had been an organizer for the purse seiners of the Fishermen's Union on Canada's west coast. Serving with the MacPaps, Jim was shot through the ankle on April 1, 1938. His wound was dressed at a first-aid station. The next morning, Jim found he was on his own behind the lines, able only to hop on one foot or to crawl. Jim spent some time in a deserted farmhouse with a Frenchman well supplied with grenades and wine. An Argentinian joined them. Jim and the Argentinian decided to leave the Frenchman because of his disconcerting habit of throwing grenades at imaginary enemies when he got drunk. Then Jim lost the Argentinian one night when a patrol fired at them. After nearly eleven weeks, Jim was betrayed by a farmer. The Civil Guard rounded him up from the deserted building in which he had taken refuge.

Jim arrived at San Pedro in July with Tom Brown and an Italian prisoner. Two months later he followed Harry Kleiman to Zaragoza Provincial Prison to face unknown charges. There he had to wash the tiled entrance hall and corridors each morning and peel potatoes out in the open—a painful chore after the weather turned cold. Then, with Blair and Kleiman, Jim was moved to Burgos Provincial Prison and to Valdenoceda; although held for court-martial, he was never tried. Jim's most vivid recollection of Valdenoceda was the escape attempt by two Germans. One, Hans, was bayoneted to death. Jim and Randulf Dalland had to put his body into a box for burial outside the cemetery walls.

Soon after that midnight in February 1940 when Blair and Kleiman were taken away, Jim Cameron was trucked to Burgos Provincial. There he met Tom Jones, who had been transferred from Burgos Central, and they were taken to Bilbao until their release was arranged. The trip back to England was a series of mishaps, and when they reached England on April 1, 1940, Jim found there was no work for him, even though England had been at war with Germany since September 1939. Canada wouldn't let him return, and so he lived on a small weekly allowance from the International Brigade Association.

Cameron became thirty years old on July 5, and since thirty-year-olds were being conscripted, he tried to register. He was turned down, but was offered a factory job. Early in 1944, after heavy British losses at sea, he was allowed to be a seaman. At the end of the war, Jim tried unsuccessfully to return to Canada.[8] He stayed at sea until 1960, and then worked in London until he retired.

John Charles "Jack" Firmin was working on a farm in Saskatchewan, Canada, in 1936 for five dollars a month. When he heard of the fight people of Spain were putting up against the fascist invaders, Jack volunteered. He reached Spain early in 1938, and enlisted, but with a fever, so he was sent to a hospital. When a call came for men to go to the front, Jack mounted a truck. Dropped off in the afternoon, the men were marched all night, then were told to go to an unoccupied hill. It was not unoccupied: men "fell like ninepins." Jack was hit in the calf, then in the upper arm. Part of the flesh was hanging loose, and to support his arm, he maneuvered his hand into a pocket.

The next morning, an Italian lieutenant found him and carried him over his shoulder to his company. There Jack got a soldier to cut his pocket open with a bayonet so his arm could be laid in a less painful position. His arm was bandaged at a field hospital. Left on a stretcher overnight, he was relieved of his wallet, watch and money. Then he was trucked to a hospital, where a doctor, using no anesthesia of any kind, carved off the loose flesh and rebandaged the arm. Placed on a hospital train, Jack fainted. When he came to, a doctor said, "So, you have awakened. Thought we had lost you."

At a hospital in Zaragoza, an elbow-to-shoulder cast held Jack's arm out in front of him in a painful position. Several weeks later he noticed maggots were dropping out of his cast onto his bed. An orderly said it was nothing to worry about; the maggots only ate decayed flesh; they were helpful.

Moved to a military hospital at Bilbao, Jack met an Englishman with a broken wrist who had developed a fever. Although the nuns prayed over him, the Englishman was carried out in a pine box. A grenade had blown off most of a Swede's right hand; he asked an orderly to cut off the inch of flesh that still hung from one finger. The orderly cut it off with scissors, and there wasn't a sound or show of pain from the Swede. He was nicknamed "Gutsy."

When Jack's cast was removed, his arm was no longer straight. The prisoners played a game where a man would lock his fingers together for another to try to pull them apart. Unable to unlock Jack's fingers, two Spaniards unaware that one arm had been broken, took hold of his arms and pulled, breaking his bad arm. Taken to the hospital, Jack had a few aspirins before a prisoner doctor, working without X rays or anesthesia, straightened the arm and bandaged it with strips torn from a sheet. Jack thought it was a fantastic job.

After his arm had healed, Jack ended up at Valdenoceda. The portion of weevil-infested *titos* a prisoner received was determined by the size of his container. Jack had only a sardine can given him by a Basque prisoner in Bilbao, and it was his only utensil until he left Spain. After Valdenoceda, Jack had to spend three weeks at Ondarreta. Then freedom, a hot bath, and new clothes, after which Jack happily joined the other freed Internationals on a train to Paris.

One freed prisoner had had his leg amputated between the knee and hip; a jolt caused the stub to bleed. At Bordeaux, Jack carried the man off the train to a nearby Red Cross station. They asked the amputee if he had any money. He had none, but Jack said he had a dollar. They rebandaged the amputee's leg, and took Jack's last dollar.

Jack sailed on the *Duchess of York* from Liverpool, ten years after he had emigrated on it to Canada. X-rays arranged by Friends of the Mackenzie-Papineau Battalion showed osteomyelitis had begun in the broken humerus. The surgeon who repaired the arm cautioned Jack to be careful as he had been able to leave only a thin section of bone in one area.

Jack worked as a hydraulics specialist until he was forty, when he felt he could serve his fellowman better as a minister. As Reverend Firmin, he has been very helpful to people in distress, including drug addicts and alcoholics. His prison experience, he believes, has made him more effective. He expressed it this way: "I am a firm believer in being a doer of Christ's word and not just a sayer."[9]

*   *   *   *   *

The departure of the eleven Americans left about four hundred Internationals at San Pedro. Plans to send 82 prisoners to Germany in May 1938 had been aborted when the Duke of Alba reported strong protests in London.[10]

Some nationalities had left San Pedro before the eleven Americans. On March 1, 1939, seventeen French prisoners had been released, including Frederic Jacosta; another twenty-one Frenchmen were freed on August 25.[11] All Norwegians had gone to Bilbao on July 5, 1939, and eventually were released, including Randulf Dalland.[12] Holland asked for its citizens on August 11, 1939; Franco's staff replied on October 4 that twenty-one were to be court-martialed and four were free to leave, including Alex de Seume.[13]

Manuel Abarrca Moreno, a Cuban lieutenant in the 205th Brigade in northern Spain, had been captured on the high seas when Franco's navy captured the *Montseny* after the fall of the North. He escaped from the prison at Gijón, but was picked up and sent to San Pedro, where he was highly regarded. Senetenced to death on July 8, 1939, he was executed soon afterward.

Five Belgians were released on October 14, 1939. On November 16, 1939, Hassan sent a long letter to Franco, asking that those left at San Pedro, whose detention was a burden on Spain now that the war had ended, also be released.[14]

But Franco formed the remaining prisoners into a labor battalion. They left San Pedro on November 29, 1939, to lay water mains and build streets for a new Belchite west of the old city. Housed in the wrecked seminary building south of the old city, with no lights and no heat except from small wood fires, the prisoners received little food, poorly prepared.

Guards were given a bonus and a home leave if they shot a prisoner trying to escape. Karl Heckhausen, a German, was shot by a guard when he looked out a window. And Tanky was there.[15] but the prisoners were being paid for their work, two cents a day.[16]

On the afternoon of December 10, twenty-seven Cubans at Belchite were told they were free. They were to take the train to Zaragoza, and then to Bilbao, to catch the *Marqués de Comillas*, sailing the next day. The twenty-seven men ran to the Belchite station, only to find the train had left. They then walked the twenty-six kilometers to Zaragoza, where again they missed the train and had to wait until nine the next morning. They arrived at Bilbao that night. Fortunately, the ship's sailing had been delayed. They received a warm welcome in Havana three weeks later.[17]

The Portuguese prisoners, four from Holland (including Alex de Seume), and the Peruvian doctor, Roberto Luna Rubinoz, also were claimed by their governments in December.[18]

*   *   *   *   *

Bob Steck, as head of the VALB committee to aid the prisoners, sent letters for the Internationals at San Pedro to the embassy in Madrid. Since the camp was closed, the embassy was told to forward the letters to the Ministry of the Army, General Inspection of Concentration Camps. The embassy did so, and sent Steck a letter that it could not guarantee their delivery.[19] Steck had already sent the State Department $5 each for five of the prisoners, and $10.87 for Bela Lustig. Funds for the first five were returned because they were not US citizens.[20]

Valb initiated a Conference for the Release of International Prisoners in French and Spanish Prison Camps. It was held in New York City and attended by seventy-five fraternal and labor organizations.[21] Plans made to send them funds and transport them to Mexico were stymied by the refusal of the State Department to transmit funds and to issue transit visas.

*   *   *   *   *

On his return to Holland, Alex de Seume held a news conference on the plight of the prisoners at Belchite. Letters and packages were sent to the Dutch prisoners, providing food and keeping them informed about the war.

Olaf Domnauer's parents obtained their son's release as a Swedish citizen through the papal nuncio. The priest at Belchhite gave Domnauer travel documents to go to Irún on May 30, 1940. A year later he left Spain for the United States after spending time in Ondarreta and a Bilbao prison.[22]

An order came in August 1940 to take Hassan to the Turkish embassy in Madrid. He was escorted by Father Molina, who had developed great respect for him. When the Turkish ambassador refused to accept Hassan, they went to the American embassy, where they received sympathy but no help.[23] Hassan had to return to the labor battalion.

In June 1941 Hassan and Father Molina went to Barcelona, hoping to arrange Hassan's departure from Spain. They were unsuccessful, but Hassan was told he was free to remain in Barcelona. He married a Catalan and became part of the anti-Franco underground. Arrested, he was sentenced to death, but his sentence was commuted, and he was sent to a prison in the Canary islands. His wife and son moved there, and he was released in 1952.[24]

At Valdenoceda, one of the Spanish trustees serving a life sentence informed the Mexican Roberto Vega that a letter had come from the American ambassador asking about Vega's health. The trustee, although directed to destroy the letter, had placed it in Vega's file. After eighteen months at Valdenoceda, Vega was court-martialed and sentenced to death for "support of the rebellion." Taken to Burgos to be executed, he was sent instead to join the Internationals at Belchite on February 16, 1941. Vega believed the ambassador's letter had tipped the scales in his favor.

Taken with others to a gravel quarry, Vega was given a pick and shovel and told to dig out ten cubic feet of stones. Poor food and lack of exercise had not prepared him for this; before the day had ended, his hands were bleeding. He had met the quota only with the help of others, saving him from a severe beating.

Unable to rise the next morning when the bugle sounded, Vega was hauled before the captain, who ordered that he forgo the morning "coffee" and dig out twice as much. Only the help of his comrades enabled him to meet the doubled quota. His first eight days were sheer agony. Fascist sadism extended to the use of the outdoor toilet. After dark one had to go out naked, regardless of the weather, and anyone who took more than a few minutes was shot at by the guards.[25]

Seven prisoners escaped at Belchite. Heinz Jordan, a German, and Josef Stadler, an Austrian, reached Lisbon, where the police picked them up. The German consulate having reported that they had lost their citizenship, the police offered to free them if they left Portugal. They wrote to Bob Steck, asking if he could obtain travel documents for them from the State Department; the Department refused to grant them.[26]

In January 1941, Franz Klatecky, from Dusseldorf, and two others managed to get away. Otto Gundlach, a German, and Ferdinand Yanda, a Czech, escaped together. Yanda succeeded in stowing away in Seville on a boat for Australia; he was interred there for the duration of World War II. When the war ended, he went to the German Democratic Republic.[27]

Early in May, the Internationals were moved to Palencia. The first stop was at the Zaragoza railroad station, where impressive precautions were taken against escape. A cordon of Civil Guards formed the first ring around the station, then a cordon of cavalry, then one formed by the Mobil Police, and then a ring of soldiers. Even so, the prisoners could hear the loud cries of the women who were trying to break through the cordons. The prisoners joked, "Not even Hitler himself would have been received with such a demonstration. Are we so important?"[28]

At Belchite, the prisoners had been told that Palencia would be a better place. Vega describes their new life:

Our new home was a powder magazine under construction. We had to live in caverns 75 feet underground and without the benefit of fresh air. From the long interior passageways a fine dust spread which entered our lungs and caused many respiratory illnesses.

The food was vile. . . . there was no opportunity to wash. . . . This was the most terrible place I experienced. . . . In this hell, water was an article of luxury. A group of workers, loaded down with canteens, had to travel several kilometers to search for water, escorted by soldiers truly without souls.

Vega followed his guard above ground, wondering why his name had been called out. The counselor of the Cuban embassy, who was waiting for him, informed him that he was free. Then the counselor took him to Palencia, bought him new clothes, provided a bath and a meal, and introduced him to two Mexicans who had been at Valdenoceda with him. The three were taken to Bilbao, where they boarded the *Marqués de Comillas*. In Mexico, Vega was honored with a request by Don Manuel Avila Comacho, the president of Mexico, to become a member of his military staff. His mother pleaded with him to leave the army, so Vega turned down the appointment. In 1944, Vega enlisted in the U.S. Army. Decorated several times, he returned to Mexico in 1947.[29]

Vega was lucky to have left Palencia. A typhus epidemic broke out in July; of the twenty who contracted it, nineteen died. Karl Loesch was the survivor. Karl Graf, a German International who had volunteered to take care of the ill, caught typhus and paid with his life. Yet when Kurt Scheffler and other German Internationals were offered their freedom if they would join the Spanish Foreign Legion, not one accepted.[30]

In October 1941 the Gestapo offered to take all Germans, Austrians and Poles to work for pay in Germany; seventeen Germans and Austrians and nine Poles accepted.[31] Several months later a group of Internationals were taken from Palencia and put on a train. Herman Streit, certain they were on their way to death in Germany, decided to escape. Together with Max Strommer, an Austrian, and Paul Wondzinaky, another German, he planned to climb out a window while the train was moving at night. They tacked a blanket up over the window to make it more difficult for the guards, who were eating and singing, to see them.

Strommer went out first, then Streit, but Wondzinaky could not get out because a guard became suspicious and ordered the window closed. It wasn't until the train arrived at the concentration camp at Miranda de Ebro the next morning that the guards learned that two had escaped.

Max Stommer reached Portugal safely and managed to get to South America. Streit waited for the others, as agreed, but when they did not show up, he started to walk to Portugal. After talking himelf through several unpleasant encounters and nearly drowning while trying to cross the Duero River, he arrived at the Portuguese border. But that evening he ran into two Civil Guards. After letting him go by, they turned around and asked for his identification papers. Streit said he had left his papers in the railroad station.

Suspicious, they took him there, and when he couldn't find his papers, arrested him. Since it was Sunday, they held him in the fire house, and children brought him food and water. Taken to Civil Guard quarters the next day, he asked to be treated as a prisoner of war, and was put in leg irons.

Several weeks later, a lieutenant offered to remove the irons if he promised not to escape. Streit gave the promise, the irons were removed, and he was sent to Miranda de Ebro and turned over to the Gestapo. Taken to Germany, he worked for six weeks in Cologne. Before he and Karl Frank from San Pedro and two others could carry out a plan to seize some weapons, Streit was arrested. Interrogated for three months in Leipzig, he was tried in Breslau for treason because of acts committed in 1934. The maximum penalty for these acts in 1934 had been two years. And that was Streit's sentence.

But the day came when the Gestapo took him to the most feared concentration camp, Mauthausen. Streit managed to be assigned to the hospital, where an illegal organization existed. He was able to save some men by giving them new names so that they were never called for the gas chambers. When they knew liberation was near, they obtained guns to defend themselves in case the guards decided to kill them. On the last few nights Streit slept with a machine gun and two pistols under his mattress. When they heard their liberators were only a day away, the prisoner leadership decided that if they were all called into the assembly area, no one should go. When no one answered the assembly order, the guards, afraid to go into the barracks, fled Mauthausen.[32] The GDR gave Streit responsibility for the collection of produce from agricultural collectives and cooperatives.

Karl Loesch also escaped from Palencia and reached Portugal, where he spent the war years, part of the time in prison. He returned to the GDR and served as its first ambassador to Cuba.[33]

When the Nazis occupied western Europe, some Allied troops and Internationals who had been interred in France escaped into Spain, only to be held in the Miranda de Ebro concentration camp. Most Germans and Austrians were sent to Germany. On October 23, 1941, the approximately six hundred foreign prisoners at Miranda were asked by the German consul, accompanied by two Gestapo agents, to volunteer to work in Germany. The consul especially wanted the nineteen Czechs. They refused on the ground they were non-Aryan (not true), and were upheld by the Spanish officials and by Dr. Formanek, the Czech chargé d'affaires in Madrid.[34]

The British government, to thwart this German effort to recruit manpower, provided visas to the French and Belgians if they stated they were Canadians. On November 21, 1941, Arthur Yencken reported from the British embassy in Madrid the approximate number of foreigners at Miranda and Palencia:

Nationality	Miranda	Palencia	Elsewhere
Poles	362	26	—
Belgians	150*	4	—
Dutch	6	20	15
Czechoslovaks	19	11	—
Yugoslavs	12	12	10
Greeks	1	6	—
"Canadians" (mostly Free French and Belgians)	90†	—	30†
Austrians	2	7	—

*indicates their release to England had been promised.
† = Approximate.

Yencken did not list Germans, Bulgarians, Hungarians, and Central and South Americans; they had not come from nations allied with Britain in its war against Germany and did not, in his opinion, merit aid. Winter clothing and weekly food packages were being sent to the Poles from Britain by the Polish legation.[35] Yencken recommended that similar help be provided all prisoners from Allied countries until arrangements were completed for their release; in view of the "extremely hard conditions," the prisoners at Palencia should be helped, he felt, but only with half as much as the others. Since the supplies could not be bought in Spain, the governor of Gibraltar would provide eight two-ton trucks, of which two would carry aid for the prisoners.[36]

Among those arriving at Miranda from Palencia were five Germans. Three were posing as Dutch: Wilhelm Reitz, alias Joop de Kat; Heinz Hauser, alias Wilhelm Foliant; Alfred Richter, alias Robertus Van Dregt. Karl Kormes claimed to be a Pole, as did Rudi Kampf, who had been in the hospital.[37]

On March 25, 1942, 2616 pesetas, 50 packets of Portuguese tobacco, 32 blocks of chocolate, and 4 packets of tea arrived at Miranda for the International Brigaders, sent by the British International Brigade Association (IBA) and delivered by the Unitarian Service Committee and the British military attaché.

Karl Kormes informed Jack Brent, secretary of the IBA, that everything had been divided up equally among the Internationals who had been at Palencia, those who had not received help at Miranda, five who were in prisons, and the Internationals who were free in Madrid and Barcelona but had no country to go to. The Dutch, Czechs, Estonians, and Yugoslavs did not take a share because they had been receiving regular help from their diplomatic representatives in Britain.

Kormes added that fifteen Internationals were free in Madrid and Barcelona, and fifteen more were free to leave Miranda if they could leave

Spain the next day. Kormes thought they could leave if a diplomat asked for their release in Gibraltar or Portugal. He suggested efforts be made to free the Polish doctors Joseph Leitner and Arthur Lilker.

Kormes also observed that every week Frenchmen, Belgians, and others were leaving as Englishmen or Canadians. There were many at Miranda who were neither British subjects nor Internationals, but were "mercenaries against whom we have fought in the defense of democracy with arms in hands and against whom we are willing to fight again." Why was the British embassy helping them on the ground of "special merits?"[38]

More tobacco and eight hundred pesetas for the Internationals arrived at Miranda in August 1942. In a letter to Jack Brent Kormes told of the difficulty he was having in getting a letter out to him, of the British embassy still showing no interest in the Internationals, and of the law that all Spanish labor battalions were to be dissolved by the end of 1942.[39]

In October, eleven Dutch Internationals, including Wilhelm Folliant (Heinz Hauser) and Robertus van Dregt (Alfred Richter), were sent to Curaçao in the Netherlands West Indies.[40] Appendix 5 gives the number of each nationality at Miranda, unless otherwise specified, after the Dutch had left.[41]

Of the remaining ten Dutchmen, one died and nine were taken to England to join the Dutch Brigade in 1943.[42]

Bela Lustig was taken to Bari, Italy. He escaped to Yugoslvia, where he fought with the partisans. He later returned to Hungary with a partisan group. At the end of the war, he joined the military police and rose to the rank of colonel. During a purge that affected Spanish veterans, he was dismissed. He earned a living with a horse and wagon until he died in an accident.

Karl Kormes reached Gibraltar in 1943, then Africa, where he joined the OSS and served with Milton Wolff and Irving Fajans. Then he joined the fighting on the Eastern Front in 1945 that destroyed the Nazi Army. He served the GDR in many capacities, including ambassador to Yugoslavia and Ecuador.[43]

Georg Heinzmann, having refused to join the German Army, was put in the Sachsenhausen concentration camp. He survived three years' imprisonment and then joined in building the GDR.[44] Rudi Kampf survived the war and lived in Dresden until his death. Alfred Richter was held in Curaçao until 1947, and eventually reached the GDR.

Wilhelm Fellendorf (Arthur Karlsson) returned to the Soviet Union in 1939. On May 17, 1942, he and Erna Eifler parachuted into eastern Prussia to organize anti-Nazi activity. They reached Hamburg, where they contacted an existing group. Both were caught by the Gestapo in October; they were sentenced to death and executed. Wilhelm's mother, Kathe, was arrested in December for having hidden her son; she was executed on March 15, 1944.[45]

25 Reflections Fifty Years Later

AT SAN PEDRO DE CARDEÑA, we suspected that our State Department was on Franco's side. But when I began to dig into the diplomatic archives at Washington, DC, I was surprised how much it had done for us. As I dug deeper, I found we and the Republic had both friends and enemies in the State Department.

Our friends, who understood the danger of fascism, were Ambassador Claude Bowers, Adolph A. Berle, and Sumner Welles. Our Enemy was the most powerful official, Secretary of State Cordell Hull, who was determined to see Franco win, as Douglas Little documents in *Malevolent Neutrality*. Hull ran a tight ship, and sharply curtailed attempts to aid us while using deceit and secrecy to allow Franco to obtain the gasoline and military trucks he had to have to destroy the Republic.

Only after Franco had won did Hull respond to public pressure and allow the embassy staff in Spain to act vigorously to free us. Ambassador Alexander Weddell and his wife, Counsellor Robert Scotten, and, especially, Earl T. Crain, went out of their way to relieve the hardships and suffering of the Americans still held after the end of the war and to obtain their release.

*　　*　　*　　*　　*

During World War II, the second war against fascism, the Americans who had been prisoners in the first war took delight in striking back at the fascists in an army with equal or superior firepower. How much we were allowed to contribute to the fighting depended, with the help of officers who recognized the value of our battle experience, on the extent to which we were able to evade the restrictions put on us for having fought the fascists too soon. Several of us reached the rank of captain, but others, where commanders didn't know what the war was about, were not allowed to advance beyond the rank of private or to go overseas. Information about military service is not available for all former prisoners. Here is a summary of what is known:

Elias Balagurchik   Army. Not permitted to go overseas.
Leo Berman   Army. Later smuggled arms to Begin's "terrorists" in Palestine.
Tom Brown   Army.
Richard Browne   Merchant Marine officer.
Homer Chase   Paratroop staff sergeant, dropped around Wesel and the Bulge.

Van Chase   Turned down by Army; served in Merchant Marine.

Morris Conway   Merchant Marine

Whitey Dahl   Led planes across the Atlantic, Brazil to Ascension Island.

George Delich   Not allowed to return to US. Served in OSS.

Norman Dorland   Merchant Marine, Murmansk run, awarded three decorations.

Lawrence Fant Doran   Army.

Howard Earl   Army.

Carl Geiser   Foreman and inventor, aircraft instrument plant.

Henry Giler   Navy. Helped invade Guam, Leyte, Luzon, and Okinawa.

Samuel Grant   Air Sea Rescue Service of the Air Force. Captain.

Frank Grodzki   Army. Discharged because of wounds received in Spain.

Maurice Gurko   Army.

Charles Hall   Army. Rose to captain in India-Burma-China theater.

Stanley Heinricher   Army. Sergeant-major in Engineering Combat Battalion.

Charles Keith   Merchant Marine, on Murmansk run.

David Kelly   Merchant Marine.

Sol Lerner   Army. Train brakeman in European theater.

Jack Mail   Merchant Marine.

Herman Lopez   Marine Corps.

Martin Maki   Fought across Europe to Czechoslovakia. Ran Polish POW Camp.

Henry Megquier   Army Signal Corps.

Fred Miller   Merchant Marine.

Ignatz Moskowitz   Army. Died in a Japanese POW Camp.

Lou Ornitz   Army. Fought in European theater with 3rd Infantry Division.

Max Parker   Army. 3rd Armored Division, radio operator.

Gene Poling   Information and Education Division, 4th Army, Fort Hood, Texas.

Joseph Radacoy   Army. Wounded.

Sam Romer   Army. Meteorologist. Civilian consultant to MacArthur in Tokyo.

Sidney Rosenblatt   Army. Motorcycle courier, died after running over a mine.

Kenneth Shaker   Captain. Commanded a parachute company at Anzio and the Bulge.

Max Shufer   Physicist at National Bureau of Standards.

Fred Stanley   Merchant Marine officer.

Bob Steck   Army Intelligence.

Jack Steinberg   Army.
Alwyn Stevenson   Army.
Frederick Stix   Army.
Leon Tenor   Army. 147th Infantry Division.
Richard Thompson   Army. Lost a leg in Europe to an antipersonnel
    mine.
Hy Wallach   Signal Corps of 15th Air Force and 5th Army in Africa and
    Italy.
Joseph Young   Merchant Marine officer.

*   *   *   *   *

What determines how steadfast an individual will be in the front line when facing the enemy? Part of the answer may be found in a study made by the US War Department in the latter part of WWII to find out why so many men were being sent back from Europe due to nervous and mental breakdowns. It found that young men who had grown up in low income neighborhoods made tougher and more reliable front-line combat troops than those from middle-class families. The army IQ tests were weeding out some of the best fighters![1] (Now we know IQ test results are a better measure of education than of innate intelligence.)

But that study tells only half the story; a soldier must also have a strong belief that what he is fighting for is worth his risking his life. My experiences as commissar and as prisoner taught me that neither strong background nor strong belief alone was enough, but with the two together, you have a cool and determined soldier who can stand up under the truly horrible stress of front-line combat, and of captivity.

My experiences in Spain and since have taught me the value—and the limitations—of democracy. For example, an army operating democratically is quite ineffective, as the Anarchists demonstrated in Catalonia. As described before, an attempt to have a communist group in San Pedro function democratically led to poor performance.

For democracy in a country to work well, its ruling bodies must be a cross section of the people. When they are badly skewed toward the wealthy, the ruling bodies will see the national good as the interests of the wealthy, and make wealth not trickle down, but pour up, and see any threat to their wealth as a threat to the nation. If it becomes serious enough, they will finance and organize violence to terrorize the dissident movement and its leaders, as in El Salvador, Chile, and South Africa, where democracy exists only for the wealthy and powerful. The oppressed people use legal forms of action when possible, and illegal and secret forms where necessary, in their struggle for democracy and a better life. A ruling class that uses violence and terror against its population can expect a violent reaction.

Fifty years have passed since Hitler and Mussolini invaded Spain to help its wealthy and powerful, who were seeking to overthrow Spain's democratic government.

Young Americans following in our footsteps today have to face the unpleasant fact that it is our own government that is helping the wealthy and powerful in Latin American countries, supplying them with arms, military training, and money, all paid out of our taxes, to kill the leaders who are struggling toward these goals, and to terrorize the rest. In the 1930s, oil, gasoline, and trucks from the United States made Franco's victory possible. But there was not the open and blatant help to the reactionary forces that the Reagan administration is giving today.

Note a similarity: those who opposed the Republican government of Spain falsely claimed it was a tool of Moscow, that Franco was waging a war against godless communism. We hear the same false cry today, that we have to support dictatorships and even overthrow the government of Nicaragua, for the same reason.

But there is an important difference. In Spain, except in the North, the Catholic Church supported the fascist overthrow of the Republic. Today the struggle for jobs, food, housing, medical care, and education receives strong support from Catholic leaders in much of Latin America, and in the United States.

*   *   *   *   *

When we went to Spain fifty years ago, our goal was to stop fascism before it could spread further and threaten our country. We failed to do so. Young Americans today face an infinitely more serious situation. It is the probable extinction of life on our planet.

Scientists warn that the explosion of even a small part of our nuclear arsenal may bring on a nuclear winter which will destroy all life—human, animal, and plant.[2] Even worse, this nuclear holocaust is very likely to be set off by accident through equipment failure, or an individual's deciding to bring about Armageddon.[3]

To prevent the destruction of life on our planet,[4] tens of millions of young Americans must swing into political action, mobilizing the churches, trade unions, and all people's organizations to prevent a nuclear holocaust. When we lost our fight in Spain because of the actions of Secretary of State Hull, Congress, and the Catholic hierarchy, the cost was World War II. If you lose your fight to outlaw first-strike plans and abolish all atomic weapons, the cost will be your life, and four billion more.

Appendices

Appendix 1: Summary of Brief on Diplomatic Protection Presented to the State Department

Prepared by Herman E. Cooper

The Americans were enlisted members of the Abraham Lincoln Brigade supporting the duly recognized government of Spain. They have neither taken an oath of allegiance to Spain, nor have they renounced or forfeited their citizenship. The State Department has failed to ascertain the fate of these Americans except to report that Edward Freed is probably still alive. Some may have been executed, and the rest face life imprisonment or death unless the arm of diplomatic protection is extended to save their lives, mitigate their punishment and possibly effect their release and return to this country.

The brief cited Supreme Court and other references holding that it is both the right and duty of the State to extend diplomatic protection to its citizens abroad when they are deprived of their rights by other states or powers without warrant in international law. It demonstrated the well-established principle that denial of justice, even the probability that justice might be denied, was historically considered sufficient ground for State Department intervention. It quoted references where unreasonably harsh treatment without fair trial according to international standards of law constituted "denial of justice" and warranted diplomatic interposition. It referred to a recent instance when the German Government arrested Lawrence Simpson, a seaman on the SS *Manhattan,* charged him with high treason and threw him into a concentration camp. As a result of interposition by the State Department before the trial, Simpson was found guilty only of disseminating propaganda material, his sentence was commuted, and Simpson was released.

The brief quoted Daniel Webster in 1874 that it is the duty of the government to see that its citizens when prisoner of war "are treated according to the usage of modern times and civilized nations." It also quoted Secretary of State Knox's protest and intention in 1910 "to hold personally responsible the men who were to blame for the torture and execution of two Americans in the service of Estrada, an unrecognized revolutionist, who were summarily executed upon capture by government troops without a fair trial. It also called attention to Secretary of State Hay's protest in 1900 to the British Government over the treatment accorded American citizens who were taken prisoner while serving with the Boers in South Africa.

The brief discussed the State Department argument that a person voluntarily entering the military service of a foreign government owes that government temporary allegiance, must look to that government for protection and cannot expect his own government to intercede on his behalf. It quoted decisions which established that a citizen is entitled to diplomatic protection until it is determined that he has denationalized himself by naturalization in a foreign state, renounced his citizenship, or taken an oath of allegiance to a foreign state. It always has been held that enlistment in the military service of another government does not constitute expatriation unless accompanied by an unconditional oath of allegiance. The members of the Lincoln Battalion did none of these.

It analyzed the two statutes which provide penalties for enlistment in foreign service. "Sec. 22 (Criminal Code, Section 10, Amended), Enlisting in Foreign Service: Exceptions" specifies a penalty only if the individual enlists inside the territory or jurisdiction of the United States. None of the volunteers enlisted in the United States and the statute does not apply. "Sec. 25. (Criminal Code, Sec. 13, Amended.) Organizing Military Expedition against Friendly Power" provides a penalty for anyone who aids or takes part in an expedition against a friendly power. This statute obviously does not apply to citizens helping the Republic, a friendly power. [Guy Castle and Arthur Krock's son had broken this law, though neither Cooper nor FALB were aware that Castle and Krock were fighting for Franco.]

The restrictions in the Neutrality Act were clearly limited to restraining commerce between the United States and Spain by an embargo and placed no restrictions on the military service rendered by the volunteers.

The brief noted in regard the illegal use of passports: "Assuming, but not conceding that these American nationals proceeded to Spain in technical violation of the terms of their passports, as contended by the Department of State, they would not have lost their citizenship, nor have been deprived of diplomatic protection by such an act." It pointed out that the regulation that passport applicants take an oath that they did not intend to go to Spain did not go into effect until March 11, 1937, and these volunteers were captured on February 15, 1937. Furthermore:

The test is citizenship—not the possession or lack of possession of a passport. Since the lack of a passport does not deprive a citizen of diplomatic protection, his breach of the conditions of a passport can certainly not accomplish that forfeiture.

The brief concluded with:

In the absence of any definite knowledge as to the present conditions of the nineteen nationals here involved, a positive duty rests upon the Department of State to utilize all available means for ascertaining whether or not they have been executed, and if alive, the condition of their incarceration. It is notorious that Generalissimo Franco invariably penalizes activity on behalf of the duly constituted government of Spain by volunteers of other than Spanish nationality, with summary execution or harsh and unusual treatment as prisoners of war. This practice may well have extended to the nineteen nationals here involved.

The first expression of diplomatic interposition in this connection would therefore be the investigation of their status. If still alive, these Americans are entitled to have diplomatic protection extended to them. This should consist of mitigating and ameliorating the conditions of their imprisonment and of obtaining fair trials with a view to their release and return to this country.

This procedure is warranted by the precedents cited and the established principles of international law.

A copy of this brief is in the National Archives under 852.2221/746.

Appendix 2:
Nationalities at San Pedro de Cardeña on September 10, 1938

THE NUMBERS below are based on the list issued by Franco's military headquarters on September 10, 1938. The country of birth appeared to be accurate except for the five pseudonymous Germans, but some military units specified were in error and have been corrected. The number who emigrated to other countries before going to Spain are shown.

Country of Birth		Total	Civilians[a]
Algiers		4	
Argentina		39	10
Austria		28	
Belgium		5[b]	
Bulgaria		3	
Canada		18	
Chile		4	
China		1	
Cuba		41[c]	11
Czechoslovakia		15	
Danzig		1	
Denmark		8	1
Estonia		3	
Finland		2	
France		59[d]	5
Germany		48[e]	
Great Britain			
England	35		1
Scotland	14		
Wales	3		
Total		52[f]	
Greece		5[g]	
Holland		20[h]	
Hungary		8[i]	
Ireland		15	
Italy		19	4
Latvia		1	
Mexico		2	
Morocco, French	2		
Spanish	2		
Total		4	
Norway		7	
Peru		1	
Poland		39[j]	
Portugal		58	4
Romania		2	
Russia		3[k]	
Saar		2	

South Africa	1	
Spain	5^m	2
Sweden	15^n	
Switzerland	13	
Tunisia	2	
Turkey	2	
United States		
Philippines	2	
Puerto Rico	1	
Mainland	76	4
Total	79°	
Uruguay	1	
Yugoslavia	16^p	1
Not recorded	2	1
TOTAL	653	44

Notes: [a]Included in total   [b]One left from USA   [c]Eight were in Spain before 1936   [d]One left from USA   [e]Includes the five pseudonymous Germans   [f]Two left from Canada   [g]Two left from USA   [h]Excludes three pseudonymous Germans   [i]One left from USA   [j]Excludes one pseudonymous German   [k]One left from Holland   [m]All were foreign citizens   [n]excludes one pseudonymous German   [o]Nine had emigrated to the USA   [p]One left from USA

The number of prisoners from each brigade is shown below. Special Services includes International Brigaders who were attached to a military unit above the brigade level, such as transport, communications and medical.

Brigade		Total
11th—German, Austrian, Swiss		160
12th—Italian		6
13th—Poles, Slavs		32
14th—French		38
15th—British Battalion	65	
Lincoln Battalion	58	
Spanish Battalion	26	
Mackenzie-Papineau Battalion	31	
Brigade staff and services	17	
Total		197
129th—Central European		18
Special services		28
TOTAL INTERNATIONAL BRIGADERS		479
Foreigners who served in Spanish units*		130
Sailors from captured or sunken ships		3
Civilian foreigners accused of supporting the Republic†		41
TOTAL OTHERS		174
TOTAL AT SAN PEDRO DE CARDEÑA ON SEPTEMBER 10, 1938		653

*The number who came to Spain after July 18, 1936, is not known. Many of these were in Spain when the revolt broke out.

†Six were born in the United States. Most of the rest were born in Argentina, Portugal, France and Italy. Included in this figure are the two Frenchmen who came to Spain to buy oranges.

Appendix 3: Thirty-one Canadian Prisoners Exchanged on April 5, 1939

These names have been checked against those reported at Ondarreta Prison by Colonel C. C. Martin on March 9, 1939, in FO 371/24123 W4658, and against the signatures collected by Frank Blackman on the back of a postal card photo of thirty of the freed prisoners at Le Havre, and by Lee Burke, MacPap secretary.

Name	Place & Date of Birth		Left from	Military unit
Bowzailo, Harry	Austria	9–12–01	Edmonton, Alta.	MacPap
Blackman, Frank	Edmonton	5– 3–13	Valemount, B.C.	MacPap
Bowen, Cromwell	Toronto	3–15–95	Toronto	MacPap
Cunningham, George	Scotland	12–30–12	Toronto	British
Delaney, Jerry	Halifax	4– 2–09	Vancouver	MacPap
Dickie, Bob	Aberdeen	2–12–02	Kirkland Lake	MacPap
Dufour, Paul	Montreal	9– 4–18	Montreal	MacPap
Elendiuk, Nicolas	Minetova	4– 2–11	Winnipeg	MacPap
Gray, Arthur	Toronto	1896	Toronto	MacPap
Hansbout, Urbain	Antwerp	1–25–02	Winnipeg	British
Harrost, Steve	Poland	12–26–05	Toronto	13 Brig Medical
Hesketh, Harry	England	2– 1–06	Vancouver	MacPap
Hill, George	Toronto	11–24–08	Toronto	MacPap
Hilton, Percy	England	2– 9–03	Toronto	MacPap
Hoffheinz, Arthur	Cambden, B.C.	4– 8–07	Cumberland, B.C.	MacPap
Jones, J. E.T.	Montreal	5–22–96	Montreal	15 Brig Phones
Kambides, John	Montreal	5– 5–13	Montreal	Lincoln
Korinski, Joseph	Ottawa	2– 8–12	Ottowa	15 Brig Medical
Madsen, Neils	Denmark	12–11–99	Vancouver	Lincoln
Malicki, Michael	Poland	3–19–02	Toronto	MacPap
Mangotic, Anthony	Yugoslavia	6–19–14	Schummaker, Ont.	Lincoln
Markowski, George	Poland	11–20–04	Toronto	MacPap
Martilla, Helge	Finland	11– 1–02	Vancouver	MacPap
Medgyesi, Charles	Hungary	3–19–96		12 Transp. Co.
Moskaluk, Peter	Poland	11–12–07		15 Brig Armory
Nunemaker, Willis	Welland	5– 6–14	Vancouver	MacPap
Paivio, Jules	Ontario	4–30–17	Ontario	MacPap
Prokopink, Nick	Romania	11–15–97	Toronto	MacPap
Scott, Paul	Toronto	6– 6–16	Montreal	15 Brig Span Bn.
Wilson, Leslie W.	Kenora, Ont.	1–20–12	Vancouver	MacPap
Wood, Frank	Vancouver	9– 5–15	Vancouver	British

Appendix 4: Americans Exchanged on April 22, 1939

Military unit code: B, British Battalion; C, Civilian, farmer or laborer; H, Headquarters or auxiliary unit of 15th Brigade; L, Lincoln Battalion; M, Mackenzie-Papineau Battalion; N, Republican military unit in Northern Spain; S, Spanish Battalion in 15th Brigade; T, Transport Battalion

SP# refers to the position on the list of September 10, 1938. Those without an SP# arrived at San Pedro after this date. An asterisk before a name indicates that this man joined us after November 12, 1938; that is, he was not listed by Bay on November 12, 1938.

SP#	Name	Birthplace	Birthday	Mil. Unit
*	Alvarez Fernández, Antonio	Springfield, Ill.	4–19–19	C
*	Alvarez Rodríguez, Julio	Cherryvale, Kans.	3–26–16	C
	Anderson, Ray	Lake City, Minn.	8–25–08	L
31	Antiros, Peter	Athens, Greece	1– 1–09	L
320	Argirakis, Matthew	Greece	10–15–98	L
19	Arranz Díaz, Avelino	Tampa, Fla.	11–10–11	N
39	Balagurchik, Elias	New York, N.Y.	9–26–13	S
	Borer, Fred	Booneville, Ind.	1–29–00	L
86	Brown, Tom	St. Louis, Mo.	2– 5–11	T
58	Busto Bango, Luis	Grasselli, W.Va.	5–13–16	N
138	Calleja Bode, Manuel	Tampa, Fla.	2–18–10	N
*	Canales Zerro, Victor	Barre, Vt.	5– 3–19	?
161	De la Casa, Jesus	Philadelphia, Pa.	9–17–17	N
146	Colon González, Gonzalo	Morovis, P.R.	5–28–98	B
163	Delich, George	Yugoslavia	2–15–98	L
*	Díaz, Serino	Morenci, Ariz.	4–27–13	?
178	Dykstra, Matthew	Passaic, N.J.	11–22–08	H
182	Earl, Howard	Santa Monica, Calif.	8– 8–07	B
190	Fajardo, Mark	Philippines	3– 1–05	127 Brig.
193	Fernández Fernández, Alfonso	Tampa, Fla.	1–10–13	C
405	García Menéndez, Amador	Zeising, W.Va.	4–21–16	C
408	García Menéndez, Marshall	Spain	8–15–00	H
409	Garcí Vásquez, Ramón	New York, N.Y.	8–22–11	C
208	Geiser, Carl	Orrville, Ohio	12–10–10	L,M
	Gerhardt, Julius	Chicago, Ill.	2–21–03	?
421	Giler, Henry	New York, N.Y.	1–16–15	L
	Gonzalo Fernández, Alfonso			
422	Grant, Samuel	Portland, Oreg.	12–18–13	L
423	Graver, William	New York, N.Y.	5–21–98	L
425	Grigas, Joseph	Worcester, Mass.	2–15–15	L
426	Grodski, Frank	Brooklyn, N.Y.	8–17–10	?
427	Gurko, Maurice	Chicago, Ill.	10–18–11	L
430	Hall, Charles	Canning, S.Dak.	7–12–14	L
431	Hannigan, Walter	Altoona, Pa.	12– 5–95	L
435	Heinricher, Stanley	Pittsburgh, Pa.	1–16–13	L
437	Higgins, John	New York, N.Y.	4–30–10	L
439	Hodge, Edward	Paris, Ky.	7–17–09	M

265	Jenkins, John Hollis	Galveston, Tex.	1– 9–06	L
448	Johnson, Edward	Lynchburg, Va.	2–10–01	B
452	Keith, Charles	Rutland, Vt.	8– 1–11	L
453	Kelly, David	Johnstown, Pa.	4–20–03	L
455	Koneski, Sam	New Kensington, Pa.	10–11–09	L
	Lemke, Otto	New York, N.Y.	7–21–08	L
460	Lerner, Sol	New York, N.Y.	8–23–12	L
	Lionetti, Marzo Guissepe	Italy	5–28–99	?
463	Logan, John	Boston, Mass.	4–16–05	L
315	Lopez, Herman	Puerto Rico	10–28–15	L
478	Mail, Jack	San Francisco, Calif.	4–18–09	L
321	Maki, Martin	Newberry, Mich.	7– 4–11	L
331	Meguier, Henry	Mobile, Ala.	6– 3–00	H
497	Miller, Fred	Detroit, Mich.	1–28–05	L
335	Moskowitz, Ignatz	Hungary	1–10–03	L
356	Panaszewicz, John	Iron River, Mich.	9– 9–11	L
519	Parker, Max	New York, N.Y.	4–25–12	T
	Pérez Fernández, Angel	Neodesha, Kans.	9–12–14	?
*	Pérez, Juan	Imperador, Panama Canal	5–16–10	?
226	Piekarski, John	Poland	3–12–98	L
229	Polansky, Sam	Newark, N.J.	6– 7–14	L
529	Poling, Eugene	Lone Wolf, Okla.	8–26–08	M
232	Pringle, Claude	Halifax Co., Va.	1–22–94	M
360	Raacke, Peter	St. Louis, Mo.	3–28–08	L
361	Radacoy, Joseph	Hutchinson, W.Va.	3–26–16	L
540	Riffe, Herman Carl	Portsmouth, Ohio	8–11–18	L
	Ribera Vásquez, Ferdinand	Catano, P.R.	7–12–12	?
554	Rosenblatt, Sidney	New York, N.Y.	10–30–15	L
	Salvini, Frederick	Italy	4– 9–98	?
391	Severdia, George	Clifton, N.J.	12– 9–15	S
535	Shufer, Max	Boston, Mass.	9– 7–14	L
575	Stanley, Fred	Oden, Tex.	12–15–16	L
588	Thompson, Richard	Newport, N.H.	8–18–17	11th Brig.

The ten Americans who were returned to San Pedro were:

576	Steck, Robert	Rock Island, Ill.	7–29–14	L
577	Steinberg, Jack	Philadelphia, Pa.	1–19–17	L
398	Stevenson, Alwyn	Bridgeport, Conn.	9– 1–16	L
579	Stone, William Clark	Chicago, Ill.	8–22–11	L
586	Tenor, Leon	Beaver Falls, Pa.	5– 7–11	L
591	Tobman, Morris	Russia	3– 5–10	L
593	Toole, Samuel	Muncie, Ind.	10–18–13	L
645	Wallach, Hyman David	Poland	2–14–14	L
649	Young, Joseph	Bellefonte, Pa.	7–20–14	L
652	Ziegler, Albert	New York, N.Y.	5–26–15	L

In Spain, Matthew Argirakis was known as Chris Maisanes, Henry Giler as Michael Goodwin, and Max Shufer as Irving Rabinowitz.

Appendix 5: International Brigade Prisoners at Miranda de Ebro Concentration Camp in November 1942

Compiled from a list smuggled out of Miranda by Adolf Redig, a Pole

Nationality	Number	Notes
Argentinian	24	Release arranged. Two are invalids
Belgians	4	
Brazilians	3	
British	1	Willi Heriberg, invalid
Bulgarians	3	
Chileans	1	Francisco Arbos Siura
Chinese	1	Chang Aking, free in Madrid
Cubans	3	
Czechs	3	One invalid
Egyptians	1	José Díaz Alonso
Estonians	6	
Filipinos	1	Agilino Belmonte Capiodist
French	12	Release arranged for three
Germans	1	Alvin Sass
Hungarians	12	Includes Bela Lustig, an invalid
Hollanders	10	Release arranged
Italians	8	
Lithuanians	3	One had come to Spain from Canada
Panamanian	1	José Rodríguez Castro
Poles	31	Includes three invalids, and Doctors Leitner and Lilker
Portuguese	2	
Romanian	2	One invalid
Swiss	2	Fred Stark, and Rudolph Zigg at Zaragoza Prison
Ukrainian	2	
USA	1	Samuel Swanson, Palencia Asylum. [Not mentioned in VALB files.]
Yugoslavs	15	One at Zaragoza Prison
No Nationality	13	Includes 9 Germans, among them Rudi Kampf and Otto Maassen, and three Jews whose nationality had been revoked

Appendix 6: American Volunteers Captured in Spain

An accurate count of the American volunteers captured and taken alive is available. But an accurate count of those killed upon capture cannot be made. The report of the missing based on battalion records in the Marxist-Leninist Institute in Moscow has been purged of the names of those reported killed and those who returned home. Six aliens who lived in the United States before leaving for Spain to join the International Brigades are treated as American volunteers.

It has not been possible to obtain the names of captured and killed in the following instances:

1. The two trucks that ran into the fascist lines at Jarama in February 16, 1937.
2. The headquarters staff members shot at Belchite on March 10, 1938.
3. Those captured at Hijar the second week of March 1938.
4. The ambulance driver and the wounded captured at Muniesa in March 1938.
5. Those who were captured with Bill Miller and escaped during the retreat from Gandesa.
6. Those captured with Jack Cooper and Howard Goddard who convinced their captors to surrender to them across the Ebro in July 1938.
7. An unknown number who were machine-gunned in the Sierra Caballs on September 7, 1938.

Without these names, the identities of 287 who were captured are known (which may include some from Groups 2, 3 and 4 above) including some who were in Spain before the uprising. The table below shows what happened to them.

Table 6-1

Killed	173
Exchanged	86
Freed	20
Escaped	5
Died of illness	2
Left in Spain	1*
TOTAL	287

*Peter Matas, who departed from Seattle, was left in Spain by the State Department because he was an alien.

Those who left Spain gained their freedom on the following dates. In the table below, the "Freed code" gives the number freed on that day, and is used in Table 6-2 to show when each individual was freed.

Freed code	Date exchanged or freed
14	October 8, 1938. Exchanged.
71	April 22, 1939. Exchanged.
11	August 25, 1939. Freed.
6	February 22, 1940. Freed.
2	March 24, 1940. Freed.
1B	End of October, 1938. Exchanged among first 100 British.
1C	April 26, 1939. Freed with Canadians.
TOTAL: 106	Includes 13 who were in Spain before the uprising, and Dahl.

Table 6-2: Americans Who Survived

Name, age, birthplace, military unit, date passport issued. Freed code.

At Brunete, July 1937   *Code*

ORNITZ, Lou Noah, 26, Brooklyn, N.Y. Mil. transport. pp on 2/13/37.   14

At Teruel, January 1938

ANDREASEN, Alf, 36, Bergen, Norway. From Brooklyn. Left N.Y. 6/5/37.   2
BARR, Reuben, 35, Lincoln. Sentenced to death.   2
MADIS, Peter, Greece. Left Portland, Oreg. Alien, left at Valdenoceda.

At Belchite, March 10 to 17, 1938

ANTIROS, Panos, 1/1/09, Athens, Greece. Left from New York, N.Y. 8/14/37.   71
BARR, Charles, 9/14/19, Steubenville, Ohio. Sailed 9/25/37.   14
BELAU, Carl Gustav, 30, St. Paul, Minn. pp on 7/27/37.   14
BERMAN, Leo, 25, Newark, N.J. pp on 5/11/37.   14
BLAIR, John Clarence, 40, Swanville, Minn. pp on 5/4/37.   6
BROWNE, Richard, 19, Kansas City, Mo. pp on 6/1/37.   14
CHASE, Homer, 1/29/17, Washington, N.H. pp on 2/24/37.   14
EARL, Howard, 8/8/07, Santa Monica, Calif. pp on 1/12/38.   71
GARCIA MENÉNDEZ, Marshall, 8/15/00, Asturias, Spain. 15th Brig Staff.   71
GILER, Henry, 22, Brooklyn, N.Y. Lincoln. pp on 7/2/37.   71
HALL, Charles, 7/12/14, Canning, S.Dak. Lincoln. pp on 8/11/37.   71
HANNIGAN, Walter, 12/5/95, Altoona, Pa. Lincoln. pp on 5/27/37.   71
HAUSMAN, Carl, From San Francisco, Calif.   1B
HIGGINS, John, 4/30/10, New York, N.Y. Lincoln. pp on 12/4/37.   71
KACHADORIAN, David, 38, Turkey. Left from Boston 6/5/37. Lincoln.   14
KONESKI, Sam, 10/11/09, New Kensington, Pa. Lincoln. pp on 9/30/37.   71
PIEKARSKI, John, 40. Poland. Left from Brooklyn, N.Y. pp on 12/16/36.   71
RADACOY, Joseph, 3/26/16, Hutchinson, W.Va. Lincoln. Sailed 10/23/37   71
RIFFE, Carl Herman, 8/11/18, Portsmouth, Ohio. Lincoln. Sailed 9/17/37   71
ROMER, Sam, 26, Detroit, Mich. MacPap. Eugene Debs Column. 5/11/37   14
ROSENBLATT, Sidney, 10/30/15. New York, N.Y. Lincoln. pp on 5/21/37.   71
SEVERDIA, George, 12/8/15, Clifton, N.J. Spanish. pp on 2/2/37.   71
SHUFER, Max, 9/7/14. Bronx, N.Y. Lincoln. Sailed 6/37   71
STIX, Frederick, 11/3/14, Suring, Wis. Sailed 2/11/37.   14
STONE, William Carl, 8/22/11, Chicago, Ill. Sailed 12/24/37.   11
TENOR, Leon, 26, Beaver Falls, Pa. Transmissions. Sailed 3/10/37.   11
TOOLE, Samuel Coleman, 19, Muncie, Ind. 15 Br. Ord. Sailed 9/15/37.   11
ZIEGLER, Albert, 5/26/15, New York, N.Y. Seaman. Summer of 1937.   11

TOTAL AT BELCHITE: 28

At Gandesa, March 30 to April 14, 1938

ACEVEDO MONDRAGON, Servando, 49, Philippines. MacPap. S. 7/21/37.   71
ACKEN, Edgar Lawrence, 11/18/06, Milburn, N.J. pp on 12/22/36.   14
ARGIRAKIS, Matthew, 11/1/97, Kios, Greece. Lincoln. Left N.Y. 1/26/37.   71
BALAGURCHIK, Elias, 9/26/13, New York, N.Y. Spanish. pp on 6/22/37.   71
BRALEY, Roger Lancaster, 34, Newport, R.I. pp on 1/5/38.   14
BROWN, Tom, 27, Wichita Falls, Tex. pp on 2/18/37.   71
CHASE, Van Rensalaer, 1/6/14, Calgary, Canada. 15th Brig Transm. 5/29/37   14
COLON GONZÁLEZ, Gonzalo, 5/28/98, Puerto Rico. British. Stowaway. 1/38   71
CONWAY, Morris, 4/21/08. Olympia, Wash. MacPap. pp on 7/23/37.   14
DELICH, George, 2/15/98, Yugoslavia. Lincoln. Sailed 4/14/37   71
DORAN, Lawrence Fant, 25, Los Angeles, Calif. Death Sentence. Sailed 2/12/38. 6
DORLAND, Norman, 25, St. Paul, Minn. 15th Brig. Staff. Sailed Spring '37.   14
DYKSTRA, Matthew, 29, from Los Angeles, Calif. pp on 3/17/37.   71
FAJARDO, Mark, 33, Philippines. 127th Brig. Sailed 2/38.   71
GEISER, Carl, 12/10/10, Orrville, Ohio. MacPap. pp on 3/29/37.   71
GERHARTT, Julius, 34, Romania. Left from Chicago. Sailed 5/1/37.   71
GRANT, Samuel, 11/8/13, Portland, Oreg. Lincoln. pp on 8/2/37.   71
GRAVER, William, 5/21/98, New York, N.Y. Lincoln, pp on 8/4/37.   71
GRIGAS, Joseph, 2/15/15, Worcester, Mass. Lincoln. pp on 2/10/38.   71
GRODSKI, Frank, 6/17/10, Brooklyn, N.Y. Lincoln. Sailed 2/17/37   71
GURKO, MAURICE, 10/18/11, Chicago, Ill. Lincoln. Sailed 1/18/38   71
HARRIS, Sydney, 22, Leeds, England, from Chicago, Lincoln. Sailed 11/6/37   1C
HEINRICHER, Stanley, 1/16/13, Pittsburgh, Pa. Lincoln. pp on 11/9/37.   71
HODGE, Edward, 7/17/09, Paris, Ky. MacPap. pp on 7/29/37.   71
JENKINS, John Hollis, 1/9/06, Galveston, Tex. Lincoln. pp on 1/11/38.   71
JOHNSON, Edward, 1/10/91, Lynchburg, Va. Lincoln. pp on 2/15/37.   71
KEITH, Charles, 8/11/15, Rutland, Vt. Lincoln. pp on 4/5/34.   71
KELLER, Fred, 25, from New York, N.Y. pp on 6/1/37. Escaped.
KELLY, David, 24, Johnstown, Pa. Sailed 10/2/37   71
KERHLICKER, Anthony, 8/23/07, Polk Co. Iowa. Death Sent. pp on 6/4/37.   6
KLEIMAN, Harry, 8/8/12, Ukraine. MacPap. pp on 6/30/37.   6
LEMKE, Otto Ernest, 7/21/09, New York, N.Y. Sailed on 6/20/37.   71
LERNER, Sol, 8/23/12, New York, N.Y. Lincoln. pp on 1/25/37.   71
LISTHAEGHE, Gustav, 9/28/14, East Moline, Mo. 11th Brig. Died at San Pedro
LOGAN, John Monroe, 4/16/05, Boston, Mass. Lincoln. pp on 7/30/37.   71
LOPEZ, Jules Herman, 10/28/15, Cabo Rojo, Puerto Rico. Lincoln.   71
MAIL, Jack, 4/8/09, San Francisco, Calif. Lincoln. pp on 9/14/37.   71
MAKI, Martin, 7/4/11, Newberry, Mich. Lincoln. pp on 4/22/37.   71
MEGQUIER, Henry, 6/3/00, Mobile. Ala. 15th Brig Transm. pp on 9/28/37.   71
MILLER, Fred, 1/28/05, Detroit, Mich. Lincoln. pp on 3/19/37.   71
MILLER, William Colfax, 26, from Hollywood, Calif. pp on 12/30/37. Escaped.
MOSKOWITZ, Ignatz, Hungary. Left Jersey City, N.J. Lincoln. pp 10/24/33.   71
OPARA, Rudolph, 21, Cleveland, Ohio. Lincoln. Death Sentence.   6
PANASZEWICZ, John, 9/9/11, Iron River, Mich. Lincoln. pp on 2/4/37.   71
PARKER, Max, 4/25/12, New York, N.Y. Transport. pp on 2/13/37.   71
POLANSKY, Samuel, 6/7/14, Newark, N.J. pp on 9/28/37.   71
POLING, Eugene Debs, 8/26/08, Lone Wolf, Okla. MacPap.   71
PRINGLE, Claude, 1/22/94, Halifax Co. Va. MacPap. pp on 4/19/37.   71

RAACKE, Peter, 3/28/08, St Louis, Mo. Lincoln.　　　71
SHAKER, Kenneth, 23, from Hartford, Conn. pp on 6/28/37. Escaped.
STANLEY, Fred, 12/15/16, Oden, Tex. Lincoln.　　　71
STECK, Robert, 7/29/14, Rock Island, Ill. Lincoln. pp on 2/11/37.　　　11
STEINBERG, Jack, 1/25/17. Philadelphia, Pa. Sailed on 2/5/38.　　　11
STEVENSON, Alwyn, 9/1/16, Bridgeport, Conn. Lincoln. Sailed 10/2/37.　　　11
THOMPSON, Richard, 20, Newport, N.H. pp on 4/20/37.　　　71
TOBMAN, Morris, 3/5/10, Russia. Lincoln. Sailed on 2/20/37.　　　11
WALLACH, Hy, 2/14/14, Poland. Left from New York. Lincoln.　　　11
YOUNG, Joseph, 7/9/14, Bellefonte, Pa. Lincoln. Sailed 2/20/37.　　　11

TOTAL AT GANDESA: 59

Across the Ebro, July 25 to September 27, 1938

ANDERSON, Ray, 30, Lake City, Minn. From Los Angeles, Calif. pp on 1/10/38. 71
BORER, Fred, 38, Booneville, Ind. pp on 2/12/37. Lincoln.　　　71
COOPER, Jack, Cleveland, Ohio. His captors surrendered. Lincoln Sailed 6/37.
EPAILLY, Raymond, 23, Los Angeles, Calif. pp on 7/8/37. Died Guernica hospital.
GODDARD, Howard, 26, from Los Angeles, Calif. Captors surrendered to him.
LIONETTI, Marzo Guiseppe, 6/28/99, Italy. Left from New York, N.Y.　　　71
SALVINI, Fred, 4/9/98, Italy. Left from New York, N.Y. pp on 1/12/37.　　　71

TOTAL: 7

Captured and Survived in the North of Spain

ALVAREZ, Calvett Joaquin, 3/1/14, Tampa, Fla. Communications in Gijón.　　　71
ARRANZ DIAZ, Avelino, 11/10/11, Tampa, Fla. First aid, Asturias.　　　71
RIBERA VASQUEZ, Ferdinand, 7/12/12. Cantano, P.R. Stowaway 6/37.　　　71

American citizens in Spain before July 17, 1936 and exchanged with us

ALVAREZ FERNANDEZ, Antonio, 4/19/19, Springfield, Ill.　　　71
ALVAREZ Y GONZALEZ, Bernardo, 8/26/13, Tampa, Fla.　　　11
ALVAREZ RODRIGUEZ, Julio, 3/26/16, Cherryvale, Kans.　　　71
BUSTO BANGO, Lewis, 5/13/16, Grasselli, W.Va. 6th Supply Co. Asturias.　　　71
CALLEJA BODE, Manuel, 2/18/10. Tampa, Fla. 208th Bn. Asturias.　　　71
CANALES ZERRO, Victor, 5/3/19, Barre, Vt.　　　71
CASA, Jesus (Andy) de la, 9/7/17, Philadelphia, Pa. 274th Bn. Asturias.　　　71
DIAZ, Serino, 4/27/13, Morenci, Ariz.　　　71
GARCIA, Amador, 4/21/16, Zeising, W.Va.　　　71
GARCIA VASQUEZ, Ramón, 8/22/11, New York, N.Y. Farmer.　　　71
GONZALO FERNANDEZ, Alfonso, 1/10/13. Tampa, Fla. Farm worker.　　　71
PEREZ FERNANDEZ, Angel, 9/12/14, Neodesha, Kans.　　　71
PEREZ, Juan, 5/16/10, Imperador, Canal Zone, Panama.　　　71

TOTAL: 13

Aviator released (not a volunteer)

DAHL, Harold, "Whitey," 28, downed July 1937, sentenced to death.   6

Table 6-3: Americans Killed After Capture

Name, Age, Birthplace, Date Passport Was Issued or Sailing Date.

At Madrid—December, 1937

DELGADO DELGADO, Carmelo, executed by a firing squad on April 29, 1937.

At Brunete—July 1937

BRADBURY, Philip Walton, 37, from Chicago, Ill. pp on 4/9/37.
CHESTNA, William, 32, Corona, N.Y. pp on 5/4/37.
ENTIN, Bernard, 22, Brooklyn, N.Y. pp on 3/10/37.
GOOD, Henry Paul, 30, Lexington, Neb. pp on 3/22/37.
GRACHOW, Leo, 23, Binghampton, N.Y. Sailed 2/20/37.
GREENFIELD, Mitchell, 28, Ohio, from New York, N.Y.
ROBEL, Charles Edward, 23, San Pedro, Calif. pp on 3/10/37.

At Teruel—January, 1938

FLORES GONZALEZ, Antonio. 24, Boston, Mass.
LASHER, Benizon, 23, New York, N.Y. pp on 5/28/37.
SHAPIRO, Henry, 26, Boston, Mass. pp on 7/22/37.
TAYLOR, Clyde Donald, 21, from Louisville, Ky. pp on 4/20/37.

At Belchite—March 10 to 17, 1938

ABRAMOVITZ, Nathan Joseph, Youngstown, Ohio. 8/12/13. pp on 4/24/37.
BENNET, Robert Lee, 37, Chicago, Ill. pp on 1/14/38.
BERSERIE, John, 22, New York. Interviewed by Carney after capture.
BLOOM, Maurice, 26, New Rochelle, N.Y. pp on 10/13/37.
BRIAN, Levi Earl, 32, from Philadelphia, Pa.
CHAKIN, Abraham Alfred, 34, New York, N.Y. pp on 6/20/35.
CORRIGAN, John Horton, 22, Newark, N.J. pp on 2/10/37.
DAVIS, Jessie Jefferson, 51, Louisville, Ky. pp on 4/12/37.
DUBOVICH, George, 27, from Duluth, Minn.
ECKER, Morris, 25, New York, N.Y. pp in San Francisco on 6/18/38.
FORS, Charles, 33, born in Finland, from Detroit, Mich. pp on 3/4/37.
FORSYTHE, Thomas Benton, 45, from Washington, D.C. pp on 7/23/37.
GOEPEL, Hans.
HAMPKINS, Lt. Peter, 43, Racine, Wisc. pp on 8/26/35.

JACOBS, Edward Deyo, 25, Highland, N.Y. pp on 2/4/37.
JENNINGS, Walter, 40, New Haven, Conn.
KAHLE, Harland, 23, from Ann Arbor, Mich. pp on 8/27/37.
KATZ, Jacob, 25, New York, N.Y. Left Washington, D.C. pp on 7/2/37.
KEMPPAINEN, Oivo William, 26, Newport, N.H. pp on 6/25/37.
LAW, Norman Emmet, 28, Hammond, Ind. pp on 12/14/37.
MACEACHRON, Paul Norton, 23, Des Moines, Iowa pp on 5/27/37.
MADSEN, Martin, 32, born in Norway. Left from New York, N.Y.
MARTINEZ, Felipe, 22, Puerto Rico.
MASSEY, Marion Burton, 21, Bothell, Wash. pp on 8/21/37.
NEAFUS, Ralph L., Clovis, N. Mex. From Ann Arbor, Mich. pp on 6/10/37.
PASHT, William, 21, Chicago, Ill.
PETERSON, John Lloyd, 23, San Fernando, Calif. pp on 9/16/37.
PILATO, Fred, 23, from Long Island City, N.Y.
RAMER, Aaron, 29, New York, N.Y. pp on 2/18/37.
RAUERT, Henry, 53, Buffalo, N.Y. Left from Santa Fe, N. Mex. pp on 6/25/37.
REEVES, Otto, 24, Dayton, Ohio. Left from Oakland, Calif. pp on 5/7/37.
ROSENSTEIN, Joseph, 23, Lima, Ohio. Left from Detroit, Mich. pp on 2/1/37.
RYANT, Reuben, 23, Montreal, Canada. Left from New York.
SEDLACEK, James, 39, Chicago, Ill. pp on 1/8/37.
SUMMERS, Thain, 25, from Seattle, Wash. pp on 4/26/37.
SUNDEEN, Walter, 25, Cleveland, Ohio pp on 12/8/37.
TAYLOR, Douglas, 29, New York, N.Y. pp on 5/26/37.
TICER, Leon Norvell, 23, Alfalfa, Okla. pp on 3/13/37. Interviewed by Carney.
TROYER, Burl Eugene, 23, New Jersey.
WALLACE, Joseph Charles, Jr., 21, Chicago, Ill.
YEAGER, Norbert Terry, 34, New York, N.Y. pp on 7/19/37.

TOTAL: 41 killed during retreat from Belchite.

At Gandesa, March 30 to April 14, 1938.

ALBERT, Reuben, 12/10/10, Rochester, N.Y. pp on 1/7/38.
ANDERSON, Erick Bernard, 28, from Boston, Mass. January, 1938.
BACKMAN, Osmo Henry, Canada. Left from Brooklyn, N.Y. pp on 3/20/37.
BLANK, John, 42, Russia. Left from New York.
BOWERS, Edward, 37, Elba, Ohio. pp on 3/10/37.
BRUDZINSKI, Czeslaw, San Pedro, Calif. pp on 1/18/38.
BUCKNELL, Leslie
BURNING, John, 23, Chicago, Ill. pp on 8/21/37.
CARTER, Barton, 22, Newton, Mass. pp on 6/22/35.
CHAIT, Jacob Jack, from New York. pp on 1/25/38.
COLVER, Robert, 26. New York, N.Y. MacPap Bn. Secy. pp on 5/13/37
CONNELLY, William Julius, 24, Escanaba, Mich.
CONTENTO, Roger, 24, Brooklyn, N.Y. pp on 1/31/38.
COOK, Walter, 32, Wilmington, Calif. pp on 1/25/38.
COOK, Frederick Joseph, 22, Baltimore, Md. pp on 6/7/37.
COSTANZA, Frank Carl, 26, Knoxville, Pa. pp on 7/26/37.

CROMWELL, Frederick William, Jr., 27, Oakland, Calif. pp on 1/10/38.
CROSS, Donald Ellis, 25, San Francisco, Calif. pp on 4/7/37.
DELANEY, Andrew, 26, Dublin, Ireland. Left from New York.
DINARDI, John, 24, New York, N.Y.
DOTY, Bennet Jeffries, 35, Biloxi, Miss. pp on 2/17/38.
ELLIOTT, Theodore Roy, 27, Seattle, Wash. pp on 1/19/38.
FINKELSTEIN, Norman, 21, New York, N.Y. pp on 7/13/37.
FOUCEK, Albert, 23, Anoka, NE. pp on 5/19/37.
FRIEDMAN, Maurice Wolf, 19, Los Angeles, Calif. pp on 12/31/37.
GARCIA, González Samuel, 28.
GLUCK, Max, 27, from Los Angeles, Calif. pp on 1/28/38.
GOLDBERG, Arthur, 25, New York, N.Y. pp in San Francisco on 6/18/37.
GOLDBLATT, Moses, 25, Uncasville, Conn. pp on 7/7/37.
GOLDMAN, Samuel, 33, Cleveland, Ohio pp on 5/21/37.
GOMEZ, Maximo, 35, St. Louis, Mo. pp on 12/21/37.
GRAY, Robert, 25, Piqua, Ohio pp on 5/28/37.
GUNNING, James Adrian, 25, New York, N.Y.
GUREVITZ, Edgar, 23, Chicago, Ill. pp on 1/6/37.
GUSTAFSON, Bernard Karl, Westfield, Mass. pp on 1/28/37.
HASLAN, Robert, 23, from New York, N.Y. pp on 6/29/37.
HEEB, Harry Jack, 25, Cincinnati, Ohio pp on 5/6/37.
HERSCH, Arthur, 29, Poland. Left from New York, N.Y. pp on 1/24/38.
HOLMES, Robert Hale, 22, Chicago, Ill. pp on 1/21/38.
HOUSE, Edward, 22, Cleveland, Ohio. pp on 11/5/37.
HUNT, Hugh Maxwell, 25, Deer Park, Wash. pp on 6/2/37.
JACKSON, Ray Jr., 31, Syracuse, Kans. pp on 2/9/38.
JOHNSON, Earl Raymond, 32, Riverton, Wash. pp on 9/4/37.
JOHNSON, Lloyd Edward, 42, St. Paul, Minn. pp on 3/29/37.
KANTOLA, Olavi, 25, Hancock. Mich. pp on 2/4/36.
KAUFFMAN, Alfred, 33, from Philadelphia, Pa. pp on 4/26/37.
KAZOGLIS, Peter, 32, Greece. Left from Fitchburg, Mass.
KONDELL, Herman Leo, 27, Brooklyn, N.Y. pp on 3/12/37.
LAUKKONEN, Lauri Armas, 27, from Marquette, Mich. pp on 8/6/37.
LEIGHTON, John Stuart, 22, Seattle, Wash. pp on 6/7/37.
LOESCH, Victor, 27, North Dakota. Left Los Angeles, Calif. pp on 1/24/38.
LORRAINE, Sidney Hotchkiss, 24, Houston, Tex. pp on 10/5/37.
LOVEMAN, Eugene Jacob, 26, Brooklyn, N.Y. pp on 2/23/37.
MALE, Douglas Wayne, 23, Athens, Ohio. pp on 6/5/37.
MALLON, John Thomas, 26, Brooklyn, N.Y. pp on 6/9/37.
MANN, Harold Mulford, 30, Kansas City, Mo. pp on 10/14/37.
MANNING, Robert, 28, Seattle, Wash. pp on 8/6/37.
MANSON, Burton Robert, 21, New York, N.Y. pp on 7/3/37.
MATSON, Eric, 35, Finland. From New York.
MATZ, Morris, Binghamton, NY pp 3/18/37.
MELEN, Karl, 32, Sweden. Left from Barre, Vt.
MERONIA, Purfil, 30, Osage, W.Va. pp on 8/19/37.
MICHALCHIK, George, 41, Poland. Left from New York, N.Y. pp on 7/14/37.
MITCHELL, Andrew, 30, from Battle Creek, Mich. pp on 7/12/37.

MOORE, Paul, 40, from Los Angeles, Calif. pp on 1/27/38.
MUSCALA, Edward Ferdinand, 26, Minneapolis, Minn. pp on 7/27/37.
NEEL, Clyde Harvey, 27, Jacksonville, Fla. pp on 6/26/37.
NELSON, Joseph, 28, Virginia.
NELSON, Kenneth Frederick, 22, Seattle, Wash. pp on 1/18/38.
NELSON, Marvin, 28, Menoska Mills, Calif. pp on 1/31/38.
NIEZGODA, Adam John, 26, Toledo, Ohio pp on 8/19/37.
NIVALA, Robert Kustav, 23, Tamarack, Minn. pp on 8/3/37.
NORIE, James Lester, Jr., 35, from Seattle, Wash. pp on 6/8/37.
PAPACOSTAS, Georgio Giovanni, 24, Detroit, Mich.
PROWELL, Alphaeus Danforth, 33, Boonesville, N.C. pp on 8/2/37.
RADIN, Walter Jack, 22, Los Angeles, Calif. pp on 1/28/38.
RAMATOWSKI, John Augustus, 24, St. Louis, Mo. pp on 5/19/37.
RICHARD, Ferdinand, 32, Honduras. Left from New York.
RICHMAN, Morris, 32, New York, N.Y. pp on 2/26/37.
ROSS, Charles Oliver, 26, Baltimore, Md.
SAMUELS, Carl, 22, Philadelphia, Pa.
SANDIFORD, Fred F., 24, England. Left from Chicago, Ill. pp on 7/27/37.
SANSONE, Joseph, 30, St. Louis. pp on 6/10/37.
SCHWARTZ, Max, 24, Brooklyn, N.Y. pp on 1/19/38.
SEELMAN, Theodore, 36, from Chicago, Ill. pp on 1/25/35.
SELBY, Vernon, 35, Chesterton, Md. Ex-West Pointer. pp on 9/20/37.
SHAHINIAN, Harold, 23, Chicago, Ill. pp on 6/1/37.
SHAPIRO, Manuel, 20, from Philadelphia, Pa. pp on 5/19/37.
SIEVE, Horace Lionel, 21, Brooklyn, N.Y. pp on 5/29/37.
SKIFSTROM, John Raymond, 25, Hamtramck, Mich. pp on 3/29/37.
SORENSON, Walter, 44, Racine, Wisc. pp on 6/10/37.
TAUB, Jack Isadore, 22, San Francisco, Calif. pp on 1/11/38.
TITELMAN, Nathan, 27, Camden, N.J.
WATKINS, Franklin Lee, 36, Philadelphia, Pa. pp on 1/30/37.
WATTS, Robert Charles, 37, Somerville, Mass.
WEBER, Robert R., 34, Russia. Left from New York, N.Y. pp on 1/5/38.
WEIL, Max, 22, New York, N.Y. pp on 2/2/37.
WEIR, Harry Oscar, 22, New York, N.Y. pp on 1/19/38
WEISS, Jacob, 27, Brooklyn, N.Y. pp on 2/20/37.
YICK, Dong Hong, 27, China. Left from the USA.

TOTAL: 99 killed in retreat from Gandesa.

Across Ebro, July 5 to September 6, 1938

MULLINGER, Cole, Cecil, 25, Montery, Calif. pp on 3/20/37.
LIFFLAND, Jack, 33, Brooklyn, N.Y.
MURPHY, James Patrick, 32, Bronx, N.Y. pp on 4/3/36.
WHEELER, Wilbert Lapointe, 38, from Seattle, Wash. pp on 1/21/38.

At Sierra Caballs, September 7, 1938.

ARNOLD, Jack, reported by Herman Rosenstein.

CAMNITZ, Ben, 33, from Milwaukee, Wis. pp on 4/14/37.

DUNOS, Edward A., 27, New Jersey. Left From New York, N.Y. pp on 7/18/38.

FUNK, Julius, 31, Hungary. Left from Detroit, Mich. pp on 2/16/37.

GAROFOLA, Patrick J., 26, St. Paul, Minn. pp on 2/10/37.

GROSSNER, Samuel, 21, New York, N.Y. pp on 4/24/37.

HARDY, Philip Henry, 35, Seattle, Wash. pp on 2/8/38.

HELLMAN, Leonard David, 22, Bronx, N.Y. pp on 7/21/38.

HOLTZCLAW, Leonard Martin, 22, Bronx, N.Y. pp on 2/2/38.

LEISEROWITZ, Sol, 21, Bronx, N.Y.

MARKOWITZ, Sam, 21, Pittsburgh, Pa.

MARTIN, James Hamilton, 26, Garden City, N.Y.

RIFKIN, Irving, 21, Brooklyn, N.Y. pp on 5/25/38.

ROSENSTEIN, Sidney, 25, Cleveland, Ohio. pp on 7/19/38.

TOTAL: 14 killed at Sierra Caballs on September 7, 1938.

Others

KUNTSLICH, Cecil Alex, 29, Passaic, N.J. Guerrilla, executed May, 1938. pp on 2/2/37.

PURCHIK, Harry, 22, Bronx, N.Y. Guerrilla or truck driver, captured on 3/23/38. pp on 5/4/37

Notes

Guide to the Notes   All notes beginning with a /xxx or a name followed by a /xxx refer to documents in the National Archives, Record Group 59, General Records of the Department of State, Decimal File 1910–1939, and have the prefix 852.2221. For all documents having a different prefix, such as 852.00, the prefix is given before the /xxx. Researchers will find in the books of Purports, prepared by the archives, a numerical list of every document, along with the names of the sender and receiver, the date it was sent, and a very brief summary of the contents of the document, all very useful for locating additional pertinent documents.

All notes beginning with FO371 refer to documents of the British Foreign Office at Kew. The first six numbers identify the volume, and the numbers preceded by W refer to the item. In a few instances, page numbers are given to identify a portion of a long document.

The location of letters and memoirs is described in Section 4 of the Bibliography, "Prisoner Collections."

References to books are given in shortened form. If the author has only one book listed in the Bibliography, only the author's name and the page reference are given. Where the author has two books listed, the title is also given. For the works of Arthur H. Landis, all references to *The Abraham Lincoln Brigade* are identified by *ALB;* references to *Spain! The Unfinished Revolution* list that title.

Chapter 1: Why Did We Go to Spain?

1. Confederación Española de Derechas Autónomas, a Catholic party.
2. *Documents on German Foreign Policy, 1918–1945,* Series D. vol. 3, p. 13.
3. For a graphic description of the trip of the 96 from New York to Spain, see Edwin Rolfe, *Lincoln Battalion,* pp. 18–37.
4. A more detailed account of how the State Department, Congress, and large corporations aided the fascist side may be found in Arthur H. Landis, *Spain! The Unfinished Revolution,* pp. 204–09.
5. When fully manned, a brigade consisted of four battalions of 600 men each. With its staff and auxiliary services, it numbered about 3,000. A division usually had three brigades, and with its staff and services numbered about 10,000. An army corps usually had three divisions with about 35,000 men. Three army corps made up an army of about 100,000 men.

Chapter 2: A Short History of the First War Against Fascism

1. Soviet War Veterans Committee, *International Solidarity with the Spanish Republic,* pp. 312–13.
2. Ramón Salas, *Historia del Ejército Popular de la República,* pp. 3519, 3558–64.
3. J. Alvarez del Vayo, *Freedom's Battle,* pp. 49–64.
4. Hugh Thomas, *Spanish Civil War,* pp. 979–80.
5. Thomas, pp. 527–31.
6. Enrique Líster, *Memorias de un Luchador,* pp. 355–59, provides an analysis of the casualties.
7. League of Nations, Addendum and Corrigendum to C.39.1939.IX: "Situation In Spain: Withdrawal of Non-Spanish Combatants," Geneva, January 16, 1939.
8. FO 371/24125. pp. 91–97, December 14, 1938.
9. Dolores Ibarruri, *They Shall Not Pass,* pp. 319–20.
10. Enrique Líster, pp. 392–98.
11. Thomas, pp. 889–90.

12. Líster, pp. 424–25.

13. José Manuel Martínez Bande, *Los Cien Ultimos Días de la República,* pp. 118–21.

14. See the *Daily World,* January 25, 1979, for American correspondent Art Shield's escape from an Anarchist firing squad.

15. Thomas, pp. 906–09.

16. Martínez Bande, p. 127.

17. Thomas, pp. 946–57.

18. Ramón Serrano Súñer, *Entre el Silencio y la Propaganda,* pp. 273–77.

19. Gabriel Jackson, *Concise History of the Spanish Civil War,* p. 539.

20. For more detailed descriptions of the war see the following books: For a concise history of the Republic and the war, see *Spain: The Glory and the Tragedy* by Robert G. Colodny. For an easy-to-read illustrated history of the war, see *A Concise History of the Spanish Civil War* by Gabriel Jackson. For a detailed history of the fighting conducted by the Americans, see *The Abraham Lincoln Brigade* by Arthur H. Landis. For a shorter and more personal history of the war, see *The Lincoln Battalion* by Edwin Rolfe. Landis and Rolfe fought in the war. For an analysis of the role of the political parties and trade unions, see *Spain! The Unfinished Revolution* also by Arthur H. Landis. For a history by an official of the Republican Government, see *Freedom's Battle* by J. Alvarez del Vayo. For what the war looked like to the soldiers in the front lines, read *Men in Battle* by Alvah Bessie. For a fascinating viewpoint by an aristocrat who served the Republic well, read *In Place of Splendor* by Constancia de la Mora. For an easy-to-read and somewhat gossipy account, read *The Passionate War* by Peter Weyden. For an account by the outstanding woman in the war, read *They Shall Not Pass: The Autobiography of La Pasionaria* by Dolores Ibarruri. For an account of the aid given to the Republic during the war by the people of all major countries, see *International Solidarity with the Spanish Republic* by the Soviet War Veterans Committee and the Academy of Sciences of the USSR. It contains a detailed account of the war material and manpower supplied by the Soviet Union. For a description of how people from all walks of life on both sides saw the war, see *Blood of Spain,* an oral history of the war by Ronald Freaser. For an account of the British battalion in the war, see *British Volunteer for Liberty: Spain 1936–39,* and for the part played by Canadians, see *Canadian Volunteers: Spain 1936–1939* by Bill Beeching, who fought in the Mackenzie-Papineau battalion.

Chapter 3: The First to Be Captured

1. *El Mundo,* July 25, 1937.

2. Santos Clemente García, taped interview, August 19, 1982 (Madrid, Spain); idem. "Camiones Americanos en la Batalla de Jarama."

3. The names of the fifteen on the two trucks have been compiled from information supplied by Randall B. Smith, chairman of the VALB Historical Committee; Paul Burns; Robert Steck, and John Tisa.

4. Irving William Rappaport to author, March 6, 1981.

5. Norberto Borges Aldama, taped interview, January 13, 1982 (Havana, Cuba).

6. A detailed description of the British Battalion's first two days in action and the capture of the thirty may be found in Bill Alexander, *British Volunteers for Liberty,* pp. 90–99.

7. The names of twenty-seven of those captured were identified in letters from Bill Alexander on November 21, 1982, and Tom Bloomfield, November 1982.

    1. Basil Abrahams, a baker from London

    2. Tom Bloomfield, a miner from Kircaldy

    3. Alfred Chowney

    4. Ted Dickinson from London, executed shortly after capture

    5. Stoel Drair

    6. Phillip Elias from Leeds, killed when reaching for a cigarette

    7. Harold Fry from Edinburgh, a former army sergeant, Company Commander

    8. Morry Goldberg from London, a cabinet-maker

    9. Jock Hunter

    10. F. Jones, Liverpool

    11. William Johnson

12. George Leeson from London, a clerk
13. Israel ("Yank") Levy from Ontario, Canada
14. Bob Maily
15. Charles Martinson
16. J. Montgomery
17. Richard Payne
18. James Pugh
19. Don Renton from Edinburgh
20. James Rutherford from Edinburgh
21. E. Robert Silcock
22. Austin Skempton
23. John Stevens from London, killed with Phillip Elias
24. Bernard Thomas
25. G. Watters
26. Charles West from Lymington
27. Grenville Wiffen

8. Bill Alexander, pp. 183–84.
9. Voice of Madrid radio broadcast, April 28, 1938, David McKelvy White Collection, New York Public Library.
10. FO 371/21287 W6098. Telegram Foreign Office to Chilton, April 8, 1937.
11. The Geneva Convention of 1929 provides that captured soldiers and officers must not be shot or tortured to obtain information, and shall be moved to prisoner camps immediately. They shall be given medical attention, and food rations equal to those provided for soldiers at base camps. Objects of value may not be taken away from prisoners. Corporal punishment and collective punishment for individual acts are forbidden.
12. NA 852.00/5124. Spanish Ambassador Fernando de los Rios to Hull, April 9, 1937.
13. Alexander, pp. 184–85.
14. Alexander to author, November 21, 1982, and November 6, 1983.
15. Hungarian General Lukács asked the Italian officers and commissars of the 12th International Brigade if they were willing to fight against Italian troops. "We are ready." "Will you respect the lives of Italians you may capture?" "We will treat them like long-lost brothers, including the fascists, and try to help them understand the truth about the situation in Spain and in Italy." See Ramón Garriga, *Guadalajara y sus Consecuencias*, pp. 125–26.
16. National Archives. US Mil. Intel. Div., War Department, 6-1-2657-S144, received May 19, 1937.
17. Enrique Líster, whose 11th Division played a leading role in the battle, gives a detailed account of the fighting, including the part played by Captain Pablito (A. I. Rodimstev), a Soviet adviser who became an outstanding general in the fighting at Stalingrad in World War II. When Miaja dressed Líster down for going beyond his orders to only stop the fascist advance, he explained, "My General, they attacked us, so we counterattacked." See Líster, *Memorias de un Luchador*, pp. 201–21. See also the *New York Times* for the contrasting accounts written during the battle by William Carney on the fascist side and by Herbert Matthews on the Republican side.
18. John F. Coverdale, *Italian Intervention in the Spanish Civil War*, p. 249, note 87, for official Italian reports.
19. *Italian Prisoners in Spain*, edited by the Spanish Embassy Press in London, published by Universal Distributors, New York, November 1937.
20. Comunicazione di Renato Bertolini al Convegno: I comunisti Italiani nella guerra di Spagna, Spezia, May 8–9, 1971, on Italians captured at Guadalajara.
21. *Documentos: La Agresión Italiana, ocupados a las unidades italianas en la acción de Guadalajara*, pp. 284–85.
22. "Statement" prepared by eight German and Czech survivors, 1969. A list of the foreign prisoners at San Pedro de Cardeña on September 10, 1938, provided missing last names and ages. Three were Frenchmen: Pierre Algrave, 21; Eugene Feltz, 24; and Alfonso Marchand, 24. The others were Alexis Christotepanowie, 37, from Yugoslavia; Alex de Seume, from Holland; Karl Spannbauer, 34, from Czechoslovakia; and Mahomet Tirouche, 34, from Algeria.
23. Germany and Italy, which had voted for the withdrawal of all foreigners on March 8 at a

meeting of the Non-Intervention Committee in the expectation of a quick Franco victory, now had to find ways to prevent the repatriation of foreign combatants. At a subcommittee meeting on March 23, Ivan Maisky, the Soviet representative, insisting on discussing the plans for withdrawal of all foreign combatants, elicited this angry statement from Count Dino Grandi: "If you want my opinion, I'll say this, not one single Italian volunteer will leave Spain until Franco is victorious." See Ivan Maisky, *Spanish Notebooks,* pp. 123–30, on how the control plan was sabotaged with England's help.

24. FO 371/21287 W5278. Scott to British Foreign Office.
25. Juan Cervera y Valderrama, *Memorias de Guerra,* pp. 87–88.
26. *Student Advocate,* New York, April 1937, pp. 3–4.
27. Marcel Junod, *Warrior without Weapons,* p. 98.
28. FO 371/21224 W11170. Chilton to George Momsey, June 12, 1937.
29. Thomas, pp. 656. Franco, alarmed by a minor Republican attack at Teruel, sent the signal to his agents. Shortly the revolt began. It may have been coincidental, for the POUM and the Anarchists may not have needed a signal from Franco. In any case, Franco benefited from the uprising.
30. For further details about the revolt and the POUM, see Arthur L. Landis, *Spain! The Unfinished Revolution,* pp. 339–48.
31. For a description of the contending groups, see Thomas, pp. 632–44.
32. For information on the causes of dissatisfaction with Largo Caballero, see Landis, *Spain!* pp. 348–51.
33. NA 852.00/5903. Charles A. Bay (Seville) to Hull. June 15, 1937.
34. Statement by eight German and Czech survivors, 1969; Karl Kormes to author, November 6, 1983.
35. NA 852.00/5591. Bowers to Hull, May 18, 1937.

Chapter 4: Captured at Brunete

1. Landis, *Abraham Lincoln Brigade* (cited hereafter as *ALB*), pp. 178–233.
2. Manuel Azaña, in *Obras Completas,* vol. 4, p. 698, wrote that at Brunete three hundred soldiers (of the 46th Division) commanded by El Campesino (Major Valentín González) were captured by the fascists and were found with their legs cut off; enraged, Campesino's men captured a battalion of Moroccans and shot four hundred of them. Enrique Líster, whose 11th Division had played a very important role at Brunete, told me the report was false.
3. According to the 15th International Brigade records at the Institute of Marxism-Leninism in Moscow, the seven captured Americans who did not survive were:
    1. Philip Walton Bradbury, 37, from Chicago.
    2. William Chestna, 21, from Bridgewater, Mass.
    3. Bernard Entin, 24, from Brooklyn, N.Y.
    4. Henry Good, 30, from Lexington, Neb.
    5. Leo Grachow, 23, from New York, N.Y.
    6. Mitchell Greenfield, 29, from Ohio.
    7. Charles Edward Robel, 23, from San Pedro, Calif.
4. Lou Ornitz to author, December 2, 1982.
5. Ornitz, *Capturd by Franco!,* pp. 1–17.
6. Ornitz to author, April 8, 1979, and December 13, 1982, and a taped interview, January 7, 1982.
7. Ornitz to author, May 24, 1979, and December 1, 1979.
8. Ornitz to author, June 24 and July 22, 1979, and December 17, 1982.
9. Dahl, Harold/3
10. *New York Times,* July 22, 1937.
11. Dahl, Harold/10.
12. Dahl, Harold/53 and 63.
13. Dahl, Harold/40 to 46.
14. Dahl, Harold/62 and 68.
15. Harold "Whitey" Dahl, "Sky Fighting Brought Me a Death Sentence," *True,* August 1940.

16. *New York Times,* October 5, 1937.
17. Dahl, "Sky Fighting."
18. *New York Times,* October 11, 1937.
19. I am indebted to Richard Sanders Allen, for much information about Dahl. Allen has a peerless collection of information about the fourteen American aviators and the planes they used while fighting for the Republic. One aviator lost his life: Ben Leider, on February 18, 1937.

Chapter 5: Quinto, Belchite and Teruel

1. Author to Sylvia Geiser, September 15, 1937.
2. Charles Nusser to author April 1938.
3. Len Crome, "Document, Walter (1897–1947): A Soldier in Spain," *History Workshop Journal* (London), Spring 1980, pp. 116–28.
4. Author to Sylvia Geiser, August 26, 1937.
5. José Manuel Martínez Bande, *La Gran Ofensiva Sobre Zaragoza,* pp. 256, 259.
6. Ibid. p. 267.
7. *Book of the XVth International Brigade,* Madrid, 1938, pp. 279, 286.
8. Author to Sylvia Geiser, September 9 and 15, 1937.
9. Author to Bennet Geiser, September 8, 1937.
10. Thomas, *Spanish Civil War,* p. 728.
11. *Volunteer for Liberty,* Madrid, September 13 and October 25, 1937.
12. Archivo del Ministerio de Asuntos Consulares, Madrid, Legajo R-1501, Expediente 22.
13. "Hossbach Memorandum," *Trial of the Major War Criminals,* vol. 25, pp. 403–14.
14. Landis, *ALB,* pp. 345–980.
15. Thomas, pp. 756–58.
16. /1713. Bucknell (Barcelona) to Hull, August 4, 1939.
17. Reuben Barr to author, July 1, 1982, June 3 and July 7, 1984.
18. /1713. Reuben admits the charge was true. At eighty-three he is still continuing his antifascist activities.
19. Stojewa, Conrad Henry/2 to 11.
20. /1760. Weddell to Hull, December 15, 1939.

Chapter 6: The Retreat from Belchite

1. Landis, *ALB,* pp. 411–41.
2. Carl Riffe, taped interview, July 27, 1982.
3. Charles Hall, memoirs, March 1978.
4. *Daily Worker,* October 21, 1938.
5. Interviews with Stix and Belau on their return to New York by Joseph North, *Daily Worker,* October 19, 1938.
6. Mike Berman, undated biography of his father, Leo Berman.
7. Joseph North, dispatch from Barcelona to the *Daily Worker* (New York) March 22, 1938.
8. *New York Times,* March 25, 1938.
9. Richard Browne, "In Franco's Prisons."
10. John Blair to author, September 17, 1977.
11. Landis, *ALB,* p. 431.
12. Arthur H. Landis, *Spain,* p. 376.
13. 852.00/7645 and 852.00/7624. Bowers and Thurston (Barcelona) to Hull, March 29, 1938.
14. /769. Bowers to Hull, March 30, 1938.
15. Thomas, pp. 812–13.

Chapter 7: Captured! Survivors and Killed

1. FALB to Eric Wendelin, June 2, 1938.
2. Mike Berman, undated biography of his father, Leo Berman.

3. Rolfe, *Lincoln Battalion*, pp. 208–09.
4. John Blair, "Experiences in Franco Prisons," 1976.
5. Castle, Guy/1–11.
6. Babsky, Sidney/1–16, 18, and 22.
7. /755. Adolph A. Berle to Wendelin, Wendelin to Passport Division, March 16, 1938.
8. Babsky, Sidney/19 and 23, March 17, 1938.
9. /755. Passport Division to Wendelin, March 18, 1938.
10. Babsky, Sidney/33, Raymond Edward Murphy to Wendelin, March 19, 1938.
11. Babsky, Sidney/42, Mr. and Mrs. Max Babsky's letter forwarded by FDR to State Department, March 19, 1938.
12. Babsky, Sidney/60, Wendelin's review of case of Sidney Babsky on May 17 in preparation for meeting teacher's union delegation.
13. Lucy Perry, memorabilia about her brother, Sidney Babsky.
14. Babsky, Sidney/60, Wendelin's review of case of Sidney Babsky.
15. Babsky, Sidney/57. Hull to Mr. and Mrs. Babsky, March 26, 1938.
16. /755. Hull's instructions to Bay, March 26, 1938.
17. /630. Hull's instructions to Bay, November 6, 1937.
18. McEachron, Paul/1, Lash to Hull, March 23, 1938.
19. Ecker, Morris/1–7; Neafus, Ralph/1–4; and Ticer, Leon Norvell/1–3.
20. /746. brief prepared by Herman E. Cooper on diplomatic protection presented on February 14 to State Department's legal adviser Ralph Hill, and his comments submitted to Hull on March 23, 1938.
21. Babsky, Sidney/48, Messersmith to White, March 28, 1938.
22. Tony Gilbert, taped interview (London), September 10, 1981.
23. Bob Doyle to author, January 15 and June 20, 1983.
24. Dougal Eggar, taped interview (London), September 9, 1981.
25. Maurice Levitas, taped interview (Durham, England), August 30, 1981.
26. John Blair, "Experiences in Franco Prisons," 1976.
27. Garry McCartney to author, March 29 and April 13, 1983.
28. Max Parker, memoirs, June 1978.
29. Stanley Heinricher, memoirs, May 28, 1978.
30. Landis, *ALB, pp. 457–58*.

Chapter 9: We Face a Firing Squad

1. Jules Paivio to author (tape), November 15, 1979.
2. Curley Wilson was erroneously reported killed by Victor Hoar, *Mackenzie-Papineau Battalion*, p. 179.
3. We were unaware of the distinction between a red cross on a white field, used by the International Red Cross and its national affiliates, and a white cross on a red field, used by military medical services. Although I do not remember which insigne was worn here, I now believe that it represented the military medical service.

Chapter 10: We Begin Our Retreat from Gandesa

1. Joseph Young, memoirs, September, 1978.
2. Stanley Heinricher, memoirs, May 28, 1978.
3. Rolfe, *Lincoln Battalion*, pp. 208–9.
4. Ramón Nicolau González, *Cuba y la Defensa de la República Española*, pp. 21–22, 163–64.
5. Frank Blackman to author, May 8, 1983.
6. Navarrese monarchists wearing red berets were known as *requetés*.
7. Cohn Haber, taped interview, 1965. Cited by Landis *ALB*, note 58, p. 644.
8. NA 852.2226/1–27. March 15–July 6, 1938.

Chapter 11: International Brigaders Behind Fascist Lines

1. Stanley Heinricher, memoirs, May 28, 1978.
2. Rolfe, *Lincoln Battalion*, pp. 208–11.

3. Archivo del Servicio Histórico Militar, Armario 10, Legajo 450, Carpeta 18.
4. Syd Harris, memoirs, July 27, 1978.
5. Ramón Nicolau González, *Cuba y la Defensa de la República Española*, pp. 163–67.
6. Bob Steck, memoirs, January 1978.
7. Archivo de Servicio Histórico Militar, Armario 10, Legajo 450, Carpeta 18.
8. Landis, *ALB*, p. 448.
9. Leonard Lamb, telephone interview, January 28, 1984.
10. Herbert Matthews, *New York Times,* April 12, 1938.
11. Fred Stanley, interview, April 27, 1979.
12. Bob Steck, memoirs, June 3, 1979.
13. Rolfe, pp. 223–24.
14. Steck, memoirs, January 1978 and June 3, 1979; and Steck to author, May 8, 1983.
15. William Miller, memoirs, September 1982.
16. Hy Wallach, memoirs, May 1983.
17. Nicolau González, pp. 130–34.
18. Martin Maki to author, February 27, 1978.
19. Eugene Poling, to author, January 21, 1984.
20. Stanley Heinricher, memoirs, June 5, 1978.
21. Bob Steck to author, March 1, 1983, on his interview with Hassan.
22. Gary McCartney to author, March 29, 1983.
23. Jules Paivio, taped interview, November 29, 1978.
24. McCartney to author, March 29, 1983.
25. Max Parker, memoirs, June 1978.
26. Archivo del Ministerio de Asuntos Consulares, Madrid, Legajo R-1346, Expediente 233.
27. /802. Bay to Hull. Peter Kemp, an Englishman who had enlisted in the Foreign Legion, in *Mine Were of Trouble,* pp. 165–67, describes how an officer gave him a choice between being shot and shooting an Irishman who had deserted to the fascist side.
28. /802. Bay to Hull, attachment.
29. For a chilling account of how bloodthirsty a Navarese Catholic priest could be, see Peter Wyden, *Passionate War,* pp. 289–90.

Chapter 12: Initiation to San Pedro de Cardeña

1. In 1942 the Cistercian Order took possession of San Pedro de Cardeña. The Cistercians believe every man should live by the sweat of his own brow. One of their first tasks was to rid the prisoners' quarters of the lice and fleas. Since that time they have rebuilt the internal areas, restored the church damaged by the storage of munitions during the war, and established a new library to replace the one damaged by a bad fire. With government and private help, San Pedro de Cardeña is becoming a national monument to El Cid Campeador, who, with his wife, was buried here. For its history up to the end of the thirteenth century, see Salustiano Moreta Velayo, *Historia de un Dominio Monástico castellano* (Salamanca: University of Salamanca, 1971).
2. Karl Kormes to author, November 6, 1983.
3. Lou Ornitz, *Captured by Eranco,* pp. 28–29.
4. Gerold Gino Baumann, *Extranjeros en la guerra Civil Española, los Perúanos,* p. 120.
5. Dr. Gabriel Ersler to author, August 22, 1982.
6. Stanley Heinricher, memoirs, June 28, 1978.
7. Herman Lopez, communication to author, April 5, 1978.
8. Max Shufer to author, February 24, 1979.
9. Herman Lopez, communication to author, April 5, 1978.

Chapter 13: Building Morale

1. British diplomat Geoffrey Thompson, in a telegram to the Foreign Office on March 14 quoted a friend: "He stated that the German barrage on Belchite was extremely effective and added that never previously in his twelve months with the Nationalist forces had he observed heavier concentration of German combatant elements—airmen, artillery, engineers—than in that area." FO 371/22639 W3421.

2. Herman Lopez account to author, June 5, 1978.
3. Partidas de Defunción #23 and #24, Archivo Parroquial de Carcedo de Burgos.
4. Stanley Heinricher, memoirs, June 28, 1978.
5. The Cistercians now at San Pedro have demolished the wall and dug up the bones of 66 Spaniards, the two Frenchmen, and eight Internationals and interred them in a common grave inside the monastery's lovely walled-in cemetery on the north side of the church. Prior Marcos knew of no other instance in which Jews were buried inside monastery grounds.
6. Archivo Parroquial de Carcedo de Burgos.
7. José María Bereciartua, *San Pedro de Cardeña, el Monasterio del Cid*, pp. 78–79.
8. Tom Entwistle to author, August 5, 1982.
9. Landis, *ALB*, p. 487. lists the thirteen points.
10. Among the sponsors were William Dodd, former ambassador to Germany; Bishop Francis J. McConnell of the Methodist Episcopal Church; Newbold Morris, president of the New York City Council; and Michael J. Quill of the Transport Workers Union. See the *ASU Peace Journal*, 1938, published by the New York District of the American Student Union.
11. Harold L. Ickes, *Secret Diary*, p. 390.
12. Archivo del Ministerio de Asuntos Consulares, Legajo 1346, Expediente 233.

Chapter 14: We Get Organized

1. Madame C. Rey-Schyrr, International Red Cross, Geneva, to author, July 1981.
2. James Moon, entry in his father's diary dated 22 August, 1938.
3. American Red Cross to Sylvia Geiser, July 27, 1938.
4. Madrid Radio broadcast, March 28, 1938, David McKelvy White Collection, New York Public Library.
5. Bob Steck, to author, February 7, 1979.
6. Frank Blackman to author, April 2, 1979.
7. FO 371/24122 W1565. British Foreign Office to Jimmy Rutherford's father, February 8, 1939.
8. NA 852.24/716 and /923. Bay to Hull, May 23, 1938.
9. Morgan Harvard, "Cultural Life in a Concentration Camp," *Volunteer* (London), vol. 5, no. 1 (January 1944).
10. Fred Stanley, interview, April 28, 1979.
11. NA 851.50/164. Bullitt (Paris) to Hull, May 9, 1938.
12. *Volunteer for Liberty*, Barcelona, May 25, 1938.
13. Thomas, *Spanish Civil War*, pp. 823–24.
14. NA 752.00114/14 and /29. Exchanges between Bowers and Hull, May 29, 1938, and June 23, 1938.
15. Archivo del Ministerio de Asuntos Consulares, Legajo 1346, Expediente 233, Items 14 and 24 and letter, Frank Ryan Release Committee to Ontiverós y Laplana, the Spanish Minister in Dublin.
16. /882A and /883. Exchange of telegrams between Hull and Bay, May 29 and 30, 1938.
17. Norman Dorland, "In Franco's Prison Camp," *New Masses*, November 22, 1938, pp. 16–19.
18. Archivo Parroquial de Carcedo de Burgos.
19. Fred Stanley, interview, April 27, 1979.
20. Robert Weinand, "Nie Vergessen," 1980, Special Collections Library, Brandeis University, pp. 24–25.
21. Maurice Levitas, taped interview (Durham, England) August 30, 1981.
22. Sean Cronin, *Frank Ryan*, p. 145.
23. Stanley Heinricher, memoirs, September 28, 1978.
24. Tony Gilbert, taped interview (London), September 10, 1981.
25. /844. Sumner Welles to Bay, April 27, 1938. /938. Bay to Hull, June 17, 1938.
26. Sylvia Geiser collection of correspondence with and about the author.
27. /938, /970, and /1029. Exchanges between Bay and Hull and Bay's report on his visit to San Pedro on June 24, 1938.

28. Tony Gilbert, taped interview, September 10, 1981.
29. Sean Cronin, pp. 145–48.
30. Archivo del Ministerio de Asuntos Consulares, Legajo 1346, Expediente 233, communication from Ontiverós to Jordana on June 13, 1938.

Chapter 15: Visitors

1. Robert Steck, memoir, August 11, 1978.
2. Henry Megquier, untitled manuscript, Special Collections Library, Brandeis University, pp. 58–59.
3. Marshall Garcia had signed twice, as M. Garcia from Canton, Ohio, and as Marshall Garcia from Los Angeles, Calif., his last residence. Five volunteers did not sign the sheets: Homer Chase from Hillsboro, N.H.; Eugene Poling from Lone Wolf, Okla.; Peter Raacke from St. Louis; Joseph Radacoy from Hutchinson, W.Va.; and Herman Carl Riffe from Portsmouth, Ohio. He also did not have the names of six Americans who were in Spain before 1936. The missing names were obtained by comparing Carney's list with Bay's list in /1078.
4. I knew the Communist Party was always short of money and could not have paid our fares. It was only while researching this history that I learned the Republic had paid our fares across the Atlantic.
5. Robert Doyle, to author, January 15, 1983.
6. Lou Ornitz, *Captured by Franco,* p. 44.
7. Efrén Manzilla Esteban, interview (Modubar de la Cibrian, Burgos, Spain), August 25, 1982.
8. *Jaily News,* No. 15, August 11, 1938.
9. Jimmy Moon to his mother, July 14, 1938, copied in his father's diary.
10. The pamphlet was Maria Reese's *I Accuse Stalin,* a long letter she finished on October 26, 1933, in Amsterdam. It was printed by Pioneer Publishers in November 1933, with an introduction by Leon Trotsky.
11. Tony Gilbert, taped interview (London), September 10, 1981.
12. Karl Kormes to author, March 29, 1984.
13. Carl Loesch, taped interview (Dresden), July 28, 1981.
14. Herman Streit, taped interview (Berlin), July 31, 1981.
15. A detailed account of the part played by the 15th Brigade can be found in Landis, *ALB,* pp. 511–43.
16. *Volunteer for Liberty,* Barcelona, September 5, 1938.
17. *Volunteer for Liberty,* Barcelona, September 17, 1938.
18. /1029. Bay to Hull, June 28, 1938.
19. Jenkins, Hollis /9 to 11; Moskowitz, Ignatz/3 to 5.
20. State Department enclosure in letter to Sylvia Geiser, August 2, 1938.
21. /970. White to Hull, July 13, 1938. Telegram Hull to Bay, July 16, 1938.
22. NA 752.00114/31. Telegrams, Hull to Bowers, July 16, 1938, and Bowers to Hull, July 18, 1936.
23. /1026. Dunn to White, July 26, 1938.
24. *New York Times,* July 24, 1938, p. 19.
25. /1064. Telegram, Bay to Hull, July 26, 1938.
26. /1083. State Department memorandum (unsigned), July 20, 1938.
27. /1069. Wood to Hull, Moffat to Wood, July 23, 1938.
28. /1078. Bay to Hull, July 17, 1938.
29. /1077. White to Hull, July 27, 1938. The nineteen included twelve who were on the two trucks at Jarma; Leo Grachow, William Chesna, and Philip Bradbury, captured at Brunete; and Sidney Babsky, Michael Ecker, Ralph Neafus, and Leon Ticer.

Chapter 16: Fourteen Americans Leave San Pedro

1. Statement prepared by eight German and Czech survivors, 1969.
2. *New York Times,* August 6, 1938.
3. John C. Blair to author, September 17, 1977, and July 1, 1979; Martin Maki, memoirs, August 1977.

4. Archivo Parroquial de Carcedo de Burgos.
5. Jimmy Moon, to his mother, August 12, 1938.
6. Jimmy Moon to his mother, August 21, and to his father, August 29, 1938; taped interview (London), August 15, 1981.
7. /1110. US Embassy in Paris to Hull, August 1, 1938.
8. Ernest J. Swift, vice-chairman of the American Red Cross, memo, on July 29, 1938, authorizing the sending of a $500 draft to the IRC.
9. *New York Times,* August 6, 1939.
10. Ernest J. Swift to Hull, October 12, 1938.
11. /1108. Passport Division memo, August 1, 1938.
12. Maki, Martti/2 and 3.
13. Archivo del Ministerio de Asuntos Consulares, Legajo R-1346, Expediente 233; Legajo R-633, Expediente 142.
14. Norman Dorland, "In Franco's Prison Camp," pp. 16–19.
15. Albert Ziegler, Item 42, Ziegler Collection.
16. Albert Ziegler, letter in early September 1938, Item 39, Ziegler Collection.
17. Archivo Parroquial de Carcedo de Bugos.
18. Archivo del Ministerio de Asuntos Consulares, Legajo R-1051, Expediente 84, Document #9.
19. Jimmy Moon to Aunt Emily Adams, September 12, 1939.
20. William Alexander, *British Volunteers for Liberty,* p. 191.
21. Jimmy Moon to Aunt Emily Adams, September 12, 1938.
22. /1190. Bay to Hull
23. Information from Jack Jones who was a British prisoner at San Pedro.
24. The fourteen who were exchanged were:

No. Name	Place and year of birth		Occupation
1. Edgar Acken	Milburn, N.J.	1906	Journalist
2. David Kachadorian[a]	Turkey	1901	Baker
3. Charles Barr	Steubenville, Ohio	1919	Chauffeur
4. Carl Belau	Valley Creek, Minn.	1907	Laborer
5. Leo Berman	Newark, N.J.	1913	Seaman
6. Richard Browne	Kansas City, Mo.	1917	Seaman
7. Roger Braley	Newport, R.I.	1903	Seaman
8. Homer Chase	Washington, N.H.	1917	Laborer
9. Van Chase	Calgary, Canada	1914	Laborer
10. Morris Conway	Olympia, Wash.	1908	Medical student
11. Norman Dorland	Granite Falls, Minn.	1912	Seaman
12. Louis Ornitz	New York, N.Y.	1912	Labor organizer
13. Sam Romer	Detroit, Mich.	1902	Journalist
14. Fred Stix	Suring, Wis.	1914	Circus roustabout

[a] Also known as Doneg Barbarian.

Place and year of birth are from NA/1212; occupation is from NA/1108, with corrections.
25. /1283. Ernest J. Swift to Nathaniel P. Davis in State Department.
26. Mervin K. Hart to Sylvia Geiser, October 17, 1938.
27. RM20/1208 in the Militargeschichtliches Forschungsamt in Freiburg im Breisgau, West Germany, includes the order of September 9, 1938, telegraphed to the Gestapo in Burgos, to return Franz Berger, Julius Bunzman, Karl Ernst, Willi Jahn, Willi Jarosch, Rudolf Ossinger, Gunther Sauer, Otto Schleicher, Bruno Roth, and Alfred Zarth to Germany. A special German boat arrived at Vigo on September 17 to take the ten prisoners to Hamburg, Germany.
28. Manuel Aznar, *Obras Completas,* vol. 4, p. 242.
29. Landis, *ALB,* pp. 566–68.
30. Interview with Juan, Morata de Tajuña, June 1981.

31. Compiled from Landis, *ALB*, p. 568, and a microfilm made from International Brigade records at the Institute of Marxism-Leninism in Moscow.
32. FO 371/24124 W6970. M. V. Miller to Foreign Office, April 5, 1939.
33. Claude G. Bowers, *My Mission to Spain*, 393–94.
34. FO 371/22613 W12638. Chetwode to Foreign Office, September 20, 1938.
35. NA 852.00114/52. Bowers to Hull.
36. Alvah Bessie, *Men in Battle*, p. 325.
37. Elman Service to author, November 13, 1980.

Chapter 17: The Big Escape

1. Olaf Domnauer to author, August 23, 1980, and a memoir.
2. Sidney Harris, memoirs, July 27, 1978.
3. Maurice Levitas, taped interview (Durham, England), August 30, 1981.
4. Jimmy Moon to his mother, October 31, 1938.
5. NA 852.00/8531. Bowers to Hull, October 13, 1938.
6. Readers interested in the role of the Communist party of Spain during the war against fascism will find an easy-to-read description of what the Communists did in Spain in Dolores Ibarruri, *They Shall Not Pass: The Autobiography of La Pasionaria* (New York: International Publishers, 1976). La Pasionaria was a leading member of the Spanish Communist Party. Briefly, the Communist Party supported the Republican government and opposed both those who wanted to make a revolution before fascism was defeated and those who wanted to surrender to Franco.
7. /1197. Consul Bay to Hull, October 5, 1938.
8. Mike Berman, memoir about his father, Leo Berman.
9. /1231. Bowers to Hull, October 10, 1938, describing the exchange of the fourteen.
10. Samuel Romer, "I Was Franco's Prisoner," *Nation*, November 19, 1938, pp. 529–33.
11. *New York Times*, October 9, 1938. Carney's dispatch on the exchange.
12. *Daily Worker* (New York), October 15, 18, and 19, 1938.
13. *New York Times*, October 19, 1938.
14. *Daily Worker* (New York), October 29, 1938.
15. Dougal Eggar, taped interview (London), September 9, 1981.
16. *New York Times*, October 9, 1938.
17. Diary of Thomas Moon, Sr., October 26, 1938.
18. Statement prepared by eight German and Czech survivors, 1969.
19. Georg Heinzmann, taped interview (Erfurt), July 27, 1981.
20. Herman Streit, taped interview (Berlin), July 31, 1981.
21. Jimmy Moon to his mother, November 1, 1938.
22. /1291 and 1352. Bay's report to Hull on his visit to San Pedro, November 18, 1938.
23. Charles Hall, memoirs, March 10, 1978.
24. /1232. Bowers's report to Hull on the exchange, October 10, 1938.
25. /1228. Hull's instructions to Bowers, October 22, 1938.
26. /1240. Exchange of cables between Bowers and Hull, October 25, 1938.
27. /1246 and /1249. Exchange of cables between Bowers and Hull, October 31, 1938, and November 3, 1938.
28. Both Hull's telegram B-465 October 4, 1938, and Bowers's reply, 553 November 5, 1938, are missing from the National Archives. Their contents have been inferred from the summaries in Purports /1250 and /1251.
29. /1285. Bowers to Hull, November 7, 1938.
30. Geiser, Carl /19, 23, 25, and 26.
31. Sam Romer, "I Was Franco's Prisoner," *Nation*, November 19, 1938.
32. /1290. Exchange of cables between Bowers and Hull, November 18, 1938.
33. /1197. Bay to Hull, October 5, 1938.
34. FO 371/22620 W15024. Cable from British Consul R. C. S. Stevenson (Barcelona), November 15, 1938.
35. The true numbers were 88 British (including 15 Irish and 1 South African), 18 Canadians, 42 Cubans, 17 Swedes, and 13 Swiss, making a total of 178. The Republic had 237 Italians

left. The rest had been exchanged or joined the Republic. That meant there would be 59 Italians left to exchange for 81 Americans at San Pedro. At the time, exact numbers were not known.

36. /1307. Bowers's cable to Hull, November 24, 1938.
37. NA 852.00/8646. Bowers's cable to Hull, November 19, 1938.
38. Enrique Líster, *Memorias de un Luchador,* p. 357.
39. /1352. Bay's report to Hull on his visit to San Pedro de Cardeña, November 18, 1938.
40. NA 852.00114/63. Bowers to Hull, November 16, 1938.
41. FO 371/22615, pp. 137–41. Memorandum by Denys Cowan, of the Chetwode Commission, November 3, 1938.

Chapter 18: A Cold Month at San Pedro

1. Author's notes on interview with Fred Stanley, April 27, 1979.
2. Bob Steck notes on interview with Hassan, February 1983. In Author's possession.
3. Jimmy Moon, taped interview (London), August 15, 1981.
4. FO 371/24122 W22. Jerram to Foreign Office, December 24, 1938.
5. Garry McCartney to author, March 5, 1984.
6. /1359. Bowers's telegram to Hull, December 15, 1938.
7. FO 371/24122 W43. British Consul Stevenson (Barcelona) to Foreign Office, December 31, 1938.
8. Geiser, Carl/30.
9. This chapter first appeared in the *New York Times* on Sunday, December 23, 1973, under the title " 'Silent Night, Holy Night'—In a Spanish Prison Camp, 1938." Its publicaton led to the writing of this history. Corrections have been made based on information from Americans and British who were there.
10. Eugene Poling to author, March 7 and 20, 1984.
11. Henry Giler, memoirs, August 20, 1978.
12. Morgan Harvard, "Cultural Life in a Concentration Camp," *Volunteer* (London), vol. 5, no. 1, Janaury 1944.

Chapter 19: We Leave San Pedro

1. Tony Gilbert, taped interview (London), September 10, 1981.
2. Albert Ziegler (postal card) to his mother, January 18, 1939; Ziegler (postal card) to Herman Cohen, January 31, 1939.
3. Date is estimated from letter by Charles Keith, February 14, 1939.
4. Archivo Parroquial de Carcedo de Burgos.
5. American Red Cross to Murray Young, April 17, 1939.
6. Author to Sylvia Geiser, February 1, 1939.
7. L. Odier, International Committee of the IRC, to Ernest J. Swift, American Red Cross, January 27, 1939.
8. FO 371/24122 W297 (January 6, 1939), W784 (January 14), W1139 (January 20), and W1149 (January 21). Telegraphic exchanges between the British Admiralty, Consul Stevenson (Barcelona), and Jerram (Burgos) with the British Foreign Office.
9. FO 371/24122 W1276. Under Secretary E. E. Butler to Griffiths, MP, January 7, 1939.
10. FO 371/24122 W1286. Foreign Office to Jerram, January 23, 1939.
11. /1414A and /1438. The delegation included Leon Tenor's mother; Al Ziegler's mother, Ida; Sidney Rosenblatt's brother, William; Alice Citron from the New York Teachers Union, Mrs. Ward; and my wife, Sylvia.
12. Stimson to Hull, January 18, 1939. (FDR Official File Box 52). Cited by F. J. Taylor, *The United States and the Spanish Civil War,* p. 176.
13. The three letters are in Taylor, pp. 213–34.
14. Harold L. Ickes, *Secret Diary,* p. 569.
15. "Public Opinion Survey," *Public Opinion Quarterly* 3 (October 1939), p. 600, Cited by F. J. Taylor, p. 137.

16. Al Ziegler to his mother, February 14, 1939. Item 45.
17. Sidney Rosenblatt to his parents, February 15, 1939.
18. Archivo del Ministerio de Asuntos Consulares, Legajo R1051, Expediente 29.
19. Frank West, taped interview (London), September 11, 1981.
20. Jules Paivio, taped letter to author, November 15, 1977.
21. Jimmy Moon, taped interview (London), August 15, 1981.
22. FO 371/24122 W1838. Wire from Acting Consul Walsh to Foreign Office, February 1, 1939.
23. FO 371/24123 W2616 (February 6, 1939), W2941 (February 16), W3000 (February 18), and W3135 (February 20). Communications from Admiralty and Consul A. Goodden (Valencia) to the Foreign Office.
24. Maurice Levitas, taped interview (Durham, England), August 30, 1981.
25. Diary of Thomas Moon, Sr., February 4–9, 1939.
26. FO 371/24123 W3490, FO 371/24151 W3003, W3005, W3250, and W3450. Foreign Office communications, February 19–25, 1939.
27. Frank West, taped interview (London), September 11, 1981.
28. /1462a and /1462. Cables between Hull and Bowers, February 7 and 9, 1939.
29. /1505 and /1513. Cables between Hull and Bowers, February 28, 1939, and March 2, 1939.
30. Minutes of meeting of the Relatives of the American Prisoners in Franco Spain, February 9, 1939. Item 47, Ziegler file.
31. *New York Evening Post,*February 20, 1939.
32. *New York Herald Tribune,* February 20, 1939.
33. "Report—Aid to Our Boys, Relatives of American Prisoners in Spain." Item 52, Ziegler file.
34. /1683. Report of Special Agent Kinsey to the State Department on the disposition of the case of Leo Hecht, February 24, 1939.

Chapter 20: Zapatari

1. This account of the activities at Zapatari is based on notes I made immediately after my return to New York.
2. For contents of package, see page 300. The IRC delivered them within a month after the funds were sent to the American Red Cross.
3. Eugene Poling to author, March 7, 1984.
4. Minute book, American Section of the International Co-op, recorded by Herman Lopez. A copy is in the author's possession.
5. Associated Press dispatch, St.-Jean-de-Luz, France, March 3, 1939.
6. Claude G. Bowers, *My Mission to Spain,* p. 143.
7. Archivo del Ministerio de Asuntos Consulares, R-1501, Expediente 37. It includes the names of the released Frenchmen.
8. FO 371/24123 W2491 (March 7, 1939) and W4658 (March 9, 1939). Hodgson to Foreign Office.
9. /1508 and /1532. Cable exchange between Thurston and State Department, March 14 and 18, 1939.
10. FO 371/24123 W4342 (March 13, 1939) and W4991 (March 14, 1939). Goodden (Valencia) and Jerram (Burgos) to Foreign Office.
11. FO 371/24154 W6705. This is a 3000-word summary by Goodden of his activities from March 28 through April 1 in the evacuation of the prisoners and fewer than 200 Spaniards, including Casado and some twenty of his friends and staff, April 13, 1939.
12. Frank West, taped interview (London), September 11, 1981.
13. For a detailed description of the horrors of the French concentration camps during the first few months, see Joan Llarch, *Campos de Concentración en la España de Franco,* pp. 175–202.
14. L. Odier, IRC, to Ernest J. Swift, vice chairman of the American Red Cross, April 28, 1939.
15. Minute book, American Section of the International Co-op at Zapatari.
16. Author to Sylvia Geiser, April 24, 1939.
17. Associated Press dispatch, April 6, 1939.
18. Otto Hafner, taped interview (Basel, Switzerland), June 20, 1981. Otto was a prisoner at San Pedro.

19. Minutes of meeting of the Relatives of the American Prisoners in Franco Spain [April 15, 1939?]. Item 51, Ziegler file.
20. Newspaper ads. Items 55 and 57, Ziegler file.
21. /1574b and /1578. Exchange of telegrams between Hull and Matthews, April 16 and 17, 1939.
22. Archivo del Ministerio de Asuntos Consulares, Legajo R-1051, Expediente 29.
23. /1589. Bowers to Hull, April 20, 1939.
24. /1600. Pierrepont Moffat Memorandum of Conversation with Robert Murphy, Paris, April 21, 1939.
25. /1590. Matthews to Hull, April 21, 1939.

Chapter 21: Freedom

1. Archivo del Ministerio de Asuntos Consulares, Legajo R-1051, Expediente 29. The seven Cubans freed were Alberto Acosta Perez, Armando Blanco Vázques, Manuel Corcho Díaz, Heriberto Hernández Fernández, José Lazo Granados, Juan Rodríguez Bocanegra, and Dámaso Rodríguez Oliva.
2. Henry Megquier, untitled manuscript, Special Collections Library, Brandeis: University, pp. 92–93.
3. Archivo del Ministerio de Asuntos Consulares, Legajo R-1051, Expediente 24.
4. FO 371/24154 W6705. British Consul A. Goodden (Valencia) to Foreign Office.
5. /1601, Samuel H. Wiley (Le Havre) telegram to Hull, April 25, 1939, identifying seventy prisoners.
6. Megquier, p. 94.
7. Appendix 6 provides the names, places and dates of birth of the seventy-one Americans who were exchanged and the ten held back, along with the military units in which they served.
8. /1593. Bullitt (Paris) to Hull, April 23, 1939.
9. /1611. Wendelin memo on phone call from White, April 24, 1939.
10. /1606. Wiley (Le Havre) to Hull, April 26, 1939.
11. /1695. Justice Department memorandum answering Wiley's questions, July 7, 1939.
12. Art Shields's participation in the resistance to Casado's sell-out and his escape from death is told in the *Daily World* (New York), January 25, February 15, and March 15, 1979.
13. Receipt for $1,800 from Louis Fischer signed by Peter C. Rhodes, Louis Fischer Papers, Princeton University Library.
14. Geiser, Carl /37. Hull night letter to Sylvia Geiser, April 25, 1939.
15. FO 371/24124 W6889. Peterson (San Sebastian) to Foreign Office.
16. /1616. Wiley telegram listing those returning on the SS *Harding* and the SS *Ile de France*, April 28, 1939. R. B. Shipley's instructions to search us for passports, May 8, 1939.
17. Geiser, Carl/44. Hull night letter to Sylvia Geiser, April 29, 1939.
18. An excellent reproduction of this photograph appears on the cover of Folkways Record FH 5435, "Al Tocar Diana," a collection of our songs in San Pedro de Cardeña sung by Max Parker, a former prisoner.
19. Helen Padula, FALB Rehabilitation Director, to Alonzo Poling, May 4, 1939.

Chapter 22: The Americans Left Behind

1. Item 59, Albert Ziegler file.
2. Joseph Young, to author, December 26, 1983.
3. Hy Wallach, memoirs, November 16, 1979.
4. Archivo Parroquial de Carcedo de Burgos.
5. Albert Ziegler postal card to Sol Lerner, May 7, 1939. Item 68, Ziegler file.
6. Bob Steck, to author, June 15, 1979.
7. /1637. FALB letter to Hull, May 3, 1939.
8. /1621. Bowers to Hull, May 1, 1939.
9. Young, to author, March 3, 1982.

10. /1665. Matthews to Hull, May 25, 1939. Includes Crain's memorandum on his visit to San Pedro on May 15, 1939.
11. University of Illinois, 1963 file on Earl T. Crain.
12. Wallach, memoirs, November 16, 1979.
13. Ziegler postal card to Sol Lerner, June 3, 1939. Item 65, Ziegler file.
14. Sol Lerner, to author, June 7, 1979.
15. Ziegler to Lerner, June 9, 1939. Item 74, Ziegler file.
16. /1667 and /1684. Rosenblatt to Hull, June 1 and 19, 1939.
17. /1693. Crain memorandum to Weddell, June 21, 1939.
18. /1682 and /1699. Weddell to Hull, June 22 and July 1, 1939.
19. Albert Ziegler, postal card and letter. Item 66 and 67, Ziegler file.
20. Bob Steck, draft letter to Jimmy Moon in Robert Steck Memorabilia.
21. Archivo Parroquial de Carcedo de Burgos.
22. Associated Press dispatch from San Sebastian, July 26, 1939.
23. NA 852.75 National Telephone Co. /280, Weddell to Hull, July 19, 1939.
24. NA 852.75 National Telephone Co. /281. Hull to Weddell, July 22, 1939.
25. NA 852.75 National Telephone Co. /283. Weddell to Hull, July 25, 1939.
26. Newspaper clippings. Item 71 Albert Ziegler file.
27. *Volunteer for Liberty,* vol. 1, no. 4 (August 1939).
28. /1709. Welles to Bullitt, August 7, 1939.
29. Archivo del Ministerio de Asuntos Consulares. Legajo R-1051, Expediente 83.
30. /1723. Exchange of letters between Eleanor Roosevelt and Welles, August 16 and 25, 1939.
31. Archivo Parroquial de Carcedo de Burgos.
32. Ziegler postal card to Herman Cohen, August 25, 1939. Item 75, Ziegler file.
33. Young, memoirs, August 1979.
34. Murat W. Williams to author, April 6, 1985.
35. Archivo del Ministerio de Asuntos Consulares, Legajo R-1051, Expediente 83.
36. Wallach, to author, May 19, 1984.
37. /1734 and /1741. Weddell and Bullitt to Hull, August 30 and September 9, 1939.
38. Ziegler postal card to Herman Cohen, August 25, 1939. Item 75, Ziegler file.
39. Wallach to author May 19, 1984
40. /1741. Bullitt to Hull, September 9, 1939.
41. Wallach to author, May 19, 1984
42. /1721. Wiley to Hull, August 27, 1939.
43. Young, memoirs, August 1979.
44. Wallach, memoirs, November 16, 1979.
45. /1742. State Department to White, October 23, 1939.

Chapter 23: Americans in Other Prisons

1. /1693. Earl T. Crain memorandum to Weddell on his visit to Burgos Central Prison, June 17, 1939.
2. Kerlicker, Anthony/1 to 39.
3. Opara, Rudolph/1 to 47.
4. /1693. Crain memorandum to Weddell, June 17, 1939.
5. /1699. Consolidated list of American prisoners, July 1, 1939.
6. /1760. Crain's memorandum to Weddell on his visit to American POWS, December 13, 1939.
7. John Blair, to author, September 17, 1977.
8. Reverend John Firmin, taped memoir, August, 1980.
9. Roberto Vega González, *Cadetes Mexicanos en la Guerra de España,* pp. 148–87. Vega gives a graphic picture of life in the Zaragoza and Burgos Provincial Prisons and at Valdenoceda.
10. /1693. Crain memorandum to Weddell, June 17, 1939.
11. Blair, Clarence A./50 to 74.
12. Haber, Cohn/21 to 46.
13. /1760. Crain memorandum to Weddell, December 13, 1939.

14. US Embassy (Madrid) to VALB, January 10, 1940.
15. /1749. Weddell to Hull, November 4, 1939.
16. /1751. Welles memorandum of meeting with Cardenas, November 7, 1939.
17. /1768. State Department, to Robert Steck, January 27, 1940.
18. EU 852.2221/1776 and DA 852.2221 Stojewa, Conrad Henry. State Department to Robert Steck, February 5 and 19, 1940.
19. John Blair, to author, September 17, 1977.
20. Reuben Barr, to author, July 1, 1982.
21. *New York Times,* March 25, 1940.

Chapter 24: The Fate of the Other Nationalities

1. Tom Jones, taped interview (Hawarden, Wales), August 31, 1981. In author's possession.
2. Sean Cronin, *Frank Ryan,* pp. 150–60.
3. Tom Jones, memoir on Frank Ryan, February 1975. In author's possession.
4. Sean Cronin, pp. 167–256, provides a detailed account of how Ryan was taken to Germany, and his life and death there.
5. Tony Gilbert, taped interview (London), September 10, 1981.
6. Cronin, pp. 234–35.
7. Jones, memoir on Frank Ryan, February, 1975. In author's possession.
8. James Cameron, to author, August 2 and September 10, 1979.
9. Reverend John Firmin, taped memoir and letter, September 22, 1980.
10. Archivo del Ministerio de Asuntos Consulares, Legajo R-1051, Expediente 26, May 15, 1939.
11. Ibid., Expediente 37. Includes names of those released.
12. Ibid., Expediente 84 and 85.
13. Ibid., Expediente 73.
14. Ibid., Expediente 26, 27, and 29 (Includes names of Belgians and Cubans released).
15. Georg Heinzmann, taped interview (Erfurt, GDR), July 27, 1981.
16. Olaf Domnauer, to author, August 23, 1980.
17. Ramón Nicolau González, *Cuba y la Defensa de la República Española,* pp. 133–34.
18. FO 371/24506. p. 133. Commissie tot Steun aan Oorlogs-Slachtoffers (Amsterdam) report on foreign POWs in Spain. January 27, 1940.
19. Madrid Embassy Counselor Robert M. Scotten to Bob Steck, January 19, 1940.
20. SD 852.2221/1774. State Department to Steck, February 16, 1940.
21. *Volunteer* (London) May 1940.
22. Domnauer, to author, June 14 and August 23, 1980.
23. Bob Steck, notes on interview with Hassan, March 1983. In author's possession.
24. Ibid.
25. Roberto Vega González, *Cadetes Mexicanos,* pp. 187–98.
26. Heinz Jordan and Josef Stadler to Bob Steck, 1940.
27. Statement by former German prisoners, June 1969, and list smuggled out by Adolfo Redig with names of escapees, typhus casualties, and those taken to Germany, cited hereafter as Redig List.
28. Vega Gonzalez, pp. 198–99.
29. Vega Gonzalez, pp. 199–233.
30. Karl Loesch, taped interview (Dresden), July 28, 1981; Georg Heinzmann, memoir, n.d.
31. Redig List.
32. Herman Streit, taped interview (Berlin), July 31, 1981.
33. Karl Loesch, taped interview (Dresden), July 28, 1981.
34. FO 371/26934 C12526. Yencken to Foreign Office, October 31, 1941.
35. The weekly food parcel supplied to the Poles consisted of one-half kilo sardines, one-half kilo jam, 80 grams coffee extract, 250 grams chocolate, one-half tin of meat, 7 oranges, one-fourth cake soap. Yencken suggested an addition of forty cigarettes a week, a pair of socks each month and extra soap.
36. FO 371/26934 C13300. Yencken to Foreign Office, November 21, 1941.
37. Redig List.

38. Karl Kormes, to Jack Brent, secretary of the International Brigades Association in London, April 1, 1942.
39. Kormes, to Brent, November 10, 1942.
40. International Institute of History, Amsterdam to author, December 7, 1982.
41. Redig List.
42. International Institute of History, Amsterdam, to author, December 7,1982.
43. Kormes, to author, November 6, 1983; and *Puente,* March 1983, a Spanish magazine published by the GDR to promote friendship with Latin American countries.
44. Georg Heinzmann, taped interview (Erfurt, GDR), July 27, 1981.
45. Kormes, to author, February 25, 1985, and March 29, 1984.

Chapter 25: Reflections on the War

1. Elliot Duncan Cook, *All but Me and Thee.*
2. R. P. Turco, O. B. Toon, T. P. Ackerman, J. B. Pollack, and Carl Sagan, "Nuclear Winter: Global Consequences of Multiple Nuclear Explosions," *Science,* December 23, 1983.
3. Caldicott, pp. 37–44.
4. For additional sources on the danger of nuclear annihilation, see Jonathan Schell, *The Fate of the Earth* (New York: Avon, 1982); David Bradley, *No Place to Hide* (Hanover, N.H., and London: University Press of New England, 1983); and Solly Zuckerman, *Nuclear Illusion and Reality* (New York: Viking Press, 1982).

Bibliography

THIS BIBLIOGRAPHY is limited to sources containing information about prisoners and pertinent military and political matters. More extensive bibliographies on the Spanish Republic and the war may be found in Gabriel Jackson's *Spanish Republic and the Civil War, 1931–1939,* Hugh Thomas's *Spanish Civil War,* and Douglas Little's *Malevolent Neutrality.*

1. Books and pamphlets

Alexander, Bill. *British Volunteers for Liberty.* London: Lawrence and Wishart, 1982.

ALVAREZ DEL VAYO, JULIO. *Freedom's Battle.* New York: Hill and Wang, 1971.

AZAÑA, MANUEL. *Obras completas,* vol. 4. Mexico, 1968.

AZNAR, MANUEL. *Historia militar de la guerra de España (1936–1939).* Madrid, 1940.

BAUMANN, GEROLD GINO F. *Extranjeros en la guerra civil española, los Peruanos.* Lima, Peru, 1979.

BERECIARTUA, JOSÉ MARÍA. *San Pedro de Cardeña, el monasterio del Cid.* Published under the auspices of the Cistercian Order at San Pedro de Cardeña, undated [1980?].

BESSIE, ALVAH. *Men in Battle.* New York: Veterans of the Abraham Lincoln Brigade, 1954.

Book of the XV Brigade, The. Edited by Frank Ryan. Madrid: Political Commissariat, 1938.

BOWERS, CLAUDE G. *My Mission to Spain: Watching the rehearsal for World War II.* New York: Simon and Schuster, 1954.

CALDICOTT, HELEN. *Missile Envy.* New York: Morrow, 1984.

CERVERA Y VALDERRAMA, JUAN. *Memorias de guerra, 1936–1939.* Madrid, 1968.

COLODNY, ROBERT G. *The Struggle for Madrid.* New York: Paine-Whitman, 1958.

———. *Spain: The Glory and the Tragedy.* Atlantic Highlands, N.J.: Humanities Press, 1970.

COOK, ELLIOT DUNCAN. *All but Me and Thee.* Washington, D.C.: Washington Infantry Journal Press, 1946.

COVERDALE, JOHN F. *Italian Intervention in the Spanish Civil War.* Princeton, N.J.: Princeton University Press, 1975.

CRONIN, SEAN. *Frank Ryan: The Search for the Republic.* Dublin, Ireland: Repsol Publishing.

Documentos: La agresión italiana, ocupados a las unidades italianas en la acción de Guadalajara. Valencia: Ministerio de Estado, 1937.

Documents on German Foreign Policy, 1918–1945, Series D (1937–1945), vol. 3. *Germany and the Spanish Civil War, 1936–1939.* Washington, D.C.: Government Printing Office, 1950.

FRASER, RONALD. *Blood of Spain: An Oral History of the Spanish Civil War.* New York: Pantheon Books, 1979.

GARRIGA, RAMÓN. *Guadalajara y sus consecuencias.* Madrid: G. del Toro, 1974.

HOAR, VICTOR. *The Mackenzie-Papineau Battalion*. Toronto, Ont.: Copp Clark, 1969.
IBARRURI, DOLORES. *They Shall Not Pass: The Autobiography of la Pasionaria*. New York: International Publishers, 1966.
ICKES, HAROLD L. *The Secret Diary of Harold L. Ickes*, Vol. 2, *The Inside Struggle, 1936–1939*. New York: Simon and Schuster, 1954.
JACKSON, GABRIEL. *A Concise History of the Spanish Civil War*. New York: John Day Company, 1974.
————. *The Spanish Republic and the Civil War 1931–1939*. Princeton, N.J.: Princeton University Press, 1965.
JUNOD, MARCEL. *Warrior Without Weapons*. London, 1951.
KEMP, PETER. *Mine Were of Trouble*. London: Cassel, 1957.
LANDIS, ARTHUR H. *The Abraham Lincoln Brigade*. New York: Citadel Press, 1967.
————. *Spain! The Unfinished Revolution*. Baldwin Park, Calif.: Camelot Publishing Co., 1972.
LÍSTER, ENRIQUE. *Memorias de un luchador*. Madrid: G. Del Toro, 1977.
LITTLE, DOUGLAS. *Malevolent Neutrality*. Ithaca, N.Y.: Cornell University Press, 1985.
LLARCH, JOAN. *Campos de Concentración en la España de Franco*. Barcelona: Producciónes Editoriales, 1978.
MAASSEN, HANNS. *Die Messe des Barcelo*. Berlin: Verlag Tribüne, 1977.
MAISKY, IVAN. *Spanish Notebooks*. London: Hutchinson, 1966.
MARTÍNEZ BANDE, JOSÉ MANUEL. *La gran ofensiva sobre Zaragoza*. Madrid: Libreria Editorial San Martín, 1973.
————. *Los cien ultimos días de la República*. Barcelona: Caralt, 1973.
MEGQUIER, HENRY. Untitled typed 100 page manscript describing our life at San Pedro de Cardeña and our release, 1939. Special Collections Library, Brandeis University.
MORA, CONSTANCIA DE LA. *In Place of Splendor*. New York: Harcourt, Brace, 1939.
MORETA VELAYO, SALUSTIANO. *Historia de un domino monástico castellano*. Salamanca: University of Salamanca Press, 1971.
NICOLAU GONZÁLEZ, RAMÓN. *Cuba y la defensa de la República española (1936–1939)*. Havana: Editora Política, 1981.
ORNITZ, LOU. *Captured by Franco*. New York: Friends of the Abraham Lincoln Brigade, 1939.
ROLFE, EDWIN. *The Lincoln Battalion*. New York: Veterans of the Abraham Lincoln Brigade, 1939.
RYAN, FRANK. *Book of the XVth Brigade*. Madrid: War Commissariat, 1938.
SALAS LARRAZABAL, RAMÓN *Historia del ejército popular de la República*. Madrid: Editora Nacional, 1973. Four volumes, pages numbered consecutively.
SERRANO SÚÑER, RAMÓN. *Entre el silencio y la propaganda: La historia como fué. Memorías*. Barcelona: Editorial Planeta, 1977.
SOVIET WAR VETERANS COMMITTEE, ACADEMY OF SCIENCES. *International Solidarity with the Spanish Republic*. Moscow: Progress Publishers, 1975.
TAYLOR, F. J. *The United States and the Spanish Civil War*. New York, 1956.
They Fought in Franco's Jails. London: Communist Party of Great Britain, August 1939.
THOMAS, HUGH. *The Spanish Civil War*, 3d ed. London: Penguin Books and Hamish Hamilton, 1977.
Trial of the Major War Criminals before the International Military Tribunal, vol. 25. Nuremberg, Germany: International Military Tribunal, 1947.
VEGA GONZÁLEZ, ROBERTO. *Cadetes mexicanos en la guerra de España*. Mexico City: Colección Málaga, S.A., 1977.

Volunteer for Liberty. A complete file of *The Volunteer for Liberty,* the official organ of the English speaking Battalions of the International Brigades, published by the Veterans of the Abraham Lincoln Brigade, New York, 1949.

WEINAND, ROBERT. Nie Vergessen [Never Forget]. Undated Manuscript. Special Collections Library, Brandeis University. In 166 typewritten pages Weinand describes his capture, life at San Pedro, transfer to Germany, and survival for three years in the most feared concentration camp, Dachau.

WYDEN, PETER. *The Passionate War.* New York: Simon and Schuster, 1983.

2. Articles and Magazines

BROWNE, RICHARD. "In Franco's Prisons." *Fight against War and Fascism,* monthly organ of the American League Against War and Fascism, New York.

CLEMENTE GARCÍA, SANTOS. "Camiones americanos en la batalla de Jarama." *Actualidades,* June 9, 1975.

CROME, LEN. "Walter (1897 to 1941): A Soldier in Spain." *History Warkshop: A Journal of Socialist Historians* (Oxford, England), Spring 1980, pp. 116–28.

DAHL, HAROLD "WHITEY." "Sky Fighting Brought Me a Death Sentence." *True,* August 1940.

DORLAND, NORMAN. "In Franco's Prison Camp." *New Masses,* November 22, 1938.

HARVARD, MORGAN, "Cultural Life in a Concentration Camp." *Volunteer* (London), vol. 5, no. 1 (January 1944).

Jaily News. Newspaper handwritten by English-speaking prisoners at San Pedro. The only known surviving copy is No. 15, August 11, 1938, in the Special Collections Library at Brandeis University.

ROMER, SAMUEL, "I Was Franco's Prisoner." *Nation,* November 19, 1938.

"Statement." A nine-page document prepared at Neustadt/Harz, June 27–29, 1969, by seven Germans and a Czech who were at San Pedro and survived World War II (Georg Heinzmann, Karl Kormes, Hermann Maschke, Hanns Maassen, Kurt Scheffler, Kurt Schwotzer, Karl Spannbauer, and Alfred Richter). Special Collections Library, Brandeis University.

The Student Advocate, New York: American Student Union, 1937–38.

3. Archives

The Abraham Lincoln Brigade Collection in the Special Collections Library, Brandeis University, is the principal depository for the Veterans of the Abraham Lincoln Brigade. It contains numerous letters, photographs, posters, and scrapbooks, as well as a very large multilingual collection of books, pamphlets, and articles about the war.

David Mckelvy White Collection, New York Public Library, has letters and memorabilia from veterans and copies of their publications on microfilm. It has copies of the daily radio broadcasts made in Madrid during the war by veterans Sidney Kurtz and David M. Miller.

The National Archives, Washington DC, Record Group 59, General Records of the Department of State, Decimal File, 1910–1939, has a large collection of information about captured Americans.

Public Records Office, Kew, Surrey, England, FO 371, General Political Correspondence of the Foreign Office, 1914–1945, had a large collection of communications about prisoners in Franco Spain. Unfortunately, preceding its recent transfer to a new building, the records were sanitized and many that appear in the Index about San Pedro are no longer available. Those related to Italians held by the Republic are fairly complete.

Archivo del Ministerio de Asuntos Consulares, Madrid, has the correspondence between Franco Spain and foreign countries about prisoners.

Archivo de Servicio Histórico Militar, Madrid, contains the daily military reports, photos, maps, and intelligence reports for the Franco Army and some captured Republican material. The only references I found to capture of Internationals were in the daily Parte Oficial de Guerra issued by Franco's General Headquarters. No names or numbers were kept of Internationals captured and killed.

Archivo Histórico Nacional, Salamanca, has the Republican records captured during the war or found later. It includes fairly complete records of the International Brigades medical service, both of the patients and the staff, and of reports issued at ten-day intervals at Albacete for each brigade, with the names of all officers and number of enlisted men plus the location of each wounded officer and number of enlisted men in each hospital. An attempt to make an alphabetical list of all Internationals yielded some 12,000 names. It has enlistment cards filled out by hundreds of Italian and French volunteers, mostly anarchists, between September 1936 and February 1937 in Barcelona, assigned to anarchist and POUM units.

Archivo Parroquial de Carcedo de Burgos, Partidas de Defunción, has the records of fifty-eight Spaniards and ten foreigners who were buried outside the east wall of the monastery at San Pedro. Usually included are date and place of birth and parents' names, whether he received the last rites, and date of death. Cause of death is seldom given.

Hemoreteca Municipal, Madrid, has files of both Republican and fascist newspapers issued during the war.

Archive of the International Red Cross at Geneva has the reports of its agents who visited San Pedro and Republican prison camps. Permission to see a report required waiting up to six months and giving IRC the right to censor the manuscript. Its file of 55,000,000 names (in 1981) of prisoners and refugees is open only to relatives. Copies of published material may be had without cost.

Bundesarchiv (Koblenz), Auswartiges Amt (Bonn), and Militargeschichtliches Forschungsamt (Freiburg im Breisgau) had few or no Gestapo records. Archivists in each believed the records were in the German Democratic Republic; there I was told they were in the Federal Republic of Germany. I was unable to find the records the Gestapo made of us or the report by the sociologists. I was told the Americans had seized forty-five tons of records, microfilmed some in England, then returned all of them to the Federal Republic, but much was still not cataloged. I had the privilege of interviewing five Germans from San Pedro—Robert Weinand in Essen, Federal Republic; and Georg Heinzmann in Erfurt, Karl Loesch in Dresden, and Herman Streit and Alfred Zarth in Berlin, German Democratic Republic.

4. Prisoner Collections

Families maintained extensive collections of letters, documents, clippings and memorabilia, and these have been given to the Special Collections Library at Brandeis, along with all documents, manuscripts, memoirs, and letters to the author listed in the notes, except as noted. They include family collections for:

Sidney Babsky   Robert Steck
Carl Geiser   Leo Torgoff
Walter Fairbanks Grant   Albert Ziegler

They also include memoirs by and about:

Leo Berman   Bill Miller
John Blair   Max Parker
Charles Hall   Bob Steck
Syd Harris   Hy Wallach
Stanley Heinricher   Joseph Young
Martin Maki

Index